Vietnamese Communists' Relations with China and the Second Indochina Conflict, 1956–1962

Vietnamese Communists' Relations with China and the Second Indochina Conflict, 1956–1962

ANG CHENG GUAN

McFarland & Company, Inc., Publishers
Jefferson, North Carolina, and London

The present work is a reprint of the library bound edition of Vietnamese Communists' Relations with China and the Second Indochina Conflict, 1956–1962, *first published in 1997 by McFarland.*

LIBRARY OF CONGRESS CATALOGUING-IN-PUBLICATION DATA

Ang, Cheng Guan.
Vietnamese communists' relations with China and the second Indochina conflict, 1956–1962 / by Ang Cheng Guan.
p. cm.
Includes bibliographical references and index.

ISBN 978-0-7864-7373-1
softcover : acid free paper ∞

1. Vietnam (Democratic Republic)—Foreign relations—China. 2. China—Foreign relations—Vietnam. 3. Vietnamese Conflict, 1961–1975. I. Title.
DS560.69.C5A54 2012
327.597051—dc21 97-27418

BRITISH LIBRARY CATALOGUING DATA ARE AVAILABLE

On the cover: Details of Vietnamese and Chinese flags (iStockphoto/Thinkstock); background: China and Vietnam map (© 2012 Comstock/JupiterImages)

Manufactured in the United States of America

McFarland & Company, Inc., Publishers
Box 611, Jefferson, North Carolina 28640
www.mcfarlandpub.com

Acknowledgments

This book is a revision of a doctoral dissertation written in the School of Oriental and African Studies, University of London. I wish to express my thanks to Professor Ralph B. Smith. It was my good fortune to have had the opportunity to study under him.

Parts of Chapter 5 were first published as "Vietnam: The Decision to Resume Armed Struggle in the South, Summer 1958–Summer 1959," *War & Society* 15, no. 1 (May 1997), pp. 101–118. Parts of Chapters 4, 5, and 6 were first published as "The Huong Lap and Phu Loi Incidents, and the Decision to Resume Armed Struggle in South Vietnam (January–April 1959)," *South East Asia Research* 4, no. 1 (1996), pp. 3–22. My thanks are due these two journals for allowing me the use of that material in the present work.

I wish also to record my gratitude to the following for their help, encouragement, and advice: First and foremost, Dr. Ong Chit Chung; Chen Jian, Carlyle Thayer, Qian Jiang, Han Suyin, Douglas Pike, James R. Reckner, Tao Wenzhao, Xie Yixian, Lin Zhonghan, Peter MacDonald, John Peaty, Christina Goulter, Geoffrey Warner, Ian Nish, Pham Kim Vinh, Keith Taylor, and my UCL friends.

Having said that, any mistakes and shortcomings in this book are my own.

Contents

Acknowledgments v
List of Abbreviations ix
Introduction 1

Chapter One: January 1956–July 1956 11
Chapter Two: August 1956–December 1956 31
ChapterThree: January 1957–December 1957 49
Chapter Four: January 1958–December 1958 73
Chapter Five: January 1959–May 1959 93
Chapter Six: May 1959–December 1959 115
Chapter Seven: January 1960–July 1960 133
Chapter Eight: August 1960–December 1960 155
Chapter Nine: December 1960–October 1961 179
Chapter Ten: October 1961–July 1962 205
Conclusion 231

Notes 237
Bibliography 291
Index 315

List of Abbreviations

AFP	Agence-France Presse
BBC	British Broadcasting Corporation
CCP	Chinese Communist Party
CDIN	Committee for the Defence of National Interests
CIA	Central Intelligence Agency
CPSU	Communist Party of the Soviet Union
CUSSDCF	Confidential U.S. State Department Central Files
DRV	Democratic Republic of Vietnam
FO	British Foreign Office Correspondence
FRUS	Foreign Relations of the United States
ISCC	International Supervisory and Control Commission
KPRP	Khmer People's Revolutionary Party
MACV	U.S. Military Assistance Command, Vietnam
NCNA	New China News Agency
NLFSV	National Liberation Front of South Vietnam
NLHX	Neo Lao Hak Xat (Lao Patriotic Front)
PLA	People's Liberation Army
PRC	People's Republic of China
RLG	Royal Laotian Government
SWB	Summary of World Broadcasts
TASS	Soviet Telegraph Agency
VNA	Vietnam News Agency
VPA	Vietnam People's Army

Introduction

I

This book examines the relationship between the Vietnamese Communists and China between January 1956 and summer 1962. The choice of 1956 as a starting point is not without justification. By 1956, it was certain that North and South Vietnam would not be reunified in accordance with the 1954 Geneva Agreements. If 1954 marked the end of one phase of the Vietnamese fight for independence, 1956 was the beginning of a new phase of the Vietnamese fight for the unification of the country. The years from 1956 to 1962 saw the Vietnamese Communists' struggle evolve from an essentially political approach to one that incorporated armed conflict; in 1959, arms began to take on a more predominant role. This period is therefore significant, for it marked the origin and the gradual escalation of the Second Indochina War. Those years also saw a gradual change in the Chinese Communists' attitude toward the intensification of the Vietnamese Communists' battle for the reunification of their country. We now know that by the summer of 1962, the Chinese were committed to assisting the Vietnamese Communists in the South. It was therefore in those years, to borrow David Marr's words, that "key attitudes were formed and vital commitments made prior to the first American combat unit touching Vietnamese soil."[1]

The relationship between the Vietnamese Communists and China was a very important one on the Communist side of the Indochina War. In his memoirs, Khrushchev recounted an incident during the concluding stages of the Conference of Communist and Workers' Parties in 1960 when the Chinese refused to sign the statement because they objected to one point in the document. Ho Chi Minh appealed to Khrushchev to accede to the Chinese because, according to Ho, China was a big country with a big party and they could not allow a schism in the Communist movement. Khrushchev retorted that the Soviet Union was by no means a small country with a small party, to which Ho Chi Minh replied, "For us it is doubly difficult. Don't forget, China is our neighbor."[2] Indeed, when one considers the geographical proximity of the two countries, the importance of that relationship becomes even more understandable. During the war, China was not only an important rear base for the Vietnamese Communists, but the most logical and efficient route for vital Soviet aid.

However, anyone studying the literature of the Second Indochina War in an endeavor to understand the decision-making processes involved will feel a sense of incompleteness, because although there is an abundance of material, historians have concentrated on the American or the non–Communist side. We know very much less about the Communist side of the war.[3]

There are possibly two main reasons why this is so. The first is the general perception, particularly characteristic of the 1950s and 1960s, that the Vietnam War was part of a wider Communist campaign to dominate the so-called Free World, and that the Lao Dong Party was but a satellite or political instrument of either the Soviet Union or China, or both. As a consequence, the possibility that the Vietnamese Communists had an independent identity was overlooked or not taken seriously. The second is the relative difficulty of obtaining access to Communist government archives.[4] This has, to an extent, led historians to focus more on the non–Communists, particularly the American side of the war, since official documents and material are more readily obtainable.

Given what we know today of Sino-Vietnamese relations, particularly from the revelations in the wake of the Sino-Vietnamese War (1979), we now realize that Hanoi was far from being a satellite of Communist China, and the assumption that the Communist side of the Vietnam War was a monolithic entity is not only simplistic, but untrue. As for the problem of inaccessible and perhaps inaccurate documentation, it will remain an enduring difficulty.[5] The controversy surrounding the authenticity of a Russian translation of a report of a purported Lao Dong Party Politburo meeting of 15 September 1972, discovered by Australian academic Stephen Morris in Moscow's Center of Contemporary Archives in 1993, is one such example.[6] Even given the passage of time, it is unlikely that we will ever be able to gain access to the complete archives of the ex–Communist governments, let alone the existing Communist ones.

However, this problem should not discourage the historian, whose duty it must be to achieve, as far as possible, a more balanced perspective of one of the longest, bitterest, most complex wars of the twentieth century.

The concentration of research on the American side of the war has produced an abundance of theses, articles, and books on the years from 1964 when American forces were directly involved in the fighting. This is clearly illustrated by a survey of the papers presented at the first conference of scholars from Vietnam and the United States held in Hanoi 25–27 November 1988 and the second conference held at Columbia University in the fall of 1990.[7] The first book written on the role of the Soviet Union in the Vietnam War using Russian sources covers the period 1964–1973.[8] As David Marr noted, the period from after the Geneva Conference till the early '60s was a sadly neglected period in recent Vietnamese history.[9]

II

To my knowledge, no other published work, either in Vietnamese or in Chinese, deals with Sino-Vietnamese relations between 1956 and 1962. There are only two books in English that deal with Communist decision-making in this period; in those books, Sino-Vietnamese relations form only a part of a broader account.

The first of the two books is Carlyle A. Thayer's *War by Other Means: National Liberation and Revolution in Vietnam 1954–1960.*[10] Although not published until 1989, the book is in fact the product of Thayer's two-volume political science doctoral dissertation, "The Origins of the National Front for the Liberation of South Vietnam," which he completed in September 1977. The published version, more than a decade later, contained some additional North Vietnamese documentation that had since become available. But there is no substantial difference between the dissertation and the book.

Thayer rightly argues that the creation of the National Liberation Front was the outcome of a complex interplay of four factors: the international environment, domestic developments in the North, the state of the party organization in the South, and the policies of both the Diem regime and the Americans. He is particularly successful in describing the last three factors. Scholars certainly owe a debt to Thayer for his thorough documentation of the thirteen plenary sessions of the Lao Dong Party Central Committee, the three politburo meetings, the 7th and 8th sessions of the National Assembly, and the three conferences of the Nam Bo Regional Committee, all of which took place between 1954 and 1959. However, the weakest link in his complex interaction model is the North Vietnam–China–Soviet Union factor, to which Thayer did not give sufficient emphasis. Thayer also stopped short at the 15th Plenary Session in January 1959. The National Liberation Front was formed on 20 December 1960, almost two years later. The 15th Plenary session can account for the decision to revive the struggle in the South, but the subsequent two years before the establishment of the National Liberation Front were not inconsequential.

It is not my intention to go over the same ground that Thayer has so admirably covered. Nor is it my primary object to rewrite the history of the National Liberation Front — though in describing Sino-Vietnamese relations during this period, it is impossible to avoid recounting the events leading to its formation. In this aspect, my research — based on documentation made available since 1989 — should further substantiate and sharpen Thayer's thesis, as well as fill in the two-year gap in his work.

The other book is R. B. Smith's *An International History of the Vietnam War*, of which Volume 1 and part of Volume 2 are relevant to my own study.[11] Although Volume 1 was published in 1983, it is actually a much later work than Thayer's. As Smith himself acknowledges, his study relies to an extent on Thayer's thesis which was not yet published as a book as well as on unpublished research on the origins of the National Liberation Front. However, *An International History of the Vietnam War* is very different from Thayer's book. Smith sets out to identify the point at which and the reasons why the Vietnamese Communists decided to return to armed struggle in South Vietnam by examining the decision-making of both the Communist and non-Communist sides. He also relates the events in Vietnam to the regional and global developments at every stage of the conflict. In the process, Smith is able to correct the imbalance of Thayer's complex four-factor interaction model. *An International History of the Vietnam War* is a seminal work, one of the first to examine in some detail the Communist decision-making during the Vietnam War and to give the Communist side of the war the equal weight it deserves. As Smith puts it, no one would write the history of a game of chess, move by move, by recording only the moves of the black player.

Again, it is not my principal object to cover the same ground as Smith's extensive study. Mine is a much more in-depth study of a special relationship on the Communist side of the war. However, in describing Sino-Vietnamese relations, it is inevitable that I address some of the same questions that Smith has asked. My own research, ten years later, using English, American, Chinese, and Vietnamese sources not then available, will further substantiate and sometimes correct some of Smith's conclusions, and sharpen others; it will answer some of the questions he raised, and highlight some of the still-contentious points in his book.

Smith was probably the first to correctly identify the importance of developments in Cambodia and Laos during this period. There is no question that Cambodia and Laos were integral to Hanoi's strategy for the reunification of Vietnam. In fact, the Vietnam War should be correctly called the Indochina War. Of the two countries, Laos was particularly important in the late '50s and early '60s. Unfortunately, scholars of the war have not given sufficient attention to the developments in Laos and Cambodia. I shall explore them in greater detail in this book.

Two other books need to be mentioned. The first is W. R. Smyser's *The Independent Vietnamese: Vietnamese Communism between Russia and China 1956–1969,* published in 1980, in the wake of the 1979 Sino-Vietnamese War.[12] By first highlighting certain major episodes within each year from 1956 till the death of Ho Chi Minh in 1969 and then applying the method of content analysis to the Communist communications between Hanoi, Beijing, and Moscow published in English, Smyser was one of the first to demonstrate that contrary to the conventional view, North Vietnam was not a puppet of China and the Soviet Union — hence the title "The Independent Vietnamese." While no one would now dispute his conclusion, Smysers's methodology, useful at the time when there was a dearth of information regarding Communist affairs, is no longer adequate today.

The second book is William J. Duiker's *The Communist Road to Power in Vietnam* (published in 1981), a pioneering study following Vietnamese Communism from its origins in the colonial period till the end of the Vietnam War in 1975.[13] *The Communist Road to Power in Vietnam* has slightly more than one chapter that covers the same period as my book. Duiker expresses regret that he was unable to make use of two important histories published in Hanoi, one on the party and the other on the VPA up till 1954. He states that new histories would presumably require revision of some of his facts and conclusions. Since 1981, Hanoi has published more than just the two official histories mentioned by Duiker. In the second edition of his book published in 1996, Duiker did attempt to update his account of this period.

In the last couple of years, several new studies have been published in English specifically on the subject of Sino-Vietnamese relations during the Vietnam War, mainly in the form of articles based on newly published Chinese sources. Leading the field is Chen Jian, who has written two articles, "China and the First Indochina War, 1950–54," which has since been published in *China Quarterly* (Number 132, December 1992) and "China's Involvement with the Vietnam War, 1964–1969" (*China Quarterly*, Number 142, June 1995).[14] There is also an article entitled "China and the Geneva Conference of 1954" by Zhai Qiang, published in *China Quarterly* (Number 129, March 1992). Although Sino-Vietnamese relations are not the main subject of Zhang Shu Guang's *Deterrence and Strategic Culture: Chinese-American Confrontations, 1949–1959* (Ithaca: Cornell University Press, 1992), Zhang provides a brief but succinct account of Beijing's policy objectives toward Indochina during the First Indochina War, 1950–1954 (Chapter 6, specifically pages 170–186). It is notable that these recent works do not focus on the period between 1956 and 1963.

III

This book is therefore the first full-length study of Sino-Vietnamese relations between 1956 and 1962. My principal contribution will be to reconstruct the events as they unfolded in Indochina and in the process shed some light on the complex relationship between the Vietnamese and Chinese Communists between 1956 and 1962, and to provide a glimpse of the patterns of decision-making on the Communist side of the Vietnam War.

No foreign policy of any country is completely independent of its domestic politics. It is also a fact that no country devises a separate foreign policy toward another with only bilateral considerations in mind. Therefore, in this study, every effort is made to keep in perspective the constant interaction of domestic politics, the role of individual leaders and political factions in both Hanoi and Beijing, and the changing international conditions that impinged on both countries.

For this book, I have made use of Vietnamese, Chinese, British, and American sources, many of which were then not available or have not yet been fully exploited by earlier scholars.

A few well-known Vietnamese primary source materials published in the late '70s and early '80s have been referred to by other scholars in the past, such as the *Socialist Republic of Vietnam Foreign Ministry White Book on Relations with China and Vietnam*, published in the wake of the Sino-Vietnamese War in 1979,[15] and *The Anti–U.S. Resistance War for National Salvation 1954–1975: Military Events,* published in 1980. There are also the memoirs of Hoang Van Hoan, Vo Bam, Truong Nhu Tang, and the letters of Le Duan to the southern comrades. To these, I have added more recent ones. Most notable are the memoirs of Tran Van Tra and Bui Tin, both high-level North Vietnamese officers; the *Lich Su Quan Doi Nhan Dan (Tap II)* ([Official] History of the Vietnamese People's Army [VPA]) published by Hanoi in 1988; and *Lich Su Cach Mang Vietnam: Giai Doan 1954–1960* by Cao Van Luong, who is also the editor of *Nghien Cuu Lich Su.* Most of these Vietnamese sources shed new light on the situation in North Vietnam but do not deal directly with Sino-Vietnamese relations. In fact, other than the polemical *White Book,* which has to be read with circumspection, the Vietnamese have not made any more revelations on the subject.

There are comparatively more Chinese source materials on Sino-Vietnamese relations. Apart from the Chinese replies to Hanoi's *White Book* in the late '70s, the most useful ones include Huang Zheng's *Ho Zhiming Yu Zhongguo* published in 1987.[16] A Vietnamese edition of this book was published in 1990. Also available is *Xiandai Zhongyue Guanxi Ziliao Xuanbian* (1986), a three-volume compilation of all the major speeches, editorials, and press reports pertaining to Sino-Vietnamese relations from both North Vietnamese and Chinese newspapers from 1949 to October 1978; and *Zhongyue Guanxi Yanbian Sishinian* (1992). The last two works are categorized as "neibu faxing" or "internally distributed works."[17]

In recent years, a number of official histories of China since 1949 have been produced, such as the speeches and letters of Mao Zedong, which were not included in the official five-volume *Selected Works of Mao Zedong* published by the Beijing Foreign Languages Press; the diplomatic activities of Zhou Enlai; and the histories of the Chinese army, air force, and navy. I have also made use of two well-known sets of documents: *Kung-tso Tung hsun* ("Bulletin of Activities" of the PLA) and *Mao Zedong Sixiang Wansui* (Long Live Mao Zedong's Thoughts). These materials have not been previously tapped by scholars working on Sino-Vietnamese relations.

I have also referred to many first-person accounts and memoirs of those who in one way or another were involved in the diplomacy of the '50s and '60s. Memoirs or recollections on the Chinese side include those by Peng Dehuai, Nie Rongzhen, and Chen Geng (one of the Chinese military advisers to North Vietnam); Chinese Foreign Ministry officials, including Liu Xiao (China's ambassador to the Soviet Union in the '50s), Wu Xiuquan (a senior official in the Chinese Ministry of Foreign Affairs), and Wang Bingnan (China's representative to the Sino–U.S. ambassadorial talks); and personalities closely associated with Mao Zedong, including Li Yinqiao (commander of Mao Zedong's bodyguard from 1947 to 1962), Shi Zhe (Mao Zedong's translator), and Dr. Li Zhisui (Mao's personal physician, 1954–1976).

I have also consulted the memoirs of many other leading personalities in the Communist camp: Khrushchev, Andrei Gromyko, Fedor Burlatsky (Khrushchev's adviser), Aleksandr Kaznacheev (Soviet ambassador to Burma in the '50s), Mieczyslaw Maneli (member of the Polish delegation to the International Commission for Supervision and Control for Vietnam), Veljko Micunovic (Yugoslavia's ambassador to the Soviet Union in the '50s), Janos Radvanyi (a Hungarian diplomat who was director of the Asia and African Department of the Hungarian Ministry of Foreign Affairs in the '50s), Marek Thee (member of the Polish delegation to the International Commission for Supervision and Control for Laos), Enver Hoxha (secretary-general, Albanian Communist Party), Jan Sejna (chief of staff of the Czech Army and assistant secretary of the top-secret Czech Defense Council), and Oleg Penkovsky.

On the Cambodian side, there is Sihanouk's account as well as the *Black Paper: Facts and Evidences of the Acts of Aggression and Annexation of Vietnam against Kampuchea* published by the Khmer Rouge government in September 1978. On the non–Communist Laotian side, I have consulted the accounts by Sisouk Na Champassak (a leading Laotian politician in the '50s) and Prince Mangkra Souvannaphouma (son of Souvanna Phouma); also, Arthur Lall (head of the Indian delegation to the 1962 Geneva Conference on Laos) and Sirin Phathanothai. (For details, see bibliography.)

I also made the most thorough use of the *Summary of World Broadcasts* for this period. The *Summary of World Broadcasts* (*SWB*), which contains press translations and monitored radio broadcasts from the Communist countries on a daily basis, is published by the British Broadcasting Corporation (BBC). The greatest value of the *SWB* to the historian is its detailed record of public events and developments, which is unsurpassed by any other form of documentation. It therefore enables the historian to reconstruct events in a chosen period with a degree of detail otherwise not possible. One should be aware, however, that the original objective of the *SWB* was to provide the British government with information which it could use to formulate its foreign policies. Thus there is a tendency for the reports selected for translation and release to be biased toward foreign policy. Generally domestic issues are translated only if they are thought to have value for foreign policy consideration. Also, it must be remembered that the *SWB* provides only authorized information that may be difficult to obtain outside the closed Communist countries but is nevertheless public knowledge within those countries.

I have also made full use of the British Foreign Office General Correspondence (*FO* 371). To my knowledge, this is the first time that the official British sources for this period have been used for the study of Sino-Vietnamese relations and the Communist side of the Vietnam War between the years 1956 and 1962.

A diplomat stationed in a foreign country is often described as the "eyes and ears" of his government. In the words of Sir Humphrey Trevelyan, "Apart from negotiating, the ambassador's basic task is to report on the political, economic and social conditions in the country in which he is living, on the policy of its government and on his conversations with political leaders, officials and anyone else who has illuminated the local scene for him."[18] During the period under study, the British government had embassies in the Soviet Union, China, South Vietnam, Laos, and Cambodia, and a consulate office in North Vietnam. The British Foreign Office General Correspondence (*FO* 371) contains situational reports that were sent to the Foreign Office on a regular and ad hoc basis. Apart from many special reports, there are routine weekly roundups of events (for Laos), fortnightly summaries (for China), monthly reports (for Vietnam), and annual summaries (for all the countries). There are also the weekly reports from Geneva during the duration of the 1961–62 Geneva Conference on the Settlement of the Laotian Question. The quality of the reportage inevitably depended on the caliber of the diplomatic staff, particularly the ambassador or, in the case of North Vietnam, the consul-general, and in China, the chargé d'affaires. The reader will find that the British Foreign Office General Correspondence is indeed a very rich source of information. Until such time as the historian can get access to the archives of the Communist countries, the *FO* 371 series is definitely invaluable for the study of this period.

I have also consulted the Confidential U.S. State Department Central Files (*CUSSDCF*), which have been declassified for the years 1956–1962. The files for this period are not as informative as the British Foreign Office General Correspondence for the same period. Perhaps it is a reflection of the level of United States' interest in Indochina during this period. But as the United States became more deeply involved in

South Vietnam beginning in the early '60s, the quantity of the reports increased.

In conjunction with the *CUSSDCF*, I have also made use of the U.S. State Department's *Foreign Relations of the United States* (*FRUS*) series, which is essentially an official historical record of U.S. foreign policy decision-making and diplomatic activities. In late 1991, President George Bush ordered that the *FRUS* volumes should be published no more than 30 years after the events they record and also passed new regulations to ensure the fullest declassification of the documents. *FRUS* Volume 16 (published in 1992) covers Cambodia and Laos up till 1960; and Volume 24 (published in 1994) covers the Laos Crisis from 1961 to 1963. The Vietnam series of *FRUS* presently available covers the period up till 1964. I have consulted Volume 1 (published in 1988), which covers the year 1961, and Volume 2 (published in 1992), which covers the year 1962.

Last but not least, I have made use of U.S. intelligence reports and captured Communist documents. Captured documents during the Vietnam War and U.S. intelligence reports in the '60s occasionally throw light on the '50s and early '60s. Most notable is the U.S. Department of State's *Working Paper on North Vietnam's Role in the South* (27 May 1968), which contains amongst others the CRIMP Document, captured during Operation CRIMP in January 1966. I have also made use of the Race Documents collected by American scholar Jeffrey Race, although they do not fall into the category of U.S. government documents.

All this information, used judiciously, should provide a better understanding of the Communist side of the Indochina War and a more even account of Sino-Vietnamese relations between 1956 and 1962. As John Tosh put it, "Each type of source possesses certain strengths and weaknesses; considered together, and compared one against the other, there is at least a chance that they will reveal the true facts — or something very close to them."[19]

One

January 1956–July 1956

I

According to the Final Declaration of the 1954 Geneva Conference regarding Vietnam, general elections should be held two years later in July 1956 under the supervision of an international commission composed of representatives of the International Supervisory and Control Commission (ISCC). It was further stipulated that consultations between the North and the South on the impending general election were to commence a year earlier, from 20 July 1955. On 7 June 1955, Pham Van Dong stated that Hanoi was ready to hold consultations with South Vietnam to discuss the general election. However, on 16 July, Ngo Dinh Diem declared in a broadcast that as South Vietnam did not sign the Geneva Agreements, it was therefore not bound by them. Two days later, on 19 July, Dong sent a note to Diem asking him to nominate delegates for a consultative conference. But on 10 August, Diem reaffirmed his declaration of 16 July and rejected any talks with the North. On 21 September, he issued a second statement declaring that there would be no question of a conference or any negotiations with the Communists. Two weeks later, on 4 October, Diem announced that an elected assembly would exist in South Vietnam by the end of the year. Following that, on 23 October 1955, he proclaimed South Vietnam a republic with himself as President.[1] Pham Van Dong continued to urge the cochairmen of the 1954 Geneva Conference to convene the consultative conference as stated in the provisions of the Geneva Agreements.[2] When it was made known by Ngo Dinh Diem in December 1955 that unilateral elections were to be held in South Vietnam during March 1956, his statement was immediately denounced by the Vietnamese Communists.[3]

Despite Diem's intransigence, many Vietnamese Communists, particularly the rank and file, looked forward to July 1956 when the reunification of North and South Vietnam would take place. Since the conclusion of the Geneva Conference, that was what they had been told by the leadership, time and again, to expect. The Vietnamese Communist leadership, however, knew from the beginning that the general election stipulated in the 1954 Geneva Agreements would not take place and there would not be a peaceful reunification. At a meeting in Spring 1959, Le Duan told Janos Radvanyi that no one in Hanoi had been surprised when the election was not held. In fact, the election was never expected to be held and the reunification of the North and South could come about only by military means. The election issue was kept alive because it had great propaganda value.[4]

As early as the 6th Plenary Session of the Lao Dong Central Committee from 15 to 18 July 1954, which took place even before the Geneva Conference ended, Ho had already identified the Americans as the main and direct enemy of the Vietnamese, Cambodians, and Laotians. In his view, the Vietnamese people must concentrate their strength against the Americans.[5] According to the *Lich Su Quan Doi Nhan Dan Viet Nam*, the 6th Plenary Session marked the beginning of a new period in the history of the Vietnamese people — the period of resisting the Americans to save the country. The Vietnamese people and army were confronting a new aggressor that possessed the greatest economic potential and the most powerful armed forces of all the imperialist powers. The Americans were the most influential and dangerous counterrevolutionaries they had ever confronted.[6] The Vietnamese Communists thus knew what they were challenging and that the United States was not an opponent they could take lightly. The strategy was to rebuild as quickly as possible the economy of the North, which had been badly damaged by the many years of struggle, and to lay the foundation for socialism so as to make the North a strong base for the unification of the country. At the same time, the Vietnamese People's Army (VPA) was to be transformed into a modern and regular revolutionary army. This in itself was expected to be a long and arduous process. The army was expected to be responsible for the security of the country and also had to partake in the reconstruction of the economy. The first target was to restore the war-shattered economy in three years (1955– 1957).[7] In short, at the 6th Plenary Session, the Hanoi leadership implicitly acknowledged that it was unlikely that they could reunite the country in 1956. Two years after the 6th Plenary Session, the perception of the Hanoi leadership had not changed.

The political and diplomatic facade had to be kept up for three reasons. First, as Le Duan recalled some years later, it had propaganda value as it put the North Vietnamese on the legal high ground and presented them as the injured party. Second, the Hanoi leadership had to show the majority of the Communist cadres who had been told to expect reunification in 1956 that efforts were being made towards that end. Third, it served as a cover for Hanoi's preparation in the North for an eventual confrontation with the United States–Diem regime as envisaged at the 6th Plenary Session of the Lao Dong Central Committee.

II

Despite their differences with the Chinese in the summer of 1954,[8] after the Geneva Conference had ended the Vietnamese Communists still consulted Beijing as to which strategy to adopt to ensure the unification of Vietnam.[9] Like the Vietnamese Communists, the Chinese also thought that it would be impossible to reunite the country by elections as stipulated in the Geneva Agreements. In their view, it was imperative that the Vietnamese Communists prepare for a protracted struggle. They recommended their own experience that had been successful against the Guomindang, which was to lie low for a long time, muster strength, keep in touch with the people, and wait for an opportunity.[10] According to Hoang Van Hoan, the Hanoi leadership decided to accept the Chinese recommendation.[11]

We can now confirm that in the early '50s, the Chinese had provided military assistance to the Vietnamese Communists in their war against the French. In July/August 1955 (at around the period when consultations between Hanoi and Saigon on the 1956 general election should have started), Beijing decided that it was time to withdraw their military advisers who had been sent to North Vietnam in July/August 1950. The withdrawal was to be carried out in three phases — in September/October 1955, at the end of 1955, and in spring 1956. As requested by the North Vietnamese leaders, the military advisers would be replaced by military specialists to help in the modernization of the VPA.[12]

By the beginning of 1956, the Chinese were poised to launch the first of their two economic "leaps forward."[13] On 12 January 1956, Mao Zedong's updated preface of his book, *Socialist Upsurge in China's Countryside*, was published. In it, Mao criticized those who underestimated the possibilities of speeding up production in all aspects of the economy.[14]

At the Supreme State Conference on 25 January 1956, Mao stated that China's First Five-Year Plan could either be accomplished ahead of schedule or in excess of the projected targets.[15] What was foremost in Mao's mind at the beginning of 1956 was accelerating the pace of the economic development of China. A peaceful international environment was a prerequisite for economic reconstruction.[16] In fact, as early as September 1955, in his summation speech at the 6th Expanded Plenary Session of the 7th CCP Central Committee, Mao had already said that China needed a period of peaceful construction and that it was the duty of the Ministry of Foreign Affairs, the International Liaison Department, and the army to ensure that a peaceful environment existed.[17]

Thus Zhou Enlai's political report to the Chinese People's Political Consultative Conference on 30 January 1956 emphasized China's desire for peace and her willingness to abide by the Bandung and Geneva spirit. In his report, he advocated the holding of a Far Eastern conference on the unification of Korea, repeated the Chinese proposal first made on 30 July 1955 for a collective peace pact within the countries of both Asia and the Pacific, reviewed Chinese efforts to normalize relations with Japan, and supported the Soviet proposal for the conclusion of a Soviet-U.S. treaty of friendship. According to Zhou, China was not hostile to the Americans. On the contrary, China was more than willing to live in friendship with them. What the Chinese opposed was the American military threat. Given a choice, China would prefer to live in peace, but she would fight if her national security was to be threatened.[18] There were indications during this time that despite China's public affirmation that it would take Taiwan by force if necessary, it was unlikely that they would do so. The preference was for a negotiated settlement.[19]

It was also in this report that Zhou made known the Chinese proposal that the Geneva Conference on Indochina be reconvened and enlarged to include members of the ISCC in Vietnam so as to ensure the implementation of the Geneva Agreements in Vietnam.[20] The Chinese suggestion was first made by Zhou in his letter of 25 January 1956 to the two cochairmen of the 1954 Geneva Conference. He was responding to the written request made by the latter on 21 December 1955 asking for suggestions on how to improve the implementation of the Geneva Agreements on Vietnam.[21] Zhou's suggestion was therefore consistent with the policy of peaceful coexistence that the Chinese had been pursuing since the Afro-Asian Conference in Bandung in April 1955.[22] On 13 January 1956, the second group of Chinese military advisers who had been sent to North Vietnam in July/August 1950 returned to China.[23]

There is no indication that the Chinese discussed their proposal with the North Vietnamese prior to their letter of 25 January to the two cochairmen. They had so far supported the North Vietnamese call for the convening of the consultative conference.[24] We do not know whether Ton Duc Thang, chairman of the Standing Committee of the National Assembly of the DRV, was informed about it. Thang was in Beijing from 9 to 11 December 1955 before leaving for the GDR to attend the 80th birthday celebration of President Pieck. While in Beijing, he attended a banquet given in his honor by Peng Zhen, vice-chairman of the Standing Committee of the National People's Congress.[25] He was in Beijing again from January 24 to 28, this time at the invitation of Liu Shaoqi,[26] and he met Mao and Zhou on 24 January.[27] The Chinese proposal was quoted by the *Voice of Vietnam* with a commentary in support of it on 31 January, the day after it was made public.[28]

The Soviet ambassador to China, Pavel F. Yudin, met Zhou Enlai on 26 January with a message from the Soviet government regarding Vietnam. We do not know the content of the message except that at this meeting, Vietnam was discussed.[29] Then on 3 February, the Soviet Union declared its support for the Chinese proposal, which it described as "noble and important."[30] On 5 February, Truong Chinh and Le Duc Tho arrived in Beijing. They stayed for four days before leaving on 9 February for Moscow to attend the 20th Congress of the CPSU.[31] It was very likely that they would have discussed the Chinese proposal during their stay in Beijing. Given that both China and the Soviet Union favored a new conference, Pham Van Dong eventually responded on 14 February 1956, the date of the opening of the 20th Congress of the CPSU, to the cochairmen's request of 21 December 1955. He too suggested that a new and enlarged Geneva Conference should be held to discuss the enforcement of the 1954 Agreements.[32]

The 20th Congress of the CPSU was a landmark congress for two reasons. First, on 24 February, just before the congress was to close on 25 February, Khrushchev delivered a speech denouncing Stalin at a special closed-door session. Second, it was during this congress that Khrushchev spelled out the revised guiding principles of Soviet foreign policy. The new Soviet position was that there could be peaceful coexistence between the socialist and capitalist camps; war was not inevitable and the transition to socialism could be nonviolent and take different forms for different countries.[33] According to Khrushchev, when it was said that the socialist system would win in the competition between the two systems, it by no means signified that the victory would be achieved through armed struggle. Rather, the certainty was based on the fact that the socialist mode of production possessed decisive advantage over the capitalist mode of production. There were only two ways — either peaceful coexistence or the most destructive war in history. There was no third way.

According to the French Foreign Ministry, the Russians, in contrast to the Chinese, were not concerned about the elections in Vietnam and appeared to be deliberately refraining from pushing the case.[34] Indeed, the Soviet Union had so far not paid too much attention to Southeast Asia. Southeast Asian affairs were largely left to the discretion of China. There seems to have been an agreed division of responsibilities in the international sphere between both countries. Some time in 1955–1956, a gentlemen's agreement initiated by the Russians was apparently reached in secret between the two countries whereby Burma, Thailand, Laos, Cambodia, Malaya, and Vietnam would be in the Chinese sphere of operations. The Russians promised not to challenge Chinese leadership of the Communist movements in those countries. India, Afghanistan, and all of Asia to the west of these countries would be in the Russian sphere. The exception was Indonesia, which fell within both the Russian and Chinese spheres of interest.[35] With this arrangement, the Russians could concentrate their attention on issues nearer home. At the beginning of 1956, the Soviet Union had far more important concerns than the problem of Vietnam, notably its own 20th Congress. Nevertheless, in a note to its British counterpart on 18 February (while the 20th CPSU Congress was still in session), the Soviet Union stated that it shared the views of both China and North Vietnam on the expediency of reconvening the Geneva Conference. It even included a draft message addressed to all the members of the 1954 Geneva Conference and the supervisory powers regarding the proposed conference.[36] On 23 February, a *Nhan Dan* editorial presented the argument that if South Vietnam — a strategic region in Asia and particularly in Southeast Asia — was transformed into an American colony and military base, it would only turn the region into a hotbed of war. It was therefore imperative that the Geneva Conference be reconvened.[37]

III

Meanwhile, on 10 February 1956, it was announced that Sihanouk was to visit Beijing on 13 February at the invitation of Zhou Enlai. The announcement added that the Chinese premier fully understood that

Cambodia's policy of neutrality prevented her from taking sides in the dispute between China and Taiwan. The Chinese also accepted the fact that Cambodia could not take any steps toward the recognition of the PRC until the dispute was resolved.[38] (Taiwan retained its consulate in Cambodia until 1958.) The visit appeared to have achieved the objectives of both parties. A joint Sino-Cambodian communique that reaffirmed the Five Principles of the Bandung Conference and that advocated the settlement of international disputes by peaceful means was signed on 18 February.[39] The Chinese told Sihanouk that neutrality was the best course for Cambodia and assured him that they would support Cambodia's independence and neutrality. Sihanouk assured the Chinese that Cambodia would remain neutral and would not resort to SEATO for protection. In return, China would restrain North Vietnam from interfering in Cambodia's domestic affairs.[40] Sihanouk's trip to Beijing was a great contrast to his visit to Manila in January 1956 where he was pressured (but unsuccessfully) to place Cambodia under the protection of SEATO and abandon his policy of neutrality.[41]

The Vietnamese Communists appeared pleased with Sihanouk's visit to China. They were themselves keen to establish diplomatic relations with Cambodia and had in fact approached Nehru as their intermediary.[42] They endorsed Sihanouk's policy of neutrality and Cambodia's compliance with the Geneva Agreements and her refusal to join any military alliance.[43] The *Nhan Dan* editorial of 20 February described the establishment of friendly relations between China and Cambodia as helpful to the enforcement of the Geneva Agreements.[44] In their effort to develop good relations with Sihanouk, the Vietnamese Communists encouraged their Cambodian counterparts to exercise restraint. According to David P. Chandler, during this time Saloth Sar "was working with fellow members of the Indochina Communist Party ... to protect its Cambodian leaders Tou Samouth and Sieu Heng and to lay the groundwork, when the time was ripe and permission came from Vietnam, for a larger and better organized Cambodian Communist Party."[45] In April 1956, at the 3rd Sangkum Congress, the Pracheachon proposed a coalition government that would include itself, the Sangkum, and other political parties.[46]

IV

The North Vietnamese, Chinese, and Russians continued to condemn Diem's preparation for the unilateral election in South Vietnam. But despite all the denunciations, the so-called "separatist" and "fascist" election was carried out on 4 March 1956. Apparently there were some attempts by the Vietnamese Communists to sabotage the election, but they were not extensive enough to disrupt it.[47] The inability of the Vietnamese Communists to take widespread and coordinated action to foil the election indicated that the Hanoi leadership was still not able to force the pace for unification.[48] According to the evaluation of the U.S. Country Team, Diem's policies and actions in the South had caused the Vietnamese Communists to lose much of their broad base of support in certain areas where they used to be strong. The Country Team further reported that the consolidation of the South Vietnamese government's position and the improved local security particularly in the central provinces had sharply reduced the Communist resistance potential. The Vietnamese Communists' subversive capability in the South had gradually declined since mid–1955.[49]

Five days after the South Vietnamese National Assembly election, on 9 March, the British government replied to the Soviet note of 18 February. The British view was that it was premature for the cochairmen to propose such a conference. The British suggested that they first seek further clarification of the views of the other countries concerned. Following that, the two cochairmen could then meet to discuss whether or not a new conference was profitable.[50] Throughout this time, Truong Chinh and Le Duc Tho were still in Moscow, although the 20th Congress closed on 25 February 1956. On 13 March, they returned to Beijing. It was reported that they were received by the Political Bureau on the next afternoon.[51] They stayed on in Beijing till 20 March before returning to Hanoi.[52] Although we still do not know about the activities of Truong Chinh and Le Duc Tho during their very long stay in both Moscow and Beijing, it is very likely that the issue of the unification of Vietnam was discussed.

Meanwhile, in mid-March 1956, the head of the Chinese Military Advisory Mission to North Vietnam, Wei Guoqing, and the last batch of Chinese military advisers who had been sent to North Vietnam in the early '50s returned to China.[53] The departure of these Chinese advisers did not mean the end of the close ties between the PLA and the VPA. We should recall that they were replaced by Chinese military technicians and specialists. In April 1956, a Chinese military delegation led by (four-star) General Chen Geng, deputy chief of the PLA General Staff and member of the National Defense Council, visited North Vietnam. In 1950–51, Chen was the deputy-commander of the Southwest Military

Command and commander of the Yunnan Military.[54] We now know that he was also one of the Chinese military advisers sent to assist the North Vietnamese in June 1950.[55] Chen and Ho Chi Minh had close ties. We do not know about the activities of the delegation in North Vietnam except that Chen Geng returned to China on 3 May 1956.[56]

On 23 March 1956, soon after Truong Chinh and Le Duc Tho returned to Hanoi, it was announced that Soviet Deputy Premier Anastas Mikoyan would be visiting Hanoi in early April. On the same day, the Indian government wrote to the two cochairmen informing them that an agreement had been reached between the French and the South Vietnamese authorities on the evacuation of the French Expeditionary Corps from South Vietnam and that there would be no French High Command in the South after 15 April 1956. The Indians expressed their concern that the South Vietnamese authorities had stated that they were not prepared to assume the legal obligations of the French High Command as successors of the French in the South. They therefore asked the two cochairmen to consider the grave situation as early as possible, and before 15 April.[57] The North Vietnamese insisted that regardless of whether there were French troops on Vietnamese soil, the French government was obliged to uphold the spirit and letter of the Geneva Agreements.

Sometime between 18 March 1956 and the arrival of Mikoyan in Hanoi, the North Vietnamese leadership discussed a 14-point plan of action that had been drawn up by Le Duan and adopted by the Nam Bo Committee.[58] The setbacks suffered by the Communist cadres in the South and their increasingly low morale had prompted Le Duan to present this 14-point plan.[59] The plan recommended that military action be used in support of other activities in the South, that support bases and more battalions be created, and that the military organizations in the interzones be consolidated. Cambodia was considered to be strategically important and it was proposed that budgetary assistance should therefore be increased and senior cadres should be seconded to Cambodia. Part of the plan also included the creation of a support base to aid activities in Cambodia and the consolidation of the leading organizations there. In sum, the plan recommended a more aggressive and militant approach to complement the political struggle in the South.

The leadership's reply to Le Duan and the Southern cadres was that they should in the meantime exploit the agrarian issues in the South until a more long-range strategy could be worked out.[60] The Hanoi leadership turned down the 14-point plan, possibly because, firstly, it did not see itself strong enough to step up the military struggle in the South at this point. Secondly, even if it had wanted to back the plan, it would still need to discuss the matter with China and the Soviet Union. Mikoyan was expected in Hanoi soon. Both countries as we have noted were not in favor of any moves that could lead to a new military confrontation. Furthermore, North Vietnam had just over a month ago publicly committed itself to a new diplomatic solution initiated by China and supported by the Soviet Union.

Since the end of the 1954 Geneva Conference, the Russians had advocated that both North and South Vietnam should coexist peacefully and engage in friendly economic competition with each other. Their belief was that the socialist mode of production was superior to that of the capitalist South. Therefore the latter would naturally and in time yearn to be unified with the North.[61] The Soviet approach was reiterated at the recent 20th CPSU Congress. According to Hoang Van Hoan, the Lao Dong Central Committee was not in favor of the Soviet proposal.[62] Nevertheless, on 31 March 1956, a few days before Mikoyan was due to arrive in Hanoi, the Vietnamese Politburo issued a statement endorsing the resolutions of the recent 20th CPSU Congress.

Mikoyan arrived in Hanoi on 2 April 1956. He was the highest ranking Soviet leader so far to visit North Vietnam and it was described as "an event of great significance."[63] The importance of the Soviet Union to the Vietnamese Communists was best described in an article by Ton Duc Thang eulogizing the visit. He wrote: "The two words "Soviet Union" were sacred for the Vietnamese people. Confidence in the Soviet Union remained a source of moral strength to the Vietnamese people."[64] Indeed, no effect was spared to create an impression on the esteemed visitor.[65]

In his short speech on arrival, Mikoyan wished the Vietnamese people success in their efforts to heal the wounds of war and to raise their material and cultural standards, as well as in their struggle for the peaceful unification of their country through free and democratic elections.[66] According to Colonel Huong Van Ba, an artillery officer in the VPA, sometime before July 1956 he heard a speech made by a visiting Russian dignitary in Hanoi and the message was the same: that the North should build a strong and wealthy socialist state, and eventually the South would follow.[67] The Russian dignitary referred to could have been Mikoyan.

Two days before Mikoyan's arrival on 30 March 1956, the Soviet Union had responded to the British note of 9 March. The Russians did not object to the British proposal of preliminary discussions between the two cochairmen and proposed that they be held in London within the next few days, "inasmuch as any postponement of the discussion of this question makes more difficult the implementation of the Geneva Agreements." The discussions would also look into the problem brought about by the withdrawal of the French High Command from the South.[68] Mikoyan's visit therefore provided the opportunity for the Hanoi leadership to clarify with the Russians the implications of the resolutions of the recent 20th CPSU Congress for the Vietnamese. We still do not know what was discussed, but evidently the discussions were unexpectedly long and drawn out. On the morning when Mikoyan was to visit Haiphong, the entire population there began to assemble at 4:30 A.M. Only at 10:30 were they told by the authorities that the visit was canceled due to pressure of work in Hanoi.[69] Significantly, Mikoyan ended his visit to Hanoi on 6 April without signing a joint communique, which suggests that the North Vietnamese and the Russians could not reach a unity of views. After Hanoi, Mikoyan visited Beijing and Ulan Bator (Mongolia). In both these capitals, however, joint communiques were signed.[70]

Meanwhile, in early April, at a special conference attended by senior party officials in Nam Bo, a further evaluation of the situation in the South was made. Having taken into consideration Hanoi's rejection of Le Duan's 14-point plan, this time it was decided that the tactical use of violence concurrently with political operations — in accordance with the September 1955 instruction of the Central Committee of the Lao Dong Party — had so far not achieved much positive result and, from the standpoint of the DRV's international diplomacy, any further use of violence would be inappropriate. The emphasis should therefore shift away from that of a military struggle to an economic struggle.[71]

Despite this conclusion, there is evidence that the Southern Communist leaders were less than happy with the strategy thrust upon them by the Hanoi leadership. A supplement to a special number of a Communist newsheet, *Nouvelles du Peuple* (dated April 1956), meant for circulation in the South included an old document that explained in some detail Communist policy and tactics in South Vietnam and the program of the Fatherland Front. We know that this document was written sometime earlier, although we cannot ascertain the exact date, and that it was redistributed in April 1956. This document first came into the hands of a USIS cinematography team at Vinh Long sometime after 20 July 1954. The British believed it was probably given to the USIS team by the French Surete who had captured it in a raid. The British were of the view that the material was genuine and was intended for use by the Communist cadres in the South.[72] It was clear from this document that the Communists were intent on first consolidating the North, while at the same time encouraging the sects or anyone else so disposed to create armed disturbances. It recommended against propagating the idea of a military intervention from the North and terrorizing of the population. In Section 6, the writer appeared obliged to deny that there was either hypocrisy or opportunism in the Communist Party policy. The recirculation of this old document tells us two things: first, that the policy established by the Hanoi leadership at the 6th Plenary Session had remained unchanged and second, there was the need in April 1956 to impress this strategy upon the Southern cadres.

Also in April, Chinese Vice-Premier Chen Yun visited Hanoi at the invitation of Ho Chi Minh and the Central Committee of the Lao Dong Party to discuss the economic strategy for North Vietnam. North Vietnam at this time was experiencing a serious problem of food shortage and high unemployment. It did not have any financial infrastructure. Neither did the country have a pool of technically skilled personnel. The country was therefore not ready for the development of heavy industry. Chen Yun's proposal, which was accepted by the North Vietnamese leadership, was to concentrate on agriculture before industry, and to establish light industry before heavy industry. Agricultural development would help alleviate North Vietnam's food shortage and also provide raw materials for the light industry. Chen Yun also proposed the construction of a number of light industries that required minimum investment but could yield quick returns. In mid-July 1956, an agreement was signed between Beijing and Hanoi whereby Chinese specialists in various fields were sent to North Vietnam to help in the rehabilitation of the North Vietnamese economy.[73]

V

While the Vietnamese Communists were doing all they could short of resorting to arms to get the agreements on the unification of the North and South implemented by the July 1956 deadline, events were developing in Laos that they could not ignore. It had to do with the political survival of the Pathet Lao.[74] After the 1954 Geneva Conference, the Pathet Lao were temporarily regrouped in the two provinces of Sam Neua and Phong Saly. The Geneva Agreements had envisaged an internal Laotian political settlement in the form of a general election in 1955. But the Royal Laotian Government (RLG) and the Pathet Lao were unable to reach any understanding and on 25 December 1955, the incumbent government proceeded with a general election without Pathet Lao participation. The North Vietnamese on 24 December declared the planned unilateral election undemocratic and "entirely contrary to the letter and spirit of the Geneva Agreements." They expressed their desire to have good neighborly relations with Laos and were deeply concerned with the developments there.[75] The Chinese shared the same sentiment. They saw the hand of the United States behind the election and spoke of an American plan to turn Laos into a U.S. military base and colony. To the Chinese, the solution of the Laos question was vital to the security of Indochina as well as the whole of Asia.[76]

Despite the boycott by the Pathet Lao and apparently some small-scale effort by the Communists to disrupt it, the election was smoothly carried out. The Communists' propaganda had failed. There was no evidence that any major plan was drawn up to wreck the election.[77] Despite having condemned the December election, Pham Van Dong sent a congratulatory message to the RLG through the International Supervisory and Control Commission on the occasion of the admission of Laos into the United Nations on 14 December 1955.[78]

Soon after the unilateral election, between 6 and 14 January 1956, the Pathet Lao held a conference at Sam Neua and established the Neo Lao Hak Xat (NLHX or the Lao Patriotic Front). This new front replaced the Neo Lao Itsala, founded in 1950. It was to be a broad united front comprising both ethnic and nonethnic Laotians. The NLHX was essentially modeled along the lines of the Vietnamese Fatherland Front. The proceedings of the conference were closely followed and duly reported by the North Vietnamese media, notably the opening of the Conference on 7 January, Souphanouvong's inaugural speech on 10 January, and the formation of the NLHX as well as its 12-article program on 14 January. The DRV Fatherland Front sent its greetings to the Pathet Lao on 11 January. In its message, it stressed the historic importance of the conference and referred to the close unity between the Vietnamese and the Laotians who had for a long time past fought side by side against a common enemy.[79] A *Nhan Dan* article of 16 January described the formation of the NLHX as an important stage in the history of the Laotian people's struggle for national independence.[80] Given the close links between the Pathet Lao and the Vietnamese Communists and judging from the leading personalities in the NLHX, there is no doubt that the new front had the full blessings of the Vietnamese Communists. On 15 January, the Chinese also greeted the formation of the new front with enthusiasm and described it as a "great event in the political life of the Laotian people" that "conformed to the aspirations of the Laotian people and reflected the growing democratic forces in Laos." The Chinese further urged the RLG to resume its negotiations with the Pathet Lao fighting units so as to reach a political solution in accordance with the Geneva Agreements.[81]

With the Laotian election over and none of the four Laotian parties having a clear majority, the North Vietnamese and Chinese could only wait and watch how the new government would be formed. Expressions of support were for the recently reconstituted Laotian Patriotic Front rather than the Pathet Lao per se.[82] The Vietnamese Communists in fact intimated to the Indians that they had no wish to upset the Geneva Agreements on Laos.[83] Pham Van Dong also told the Indian chargé d'affaires in Hanoi that he was willing to exercise his "good offices" to help settle the Pathet Lao problem, and he also renewed his invitation to Katay Don Sasorith (who was the pro–Western Laotian prime minister from October 1954 till the recent election) to visit Hanoi. The Indians on their part advised the North Vietnamese against linking the unification issue with the Pathet Lao problem by pointing out that a settlement in Laos would improve the atmosphere for the settling of the unification issue.[84] That the Pathet Lao did not resort to open fighting during and after the December elections and the subsequent formation of the NLHX, as well as the conciliatory attitude of the North Vietnamese, showed that the Hanoi leadership had an overall strategy in Indochina of which the Chinese approved.

According to the Chinese, as a neighbor China welcomed a Laos that would live peacefully and cooperatively with all her neighbors as a completely sovereign and independent member of the big family of Asian nations. They also indicated to the Laotian premier-designate that so long as the Laotian government strictly adhered to the Geneva Agreements, a basis would exist for the settlement of the political issues, particularly the integration of the Pathet Lao forces into the country's political life.[85]

Almost two months after the elections, it was confirmed that Prince Souvanna Phouma would form the new government. On 20 March, he pledged to bring about the national reconciliation in accordance with the Geneva Agreements. There was no more mention of Laos in the North Vietnamese media until 10 April, when they reported that the Pathet Lao had called for the reconvening of the political conference with the RLG. We should recall that during this interval of time, the North Vietnamese were preoccupied with the visit of Mikoyan and they also had to decide on the 14-point plan submitted by Le Duan. On 11 April, the Vietnamese broke their long silence and came out in full support of the Pathet Lao proposal, which they described as a "new effort showing the constructive spirit of the Pathet Lao forces." They further expressed hope that the RLG would act in full accordance with Souvanna Phouma's pledge.[86] Again, the North Vietnamese position was in keeping with their policy regarding South Vietnam and Cambodia.

VI

We should recall that the Russians had agreed to meet their British counterpart in London to discuss the problem of the reunification of North and South Vietnam. On 5 April, which was the eve of Mikoyan's departure from Hanoi, the British replied to the Soviet Union with the proposal that the first meeting between Lord Reading and Gromyko take place on 11 April.[87] The London Talks between Gromyko and Lord Reading were publicly welcomed by the Vietnamese Communists. The Vietnamese again urged the two cochairmen to convene a new Geneva Conference.[88] However, there is indication that the Hanoi leadership might have been quite skeptical as to how much another conference could achieve. A document purportedly issued to senior Southern cadres in late spring 1956 by the Lao Dong Party Central Committee for their general guidance stated that although England, Russia, France, China, and India were trying to arrange a second Geneva Conference, the solution to the Vietnam problem would depend basically on the actual strength of the Vietnamese Communists. The North would have to make plans to solve the military, political, and economic problems of the South.[89]

Despite all their expressions of support, the Russians showed only a minor interest in the Far East during the London Talks. They were evidently more concerned about developments in the Middle East than in Indochina.[90] The outcome of the talks was most disappointing to the Vietnamese Communists. As the official British record put it, "Since the Government in South Vietnam adhered unflinchingly to the position that it was not a party to the Geneva Agreement or Final Declaration, and therefore under no obligation to discuss elections, and to the view that in any case it was unrealistic to think that any elections held in Communist North Vietnam could be free, there was nothing that could be done."[91] A tacit understanding was reached between the two cochairmen that there was no point in holding a new conference and that reunification would have to be postponed indefinitely. They also absolved the French of any further obligation for the execution of the Geneva Agreements.[92]

The Soviet Union, apart from playing its role as cochairman of the 1954 Geneva Conference, appeared content to let the Chinese take the initiative in Indochina during this period. It paid hardly any attention to Laos. In the British note of 5 April to the Soviet Union regarding the meeting of the cochairmen in London during April 1956, they had proposed to discuss Laos as well.[93] But in London, the Russians refused to put any pressure on the Pathet Lao to conclude a political settlement.[94] This is not to say that they were completely uninterested in the region. In April they approached Sihanouk regarding the establishment of a Soviet embassy in Phnom Penh, but they were unsuccessful.[95] At the end of June, they offered de jure recognition to the Laotian government and suggested an exchange of diplomatic missions as well as the development of cultural and economic ties. They appeared rather anxious for a Laotian response to their offer.[96]

Following all this, in Hanoi, the North Vietnamese leadership held the 9th Plenary Session (enlarged) of the Lao Dong Central Committee from 19 to 27 April 1956. During this plenary session, the resolution of the 20th CPSU Congress was once again acclaimed. However, the Vietnamese Communists, like the Chinese, had reservations about Khrushchev's repudiation of Stalin. Ho's view was similar to that of the Chinese as expressed in an article in the *Renmin Ribao* of 4 April 1956, "On the Historical Experience of the Dictatorship of the Proletariat."[97]

But whereas the Chinese, and particularly Mao, paid great attention to the denunciation of Stalin, the Vietnamese Communists were more concerned about the question of the inevitability of war and its implications for their struggle for national reunification. In his closing speech at the plenary session on 27 April, Ho Chi Minh did not discount the possibility of resorting to armed struggle to achieve reunification. According to Ho; "Although it is possible that certain countries may achieve socialism by peaceful means, we must understand that in those countries where the administrative machinery, the military powers and the secret police of the bourgeois class are still powerful, the proletariat must prepare for an armed struggle. While noting the possibility of achieving the territorial unification of Vietnam through peaceful means, we must not forget [that] the American imperialists and their lackeys still occupy one-half of our national territory and are preparing for war. That is why, while holding high the flag of peace, we must be prudent and vigilant."[98]

From the same speech, we know that during this period Ho was also concerned with the differences within the Hanoi leadership. He believed that if they were not resolved, they could weaken the collective leadership.

Unfortunately, we still do not have enough information regarding the specific problems within the North Vietnamese leadership during this period. It was likely that the issue of reunification was one of them.

In China, the primary concern was still for the economy. On 25 April 1956, Mao made a speech at the enlarged meeting of the Political Bureau of the Central Committee of the CCP in which he expounded on "the ten major relationships."[99] In the speech, Mao spelled out the ten major relationships in socialist revolution and construction and set forth the principles underlying the acceleration of economic development in China. Of the ten relationships, the one that is most pertinent to this study is the relationship between economic construction and defense construction in which Mao said that China needed the atom bomb to protect itself. According to Mao, the only reliable way to have the bomb was to cut military and administrative expenditures down to appropriate proportions and increase expenditures on economic construction. In his words, "We must strengthen our national defense, and for that purpose we must first of all strengthen our work in economic construction."[100]

VII

On 8 May, the Geneva cochairmen addressed a message to both North and South Vietnam urging them to make every effort to implement the Geneva Agreements and to prevent any violations of the military provisions and also to ensure the implementation of the political provisions embodied in the Final Declaration.[101] Both the North and South Vietnamese governments were invited to let the cochairmen know, either jointly or separately but as soon as possible, their views about the time required for the opening of consultations on the holding of the national election.[102] The Russians were more concerned about the preservation of peace than about the unification of Vietnam. After receiving the cochairmen's message, the Chinese, although they were the first to propose the idea of a new Geneva Conference, stopped calling for a conference. Having been led by China and the Soviet Union to support the idea of a new Geneva Conference, the Vietnamese Communists were again let down by their mentors, who once more failed to back them to the end.

After the outcome of the London Talks was made known, it was obvious that there would be no general election in July 1956 or even in the near future. However, the North Vietnamese continued to give the impression that they were optimistic of a peaceful unification of the country. In response to the cochairmen's message, Pham Van Dong on 11 May dispatched yet another letter to Ngo Dinh Diem calling for consultations on the election. In the letter, Dong also pledged to maintain peace.[103] Diem, with the support of the Americans, opposed a national election and never replied. Diem's insistence that the South Vietnamese government was not bound by the Geneva Agreements was already public knowledge. Notwithstanding that, on 4 June Dong wrote to the cochairmen and expressed North Vietnam's readiness for immediate consultations.[104]

The Chinese continued to give verbal support for the North Vietnamese cause. They declared that they had always been closely concerned that the Geneva Agreements were carried out and that it was their hope that Vietnam, which was their neighbor, would become a prosperous and united country in accordance with the 1954 Agreements. They further maintained that the South Vietnamese authorities should adhere to the agreements without further delay. China would continue to strive with the North Vietnamese for the full implementation of the Geneva Agreements.[105]

The Chinese at this time were very concerned about their economy as was reflected in the proceedings of the 3rd Session of the 1st National People's Congress held in Beijing June 15–30. The main attention of the congress was focused on economic issues, improvement of the conditions of the intellectuals, science, and education. As for foreign relations, the emphasis was again on the need for peaceful coexistence. Zhou Enlai's speech on foreign policy was conciliatory in tone. He urged improving Sino-Japanese relations and a peaceful solution of the Taiwan issue.[106] According to Zhou, the absence of diplomatic relations need not prevent the strengthening of cultural and economic ties.

The Chinese as well as the Russians could easily continue giving moral and verbal support from a distance. But the North Vietnamese leadership was faced with a problem. What they had to grapple with in 1956 in particular was not so much that the reunification could not take place as stipulated. Rather, it was how to convince the Southern cadres who had gathered in the North, as well as those who had been instructed to remain in the South, that the leadership had a more long-term plan to reunite the country. For this plan to be successful, it had to be kept absolutely secret.[107] This was not an easy task. According to an official North Vietnamese history, during this period, "the struggle of the people in the South to achieve the unification of Vietnam became increasingly fierce.... The revolutionary movement demanded guidance that was appropriate to a situation that was undergoing new development." In response, the politburo held a meeting on 8–9 June 1956.[108] On 19 June, Ho wrote a letter to the South Vietnamese cadres who had regrouped in the North and told them that the North was the foundation of their struggle to achieve the liberation and reunification of their country; and therefore whatever was done for North Vietnam was not only to increase the strength of the North but that of the South as well.[109] On the same day, the Politburo issued a directive that clarified the role and responsibility of the Southern cadres in their revolutionary struggle. According to the directive, the struggle at that point of time was essentially a political and not a military struggle. Therefore, they should resort to arms only in situations that called for self-defense. The plan was to concentrate on the development of the armed forces to a point when they were sure of its capability, as well as to consolidate the forces that they already control. Meanwhile, the Southern cadres were instructed to organize self-defense forces amongst the masses in order to protect the struggle and to attempt to free those cadres who had been arrested, develop more base areas, and arouse the political consciousness of the masses. The establishment of a popular front and the consolidation of the party in the South were to be the key tasks.[110]

Right up to the end of July and for sometime after, the Vietnamese Communists continued to press for a meeting to discuss the elections. On 12 July, in an interview with Leroy Hanson, the editor of *United Press*, Ho was asked what was likely to happen if nationwide elections were not held by the July 1956 deadline. His ambiguous reply was that they would continue to struggle with even greater energy to have free elections throughout the country. (The real strategy must necessarily remain a secret.) When asked if the North were willing to accept a formula under which both North and South would be regarded as separate nations recognized by the United Nations, Ho was adamant that Vietnam was a whole from the North to the South and it must be unified. Just as the USA could not be divided into two, neither could Vietnam be divided into two separate nations.[111] In any event, the elections failed to take place and the Vietnamese, Chinese, and Russians all allowed the July 1956 deadline to pass by somewhat uneventfully.[112]

Two

August 1956–December 1956

I

In the second half of 1956, the Hanoi leadership had to grapple with two sets of problems Firstly, it had to deal with problems in the North. Apart from trying to create a more cohesive collective leadership as mentioned by Ho Chi Minh in his speech at the 9th Plenary Session of the Lao Dong Central Committee in April, Ho's letter of 1 July 1956 to the Agrarian Land Reform Committee during its conference to review Round 5 ofthe agrarian reform revealed that many serious mistakes had been committed during the latest stage of the agrarian reform.[1]

We should recall that at the 6th Plenary Session in July 1954, it was decided that the first target was to restore the war-shattered economy within three years (1955–57) and pave the way for North Vietnam's economic recovery and advance to socialism.[2] Since the consolidation of the North was seen as a prerequisite to the unification of Vietnam, the success or failure of the agrarian reform would affect the pace of reunification. By August 1956, the North Vietnamese leadership was forced to come to grips with the errors that were committed in the carrying out of the agrarian reform. On 18 August, Ho Chi Minh publicly admitted that major mistakes had been made and promised that the party would do its utmost to rectify those mistakes. He appealed to everyone to unite and to resolutely correct the mistakes.[3]

Besides the peasants, the intellectuals, particularly in Hanoi, were also disaffected. That the intellectuals were unhappy with many of the policies of the DRV was not something new, but the North Vietnamese government had so far been able to control this small group of dissidents. However, the decisions of the 20th CPSU Congress in February and the Chinese example of liberalization in the field of culture in May 1956[4] provided the impetus for the North Vietnamese intellectuals to once again express their different views. During the Hanoi Municipal Congress from the end of July to early August, the delegates were extremely critical of many of the party's policies, ranging from the shortage of consumer goods to taxation. At a conference of writers and artists held from 1 to 18 August 1956, the participants demanded not only material improvements but also freedom of expression.

Secondly, the leadership also faced pressure from certain quarters in the party who felt that the "North Vietnam first" policy needed to be balanced by more consideration for the situation in the South. While these party members did not necessarily object to the approach adopted by the Hanoi leadership, they felt that more attention needed to be paid to the problems faced by those in the South.[5] The leadership had to placate and control the Southern comrades in the wake of the failed reunification. Because of the difficulties of communication, a number of regions in the South did not receive the 19 June directive mentioned earlier. After the failure to reunite the country in July, some comrades in the Plain of Reeds (region in Kien Phong and Kien Tuong Provinces and parts of Dinh Tuong, Long An, and Hau Nghia Provinces) were already making preparations to restart armed struggle. On 18 August, the same day that Ho Chi Minh made public the mistakes of the agrarian reform in the North, the Politburo sent a letter to the Nam Bo Regional Committee that reiterated and clarified the main points of the June directive.[6] In August too, while the Hanoi leadership was preoccupied with the problems in the North, Le Duan was assigned by the Politburo to remain in the South to guide the revolutionary struggle. Le Duan had by this time already written the thesis, *"Duong Loi Cach Mang Mien Nam,"* which spelled out the path that the struggle in the South would gradually advance into a violent revolution.[7] In the same month, he traveled from U Minh (the area extending along the coast of the Gulf of Siam in An Xuyen Province) across the Plain of Reeds up to Ben Tre. Le Duan instructed the Southern comrades not to conduct any further struggle in the name of the religious sects. He also entrusted Comrade Sau Duong to write a thesis on the proper conduct of armed propaganda.[8]

II

Meanwhile, events in Laos were moving at a somewhat faster pace than before. Talks between the RLG, represented by Souvanna Phouma, and the Pathet Lao, represented by Souphanouvong, took place in Vientiane between August 1 and 4.[9] At the outset of the talks, all Hanoi papers published articles welcoming the negotiations and described the talks as a very important event. *Nhan Dan* stated that unlike past attempts, the present talks were taking place under favorable conditions.[10] On 5 August 1956, a joint-communiqué was signed between the RLG and the Pathet Lao. The communiqué stated that Laos would follow a policy of neutrality; would neither join any military alliances nor allow foreign bases on its soil other than those stipulated in the Geneva Agreements; pending a political solution, both sides would observe a ceasefire; the provinces of Sam Neua and Phong Saly would be restored to the RLG; Pathet Lao fighting units would be placed under the command of the RLG and there would be no discrimination against the Pathet Lao. It was agreed that a military and a political committee would be formed to look into the implementation procedures.[11] The next day, on 6 August, Ho Chi Minh sent a message of greetings to King Sisavang Vong on the occasion of the Laotian National Day expressing the conviction that relations between the two countries would become closer.[12] Souvanna Phouma told the correspondent of the Japanese newspaper *Yomiuri* on 7 August that he would visit China in the near future. The invitation to Souvanna Phouma to visit Beijing had been extended by Zhou Enlai through the Indian channel as early as 7 May 1956.[13] He also disclosed that Laos was considering signing treaties of friendship and trade agreements with China and the Soviet Union.[14] On 8 August, it was reported that agreement had been reached between the RLG and the Pathet Lao on general elections and the establishment of a coalition government that would include the Pathet Lao and other parties.[15] A final round of talks took place on 10 August and a supplementary communiqué to the one signed on 5 August was issued.[16]

The Vietnamese Communists hailed the success of the talks as a major victory for the people of Laos. They also pointed out that the talks had provided a good example for solving political differences through negotiations on the basis of the Geneva Agreements.[17] Likewise, the Chinese were all praises for the success of the talks. They firmly supported the agreements reached, describing them as being in line with the spirit of the Geneva Accord and a good foundation for consolidating peace and independence in Laos and for bringing about democracy and unification.[18] A few days earlier, on 6 August 1956, the Chinese government had unilaterally lifted its ban on American journalists entering China. A telegram was sent to 15 U.S. news agencies inviting them to send their reporters to China for a month's visit.[19]

Souvanna Phouma arrived in China on 20 August 1956.[20] The RLG's delegation spent a week in China. The Chinese played the perfect host as they did to Sihanouk in March. In speech after speech, the Chinese stressed their support and approval for the agreements reached at the recent Vientiane talks. They did their best to convince the Laotians that although their social systems were different, they were sincere about establishing friendly relations with Laos on the basis of the Five Principles of peaceful coexistence, just like their ties with India, Indonesia, Burma, Pakistan, and most recently Cambodia. Indeed, at the Sino-American ambassadorial meeting at Warsaw on 21 August 1956, the Chinese representative, Wang Bingnan, had proposed that talks on subsidiary issues, such as trade restrictions and other kinds of contact, could be settled before matters of principle. The Chinese were prepared for the time being to put aside the intractable issue of the renunciation of force regarding Taiwan.[21] According to Souvanna Phouma, in the only serious discussion during the visit, which lasted for two to three hours on the evening of 25 August, the Chinese leaders had welcomed the progress made in the RLG's discussions with the Pathet Lao, but had made no attempt to intervene. Zhou Enlai also compared the Taiwan issue with that of the Pathet Lao saying that he too would patiently seek a peaceful solution. Zhou spoke much about China's need for peace in order to complete her program of internal development and expressed pleasure at having a friendly Laos pursuing the same policy. He did not press for the establishment of formal diplomatic relations but suggested a border regime that would oversee local inhabitants moving within the border zone.[22] At the end of the visit, both countries signed a joint statement that expressed their mutual desire to observe the Five Principles of peaceful coexistence and to promote good neighborly relations.[23] The Sino-Laotian joint statement was hailed by the Vietnamese Communists as a new success for the Five Principles and the Bandung spirit, which showed that cooperation was quite possible among countries of different regimes.[24]

On 28 August, the RLG delegation arrived in Hanoi from China. In his speech of welcome, Pham Van Dong said that the visit had opened a new phase in the good neighborly relations between North Vietnam and Laos. The North Vietnamese put on their most amiable appearance and did their best to deny that they had interfered in the internal politics of Laos. A joint statement was also issued at the end of the one-day visit, reaffirming that the relations of the two countries would be based upon the Five Principles of peaceful coexistence and that outstanding issues between them would be settled by peaceful negotiations.[25] The Chinese declared that the talks between the RLG delegation and the DRV were "a vital contribution to peace in Indochina."[26]

The main stumbling block that prevented a national reconciliation in Laos had been the intractability of the Pathet Lao. Souvanna Phouma had gone to Beijing and Hanoi because he and the Laotian leadership believed that in order to get the Pathet Lao on board, the most effective way was to deal directly with the Vietnamese and Chinese Communists.[27] During this period, as we have seen, the North Vietnamese and the Chinese, for their own reasons, were both keen to pursue a strategy of coexistence in the region. Consequently, the Pathet Lao became more cooperative and less obdurate. The Chinese appeared satisfied with the way their ties with Cambodia and Laos had so far developed. Compared to the Chinese, the North Vietnamese appeared more anxious to establish formal diplomatic relations with their two neighbors, but they were unsuccessful. The Cambodians and the Laotians remained wary of the North Vietnamese.[28]

III

In Hanoi in September, the 10th Plenary Session of the Party Central Committee met to discuss ways of rectifying the errors that had been made in the course of the agrarian reform. According to Wilfred Burchett, the session lasted the whole of September and part of October.[29] Hoang Van Hoan described it as "the longest meeting since the founding of the Party."[30] That it was such a long session would indicate the gravity — and possibly the divisiveness — of the issues. At the end it was agreed, though not unanimously, that the Agrarian Reform Committee had failed to correctly implement the reform. A decision to draw up a resolution that would summarize the experiences gained from the debacle had to be shelved because of a lack of consensus.[31] At the 10th Plenary Session, it was decided that the unification of Vietnam would have to be further delayed and top priority was accorded to the improvement of the living conditions in the North.[32]

Meanwhile, on 20 September, the first issue of a dissident magazine entitled *Nhan Van* was published. (Between 20 September and 20

November, five issues were published.) *Nhan Van* was by no means the only dissident publication, although it was perhaps the best known. A collection of writings entitled *Giai Pham,* which was seized by the cultural authorities when it was first published on the eve of Tet, 1956, was also reprinted. From late September onward, the situation thus became grave as intellectuals through their writings and publications started to discuss themes such as individual freedom and the pursuit of democracy.[33] Initially, the party, following the lead of its two mentors, seemed prepared to accept a certain degree of openness, took the criticisms well in stride, and in fact encouraged the spirit of self-criticism. This was particularly so in the wake of the agrarian reform crisis. Much time and energy were therefore channeled to quell unrest and criticisms of the party leadership.[34]

On 29 October, the conclusion of the 10th Plenary Session was announced in the form of a communiqué in which the Central Committee admitted responsibility for the mistakes committed and stated that corrective measures had been and were being taken to rectify them. The correction of errors was now to be one of the party's major tasks.[35] On the same day, the Central Committee and the Hanoi Committee of the Fatherland Front assembled about 10,000 cadres, workers, peasants, officials, intellectuals, traders, and so on to listen to a two-hour speech by Vo Nguyen Giap on the topics of agrarian reform, democratic reforms, improvement of living conditions, and only finally, the struggle for the reunification of the country.[36] The Hanoi Radio report of 30 October on the work of the 10th Plenary Session also relegated the struggle for unification of Vietnam to third place after democratization and the improvement of living conditions.[37]

One significant result of the session was Truong Chinh's resignation as the secretary-general of the Lao Dong Party, which was announced on 29 October. The resignation of Truong Chinh, who had been the secretary-general of the party since 1941, must have seriously tested the cohesion of the Hanoi leadership. As late as 25 October, it was Truong Chinh who had addressed the National Congress of Vietnam Youth Union for National Salvation on behalf of the Lao Dong Party. In his speech, although he called upon the union to participate fully in the work of correcting the mistakes committed during the agrarian reform, he did not admit any responsibility for the mistakes.[38] But the situation was sufficiently grave and the public had to be mollified. Truong Chinh, as the main North Vietnamese leader responsible for the agrarian reforms, had to bear the brunt of it.[39] The choice of Giap — the victor at Dien

Bien Phu — as the party spokesman on 29 October could be seen as due to the need to put forward a popular figure in a bid to regain the confidence and support of the people. According to Bui Tin, Ho Chi Minh had two persons in mind who could replace Truong Chinh and carry out the rectification of the agrarian debacle — Giap and Le Duan. Ho's preference was for Giap because they had worked together for many years.[40] However, there is no evidence yet to suggest that Giap's position was substantially strengthened by the fall of Truong Chinh. In any event, Truong Chinh was replaced by Ho himself, undoubtedly the most popular figure in the North, and probably the most acceptable choice amongst the Hanoi leadership. Although Truong Chinh had to relinquish his position as secretary-general, he remained a member of the politburo and played a significant role in the rectification of the agrarian reform. In 1957 he was appointed head of the Rectification of Errors Campaign. In addition to the demotion of Truong Chinh, the other members of the Agrarian Reform Committee, both Le Van Luong and Ho Viet Thang, were dismissed from their party and government positions, and Hoang Quoc Viet was dropped from the politburo.

A question that needs to be addressed at this point is whether the failure of the agrarian reform affected Vietnamese relations with China. The Vietnamese Communists' policy of land reform was patterned upon that of the Chinese and guided by Chinese advisers since 1953.[41] According to Bui Tin, all members of the land reform group — Truong Chinh, Hoang Quoc Viet, Le Van Luong, Ho Viet Thang, and Chu Van Bien — were "disciples" of Mao Zedong and they accepted the views of the Chinese advisers completely.[42] The Chinese apparently did not agree with the conclusion regarding the agrarian reform reached at the 10th Plenary Session and felt that the Vietnamese leadership had overreacted. According to one Chinese source, the different perceptions regarding the agrarian reform represented one of the major points of divergence between the Vietnamese and the Chinese before 1965. However, it did not gravely affect Sino-Vietnamese relations.[43] There is as yet no evidence to suggest that it led to a tilt away from China toward the Soviet Union at this time. At the 10th Plenary Session, Nguyen Duy Trinh, Le Thanh Nghi, and Hoang Van Hoan were elected members of the political bureau.[44] Of the three, we are now certain that Hoang Van Hoan had very close ties with the Chinese. During this time, he was the North Vietnamese ambassador to China.[45] Nguyen Duy Trinh was also believed to be well disposed toward Beijing.[46] Also, when Hanoi completed its economic restoration at the end of 1957 and began its socialist revolution in 1958 with the launching of its three-year economic plan (1958–1960), Chinese assistance remained considerable.[47]

On 21 October 1956, it was reported that Brigadier General Nguyen Son died of cancer. Nguyen Son was the former commander-in-chief of Interzone IV, who had very close ties with the Chinese. He was a member of the CCP and had taken part in revolutionary activities in China, including the Long March.[48] It was reported that Ho Chi Minh, Pham Van Dong, and Phan Ke Toai were among the leading members of the party who paid their last respects. On 22 October, he was posthumously decorated with the War Cross. The rumor carried to the South by refugees from the North was that he had led a rebellion and was actually executed on Truong Chinh's order.[49] However, there was no evidence to ascertain that.[50] Two years later, on the anniversary of Dien Bien Phu on 7 May 1958, Nguyen Son was posthumously awarded the First Class Victory Order. Thus, until the theory regarding Son's death is confirmed by factual evidence, the award can only suggest that Nguyen Son's death was due to illness as reported.

IV

At the time the Lao Dong Party was holding its 10th Plenary Session in September, the Chinese held their 8th CCP National Congress from September 15 to 27 in Beijing, the first since 1945. The proceedings of the congress dealt mainly with internal and economic affairs. According to Liu Shaoqi in his political report, China had followed the Five Principles of peaceful coexistence in her dealing with international affairs and would continue to carry out this policy in the future. In his words, "the Chinese people and all the peoples of the world need peace."[51] Regarding Taiwan, Liu said that they would resort to force only if all possibilities of peaceful negotiation failed.[52] At the 8th Congress, it was decided that the budget for defense and administration would be reduced and the economy would have priority over defense.

In Chen Yi's report on foreign policy delivered on 25 September, he made the following points: (a) China needed a peaceful international environment in order to build itself into a prosperous, happy, socialist, and industrialized country; (b) the growing strength, unity, and solidarity of the socialist camp would be the cornerstone to safeguard peace (China considered the consolidation and development of unity and cooperation with the Soviet Union and other socialist countries as of prime importance); (c) it was the firm conviction of China that countries with different social systems should live together in peace; (d) the Chinese government was willing to establish diplomatic relations with any government that was willing to observe the Five Principles of peaceful coexistence, and that included the United States.[53] Chinese foreign policy therefore remained essentially the same as the foreign policy statement Zhou Enlai made on 28 June 1956 during the 3rd Session of the 1st National People's Congress. It was also consistent with what the Chinese had intimated to Sihanouk and Souvanna Phouma.

The role and responsibilities of the Chinese PLA were also discussed during the congress.[54] According to Peng Dehuai, the minister of defense, the most important task of the PLA was to fight imperialist aggression and to safeguard the construction of China. Peng said that China needed an environment of lasting peace to carry on socialist construction. At the same time, she needed a modern revolutionary army to meet any contingency. In order that the PLA could carry out its task effectively, there was a need for a strong reserve force as well as a regular army, which was the reason China had introduced compulsory military service in place of the voluntary military system. In the modernization of the PLA, Peng spoke of the need to master both modern military science as well as Marxism-Leninism. Learning from the Soviet Army was a shortcut toward the speedy modernization of the PLA. But he also stressed that in the process of learning, the PLA should combine what it learned from others with their own historic experiences.

Both Peng Dehuai and Tan Zheng, director of the General Political Department in the PLA, maintained that political work remained the lifeline of the PLA. But there was a difference in the perceptions of the two men. To Peng, the military commanders and the political commissars were both leaders of the troops, but once the party committees had made their decisions, they should adopt a hands-off attitude and let the military commanders exercise their initiative. It was therefore a mistake for the party committees to interfere in the daily work of the army and to take everything into their hands. On the other hand, Tan Zheng felt that although the chain of command had become highly centralized, all parts of the army should still be subjected to the supervision of local party organizations. They should not repudiate this supervision on the pretext of modernization and the centralization of the army's chain of command.[55]

We now know that there were differences between Mao on the one hand and Liu Shaoqi and Deng Xiaoping on the other, as well as amongst other personalities in the Chinese leadership during this time.[56] But at this stage they remained muted. China's policies as spelled out during the 8th Party Congress in 1956 were substantially similar to the policies the Russians adopted at their 20th Party Congress in February. In the words of Khrushchev; "I particularly admired Liu's report to the 8th Chinese Party Congress, in which he laid out the tasks confronting the Chinese people and party. He seemed to agree with the point of view held by the leaders of our own Party as reflected in the decisions of the 20th, 21st, and 22nd Soviet Party Congresses."[57] In line with the Soviet policy of discouraging any form of personality cult, at the 8th Party Congress the Chinese passed a resolution emphasizing collective leadership and removing all references to "Mao Zedong Thought" from the constitution. However, Mao's position was by no means seriously threatened by this.

What is particularly significant for us is that by the time of the 10th Plenary Session of the Central Committee of the Lao Dong Party and the 8th Congress of the CCP, both North Vietnam and China had independently and for their own specific reasons concluded that they needed a period of peaceful coexistence.

V

During the months of October and November 1956, a crisis developed in Eastern Europe, specifically in Poland and Hungary, that threatened the solidarity of the socialist bloc. In Poland, the appointment of Gomulka as first secretary of the Polish Communist Party initially did not please the Russians. Gomulka had demanded that Polish national interests should be of overriding importance. He planned to drop Soviet Marshal Konstantin Rokossovsky from the Polish Political Bureau and Foreign Ministry as an indication of Polish independence and national integrity. The Soviets feared that this would jeopardize their position and set a dangerous precedent. On 19 October, Khrushchev and other Soviet leaders flew to Warsaw. Soviet tank formations were positioned to move in as well. Under these circumstances, Gomulka was prepared to strike a deal with the Russians. In exchange for Soviet tolerance, Poland remained within the Soviet alliance. In the case of Hungary, the appointment of Imre Nagy on 23 October as the new Hungarian premier was accepted by the Russians until Nagy proceeded to support the withdrawal of Hungary from the Warsaw Pact and the holding of free multiparty elections. These the Russians could not tolerate, and on 4 November, Russian troops moved into Budapest and installed a new government under Janos Kadar.[58]

As members of the socialist fraternity, it was not surprising that the Vietnamese and Chinese Communists followed the developments in Poland and Hungary closely. Both supported the Soviet Union to the hilt. The Chinese played a significant role in the two crises.[59] According to Fedor Burlatsky, at the request of Khrushchev, Liu Shaoqi, who was respected in the Soviet Union as one of the most authoritative Chinese leaders, flew to Moscow to discuss the matter. Liu Shaoqi was in Moscow probably between 22 October and 4 November.[60] According to a Chinese source, on the request of the CPSU Central Committee, both Liu and Deng Xiaoping paid a secret visit to Moscow.[61] Although Mao concurred with the Russian decision to move troops into Budapest, he believed that Khrushchev's secret speech at the 20th CPSU Congress was the root cause of the problem.[62] This was the first time that the Chinese were involved in the political developments of an area that had always been regarded as within the Russian sphere of influence, and it raised the status of the CCP in the socialist bloc.

The crisis within the socialist bloc was over by early November, but not without some ramifications for Soviet and Chinese interests in Indochina. As a consequence of the events in Poland and Hungary, the Laotian leadership expressed doubts as to the sincerity of the peaceful coexistence policy espoused by the Chinese and North Vietnamese. We should recall that in June 1956, the Soviet Union made overtures to Laos regarding the establishment of diplomatic relations and an exchange of missions. It also granted de jure recognition to the Laotian government. The latter acknowledged Soviet recognition without at that time taking any action on its own part. The Laotian cabinet had decided on an exchange of missions when the Hungarian crisis led them to have second thoughts.[63] According to the British ambassador, Souvanna Phouma had angrily commented to him then that if one of the Communist Big Two did not hesitate to take ruthless action against a small country trying to be free, why should the other hesitate to do likewise in Asia?[64] On 14 November, the Chinese reported the statement of the prime ministers of the four Colombo Powers calling for the Soviet Union to withdraw its forces from Hungary.[65] But they failed to mention Tito's speech, which described the Russian leadership as hardened Stalinists and blamed them for what happened in Hungary. The Hungarian crisis had inadvertently put China's credibility in the eyes of the non-Communist countries to the test. The Chinese would have to reconcile their support for the Soviet actions with their proclaimed support for the Five Principles of peaceful coexistence.

VI

Meanwhile, in North Vietnam the government had to squash the Quynh Luu uprising (2–14 November 1956) in Nghe An Province, which arose as a consequence of the harsh practices of the agrarian reform and the discontent of the largely Catholic population there.[66] It was said that the 325th Division of the VPA had to be called in to put down the rebellion.[67] Order was apparently restored only on 19 November.[68] The government also resorted to repressing the more outspoken intellectuals in the cities, and on 18 December, the authorities confiscated and banned "subversive" publications — most notably, the *Nhan Van*.[69] The North Vietnamese government's move against the intellectuals coincided with the Chinese halting of their liberalization drive in the wake of the Hungarian crisis. The policy of liberalization in China was, however, not abandoned but was for the moment put on hold.[70]

The consequence of all these developments was that the struggle for the reunification of the North and South received less attention. According to U.S. State Department sources, on top of all these problems, the Hanoi leadership also had to expend considerable effort on bolstering the morale of the cadres who had regrouped in the North as well as the cadres in the South who were anxiously waiting for reunification.[71]

On 18 November, a Chinese delegation led by Zhou Enlai arrived in Hanoi, the first stop of a series of state visits to eight Asian countries.[72] Zhou was accompanied by Marshal He Long, vice-premier and vice-chairman of the National Defense Council. Traveling on the same plane as the Chinese delegation was Hoang Van Hoan and Yong Aun, head of the Cambodian economic mission to China. The first news of Zhou's visit was a brief announcement from the VNA on 16 November. A few hours later, the DRV Foreign Ministry issued a communiqué saying that the Chinese premier would arrive on 18 November at the invitation of the DRV Government.[73] This gives the impression that Zhou's inclusion of North Vietnam — the only socialist country of the eight — in his itinerary was a late decision. The news of Zhou's impending visit came in the immediate aftermath of the Quynh Luu uprising. Indeed, as we have noted above, order was not restored in the province till 19 November. However, according to U.S. officials in Saigon, Zhou's visit to Hanoi, though not well advertised, was known about in advance, although it was impossible to speculate as to whether an emergency stop would have been made in the light of the Quynh Luu uprising.[74]

On 17 November, the *Hanoi Daily* recalled the jubilant atmosphere during Mikoyan's visit in April and spoke of the same jubilant feeling for Zhou's visit.[75] The *Nhan Dan* editorial on 18 November described the visit as of great significance for the development of the sacred friendship between the Chinese and Vietnamese people and a reflection of the solidarity and single-mindedness in the socialist camp.[76] However, the British consul-general made the observation that Zhou's visit was not nearly as widely heralded as that of Mikoyan.[77]

The *VNA* did not list Truong Chinh in its report of the welcoming party at the airport, but the *NCNA* report listed him after Ton Duc Thang. Truong Chinh was still described by the *NCNA* as the Secretary of the Lao Dong Party Secretariat, but the subsequent report on the banquet in the evening described him only as a member of the politburo.[78] In his speech of welcome at the airport, Pham Van Dong spoke of the long history of friendship between the Vietnamese and the Chinese and said that the visit of Zhou would further enhance the relationship between them. Zhou, in his reply, described the friendship of the two countries as unshakable, warm, brotherly, and firm.[79] On the same afternoon, Ho received Zhou at the presidential palace. With Ho was Pham Van Dong, Phan Ke Toai, Vo Nguyen Giap, Nguyen Duy Trinh, Ung Van Khiem, and Hoang Van Hoan.[80] In the evening, Pham Van Dong gave a reception in honor of Zhou. In his dinner speech, Dong spoke of the selfless and effective help of the Chinese in Vietnam's economic reconstruction. Zhou, in turn, said that China would continue to give firm support to the Vietnamese struggle. He also referred to the Five Principles of peaceful coexistence.[81] On the morning of 19 November, Zhou attended a rally at Ba Dinh Square.[82] That afternoon, there was a meeting between Pham Van Dong and Zhou. Phan Ke Toai, Vo Nguyen Giap and the two ambassadors were also present.[83] Zhou, accompanied by Pham Van Dong, later visited the Vietnam-China Friendship Association. In the evening, he attended a banquet given in his honor by the chairman of the Hanoi Administrative Committee, Tran Duy Hung.[84] The next morning, Zhou visited the Jade Mountain Pagoda, the Pioneer's Club, the Temple of the Two Trung Sisters, and Hanoi University. Addressing the staff and students of Hanoi University, Zhou said that every state and nationality had its own good points. China would send some students and experts to study in Vietnam.[85] In the afternoon, Zhou visited the Unity Match Factory and Gia Lam Railway Works.

At a reception given by the Chinese ambassador in the evening, which Ho Chi Minh also attended, Zhou said that China would always abide by the Five Principles and opposed "great-nation chauvinism."[86] In referring to "great-nation chauvinism," Zhou was alluding to the Russian handling of the recent crisis in Eastern Europe. The Chinese view was that cooperation amongst the socialist countries should be based on equality and non-interference; and that while differences were to be expected, they should be resolved through friendly talks and consultation; if that was not possible, they should be minimized because the unity of the bloc should never be undermined. We can infer from Zhou's speech that this would be the Chinese attitude regarding their differences with the North Vietnamese over the handling of the recent agrarian reform debacle in North Vietnam. That night at the Chinese embassy, Zhou met the representatives of the overseas Chinese community living in Vietnam.

On the morning of 21 November, Zhou and He Long paid a visit to the Zhonghua Middle School in Hanoi, which had been founded by Sun Yat Sen 50 years before. Addressing the students, Zhou urged the Chinese students to study the good points of the Vietnamese people and their language. He pointed out that education for overseas Chinese should be integrated with the practical conditions in China, as well as with those in the country where they resided.[87] On that same afternoon, Pham Van Dong and Zhou resumed the talks that they had started on the afternoon of 19 November.[88] In the evening, Ho Chi Minh gave a banquet in honor of Zhou. In his speech, Ho described Zhou as a brother and a comrade-in-arms for the past 30 or more years who had shared the same joys and sorrows and worked for the revolution. Zhou thanked Ho for his speech and said that China's assistance to Vietnam referred to by Ho was not worth mentioning. The real strength of Vietnam came from her people. Zhou described Ho as his big brother and recalled that 34 years ago in Paris, Ho was his guide. They then pinned red roses on each others' coats.[89] While in Hanoi, Marshal He Long also introduced Taiji Quan to Ho and in early 1957, he sent a Chinese instructor to Hanoi to teach Ho.[90]

At the end of the four-day visit, on the morning of 22 November, a joint statement was signed in which both countries expressed deep concern over events that had caused international tension brought about by the imperialists; their satisfaction with the developments in Cambodia and Laos as well as their relations with those two countries on the basis of the Five Principles of peaceful coexistence; and their insistence that the agreements reached at Geneva in 1954 should be observed. The Vietnamese acknowledged the importance of Chinese technical assistance while the Chinese instructed their advisers in Vietnam to be industrious and as modest as the Vietnamese and not to expect special treatment. Both leaders reiterated their support for the Soviet statement of 30 October 1956 on developing cooperation between the Soviet Union and other socialist countries. Lastly, they pledged that Sino-Vietnamese relations as well as their relations with other countries would be guided by the Five Principles and that mistakes due to "chauvinism" would be resolutely prevented.[91]

Some observations on Zhou's visit were made by Canadian officials in Hanoi. A member of the Canadian delegation to the ISCC reported that Zhou was "demonstrably cool to Pham Van Dong and all but ignored him" at two receptions that the Canadian attended. Another Canadian present in Hanoi during Zhou's visit reported that the Chinese premier "was friendly to all but DRV officials and appeared to have little use for the DRV premier, Pham Van Dong." The free circulation of Truong Chinh at the receptions given for Zhou was also noted.[92]

Compared to Mikoyan's visit in April, Zhou's visit was admittedly less elaborate. But this was understandable given the domestic problems that were dogging the North Vietnamese. Zhou, in fact, arrived in Hanoi less than a week after the uprisings in Nghe An Province. Many years later, the Vietnamese Communists were to accuse the Chinese of preventing them from reunifying the country in 1956. In the *White Book*, the Vietnamese claimed that in November 1956 they were told that the partition of Vietnam could not be solved in a short time. It might take a long time; and if ten years was not enough, they should be prepared for a hundred years.[93] But as we have noted above, the Hanoi leadership had already on their own arrived at more or less the same conclusion as the Chinese that the partition could not be solved in a short time. The difference, perhaps, was that their Chinese mentor could afford to be more patient.

VII

After Hanoi, the Chinese delegation proceeded to Cambodia.[94] Zhou was in Cambodia from 22 to 27 November. There, he declared his support and respect for the country's policy of peace and neutrality and reiterated China's commitment to conduct her foreign relations on the basis of the Five Principles. He also made a point to assure the Cambodians that China opposed "great-nation chauvinism." In his address to the Cambodian Parliament on 23 November, Zhou said that China's economy was still very backward as a result of the long years of "colonialist scourge." The Chinese aim was to transform the country from a backward agricultural land into an advanced industrial one as soon as possible. Zhou thought that the transformation process would take a fairly long time and China needed a peaceful international environment.[95]

Speaking at a reception to Chinese residents living in Cambodia, Zhou exhorted them to abide by Cambodian laws and decrees and those who have not taken Cambodian nationality to refrain from taking part in political activities.[96] While in Cambodia, Zhou also referred to the issue of the unification of China. Once again, he spoke of China's intention to achieve the liberation of Taiwan through peaceful means. According to Zhou, the Chinese Communists had twice cooperated with the Guomindang, so there was no reason why they could not cooperate a third time. We should recall that Zhou conveyed the same message regarding China's desire for a peaceful unification of Taiwan to Souvanna Phouma when the latter was in Beijing in August 1956. However, there is no record of him mentioning Taiwan during his recent trip to Hanoi. Speaking to American reporters in Phnom Penh, Zhou reiterated the Chinese invitation to American journalists to visit China. (The invitation was first extended in August 1956.)[97] At the end of the visit, a joint statement was signed that reaffirmed the Five Principles.[98] Sihanouk was clearly pleased with the Chinese attitude. In his speech at the farewell party hosted by the Chinese, he spoke of Cambodia's neutrality and how it had been misunderstood abroad except for "a number of wise people," of which he identified Zhou as one of the few.[99] According to *Nhan Dan*, Zhou's visit to Cambodia had further strengthened Sino-Cambodian relations and contributed to the consolidation of peace in Asia.[100]

On the afternoon of 27 November, Zhou returned to Hanoi. He was met at the airport by a small contingent comprising Pham Van Dong, Hoang Van Hoan, the Chinese ambassador, and the Indian consul-general.[101] It was rumored that Zhou returned to Hanoi because of the tense situation in North Vietnam. But his return to Hanoi had been prearranged so that he could rejoin the long-range aircraft that was unable to land in Phnom Penh.[102] According to Indian officials in Phnom Penh, Zhou would merely change planes in Hanoi, but instead, he stayed overnight and left for India the next morning.[103]

VIII

In North Vietnam, the Lao Dong Central Committee held its 11th Plenary Session in December 1956. One of the most important lessons that the North Vietnamese leadership drew from the Hungarian episode was the necessity of leading governments to pay adequate attention to the people's living conditions and adopt a correct attitude when confronted with mistakes,[104] which further confirmed the validity of their stand that before anything else, it was necessary to put the North in order first. During this plenary session, it was asserted that the party had not fully grasped the line and policy for economic restoration laid down by the political bureau in September 1954; the general task for 1957 was thus to conclude the work of restoration and to increase production — particularly agricultural production. Light industry and handicrafts were also key areas, and trade was to play an important role. All economic policies were aimed at impressing the South.

The 11th Plenary Session also affirmed that revolution was the correct way to liberate South Vietnam.[105] At that session, it was agreed in principle that Le Duan's thesis, *Duong Loi Cach Mang Mien Nam* would serve as the basis of the three-pronged strategy: (a) the consolidation of the North, (b) sustaining the struggle in the South, and (c) winning international support for their cause.[106] Although the available official Vietnamese sources concur that this thesis served as the basis for the Lao Dong Party's revolutionary line in the South, according to Tran Van Tra it was neither formalized nor fully implemented till three years later.[107] Thus the basic strategy for the unification of the country spelled out at the 6th Plenary Session in July 1954 remained essentially unchanged.[108]

Following the 11th Plenary Session, the 2nd Conference of the Nam Bo Regional Committee took place in December. It was presided over by Le Duan and Nguyen Van Linh, the general-secretary of the Nam Bo Regional Committee. The meeting passed a resolution on the organization and activities of the self-defense forces drafted by Nguyen Minh Duong. The resolution stated that in this period during which South Vietnam was engaged in a political struggle, it was not yet time to carry out guerrilla warfare. However, due to the needs of the revolutionary movement in the South, it was necessary to have self-defense and armed propaganda forces in order to support the political struggle and eventually to use those armed forces to carry out the violent revolution. The meeting decided on the following mission: Build propaganda forces, set up secret armed units, and create base areas in the forested mountains in eastern Nam Bo, the Plain of Reeds, and U Minh; win over as many disaffected people as possible and kill traitors.[109] Nguyen Huu Xuyen was instructed to remain in Nam Bo to oversee the building up of the armed forces in the South.[110]

One of the most important decisions made at this meeting was the lifting of the restriction on the use of force in the South. According to the *Lich Su Quan Doi Nhan Dan Viet Nam*, at this meeting armed propaganda was advocated. But, it was made very clear that until the North was ready, the struggle in the South would not be intensified. In other words, the Southern cadres, although they were now given more freedom of action, were cautioned against embarking on premature adventures that were not in line with developments in the North.

Soon after this meeting, sometime around the end of 1956 or the beginning of 1957, Le Duan left South Vietnam for the North to assume the position of acting secretary-general to assist Ho in the running of the daily affairs of the party.[111] William J. Duiker believed that Le Duan was the de facto secretary-general. Tran Van Tra, in his memoir, said that from the end of 1956, Le Duan was the secretary-general.[112] According to Hoang Van Hoan, Le Duan was chosen because he had advocated some form of agrarian reforms to improve the lot of the peasants in the South and it was therefore thought that he was the right person to assist Ho in the aftermath of the agrarian reform debacle in the North.[113] Bui Tin revealed that Ho's preference for the post was Giap. But Le Duc Tho, who was influential as head of the party's Organization Department, supported Le Duan. Le Duc Tho's view in this matter was significant.[114] According to Hoang Van Hoan, Le Duc Tho was Le Duan's most trusted follower.[115] Apparently it was felt that the many years that Le Duan had spent in imprisonment in Poulo Condore identified him as the most trustworthy person to oversee the implementation of the three-pronged strategy spelled out in his thesis *Duong Loi Cach Mang Mien Nam* (which was broadly accepted at the recent 11th Plenary Session) and the eventual reunification of North and South Vietnam. According to Bui Tin, Le Duan held on to the view that war was inevitable. Thus from 1957, Le Duan's role and responsibilities were no longer confined to the narrow perspective of the South but, from a much wider vantage point, encompassing not only the North and South, but the international environment as well.

Three

January 1957–December 1957

I

Domestic concern was uppermost in the minds of the North Vietnamese Communists in 1957. The 6th Session of the DRV National Assembly (29 December 1956–25 January 1957) amplified the decisions reached at the recent 11th Plenary Session. Regarding the economy, the immediate task was to try to complete as quickly as possible the task of rectifying the mistakes made in the agrarian reform. In the area of defense, it was agreed that although peace had been restored, it had yet to be consolidated. The National Assembly approved the demobilization of 80,000 volunteers and the introduction of compulsory military service. In his address to the National Assembly, Pham Van Dong stated that peaceful coexistence would remain the cornerstone of the DRV's foreign policy. Special mention was made with regard to further improving relations with Cambodia and Laos. As for the unification of the country, Dong reiterated the call for consultations between the North and the South.[1]

Just when the National Assembly was winding up its proceedings, the North Vietnamese were confronted with an urgent problem. On 23 January 1957, 13 states submitted two draft resolutions calling upon the Security Council to reconsider the applications of South Korea and South Vietnam for membership in the United Nations. The Soviet Union, evidently without consulting Hanoi, also submitted a draft resolution of its own, proposing that the Security Council should reconsider the applications of North Korea and North Vietnam as well, thus admitting all four states as members of the United Nations. According to Wang Bingnan, who was the Chinese ambassador to Poland from April 1955 to 1964 and also the Chinese representative at the Sino-U.S. ambassadorial talks from 1955 till 1964, Khrushchev had been floating this proposal since 1956 through the Soviet ambassador in Washington. The Soviet idea was therefore well known in diplomatic circles both in the United States and China.[2] In November 1956, when Zhou Enlai was in Hanoi, he had reassured Ho Chi Minh that China would not agree to such a proposal. Describing Khrushchev's action as a "selling out," Zhou said that China would not be "a party to this betrayal."[3] (China, of course, was not a member of the United Nations, and therefore had no opportunity to vote on the resolutions.)

Another draft resolution was submitted by India and Syria, who considered that the matter required further examination and proposed that the Security Council be provided with all the relevant records so that it could consider all the applications for admission.[4] On 25 January, Pham Van Dong wrote to the members of the Security Council and the Chairman of the United Nations General Assembly arguing that South Vietnam was not a separate nation and its application for admission into the United Nations was at variance with the spirit of the Geneva Agreements. The next day, Ung Van Khiem, DRV's deputy-foreign minister, handed out copies of that letter to representatives of the diplomatic corps in Hanoi. Jean Sainteny, then the chief French representative to the DRV, was invited to the Foreign Ministry where the North Vietnamese protested against French support for the South Vietnamese.[5] The United Nations Special Political Committee on 30 January adopted the 13-power draft resolution and rejected that of the Soviet Union. In light of the committee's decision, the representatives of India and Syria decided to withdraw their joint draft resolution. The recommendation of the Special Political Committee was subsequently adopted by the General Assembly on 28 February 1957. The next step was for the Security Council to reconsider the two 13-power resolutions.[6] The resolutions were eventually discussed at the 789th and 790th meetings of the Security Council on 9 September 1957. The Russians vetoed the 13-power draft resolutions and insisted that the question of admission be postponed till after the unification of North and South Vietnam.[7]

Meanwhile, Zhou Enlai interrupted his Asian tour and returned to Beijing on 3 January 1957 after having visited North Vietnam, Cambodia, India, Burma, and Pakistan.[8] On 7 January, he proceeded to Moscow, Warsaw, and Budapest. The U.S. State Department observed that following the crisis in Eastern Europe in the summer of 1956, Moscow seemed to have gone out of the way to publicize Chinese Communist expressions of approval for Soviet courses of action.[9] Zhou's visit was hailed as "an important event in the friendship between China and the Soviet Union."[10] The invitation of the Chinese premier to visit Moscow, Warsaw, and Budapest on short notice once again underscored the growing prestige of China in the socialist bloc.

After visiting Moscow, Warsaw, and Budapest, Zhou resumed his Asian tour on 19 January, visiting Afghanistan, Nepal, and Sri Lanka before returning home on 6 February 1957. In all the Asian countries he visited, Zhou stressed the policy of peaceful coexistence and Asian-African solidarity in the fight against colonialism. After ensuring that the external conditions were conducive for China's economic construction, the Chinese refocused their attention back to their principal domestic concerns. In his report on foreign relations to the 2nd National Committee of the Chinese People's Political Consultative Conference (5–20 March 1957), Zhou expressed satisfaction with his recent Asian tour and visits to Moscow, Warsaw, and Budapest. He spoke of the general trend of the world situation toward relaxation and progress, of the varying roads to independence, the common desire for peace and friendship, and the Bandung spirit. While reiterating China's determination to safeguard its sovereignty and liberate Taiwan, he once again expressed the willingness to settle the dispute between China and the U.S.A through peaceful negotiations.[11]

Beijing did not support the Russian proposal to admit both Vietnams into the United Nations. However, there were also no reports of any Chinese protests on behalf of the North Vietnamese. We have no indication that Khrushchev discussed the Soviet proposal with Zhou while the latter was in Moscow. The "United Nations episode" did not arise till after Zhou Enlai had left Moscow on 19 January 1957. In April 1957, Pham Van Dong went to Beijing for discussions with Zhou Enlai and Chen Yun regarding North Vietnam's economic plans. Also, a delegation from the Lao Dong Party Organization Department led by Le Duc Tho spent almost four months in China, from April 1957 to July 1957.[12]

In North Vietnam, apart from the economy and the UN episode, attention was also focused on the development of the VPA. We should recall that as early as the 6th Plenary Session in July 1954, it had already been recognized that in order to deal effectively with the post–Geneva new revolutionary situation, there was the need to develop the army into a modern and regular one. The whole issue of modernizing the army was reviewed at the 12th Plenary Session of the Lao Dong Central

Committee in March 1957, at which Le Duan would have been present. At the plenary session, General Giap emphasized that for the VPA to be able to effectively carry out its missions of protecting the North and unifying the country, it must be gradually developed into a modern and regular army.[13] The leadership, while acknowledging that necessity, felt that the modernization of the army should be in tandem with the pace of the economic reconstruction of the North. They cautioned against hasty and impractical changes. Taking into account the existing limitations of the army and the economic condition of the North, they anticipated that it would be a long and arduous process. The leadership also decided that the system of voluntary enlistment was to be replaced with the system of obligatory military service. The modernization of the VPA was targeted for completion in 1959.[14] This target would suggest that Hanoi was not prepared for military action in South Vietnam or Laos before 1959 at the earliest.

The process of modernizing the VPA was carried out with the assistance of the fraternal socialist countries. All aspects of the military—staffing, training, weaponry—were gradually reconfigured along the lines of modern doctrines of warfare.[15] In 1972, Giap recalled that the resolution of the 12th Plenary Session of the Party Central Committee marked "a new step of development in the party's military theory in general and in its theory on building the armed forces in particular."[16]

Some months later, on 16 May 1957, Ho in an address to middle- and senior-ranking officers from the Ministry of Defense who were attending a reeducation class to study the decisions of the 12th Plenary Session of the Party Central Committee, disclosed that the leadership had carried out self-criticism at that session. From Ho's address, we can tell that the regularization and modernization of the army had not been smooth sailing. Ho spoke of the responsibility of regularizing and modernizing the army, as well as the need to raise the level of socialist consciousness of the VPA. He warned against individualism, meritocracy, arrogance, envy, jealousy, and the danger of dividing the people, party, and army. He stressed the need for unity between the top and bottom hierarchy, cadres and fighters, North and South, within and outside the party, the military and the people.[17]

In a separate talk to the military units at the Military Region Department, Military Region IV on 15 June 1957, Ho again warned against "falling into the hole of individualism," jealousy, and envy. He emphasized the importance of manual labor. According to Ho, while mental labor was important, manual labor was even more important. To belittle manual labor was therefore the wrong attitude to adopt. In his view, party consciousness was not yet sufficiently developed in the VPA. He called upon the army to raise their alertness, put more effort into their military training and political reeducation, and to economize. Ho again spoke of the need for unity in every part of the army, and warned against divisions between the Northern and Southern fighters.[18]

When we compare the little we know of the VPA gleaned from the above account with what we know of the PLA gathered from the proceedings of the 8th CCP National Congress in September 1956 (as recounted in Chapter 2), we can see that there was much in common in the state of affairs of both armies during this period.

The process of rectifying the mistakes made in the agrarian reform took a long time, as the Hanoi leadership had anticipated. At the end of May 1957, there were still pockets of unrest in the villages over the slow pace of redressing the injustices of the agrarian reform. Giap, Truong Chinh, and even Ho Chi Minh himself had to personally go to the villages to give talks in the attempt to revive the flagging revolutionary spirit.[19] In June, Ho visited four northern provinces of Central Vietnam — Thanh Hoa, Nghe An, Quang Binh, and Vinh Linh — and an army unit. Up till October 1957, Ho was still engaged in giving talks.[20]

II

We have noted that peaceful coexistence was a cornerstone in the strategies of both the North Vietnamese and Chinese for the realization of their respective goals. Whether there could be peaceful coexistence in Indochina to a large extent hinged on developments in Laos. This is because of the geographical propinquity of Laos with North Vietnam and China. Cambodia, on the other hand, does not share any common borders with either North Vietnam or China. Also, whereas Cambodia had a strong and effective leader in Sihanouk, who was determined to keep Cambodia neutral, the situation in Laos was more fluid and uncertain. After the successful conclusion of the Souvanna Phouma–Souphanouvong talks in August 1956 and Souvanna Phouma's visits to China and Hanoi, it appeared that the Laotian problem in principle had been resolved. According to French sources reported in British diplomatic communications, there were signs that the Vietnamese Communists were stepping up their indoctrination activities in Sam Neua and Phong Saly in preparation to pull out from the two provinces.[21] During the last quarter of 1956, the RLG and the Pathet Lao sat down to work out the practical details of the August Agreement. Finally, on 28 December 1956, Souvanna Phouma and Souphanouvong concurred that a temporary coalition government in which the Pathet Lao was to be given two portfolios in a broadened cabinet would be formed prior to the holding of a supplementary election.[22] On 31 December, Souphanouvong returned to Sam Neua to confer with his colleagues, promising to return to Vientiane in two or three weeks time to complete the negotiations.[23] The joint communiqué was greeted with approval, particularly by the Chinese. It was described as "helpful to the peace and independence of Laos" and "fully in keeping with the Geneva Agreements and the interests and wishes of all the people in Laos." The Chinese further extended their "heartfelt congratulations to the Laotian people on their great achievements in realizing the peaceful unification of Laos."[24] To the North Vietnamese, the communiqué marked a new success for the Laotians in their struggle to uphold the Geneva Agreements.

Since August 1956, the Pathet Lao had been pressing for a quick agreement. They even threatened to renew hostilities if an agreement could not be reached. When the agreement was eventually achieved, both the Chinese and the Vietnamese also expressed their approval. Therefore, it is puzzling that Souphanouvong delayed for five weeks before returning to Vientiane on 4 February 1957. We still do not have the complete picture. Some observers thought that he was summoned to Hanoi during this time to explain why he did not manage to extract more concessions from the RLG.[25] Given the close relationship between the Pathet Lao and the Vietnamese Communists, it is not unlikely that they would have conferred with each other.

What we do know is that those five weeks before Souphanouvong finally returned to Vientiane coincided with the 6th Session of the DRV's National Assembly (29 December–25 January 1957) and with Zhou Enlai's absences from Beijing. (We should recall that Zhou did not return to Beijing till 6 February from his Asian tour.) They also coincided with the period of the Soviet draft resolution to admit both North and South Vietnam into the United Nations. On 4 February, a few days after the UN Special Political Committee rejected the Soviet proposal, Souphanouvong returned to Vientiane.

Those five weeks were crucial weeks because they gave Katay Sasorith, who had returned to Vientiane from New York on 10 January 1957, time to campaign against the 29 December agreement, which was essentially an understanding reached between the two half-brothers.[26]

The interval provided Katay with the opportunity to galvanize enough support to oppose the agreement. Consequently, the RLG demanded additional written guarantees from the Pathet Lao as proof of their good faith. They also insisted that the integration of the Pathet Lao forces should precede, rather than follow, the formation of the enlarged government. Unlike Sihanouk, Souvanna Phouma was only the head of a multiparty government and was therefore obliged to take into account the views of Phoui Sananikone, leader of the Independent Party, and of the pro–West Katay Sasorith, leader of the National Progressive Party. Unlike Souvanna Phouma, who was the half-brother of Souphanouvong, Phoui and Katay did not trust the Pathet Lao.

Souphanouvong was prepared to accede to the demand of the RLG for written guarantees only if the RLG in turn accepted Chinese aid.[27] We should recall that when Souvanna Phouma met Zhou Enlai in Beijing in August 1956, there was no pressure exerted on the Laotians to accept Chinese aid or to establish diplomatic relations. This sudden demand could be seen as a tit-for-tat response to the new demands of the RLG. A guarantee that Laos would be neutral was and had always been the concern of the Chinese in particular. As Souphanouvong put it in mid–May 1957, "It was not correct to say that the Pathet Lao had insisted on the RLG's acceptance of Chinese aid as a prerequisite for cooperation, but at the same time, they did believe that non–Western aid would be a guarantee of neutrality and independence."[28] Souphanouvong was however prepared to drop his call for Chinese aid if the RLG dropped its demands for additional guarantees.[29] But the RLG refused to compromise.

On 13 May 1957, the North Vietnamese ambassador to China, Nguyen Khang, met Zhou Enlai. Zhou told Khang that Laos must be neutral and that there should not be a revolution in Laos at that point in time. The immediate priority was to consolidate North Vietnam.[30] Soon after, Hoang Minh Giam, the North Vietnamese minister of culture, who was a schoolmate of Katay when the latter was in Hanoi, stopped over in Vientiane from 19 May to 20 May on his way back to Hanoi from Cambodia. He visited Katay and Nhouy Abhay. British officials based in Vientiane were of the view that the North Vietnamese might have tried to obtain the assurance of Laotian neutrality from Katay.[31] But nothing came out of that. The government of Souvanna Phouma was toppled on 30 May 1957, which led to the suspension of the negotiations. This was followed by a political crisis that lasted for almost two months, from 31 May to 9 August 1957, in which none of the leading Laotian personalities could form a new government. Meanwhile, the issue of national reconciliation was in limbo. Thus Laos remained a cause of concern for both North Vietnam and China.

III

Domestic affairs were also the focus of attention in the Soviet Union, particularly during the months of June and July 1957, which witnessed a power struggle within the Russian leadership. During the three-day meeting of the Central Committee Presidium that began on 18 June 1957, Khrushchev managed to outmaneuver his opponents — namely, Molotov, Malenkov, and Kaganovich — who had tried to remove him from the post of first secretary of the CPSU. Khrushchev then convened a special Central Committee Plenary Session (June 22–29) and expelled his opponents. The outcome of the struggle was finally made public on 3 July.[32]

According to Liu Xiao, who was then the Chinese ambassador to the Soviet Union, the Chinese did play a major although indirect role in the struggle. Khrushchev believed that the support of the Chinese was crucial to his cause and was therefore prepared to assist China's nuclear research program in order to elicit Chinese backing. After Khrushchev's victory in July, it was said that he sent Mikoyan to brief Mao regarding the foreign policy differences between Molotov and himself and to secure Chinese support for the Soviet Union under his leadership. According to Liu, the Chinese endorsed Khrushchev's victory despite having serious reservations.[33]

As for the North Vietnamese, while the Soviet leadership was still in the balance there was always the possibility that a hardliner policy in support of the reunification of Vietnam might prevail. Now with Khrushchev in complete control, the Soviet position regarding Vietnam seemed more than likely to stay unchanged. Nevertheless, the *Nhan Dan* commentary entitled *"Union within the Party is essential to its existence"* of 5 July 1957 expressed support for the decision of the CPSU Central Committee. The news also received prominence in the other newspapers, the *Hanoi Daily* and *Thoi Moi*.[34]

IV

It was against the backdrop of the above events that Ho Chi Minh decided to visit the fraternal countries in the socialist bloc. The news of

Ho's impending tour was made known on 30 June 1957, almost immediately after the political crisis in Moscow was clearly resolved in Khrushchev's favor. Pham Van Dong was entrusted with the government's affairs during Ho's absence.[35] Ho was supposed to have left for Pyongyang by way of Beijing on 5 July. He was accompanied by Hoang Minh Giam, minister of culture, Hoang Van Hoan, and Pham Ngoc Thach, deputy-minister of health. But the departure was delayed by a day because of bad weather.[36] It was reported that he was sent off by a number of officials and members of the diplomatic corps, and specifically by Pham Van Dong, Phan Ke Toai, and Vo Nguyen Giap.[37] On the evening of 6 July, Ho arrived in Beijing and was met by Zhu De, Liu Shaoqi, and Zhou Enlai. After reviewing a full guard of honor, he was driven to the guest house accompanied by Zhu De. That evening, he was the guest of honor at a dinner hosted by the CCP Central Committee. Mao was not around when Ho arrived in Beijing. He was in Shanghai at this time. On the evening of 7 July, Ho went to the cinema with Zhu De and Luo Guibo.

When Ho was in Beijing, the 4th Session of the 1st National People's Congress was in session (26 June–17 July). During the months of May and June, Mao's "hundred flowers" policy had backfired. The CCP found its dominant position threatened by demands for the end of the CCP monopoly of power. At the 4th Session of the 1st National People's Congress, there was not even, as there was in 1956, a full-dress report on foreign affairs. The deliberations dealt exclusively with the domestic crisis.[38] During this period and for the rest of 1957, the Chinese Communists were absorbed by their domestic and economic affairs and were content to leave their foreign policy as it was. The policy of peaceful coexistence would allow them to focus on straightening the mess that they had inadvertently created at home as well as to concentrate on economic development. Sometime in July 1957, Mao was said to have told the Vietnamese Communists that reunification might take a long time and the immediate concern was to defend the existing frontier — the 17th parallel.[39] The North Vietnamese did not disagree. They too were preoccupied with domestic problems.

Ho stayed in Beijing for two nights and a day before leaving for Pyongyang on the morning of 8 July. On that same day, the Anti-Rightist Campaign in China began.[40] The Vietnamese delegation was in Pyongyang from 8 July to the morning of 12 July, when they left for Eastern Europe via Moscow.[41] Because of bad weather, Ho had to stop at Harbin on 12 July.[42] He left on the morning of 13 July and arrived in Moscow on the same day. The next day he visited the All-Union

Agricultural and Industrial Exhibitions at the Luzhniki Stadium. He was received by Voroshilov and a lunch was given in his honor on 15 July. He met Khrushchev on 17 July and departed for Prague on the same day, the first leg of his visit to Eastern Europe.[43] After visiting Czechoslovakia (17–21 July), Ho proceeded to Poland (21–25 July), the GDR (25 July–1 August), Hungary (1–5 August) and Yugoslavia (5–9 August). Two days before Ho arrived in Belgrade, it was disclosed that Khrushchev and Tito had signed an agreement of cooperation between the Soviet Union and Yugoslavia after two days of secret meetings in Romania.[44] After Yugoslavia, Ho continued to Albania (9–13 August), Bulgaria (13–17 August), and Romania (17–21 August) before returning to the Soviet Union where he visited Odessa, Stalingrad, South Crimea, Sebastopol, and Leningrad. He arrived back in Moscow on 26 August and met Khrushchev again before leaving the Soviet Union on 27 August.[45]

We do not know what transpired between Khrushchev and Ho, but it was likely that the issue of the two Vietnams' admission into the United Nations was discussed. Subsequently, at the 789th and 790th meetings of the Security Council on 9 September 1957, the Russians insisted that the question of admission be postponed till after unification. Without the opposition of the Soviet Union in the Security Council, South Vietnam would have been admitted into the United Nations and the Vietnamese Communists' cause would have been seriously affected.[46]

Ho was back in Beijing on the evening of 28 August.[47] China was now into the second month of its Anti-Rightist Campaign, which continued till July 1958. On the day of his arrival in Beijing, four leading papers in Beijing carried editorials welcoming him and also commented that during his tour, Ho had promoted mutual understanding between Vietnam and the other socialist countries as well as strengthened the unity of the socialist camp. The Chinese further expressed their resolute support for the North Vietnamese call for a consultative conference to discuss national unification through free general elections.[48] On the evening of 29 August, Ho attended a banquet given in his honor.

The next morning he left for Hanoi via Wuhan. The Yangtze Bridge in Wuhan was nearing completion, two years ahead of schedule. Built with the assistance of the Soviet Union, the Yangtze Bridge is strategically important for China because it transformed the almost impassable natural barrier between North and South China into a broad thoroughfare, thereby significantly enhancing the geographical integrity of China and reinforcing China's national defense. The bridge also improved communication between North Vietnam and China. On 15 October 1957 (just after it was officially declared open), at 11:25 A.M., the first express passenger train from Beijing crossed the bridge bound for the town of Pingxiang situated at the Sino-Vietnamese border in Guangxi Province. Pingxiang is connected to Hanoi by rail. On that same day, at 3:25 P.M., the first Beijing-bound train from the Vietnamese border also crossed the Wuhan bridge.[49]

Compared to the Vietnamese themselves, the Chinese appeared to have been particularly expressive about their closeness to the North Vietnamese during this time. *Renmin Ribao*, for example, had a fairly long commentary on the Sino-Vietnamese goods exchange and payment agreement and protocol on Chinese aid for 1957 signed on 31 July 1957, which it described as a manifestation of proletarian internationalism. According to the article, trade between China and North Vietnam took three forms: state trade, which in 1956 had risen to 13 times the level of 1952; direct trade between local trading companies on the Sino-Vietnamese border; and small-scale border trade. It also estimated that between 1955 and 1959, Chinese aid to North Vietnam would reach 800 million yuan. The article concluded that the close economic cooperation would continue with growing friendship.[50] The Chinese media also devoted much attention to the DRV's National Day. There were reports of the greetings from the Chinese leadership, Zhou's speech at the reception given by the DRV ambassador in Beijing, and the message from Lin Haiyun, the Chinese deputy-minister of foreign trade who recently signed the trade agreements with the North Vietnamese.[51] Lin's message again referred to the close economic cooperation between the two countries. There was also a radio talk on the economic achievements of the DRV. Both Mao's message and Zhou's speech particularly expressed the Chinese approval of Ho's tour of the socialist countries.[52]

Ho's visit to the fraternal countries was for the purpose of strengthening ties and gathering support for the North Vietnamese cause. According to *Nhan Dan*, "to reinforce unceasingly the close union with friendly countries is the first duty of the Party, Government and our people. It is a factor ensuring all our successes."[53] More importantly, Ho visited Beijing and Moscow at a key point in the internal developments of both countries. In China, the Communists were trying to come to grips with the unintended repercussions of the Hundred Flowers Movement, while in the Soviet Union, Khrushchev had just recently strengthened his position. By being there, Ho could personally assess the two situations and their implications for North Vietnam.

What he concluded from his visit, particularly to Beijing and Moscow, can be gleaned from his speech in Hanoi on the occasion of the

12th anniversary of the independence of North Vietnam on 2 September 1957. In that speech, he stated that as far as the North was concerned, the basic task was still to restore the economy and to progressively improve the living conditions of the people. There was the need to lay a strong foundation so that in 1958 they could proceed to build up the North under a long-term plan. As for the South, they should continue to persevere in their struggle. He again raised the proposal that contacts should be established as a first step toward a consultative conference on the general election. Ho referred specifically to the experiences of North Korea and the GDR, which were also concerned about the reunification of their own countries.[54] Thus, after his visit to Beijing and Moscow, Ho concluded that it was still not the right time to step up the struggle in the South.

V

Meanwhile, in Laos, during June and July 1957, there were three unsuccessful attempts to form a new cabinet. Two were made by Katay Sasorith and one by Bong Souvannavong. It was not till 9 August that the National Assembly approved another coalition government, which was once again headed by Souvanna Phouma. The return to power of Souvanna Phouma was warmly received by both the North Vietnamese and Chinese. The North Vietnamese saw it as "a success of the Laotian people,"[55] while the Chinese regarded it as a defeat for the United States, which had tried every means to set up a pro–American government during the cabinet crisis since 30 May 1957.[56] Souphanouvong in a statement of 13 August expressed his support for the new government under Souvanna Phouma and called upon all Laotians to support the new government.[57] Back at the helm, Souvanna Phouma tried to get the negotiations started again. Negotiations between the Pathet Lao and the RLG eventually resumed on 16 September. The condition set by the Pathet Lao earlier in the year that the RLG must accept Chinese aid was quietly dropped. We should recall that the Communists were never really serious about this requirement. It was proffered to counter Katay. Furthermore, the Pathet Lao had found that the insistence on accepting Chinese aid had aroused doubts in many nonpartisans regarding their allegiance. On 22 October, Vientiane radio reported that both parties had reached an understanding regarding the formation of a coalition government. It was agreed that the Pathet Lao would return the two northern provinces on the day of the formation of the new government; the Pathet Lao fighting forces would be integrated into the national army; those that could not be integrated would be demobilized; the Pathet Lao would surrender all the weapons in their possession; the NLHX would operate as a legal party in Vientiane; and Laos would adhere to a policy of neutrality. Souvanna Phouma and Souphanouvong finally issued a communiqué regarding the agreements on 2 November.[58] Once it became official, the North Vietnamese described it as "an important advance in the unification of Laos in conformity with the Geneva Agreements,"[59] and the Chinese hailed it as "a great victory for the Laotian people in striving for the peaceful unification of their country."[60] The Russians too, in contrast to their silent reception of the December 1956 agreement, greeted it as a cause for "rejoicing among all peoples of goodwill."[61]

The reasons as to why the Pathet Lao yielded on points to which they had held firmly until October 1957 remain obscure. One possible reason is that the Communists had come to the conclusion that any further intransigence on the part of the Pathet Lao would only result in the downfall of Souvanna Phouma. When Souvanna Phouma became prime minister again in August 1957, he committed himself to completing negotiations with the Pathet Lao in two months. If he should fail again, the National Assembly could call for his resignation. To the Communists, Souvanna Phouma was their best bet since the alternative would have to be either Phoui or Katay, both strongly anti–Communist and pro–U.S.. Both North Vietnam and China wanted very much to concentrate on their domestic concerns and certainly had no wish for an anti-Communist government in Laos.

According to U.S. intelligence reports, the Pathet Lao's intention was to keep a nucleus of hardcore cadres in North Vietnam. A group of 600 had already left for North Vietnam. Souphanouvong would lead the "legal group," or the NLHX in Vientiane, while Kaysone would be responsible for the "underground."[62] This strategy was likely to have been agreed upon by the North Vietnamese, Chinese, and the Pathet Lao. It was based on the assumption that an eventual armed struggle was a legitimate route to national liberation, a point that the Chinese strongly insisted upon at the Moscow Conference during the same month and that, as we shall see, was eventually enshrined in the Moscow Declaration of 22 November.

After the signing of the 2 November 1957 communiqué, the RLG proceeded to take over Sam Neua and Phong Saly in early December. The British ambassador to Laos was one of the foreign diplomats who was present in the official party led by Souvanna Phouma at the handing-over ceremony in Sam Neua. According to his report, the Pathet Lao regime in Sam Neua was modeled on the Communist pattern and there were still Communist slogans on the walls. Posters that were not yet removed showed Chinese and Vietnamese Communist leaders and the Pathet Lao triumvirate of Souphanouvong, Kaysone, and Singkapo. The few essential goods available came mainly from China and North Vietnam. Kaysone was said to be ill and was absent from the ceremony. His whereabouts were unknown. Also, the nominal roll of troops and lists of equipment were smaller than was admitted during the negotiations.[63] The Canadian commissioner who attended a similar ceremony in Phong Saly reported that the overt Communist influence was even stronger there than at Sam Neua. There was also no sign of Kaysone.[64] Kaysone finally appeared in Sam Neua sometime in January 1958. He was reported to have come from Hanoi.[65]

Sam Neua and Phong Saly were completely taken over by the RLG by 19 January 1958. The occupation of the two provinces by the Royal Laotian Army that began on 24 December 1957 proceeded speedily and smoothly without any incident, which came as a surprise to many foreign observers.[66] Clearly, the Pathet Lao had been instructed to be cooperative and not to create trouble.

VI

In North Vietnam, during the months of October and November, there were rumors of dissension within the leadership, specifically between Truong Chinh and Vo Nguyen Giap.[67] The generally accepted interpretation was that there was a clash between the pro-Chinese faction led by Truong Chinh and the pro-Soviet faction led by Giap.[68] In those two months, except for a brief report of a congratulatory cable that Giap sent to Marshal Malinovsky on 31 October 1957, there was a publicity blackout of his activities[69], although there was nothing unusual about Truong Chinh's activities.

The last occasion when Giap was present was during the visit of the Bulgarian government delegation from October 6 to 9. Giap was part of the reception party to welcome the Bulgarians at the airport on 6 October. On the same day, the delegation was received by Ho Chi Minh. Giap was also present. Ho Chi Minh also attended the luncheon for the Bulgarian delegation on that day, where he made a welcome speech. On 8 October, the visiting Bulgarian government and party delegations had talks with their Vietnamese counterparts, who included Ho, Truong Chinh, Giap, and Le Duan. This was the first reported public appearance of Le Duan in Hanoi. On the same day, Ho gave a lunch in honor of the visitors that Truong Chinh, Giap, and Le Duan attended.[70] This was also the last reported public appearance of Giap till 22 December 1957, when he appeared at a public meeting to mark the 13th Army Day anniversary.[71] At the evening reception to commemorate Army Day, he was accompanied by Truong Chinh.[72]

We still cannot fully account for Giap's long absence from public view during these two months. We now know from a Chinese source that in October 1957, Giap had led a military delegation to Beijing for discussions regarding North Vietnam's military plan and the issue of Chinese assistance.[73] This would partially explain Giap's absence from view after 8 October. It is also possible that Giap was in China to witness the opening of the Yangtze Bridge on 15 October 1957. We know that there were many foreign representatives, including North Vietnamese representatives, although no specific names were given.[74]

The Vietnamese media were also unusually silent about the activities of Ho Chi Minh in the later part of October. On 12 October, it was reported that he would visit Burma in spring at the invitation of the Burmese government.[75] On 18 October, the delegation from the Supreme Soviet, led by A. B. Aristov, member of the Legislative Commission of the Soviet Union and secretary of the CPSU Central Committee, arrived in Hanoi. The delegation was received by Pham Van Dong and also met Truong Chinh and Le Duan. Although the delegation was in North Vietnam from 18 to 26 October, there was no report of it having any meeting with Ho. Giap was also conspicuously absent during this time.[76] Ho, however, did receive the new Czech ambassador, Alexis Voltv, on 21 October.[77] Also around this time, two delegates from the Asian Socialist Conference were in Hanoi. They met Pham Van Dong as well as Truong Chinh and Hoang Van Hoan on 22 October.[78]

Ho was rumored to be ill during this period. According to the British consul-general in Hanoi, K. J. Simpson, on 22 October King Suramarit of Cambodia sent a goodwill message to the DRV, and political observers read significance into his wishes of good health to Ho.[79] This further fueled rumors about Ho's state of health. But on 28 October, it was announced that Ho would personally lead the North Vietnamese delegation to attend the celebration of the October Revolution.[80] He left for Moscow on 30 October, accompanied by Le Duan and Pham Hung.[81]

Meanwhile, on 26 October 1957, the Soviet government issued a brief statement that Marshal Zhukov, the Soviet defense minister, had been replaced by Marshal Rodion Y. Malinovsky.[82] This announcement was reported without comment by *NCNA* on 27 October.[83] But it was only on 31 October 1957 that it was reported that Giap had sent a cable congratulating the new Russian defense minister.[84] On 2 November, the CPSU Central Committee announced that Zhukov was also dismissed from the CPSU Central Committee and Presidium. The next day, the Central Committee issued the "Resolution of the Plenary session of the Party Central Committee on improving Party political work in the Soviet Army and Navy," which affirmed that the CPSU was the guiding and directing force of Soviet society and that the policy of the military departments must be pursued in strict accordance with party directives. It also made public the reasons for Zhukov's removal. Zhukov was accused of promoting his own "cult of personality" in the army and for trying to eliminate party control over the military.

The dismissal of Marshal Zhukov was a purely Russian affair, but it appeared to have had an indirect impact on North Vietnam. We should recall that on at least two previous occasions that we know of— on 16 May 1957, in an address to middle- and senior-ranking officers from the Ministry of Defense who were attending a reeducation class to study the decisions of the 12th Plenary Session, and in a talk to the military units at the Military Region Department, Military Region IV on 15 June 1957 — Ho Chi Minh commented that party consciousness was not yet sufficiently developed in the VPA. The regularization and modernization of the army had not been smooth and the Southern cadres in the North were anxious to return to the South. Ho called for unity within the military and exhorted everyone to consolidate their ideological viewpoint.[85]

According to Georges Boudarel, there were certain quarters within the military, believed to be close to Giap, who were sympathetic toward the intellectuals and the reformers (associated with the now-defunct publications, *Nhan Van* and *Giai Pham*) and their ideas of a more open and liberal society. Giap's position regarding this issue is, however, still unclear.[86] In the summer and autumn of 1957, many rehabilitation classes were organized to study the resolutions of the 12th Plenary Session. All these political reeducation and rehabilitation classes would indicate that party leaders were not satisfied with the level of revolutionary consciousness in the military.

The text of the CPSU resolution was published in full on the front page of the *Nhan Dan* of 5 November. Supporting the decision of the

CPSU for sacking Zhukov, the *Nhan Dan* editorial stated: "The Party's leadership constitutes the decisive factor of all our successes and progress. Yet, locally and occasionally in practical revolutionary activities, such a fundamental principle has not been thoroughly carried out.... The leadership of the Party was the determining factor of all success and progress ... and that there have been comrades who did not thoroughly understand the fundamental principles of the Party and thus deviated from and restricted the leadership principles and policies of the Party in contradiction to the policies of Marxism-Leninism."[87]

We do not know whether or not Zhukov's disgrace affected Giap personally. Giap was said to have been receiving relatively less publicity in the North Vietnamese media since late 1956,[88] around the time when it was decided to recall Le Duan to the North. There is the possibility that Le Duan and Le Duc Tho, whom we now know did not have good relations with Giap, could have exploited the Zhukov affair to discredit Giap. That could explain Giap's "absence" from late October till 22 December 1957. Zhukov and Giap shared some obvious similarities. Both were ministers of defense and they headed the army. Both were war heroes. Zhukov was known for his distrust of political intervention in military affairs, and one of the reasons given for his dismissal was that he was trying to remove party control of the armed forces.[89] The American officials based in Saigon believed that Giap too was sympathetic toward those who were in favor of a lessening of party control over the army. They further believed that the fall of Zhukov might encourage the Lao Dong Party to tighten its control over the army, through an intensification of the already ongoing political education courses under the overall charge of Nguyen Chi Thanh, head of the VPA's General Political Directorate.[90]

If there had been differences within the leadership, particularly on issues related to the army, or if Giap was in any difficulty during this period, they seem to have been resolved by the time Giap reappeared in public during the 13th Army Day anniversary on 22 December. In his Order of the Day to mark the occasion, Giap emphasized that in the process of gradually becoming a modern and regular army, the army must strictly implement every policy of the party and law of the government. He also affirmed that a weak and small nation that stood united and struggled resolutely for self-liberation could defeat a big imperialist power and that a small colonial country without any regular army could also defeat a big imperialist country.[91]

VII

Meanwhile, in November, Ho, Le Duan, and Pham Hung were amongst the Communist leaders gathered in Moscow to celebrate the 40th anniversary of the October Revolution. After this, they assembled for a conference that dealt with the important issue of intrabloc relations. This was an important issue that had become particularly controversial since the Polish and Hungarian crises of 1956. The Moscow Conference was divided into two parts: The first, from 14 to 16 November, was attended only by the representatives of the 12 Communist and workers' parties of the socialist countries (of which China and North Vietnam were two of the countries). At the end of this session, a 12-party declaration was signed. The second part of the conference from 16 to 19 November included all the other delegates who participated in the 40th anniversary celebration. At the end of the whole conference, the fraternal countries affirmed their unity and solidarity in the Communist bloc headed by the Soviet Union with the issue of the Moscow Declaration of 1957.[92]

It is notable that Ho was accompanied by Le Duan and Pham Hung, who were both closely associated with the Communist revolutionary movement in South Vietnam. In early 1957, Le Duan had returned to the North to assist Ho, and in the following year, during the 8th Congress of the DRV National Assembly (16–29 April 1958), Pham Hung was appointed vice-premier.[93] Unfortunately we still do not know about their activities in Moscow during this time, except that on 17 November, while the conference was still in session, Pham Hung left for Prague as head of a Vietnamese delegation to attend the funeral of the Czech President, Zapotocky, who died on 13 November.[94]

Mao too had traveled to Moscow to attend both the celebration and the Conference to express his support for Khrushchev.[95] When Mao arrived at Moscow airport, Ho Chi Minh was also there to welcome him. Ho stood behind Khrushchev. According to a Chinese source, Ho and Mao had established a close personal relationship since the Yenan days. After greeting Khrushchev, Mao next embraced Ho and had a brief conversation with him recollecting their last meeting in Beijing. Mao then told Khrushchev that he and Ho were relatives, implying that they were very close. In Moscow, Mao and Ho stayed in the Kremlin and he visited Ho on a few occasions.[96]

At the conference, Mao took an extremely hard line, which caught many — particularly Gomulka and Kadar — by surprise. The Chinese had since the autumn of 1956 given the impression that they were sympathetic toward the idea of greater independence of the satellite countries vis-à-vis the Soviet Union. But during the conference, Mao was the one who made the strongest and most unqualified endorsement of Soviet leadership of the bloc. Mao went even beyond the expectations of Khrushchev. According to Khrushchev, it was Mao who had demanded that the Russians revise the text of the declaration to emphasize Soviet leadership.[97] The Chinese about-face regarding intrabloc policy in November 1957 came in the wake of the successful launching of the two Sputniks (4 October and 3 November 1957). The two Sputnik successes added credibility to the Russian claim in late August 1957 that they had successfully tested the world's first ICBM. Also, on 15 October 1957, a secret agreement in which the Russians promised to assist the Chinese in their nuclear program was signed. This secret agreement was reached after a 35-day discussion between the Russians and the Chinese delegation, led by Vice-Premier and Head of the Scientific and Technological Commission Nie Rongzhen, who was in Moscow from September to mid–October 1957.[98] During the 40th anniversary celebration and the Moscow Conference, a high-level Chinese military delegation led by Marshal Peng Dehuai and including General Su Yu, chief of staff of the PLA, and Marshal Ye Jianying was in Moscow from 6 November to 3 December. One of the purposes of this visit was to discuss Soviet assistance in China's nuclear weapons program.[99] Mao's assessment was that the East was now stronger than the West as a result of the Russian technological successes — thus his famous slogan: "At present, it is not the west wind which is prevailing over the east wind, but the east wind prevailing over the west wind."[100] He expected the Soviet Union to lead in the struggle against the West. The Russians, on the other hand, had a different view. While they did make political mileage out of their military and technological success, unlike Mao they did not believe that the east wind had necessarily prevailed.

In Moscow, Mao warned Khrushchev that West Germany and Japan were the main dangers to the Communist world.[101] In the early '50s, China had tried to normalize relations with Japan based on the Five Principles of peaceful coexistence. One of China's objectives was to break the ties that Japan had with the United States and Taiwan. The appointment of Kishi Nobusuke — who was strongly committed to maintaining ties with the United States and Taiwan — as foreign minister in December 1956 and subsequently prime minister in February 1957 diminished the chances of a Sino-Japanese rapprochement. In June 1957, Kishi made his first state visit to Taiwan as prime minister, and in November of the same year he visited South Vietnam.[102] Japan was therefore a concern of not only Beijing but Hanoi as well.

According to Khrushchev, it was either during the Moscow Conference or earlier that he raised with Mao the subject of a division of labor in the international Communist movement. His proposal was that China concentrate on establishing closer contacts with the Asian countries and Africa, while Russia would concern itself with Western Europe and the Americas. Mao had declined, saying that the CPSU should be the one and only center of the international Communist movement. But in the words of Khrushchev, "as we listened to Mao pay recognition to the Soviet Union and the CPSU, we couldn't help suspecting that his thoughts were probably very different from his words."[103]

The Moscow Conference is pertinent to our present study for two reasons: What was especially significant for the Vietnamese Communists was that in contrast to February 1956 during the 20th CPSU Congress, the Russians now accepted that under certain circumstances, there could be a nonpeaceful transition to socialism. The North Vietnamese had the Chinese to thank for this change of mind on the part of the Russians.[104] Not unexpectedly, both the Vietnamese and Chinese media had only praise for the outcome of the Moscow Conference.[105] Secondly, according to Edward Crankshaw, the Moscow Conference was the first time the Chinese presented themselves as representatives of a great Communist power with a strong voice in policy making for the movement as a whole.[106]

Ho and the Vietnamese delegation were reported to have left Moscow on 21 November, the same day as Mao.[107] Before leaving, Ho gave a press conference in which he described the recent meeting as a significant event. According to him, before the Second World War there were only 4,000,000 Communists, and in 1957 there were 33,000,000—a great force capable of defending peace and fighting against war. Ho also said that the Vietnamese Communists were pleased that the Soviet Union was leading the world in conquering cosmic space and that American science had been left behind.[108]

The Vietnamese party and government delegation, with the exception of Ho Chi Minh, returned to Hanoi on 28 November. They were received at the airport by Truong Chinh.[109] Ho, on the other hand, stayed in Beijing for almost a month. His prolonged stay in Beijing was attributed to his need for a rest. We have no idea whether Le Duan and Pham Hung spent a week in Beijing after leaving Moscow before returning to

Hanoi. On 30 November, the North Vietnamese Politburo met to be briefed on the Moscow meeting by Le Duan and Pham Hung.[110] Following that, on 4 December, an extraordinary meeting of the Lao Dong Party was held to hear Le Duan's report on the recently concluded meeting in Moscow.[111] Three days later, it was again Le Duan who addressed 1,500 party officials. He told them that the Moscow Declaration and Manifesto had not only confirmed the line and created the conditions for North Vietnam to advance toward socialism, they had also shown the path of struggle for the liberation of the South. According to Le Duan, the socialist revolution in the North had just started. Among other things, they had to build a new economy, industrialize and collectivize agriculture. Meanwhile, the South remained occupied by the imperialists. The task was therefore to struggle together for the reunification of the country.[112]

On 2 December, Luo Guibo, who was the first Chinese ambassador to North Vietnam as well as the first diplomatic envoy credited to the DRV, returned to Beijing to assume his new appointment as one of the deputy ministers of foreign affairs. (We do not know for sure to what extent this move was motivated by the Chinese decision to pay greater attention to Vietnamese affairs.) Luo was seen off by Truong Chinh. On 14 December it was announced that He Wei had been appointed as the new Chinese ambassador to North Vietnam.[113] He Wei assumed his post in Hanoi on 13 January 1958.

We have no information on Ho Chi Minh's activities during his almost month-long stay in China. But he could not have failed to observe the Rectification Campaign that was sweeping across China and that involved all levels of Chinese society during this time. When he was briefly in Beijing in July and August 1957, the Rectification Movement had just started. It was also very likely that he was aware of the CCP's plan to accelerate economic development in China. During December, plans and decisions for the Great Leap Forward were already in the pipeline. On 7 December 1957, Mao told the visiting Czech military delegation that it was China's responsibility to develop a new theory and practice of Communism in Asia and that only by following this new route would China achieve the status of a first-class power. According to Jan Seljna, the first high-level military delegation from Czechoslovakia to visit China returned home on 27 December 1957 with the first hint of the Sino-Soviet split.[114] We do not know if, while Ho was in China, Mao informed him of his intention to establish China as an alternative center within the Communist movement.

Ho finally returned to Hanoi on 24 December 1957, two days after the reappearance of Giap and on the same day the RLG started the operation to resume control of Sam Neua and Phong Saly as agreed in the 2 November 1957 communiqué. On his return, the Vietnamese media made a point of mentioning that he looked well.[115]

Thus, by the end of 1957, there was no longer any uncertainty about Ho's health. If there had been a tussle between Truong Chinh and Giap as rumored, or any other differences within the North Vietnamese leadership, it was either resolved or temporarily put aside. By December 1957, Le Duan was most probably the number-two man in the Vietnamese leadership hierarchy after Ho. The British consulate-general in Hanoi had observed that since Le Duan's return from Moscow, he had always been named first among the representatives of the Lao Dong Party at public functions.[116]

VIII

At the 13th Plenary Session, which took place soon after Ho Chi Minh returned from China on 24 December 1957, Ho made clear the intrinsic relationship between the two revolutionary strategies and the two revolutionary responsibilities. According to him, the Vietnamese were concurrently engaged in carrying out two equally important revolutionary strategies: a people's democratic revolution and a socialist revolution. To belittle either of the two strategies was a mistake. The responsibility to consolidate the North and gradually advance toward socialism was a decisive factor for the victory of the revolution. The North must become a socialist society so that it might serve as a solid base in order to guarantee the reunification of the country. At the same time, the revolutionary strength of the South must be maintained and developed, for that would constitute the direct and decisive factor for the victory of the struggle in the South. In short, Ho was saying that the struggle in the South was now considered to be as important as the revolution in the North. According to the *Lich Su Quan Doi Nhan Dan Viet Nam*, Ho's speech at the 13th Plenary Session was very significant as it clarified the path along which to carry out the socialist revolution in the North and the people's democratic revolution in the South.[117] We should recall that in September 1957, Ho was still advocating a "North-first" strategy. It is highly likely that this shift was the outcome of the deteriorating situation of the Communists in the South as well as his discussions in both Moscow and

Beijing. A later North Vietnamese account noted that by the end of 1957 and early 1958, the revolutionary forces in the South — the Mekong Delta region (from Go Cong Province down to the Ca Mau Peninsula), My Tho Province, the Plain of Reeds (region in Kien Phong and Kien Tuong Provinces and parts of Dinh Tuong, Long An, and Hau Nghia Provinces), U Minh jungle (the area extending along the coast of the Gulf of Siam in An Xuyen Province), and Resistance Zone D (the region 20 miles northwest of Saigon) — suffered heavy losses as many cadres were arrested or massacred, the self-defense organizations in the countryside were broken up, the armed forces in the resistance bases had to be reduced, and the resistance army of the religious sects dwindled into a token force.[118] The Moscow Conference had implicitly acknowledged that nonpeaceful means could be adopted to achieve the reunification of Vietnam. The situation in Laos was also progressing toward a conclusion that pleased both the North Vietnamese and Chinese. More attention could now be given to the struggle in the South.

The decisions made at the 13th Plenary Session in December 1957 were carried out in 1958. At the start of the year, Ho announced that "the period of economic restoration has come to an end and the period of planned economic development has begun."[119] The target of restoring the war-shattered economy in three years (1955–1957) as spelled out at the 6th Plenary Session in July 1954 had therefore been achieved.

For 19 days, between 27 December 1957 and 14 January 1958, the Lao Dong Central Committee held a conference of high- and middle-level cadres of the party to study the Moscow Declaration as well as to discuss the current situation of the country. At the conference, more than 200 cadres at the central and provincial levels were briefed by Le Duan and Truong Chinh. It was unanimously agreed that the people's democratic revolution in the North was over, the foundations for a socialist economy had been laid, and the socialist revolution had begun.[120] The new three-year economic plan (1958–1960) was subsequently spelled out in detail during the 8th Session of the National Assembly between April 16 and 29.

At the beginning of 1958, Le Duan also met with the cadres in charge of Interzone V (that is, the southern half of Trung Bo). The Communist activities in Interzone V had declined considerably as a result of Diem's renewed efforts to exterminate the Communists, particularly at the end of 1957 and early 1958. During this meeting, Le Duan pointed out that Interzone V was divided into three regions: the towns, the deltas, and the central highlands. If the highlands were strong and stable, the deltas would be strong. Therefore, according to Le Duan's analysis, there were real and strong reasons to quickly establish small squads, or — even better still — platoon-sized armed forces to operate independently in the highlands with the objective of controlling and maintaining the party's agricultural activities there. When the time was ripe, this guerrilla movement could then complement effectively the main offensive. The cadres in charge of Interzone V were thus told to urgently build many safe base areas to assist the guerrilla activities and to guide the economic struggle in the delta and towns.[121]

Four

January 1958–December 1958

I

Vietnamese relations with China remained strong. On 11 January 1958, three protocols on the transport of goods and passengers from Yunnan along the Vietnamese railway to the other Chinese provinces and vice-versa were signed.[1] These came into effect on 1 March.[2] On 13 January, the new Chinese ambassador to North Vietnam, He Wei, assumed his post. He Wei was one of the most important officials in Guangxi Province from 1950 to 1952. From 1953 to 1954, he was the mayor of Canton and a member of the standing committee of the South China Party Subbureau, which had jurisdiction over Guangdong and Guangxi Provinces, and a member of the Central-South Administrative Committee (formerly the Central-South Military and Administrative Committee), which was responsible for Henan, Hubei, Hunan, Jiangxi, Guangdong and Guangxi Provinces. In all these capacities, he would have had contacts with the North Vietnamese. He was assistant-minister of foreign affairs before becoming ambassador to North Vietnam. On 20 January, a 20-member government trade delegation headed by Phan Anh, the minister of commerce, arrived in Beijing.[3] On 24 January, another protocol allowing the use of Haiphong to facilitate Sino-Vietnamese trade was signed.[4]

A 20-member delegation representing seven nationalities in the Viet Bac Autonomous Region led by Chu Van Tan left for Guangxi on 2 March to attend the inauguration ceremony of the Zhuang Autonomous Region and to make a one-month tour of China.[5] A protocol on Chinese aid to the North Vietnamese for 1958 and an agreement on assistance to the DRV in the construction and reconstruction of 18 industrial projects were signed on 31 March. The Chinese would help the Vietnamese to build or reconstruct 18 industrial projects between 1958 and 1960 with part of the 800 million yuan which they had committed to the Vietnamese as a gift in 1955. An agreement on the exchange of goods and payment was also reached. The amount of trade in 1958 was expected to be greater than the previous year.[6]

On at least three occasions, Ho Chi Minh made reference to China in his speeches. During a tour of Thai Nguyen (the capital of the Viet Bac Autonomous Region) on 2 March, Ho told the residents there that China not only gave the Vietnamese pumps but also sent experts to help the Vietnamese peasants in handling the pumps. He thanked the CCP and Mao and encouraged the peasants to join mutual aid teams.[7]

Addressing the Enlarged Session of the Vietnam Fatherland Front Central Committee on 19 March, he spoke of the mass gatherings and big parades held in China by the various democratic parties, showing their determination to follow the lead of the CCP.[8]

On 24 April, at a discussion on the line for North Vietnam's advance toward socialism during the 8th Session of the National Assembly, Ho Chi Minh spoke on the socialist transformation in China. He expressed the hope that Vietnamese intellectuals, industrialists, traders, and other patriotic personalities would follow the example of the Chinese in strengthening their unity to carry out the resolutions to be adopted by the National Assembly for the successful advancement of North Vietnam toward socialism. At the end of his talk, a Chinese documentary film, "Everything Has Changed," which described the socialist transformation in China, was screened.[9]

Also in April 1958, the North Vietnamese and Chinese governments reached an agreement regarding the Sino-Vietnamese boundary question. The Chinese agreed to the Vietnamese proposal to adhere to the boundary line between their two countries that had been drawn up between France and China in 1887 and 1895, until a new boundary agreement could be negotiated by North Vietnam and China.[10]

The Moscow Declaration signed in November 1957 had condemned revisionism and all dogmatic ideas contrary to Marxism-Leninism. The North Vietnamese politburo now adopted an uncompromising attitude toward the intellectuals who were critical of the Hanoi leadership. Following the example of its Chinese mentor, the politburo at the beginning of 1958 passed a resolution for the launching of a literary rectification campaign, the main target being the literary circles. In January, the journal of the Association of Writers, *Van*, was banned. The last issue to be published was issue 37 on 17 January 1958. The North Vietnamese leadership had tolerated the criticism of the writers since the first issue was launched on 10 May 1957, which coincided with the Hundred Flowers Movement in China. From March till June 1958, a campaign against the writers who had contributed to the *Nhan Van* and *Giai Pham* was carried out. In outlining the Three-Year Plan at the 8th Session of the National Assembly in April 1958, Pham Van Dong made it very clear that it was absolutely essential for intellectuals to be loyal to socialism, which meant that they must "understand the position and the role of culture and cultural organizers during the period of transition in the North, and do so from the Marxist-Leninist standpoint and by means of a Marxist-Leninist methodology and viewpoint.... This is so fundamental an issue that there is no room for compromise."[11]

We can almost be certain that by May Day 1958, Le Duan was the number-two man in the Hanoi leadership. According to normal practice, the number-two man in the party would always preside at the May Day celebration in Haiphong while Ho would be in Hanoi. In 1957 it was still Truong Chinh, but in 1958 it was Le Duan.[12] Truong Chinh was appointed deputy-premier on 29 April 1958 during the 8th Session of the National Assembly (16–29 April 1958). But one should not think that his influence had as a consequence waned. According to the Indian consul-general in Hanoi, all the new vice-ministers appointed during the National Assembly session in April were protégés of Truong Chinh.[13] In fact, Truong Chinh was the acting prime minister for about two weeks in August 1958 when Pham Van Dong was ill.[14] In the collective leadership of North Vietnam, Truong Chinh would be most likely to pay closer attention to the socialist development in the North, while Le Duan would concentrate on preparing the South for the eventual offensive, thus carrying out the dual revolution spelled out by Ho Chi Minh during the 13th Plenary Session in December 1957. Also, by virtue of their respective appointments, it would appear that Truong Chinh became more powerful in the government, whereas Le Duan was gradually becoming the dominant personality within the party. It is worth noting that Le Duan never held a government position in North Vietnam.

In China, attention remained focused on the development of the economy. The First Five-Year Plan ended in 1957. It was judged a success although it was felt that the economy could have developed even faster.[15] Mao in particular believed this to be so. In the *Sixty Articles on*

Work Methods, which he signed on 31 January 1958, he envisaged an economic upsurge in three years.[16] At the 5th Session of the National People's Congress in February, it was agreed that China could make this great leap forward.[17] One would notice that the economic development of both North Vietnam and China were moving on a parallel course. Both countries had decided upon a three-year economic plan instead of the standard five-year plans. However, the North Vietnamese did not follow the Chinese example of a Great Leap Forward, which was launched in May 1958. On 12 March, the DRV and the Soviet Union agreed to extend the most-favored nation treatment to each other.[18] A trade protocol was also signed that provided for an exchange of goods trebling that of 1957.[19] According to *Nhan Dan*, the trade agreement marked "an important step forward in the development of trade relations between the two countries" and it also testified to "the spirit of generous and wholehearted assistance of one of the most industrially advanced countries in the world toward a backward agricultural country which has just begun to build a new economy."[20] During this time, China and the Soviet Union also continued to have active trade relations.

Ho Chi Minh visited India from 4 to 13 February 1958 and Burma from 14 to 17 February to win support for the North Vietnamese cause. According to Ho before his departure, the objective of the trip was to further strengthen the friendship with the two countries and to enhance solidarity among countries in Asia and Africa.[21] As Le Duan put it, "To unify the country, we must build a really strong Vietnam, intensify the revolutionary movement of our compatriots in the South and gain the approval of peace-loving peoples throughout the world."[22] SarDesai noted that particularly after Ngo Dinh Diem's visit to New Delhi in November 1957, Indian policy toward Vietnam shifted from one of pro–North and anti–South to one of impartiality. On 7 February 1958, addressing the Indian Council of World Affairs, Ho advocated discussions between North and South Vietnam in preparation for the holding of free elections on the basis of universal suffrage and secret ballot under the supervision of the ISCC; a single parliament that would choose a national coalition government and the gradual integration of the two armies; and finally, pending the reunification of North and South Vietnam, that parties and other organizations that supported peace, unity, independence, and democracy be legalized, and normal economic, cultural, and social relations and free communications between the two zones be established.[23] In Rangoon, Ho repeated his proposals. It is notable that while both India and Burma endorsed Ho's call for the reunification of Vietnam, they did not condemn either South Vietnam or the United States for obstructing the process.[24] Returning to Beijing after a stay in Hanoi, Vladimir Popovic, the Yugoslav ambassador who was accredited to North Vietnam, disclosed that the objective of Ho's trip was to ascertain how much political support (not material support) Hanoi might have outside the socialist bloc. Popovic told the British officials in Beijing that the North Vietnamese realized that they were very dependent on the socialist bloc and would like to get away from this dependency.[25] The Indian and Burmese responses would indicate to Ho that North Vietnam had little choice but to count on the support of China and the Soviet Union.

The Chinese continued to give support to the North Vietnamese call to the South for a dialogue.[26] On 7 March, Pham Van Dong again wrote to Diem condemning the U.S. presence in the South. He also called for a meeting to discuss the reduction of troops and the establishment of mutual trade so as to promote the eventual unification of the country.[27] On 9 March, the Chinese government issued a statement giving strong support to "this opportune peace proposal initiated by the Government of the DRV."[28] The Chinese statement showed that they were equally concerned about the growing American presence in South Vietnam.

II

The Vietnamese Communists could not have managed the modernization of the VPA without the help of the Soviet Union and China, although in the *Lich Su Quan Doi Nhan Dan Viet Nam* (published in 1988), they failed to mention the Chinese at all. According to one Chinese source, between 1953 and 1963, China assisted the VPA in establishing six antiaircraft units, an engineer unit, a bridgehead unit, a tank unit and a fighter unit. Besides that, the Chinese also supplied the VPA with assault guns, military vehicles, engineering, communication, and reconnaissance equipment.[29]

The VPA was close enough to the PLA for them to play football together. The August First Army football team was in Hanoi from 21 December 1957 to attend the national sports meeting at the invitation of the Vietnam Sports Commission and the VPA.[30] It was reported that the Chinese August First Army Number 2 football team won one of two matches in Hanoi, beating the Vietnamese security forces 3-1 on 29 December 1957, and drew a game with the VPA on 1 January 1958. Pham Van Dong and Truong Chinh (whom the *NCNA* still referred to as the secretary-general of the Lao Dong Party), were both present at the occasion.[31]

In mid–March 1958, the Central Military Committee produced a new military plan. The principal objective of this plan was to come up with concrete methods to increase the security and defense of the North, particularly in the northwest and west Interzone IV, so as to be ready for the unexpected.[32] It is instructive to note that northwest and west Interzone IV adjoined the two Pathet Lao-controlled provinces of Sam Neua and Phong Saly. It was decided to adjust the target year for the modernization of the army from 1959 (decided at the 12th Plenary Session in March 1957) to 1960. This was to complement the three-year economic plan (1958–1960) that had been drawn up and would be in keeping with the decision that military development must be in tandem with the country's economic development made at the same session. This would also imply that a campaign for reunification was not expected till at least 1960.

Also in mid–March 1958, the Council of Ministers met to discuss, amongst other things, the subjects of military service, reward, military rank and salaries, the problems of building up the army reserve, and the participation of the army in production work. It was decided that there was to be a further redeployment of troops so as to concentrate more forces in economic construction. Some of the armed forces were to be transferred to farm production units so that they could directly participate in production.[33] In China in January 1958, it was reported that many PLA units had started to discharge drafted personnel and transfer them to production work.[34]

On the anniversary of Dien Bien Phu on 7 May 1958, Nguyen Son (formerly commander-in-chief of Interzone IV and a member of the CCP),[35] who had died in October 1956, was posthumously decorated.[36] This second posthumous award to Nguyen Son could be seen as another indication of the close relationship between North Vietnam and China during this time.

In the PLA (as in the VPA), the Soviet Army was still considered to be the army to emulate. On the occasion of Soviet Army Day in February 1958, Peng Dehuai spoke of the Soviet Army as possessing the "most up-to-date equipment in the world" and that it was "the example for the armed forces of all socialist countries."[37] But as the PLA became more deeply involved in the Rectification Campaign, it began to study Mao's military writings more intensively, although not exclusively.[38] It was reported on 18 May that the military academies, army schools, and units were all studying Mao's military thoughts.

In May 1958, at the 2nd session of the 8th CCP Congress (2–23 May), the Great Leap Forward was officially launched. The Chinese people were told to "go all out, aim high and achieve greater, faster, better and more economical results in the building of socialism."[39] At a reception on 19 May, Foreign Minister Chen Yi had told the representatives of the foreign diplomatic and economic missions that as China wanted to complete its socialist construction successfully, she was keenly aware of the value of peace, and was working consistently and unswervingly for the safeguarding of world peace.[40]

Between 27 May and 22 July 1958, the 2nd Enlarged Conference of the Military Affairs Committee was held and was attended by more than a thousand high-ranking cadres. At the conference, dogmatism and excessive reliance on foreign ideas were criticized, and Mao instructed the army to draw up a new set of operational manuals and systems specifically based upon the PLA's own revolutionary experience. Mao also confirmed that China would develop an independent nuclear capability. In short, it was decided at this conference that China would chart an independent course in military and strategic matters. But it did not yet mean that the Chinese were foregoing their military ties with the Russians at this point.[41]

For three days, from 31 July to 3 August 1958, Khrushchev was in Beijing on a secret visit.[42] Khrushchev was accompanied by B. N. Ponomarev, member of the CPSU Central Committee and Kuznetsov, first deputy foreign minister, who had also been the ambassador to China from 1953 to 1955. As military issues were to be discussed, Khrushchev also brought along Marshal Malinovsky. The Russians traveled incognito and were met at the airport by Mao and Chen Yi. There were altogether four meetings between Mao and Khrushchev.[43]

In his memoir, Khrushchev did not elaborate on his discussion with Mao, but he noted that: (1) The Chinese, despite all the outward protestations of camaraderie with the Soviet Union, did not trust the Russians; (2) Mao and the Russians disagreed fundamentally about the nature of a future war. To the Russian leadership, battles were no longer won by bayonets or bullets, whereas Mao maintained that given the combined population of the Soviet Union, China, and the socialist countries, the balance of power was in their favor. Mao once again warned Khrushchev of the dangers that West Germany and Japan posed to the Communist camp.[44] (By this time, any possibility of a Sino-Japanese normalization had vanished completely. On 9 May 1958, China had suspended all economic transactions and other forms of relations with Japan in reaction to the flag incident at Nagasaki on 2 May 1958.)

According to one Chinese source,[45] during the second meeting that took place on 1 August by the swimming pool in Zhongnanhai (when Liu, Zhou, and Deng were also present), Khrushchev once again proposed that China, being more familiar with the situation in Asia and Southeast Asia, should concentrate on that region, whereas the Soviet Union would concentrate on Europe since it had a better understanding of European affairs. Mao once again objected to what, in his view, was a policy of divide and rule. During this meeting, Khrushchev reiterated Soviet support for the liberation of Taiwan. At the same time, he urged Mao to refrain from constantly thinking of resorting to military means to test the resolve of the West. Mao, in turn, told Khrushchev that he should drop all liaison with the United States and drop the idea of the Five-Power Summit Conference in Geneva, which Khrushchev had proposed before coming to Beijing. On the Great Leap Forward, Khrushchev said that it was an extreme strategy.

Mao and Khrushchev failed to reach any agreement. Khrushchev had initially planned to stay in Beijing for a week but left after three days.[46] Nevertheless, a communiqué had to be issued to cover their differences. In the communiqué, which was signed on 3 August, both parties called for a summit conference on the Middle East question; they agreed to struggle against revisionism without compromise and they reiterated their support for peaceful coexistence with states of different systems, to do their utmost to ease international tension and prevent a new war disaster.[47] All the Hanoi press on 5 August duly welcomed the communiqué as showing that the socialist countries and peace-loving countries in the world were definitely strong enough to crush the imperialists.[48] Once again, the Chinese and the Russians managed to conceal their differences from the rest of the world. What is equally significant is that Khrushchev's trip to Beijing was a further indication that China was now an equal partner with the Soviet Union in the socialist bloc. This was in spite of the constant references and Chinese insistence that the Soviet Union was the sole leader of the socialist fraternity.

III

We should recall that in Laos, the November 1957 Agreement had specified that a nationwide supplementary election would be held on 4 May 1958. There were 21 seats to be contested and it was the first test of the strength of the Neo Lao Hak Xat and the effectiveness of their united-front strategy. On the eve of the elections, the editorial in *Renmin Ribao* expressed Chinese pleasure over the numerous major successes of the Laotian people in their fight for peace, unification, and independence. It added that the formation of the Laotian coalition government and the implementation of the various agreements between the RLG and the Pathet Lao fighting units, including the forthcoming supplementary elections, were important steps to the further realization and consolidation of peace, unification, and independence of the country as well as in the interests of peace for the whole of Indochina.[49]

The Neo Lao Hak Xat won 9 out of the 21 seats. They had allied themselves with the left-wing Peace Party (Santiphab, founded in 1957 by Quinim Pholsena), which won 4 seats, thus giving them a total of 13 seats out of 21. Although this did not bring about any change in the overall composition of the National Assembly, which was still controlled by the rightwing and neutralists, it showed that the Neo Lao Hak Xat should not be taken lightly. The results of the supplementary election jolted the disunited rightwing and neutralists and upset the United States considerably.[50] But the Chinese were obviously pleased. To them, the result of the supplementary election marked a new important development in Laotian political life and a new victory in the implementation of the Geneva Agreements.[51]

As early as 20 March 1958, Souvanna Phouma had informed the ISCC that the cabinet had decided on 13 March 1958 to request the withdrawal of the Commission as of 4 May, the date of the supplementary election. Souvanna Phouma explained that the RLG considered the elections as the last act in the application of the Geneva Agreement.[52] On 15 May, Souvanna Phouma informed the International Supervisory and Control commission of the successful completion of the election. The members of the ISCC were unable to agree as to whether the Commission had in fact completed its task. The Vietnamese and the Chinese Communists objected to the withdrawal of the ISCC. According to the Vietnamese, "The ISCC should continue with their task in order to defend the important provisions of the Geneva Agreements. If, as a result of foreign intervention, the situation in Laos became disturbed and if Laos were dragged into a military alliance and became a military base of a foreign power, peace in Indochina would be seriously threatened."[53]

The Chinese expressed their deep anxiety at the proposal to wind up the activities of the ISCC and were in total agreement with the Vietnamese position that it was imperative that the ISCC remain in Laos. They further stated that China as a participating country of the Geneva

Conference and a friendly neighbor of the Indochina states could not keep silent on the question.[54] An article in *Guangming Ribao* of 3 June argued that any unilateral abolition of the ISCC in Laos would affect the two other commissions in Cambodia and Vietnam. The commission must not be abolished if the Geneva Agreement on the Laotian question were to be thoroughly carried out and peace in Indochina preserved.[55] It was reported on 2 June that some Indian members of the ISCC had already left for home on 30 May and more would leave on 6 June.[56] The *Nhan Dan* editorial of 8 June stated that dissolving the ISCC in Laos would benefit only the U.S. imperialists.[57] The Chinese continued to oppose the dissolution of the ISCC in Laos in *Guangming Ribao* on 11 July and *Renmin Ribao* on 14 July.[58] After much deliberation, on 19 July the commission, with the Polish member dissenting, finally decided to adjourn sine die.[59] The Poles were evidently in collusion with the North Vietnamese and the Pathet Lao. Souvanna Phouma told an Australian official in Saigon in July that he was aware that the Pathet Lao were keeping in touch with Hanoi through the Poles.[60] On 9 August, the North Vietnamese issued another statement arguing for the maintenance of the ISCC in Laos, but to no avail.[61]

What worsened the situation for both Hanoi and Beijing was that after the election, Souvanna Phouma failed to form a new government. On 22 July, he resigned.[62] The resignation of Souvanna Phouma must have disappointed both the North Vietnamese and Chinese and forced them to reassess their strategy regarding Laos. On 15 August, a new government was formed by Phoui Sananikone. According to Phoui, the objective of his government was to preserve the independence and unification of Laos, which meant that "we must guard against the most threatening danger which will undermine our independence and unification. This danger is Communism."[63] Nevertheless, on 21 August, Pham Van Dong sent a congratulatory message to Phoui on his formation of a new cabinet.[64] Phoui, however, proved to be staunchly anti-Communist and abandoned the neutral policy that Souvanna Phouma had pursued. In September 1958, he invited Ngo Dinh Nhu, brother and adviser of Diem, to Vientiane. He declared that the visit of Nhu signified "the identical points of view and the solid friendship of the two countries." This was shortly followed by the visit of the South Vietnamese foreign minister. The Laotian Legation in Saigon was subsequently elevated to an embassy in 1959.[65] Phoui also established diplomatic relations with Nationalist China. He approved the establishment in Vientiane of a Chinese Nationalist consulate, which opened on 5 January 1959.[66]

IV

While the situation in Laos became more and more unpalatable to the Vietnamese and Chinese Communists and Sino-Soviet relations continued to deteriorate, things in Cambodia appeared more promising, at least to the Chinese. Sihanouk did not think that Beijing had formulated a forward policy with regard to Indochina. Therefore he believed that any Chinese subversive threat, insofar as Cambodia was concerned, was a very distant one. However, he did feel a sense of grave anxiety about the activities of the Vietnamese Communists.[67]

Since the start of 1958, he had been attacking the Cambodian Communists in his speeches. Although the Cambodian Communists were particularly weak in the rural areas, they were fairly active and relatively successful in the capital. In Phnom Penh, the major Communist newspaper, *Pracheachon*, had a relatively respectable circulation and was considered fairly influential. In the National Assembly elections in March 1958, the Pracheachon Party was able to put up five candidates against the Sangkum. This is not to say that they had a chance against Sihanouk and the Sangkum. From the results of the elections, it was evident that they did not. But to Sihanouk, if their activities were not checked the consequences would be serious.[68] He was particularly annoyed by the activities of the North Vietnamese and the Soviet ambassador, who he said were working energetically to subvert the Cambodian intellectuals. The North Vietnamese and the Soviet ambassador had been bribing students who failed to obtain scholarships to either the United States or France to work for Communism.[69] Sihanouk believed that the Chinese could exert pressure on the North Vietnamese to lay off Cambodia.[70]

Nevertheless, in 1958 it was the Thais and the South Vietnamese rather than the Communists who were perceived as the imminent threat.[71] On 29 and 30 May, the Cambodian government protested to the South Vietnamese government regarding the intrusion of South Vietnamese soldiers into its territory, near the Kas Kong district of Peam Chor in PreyVeng.[72] More protests followed on 15 and 19 June. It was reported that on 15 June, South Vietnamese soldiers had crossed into Cambodian territory, occupied a number of villages, and clashed with Cambodian patrols. On 19 June, the South Vietnamese were said to have moved a frontier border-marking post on Route National 19 by three kilometers and subsequently by four kilometers.[73] The South Vietnamese government denied that any of the incidents had taken place. On 27 June, a joint meeting of the Cambodian National Assembly and the Royal

Council adopted a declaration appealing to foreign countries to send observers to Cambodia to establish the truth of what it described as a South Vietnamese invasion of Cambodia. The King of Cambodia and Sihanouk also demanded that the United States order South Vietnam to withdraw its army from Cambodian territory immediately and unconditionally.[74] The Cambodians revealed that South Vietnamese regular troops had penetrated seven miles into Stung Treng Province and that since the beginning of 1957, the South Vietnamese had intruded into Cambodian territory on 29 occasions and removed the border-marking post deep into that territory.[75] On 30 June, Chinese Vice-Premier and Foreign Minister Chen Yi condemned U.S.–South Vietnam encroachment on Cambodian territory and expressed Chinese support for Cambodia.[76] One Chinese Foreign Ministry source believed that Chen Yi's expression of support helped Sihanouk make up his mind to establish diplomatic relations with Beijing.[77] The Stung Treng incident forced Sihanouk to recognize China in the hope of using Chinese support as a leverage against the South Vietnamese,[78] and possibly the Thais as well.

On 18 July Sihanouk sent a letter to Zhou Enlai proposing that Cambodia and China establish diplomatic relations. The next day, Zhou sent Sihanouk a positive reply and added that China would do its utmost to support Cambodia's defense of its independence.[79] On 23 July (just one day after the resignation of Souvanna Phouma), it was made known that China and Cambodia had decided to exchange ambassadors and that embassies would be set up in Beijing and Phnom Penh. On 27 July, a statement was issued by the Royal Council declaring its support for the government's decision to establish diplomatic relations with China. The statement also revealed that "China with its 600 million people and efficient government was giving Cambodia disinterested aid."[80]

Soon after the announcement of the establishment of diplomatic relations, Sihanouk made his second visit to China. Before he left for China, a number of "high personalities" (we still do not know who they were) had tried to persuade him to make a stopover at Hanoi, even if only for five minutes. But Sihanouk firmly refused. He then instructed Son Sann to convey his reply to those "high personalities" saying that would be going too far in annoying South Vietnam and the United States.[81]

Sihanouk arrived in Beijing on the afternoon of 15 August 1958 and stayed in China till 25 August. The visit was accorded maximum coverage by the Chinese media. For example, all Beijing newspapers on 15 August carried editorials welcoming the visit and emphasized the brilliant example of peaceful coexistence shown by the friendly cooperation between the two countries. On subsequent days, the newspapers carried reports of the activities and speeches delivered. In his speech of welcome, Zhou Enlai said that the establishment of diplomatic relations between the two countries and the visit of Sihanouk showed that a new page had been opened in the book of traditional friendly relations between China and Cambodia, and it also marked the consolidation and success of the Five Principles of peaceful coexistence. Sihanouk and Zhou had two meetings, on 17 and 24 August.[82] Zhou Enlai told Sihanouk that China was willing to allow neutral and nationalist states in Southeast Asia to remain as a buffer area between China and the West. He specifically assured Sihanouk that China would not interfere in Cambodia's domestic affairs.[83] Sihanouk met Mao Zedong on 16 August in Zhongnanhai and again on 20 August in Beidaihe.[84] In his conversations with Mao, Sihanouk observed that unlike his more flexible and moderate prime minister, Mao showed a "certain distrust for non-Communist regimes" and seemed unable to compromise as easily.[85] The Chinese also offered to provide Sihanouk with whatever military armaments and equipment he needed.[86] A joint statement was signed on 24 August that again emphasized both countries' adherence to the policy of Cambodian neutrality.[87]

The newspapers in Hanoi on 26 August carried on their front pages the news of the agreement reached between Cambodia and China. The *Nhan Dan* editorial described the joint statement as a good expression of the Five Principles of peaceful coexistence. According to the North Vietnamese, the agreement was not only a living expression of the peaceful coexistence policy and of the Bandung spirit but also a document condemning colonialism and a warning to the U.S. imperialists who were stubbornly interfering in the internal affairs and encroaching on the sovereignty of other countries.[88]

Despite Sihanouk's decision not to go to Hanoi, Cambodian–North Vietnamese relations were also making some progress during this time. In an interview with the *VNA* correspondent on 6 August, Touch Kim, the Cambodian minister of economic affairs and finance, disclosed that negotiations on a trade and payments agreement between the two countries were likely to take place in September 1958.[89] Trade talks finally took place on 12 November, and the first trade and payments agreement between Cambodia and the DRV was signed on the afternoon of 18 November 1958 in Phnom Penh.[90]

V

Meanwhile, in South Vietnam, beginning in mid–1958, Diem's renewed efforts to exterminate the Communists began to adversely affect the revolutionary movement in the South.[91] It was in this context that the proposal to launch the armed struggle in the South was raised. According to Hoang Van Hoan's account, in 1958 it was suggested inside the Lao Dong Party that armed struggle be launched against Ngo Dinh Diem, and this proposal was put forward to the CCP Central Committee. But the Chinese were of the view that the time was not yet ripe and suggested that Hanoi reconsider whether it was opportune then to expose its armed forces in South Vietnam.[92]

According to a Chinese source,[93] after the North Vietnamese completed the restoration of their economy, in 1958 they began to give more attention to strengthening the struggle in the South. In that summer, the Lao Dong Central Committee sent two documents to their Chinese counterpart for their views. These were *"Regarding the basic tasks of the Vietnamese Communists in the new phase"* and *"Views on uniting the line of struggle with the revolutionary struggle in the South."* The Chinese subsequently submitted a written reply to the Vietnamese. The same Chinese source also noted that Ho Chi Minh made a trip to Beidaihe in the summer of 1958 where he met Zhou Enlai and Deng Xiaoping to discuss how the Chinese could assist the Vietnamese Communists in their struggle against the Americans. At the meeting, Ho gave the Chinese a document regarding the strategy of the Vietnamese Communists' struggle against the Americans in the South for their opinion. We do not know the substance of the Vietnamese documents or what transpired between Ho and the Chinese leaders. It is also unclear from the Chinese account as to when precisely the documents were sent, and whether Ho's trip was made before or after the Chinese reply to the two documents. The Chinese position was that the socialist revolution in the North was the fundamental and most urgent task. As for the revolutionary struggle in the South, they continued to hold the view that the Vietnamese should lie low, build up and consolidate their military strength, win over the masses, and wait for the opportunity to strike. The same Chinese source noted that events during this period indicated that the Hanoi leadership did not disagree with the Chinese view in principle.[94]

However, at the 3rd Conference of the Nam Bo Regional Committee in August 1958, chaired by Nguyen Van Linh, it was decided that because of the current revolutionary situation in South Vietnam, it was necessary to apply some degree of military force to assist the political struggle and gradually use the armed forces to defeat the enemy. This was conveyed to the Party Central Committee in Hanoi.[95] The committee also decided to establish two revolutionary base areas: Zone A, which was situated northeast of Saigon, extending from Ma Da to Bu Champ in Thu Dau Mot Province; and Zone B, which was situated northwest of Saigon in Duong Minh Chau District, Tay Ninh Province. It was also decided to establish the Eastern Nam Bo Command, which was to be the center of the armed struggle in the South. Some of the forces in the eastern Nam Bo provinces were grouped into four companies under this command. Its formation helped the Regional Party Committee unify and centralize its leadership of the armed forces and their activities in the South.[96]

In the summer-fall of 1958, the Interzone V Party Committee held a meeting chaired by Vo Chi Cong to discuss their strategy. Bearing in mind the instructions of Le Duan at the beginning of the year, it was decided at this meeting that they would step up their activities to develop the western parts of the lowland provinces in Interzone V and the Central Highlands. The objective was to recover and expand their base of support. The plan was to build up storage bases for rice, salt, and so on, and to mobilize the people in preparation for the revolution. They would organize a number of platoons and arm them with whatever weapons they could muster. These armed troops would be used for self-defense, to support their political struggle, and to protect their economic activities and the villages. They would also attempt to free their comrades who had been arrested by the government, as well as kill those people that they considered were traitors to their cause. The committee decided that they could no longer rely solely on political struggle but "must use limited armed struggle coordinated with political struggle" in order to annihilate the enemy.[97]

Sometime in November 1958, the Lao Dong Party held its 14th Plenary Session. It was reported on 8 December that the meeting had discussed the report by Le Duan on the world situation; the report on the three year-plan (1958–1960) for economic transformation and cultural development by Nguyen Duy Trinh; and Truong Chinh's report on land reform. The 14th Plenary Session decided that "the immediate task is to step up the socialist transformation of the individual economy of the peasants and craftsmen and that of the privately run capitalist economy, and at the same time to strive to develop the state-run economy which is the leading force of the whole national economy."[98] Although it was not reported, it is highly unlikely that there was no discussion on the revolutionary situation in South Vietnam. After the 14th Plenary Session, Le Duan is believed to have left for the South on an extended inspection tour to study the situation there.[99] Meanwhile, the Southern revolutionaries were told that political struggle remained the basis of the revolution in the South. This is confirmed in a document (captured in July 1959) entitled "Situation and Tasks for 1959." This document, issued by the Nam Bo Regional Committee—despite its acknowledgment that the Diemist forces were getting stronger vis-à-vis the Southern revolutionaries — nevertheless directed that political struggle should remain the basis of the revolution in the South.[100]

VI

The Chinese bombarded the offshore islands of Quemoy and Matsu (Jinmen and Mazu) on 23 August 1958.[101] According to Liu Xiao[102], the incident occurred because of the deadlock in the Sino-American talks—the Chinese wanted to force the Americans to take them seriously. In 1993, a Soviet document disclosed that on 14 October 1959, Mao told the Soviet diplomat and Sinologist S. F. Antonov that his intention had not been the occupation of the islands but to add to the difficulties that the Americans were facing in the Middle East during that time.[103] According to Li Zhisui, Mao's personal physician from 1954 to 1976, the shelling of Jinmen and Mazu was not for the purpose of retaking the islands but to demonstrate to both Khrushchev and Eisenhower that Mao could not be controlled and to undermine Khrushchev in his quest for peace.[104]

The North Vietnamese press was initially silent about the bombardment until 29 August. Thereafter, they supported the Chinese action to the hilt. A commentary in *Nhan Dan* on 29 August strongly condemned the U.S. imperialists and their stooge Jiang Jieshi. According to the Vietnamese, Chinese territory covered Jinmen and Mazu as well as Taiwan, and the settlement of the issue fell entirely within the competence of China.[105] Truong Chinh on 1 September blamed the tense situation in the Taiwan Strait on the U.S. imperialists and reiterated Vietnam's resolute support for China.[106] At a reception in Beijing to commemorate the founding of the DRV on 2 September, Nguyen Khang, the North Vietnamese ambassador to China, stated that the Vietnamese people and government wholeheartedly supported the Chinese in their cause of liberating Taiwan, which was a part of China's territory, and determinedly opposed the U.S. imperialists' interference in China's internal affairs.[107] In general, there was a tendency in all the Vietnamese and Chinese reports on the Taiwan Strait crisis to see a parallel between American policy in that crisis and American intervention in South Vietnam, as in Pham Van Dong's statement demanding that the U.S. imperialists withdraw all their military forces from the Taiwan Strait area as well as end their intervention in South Vietnam[108]. The statement that "like the Vietnamese people's struggle for national liberation, China's struggle to liberate Taiwan enjoys the support of the whole world" was typical. On 14 September, the North Vietnamese government recognized the Chinese claim of 4 September 1958 to 12 nautical miles of territorial waters and accepted that the Spratly and Paracel Islands belonged to China.[109] On 21 September, the Vietnamese once more condemned the "blindfold" attitude of the American imperialists and quoted the saying of Mencius about someone who would see clearly a small feather in the wind but was unable to see Mount Taishan. According to the Vietnamese, the fact that the Chinese population was nearly four times that of the United States was a real factor compared to "the small feather flying about in the autumn," a reference to the smallness of Jiang Jieshi. The Chinese could therefore liberate Taiwan any time they chose, despite the presence of the American "paper-tiger."[110]

The Chinese action evidently surprised the Russians.[111] Although around the time of Khrushchev's visit to Beijing there was a sudden proliferation of rather jingoistic propaganda circulating in China regarding the liberation of Taiwan, Mao did not tell Khrushchev of his intention to bombard the offshore islands. In early September, Liu Xiao met Khrushchev in Crimea to discuss the Taiwan Straits and Middle Eastern situations. Khrushchev was very troubled by the straits crisis and felt that any further escalation of the situation was dangerous and must be prevented.[112] Khrushchev sent Andrei Gromyko, Soviet foreign minister, to Beijing on 6 September on a fact-finding mission. Mao and Zhou told Gromyko that China did not intend to attack Taiwan but only wanted to stop the United States from pursuing a "two Chinas policy," and that China alone would bear all responsibilities for the bombardment.[113]

During the crisis, the Russians duly supported the Chinese publicly, but they were surpassed by the enthusiastic support shown by the North Vietnamese. Like the Vietnamese, the Russians were silent during the first few days of the crisis. Their first direct and authoritative statement came on 31 August in *Pravda*, three days after that of the North Vietnamese. In contrast to the Vietnamese, Russian support was very cautious.[114] The Soviet Union came out in strong and unequivocal support of the Chinese only on 7 September, one day after Zhou Enlai offered to restart the dialogue between China and the United States in Warsaw. The Sino-American ambassadorial talks, suspended since 12 December 1957, eventually resumed on 15 September.[115] The rather lukewarm and tardy Russian support during the Taiwan Straits crisis was, however, not lost on the Chinese.[116] Like Jan Seljna, Liu Xiao identified 1958 as a "turning point" in Sino-Soviet relations and in addition, cited the Taiwan Straits crisis as a significant contributing factor.[117] Noted Mao scholar Stuart Schram observed that after the middle of 1958, Mao never again spoke positively of Khrushchev.[118]

A speech that Mao made at the 15th meeting of the Supreme State Conference on 5 September 1958 gives us some idea of Mao's thinking at this point of time: Mao did not think that there would be a war. However, the world situation required that it was important to maintain a "defensive insurance system." Therefore, China must prepare for war. Mao acknowledged that China had only hand mortars and grenades, whereas the enemy had hydrogen and atomic bombs. That was why China (and the Soviet Union as well) did not want to fight, and opposed fighting. China would not strike first but if given no choice would fight fearlessly. He was optimistic that even after a nuclear war, there would be enough people left to form a new government and to negotiate.[119]

By the end of October, Mao's article, "Imperialism and All Reactionaries are Paper Tigers," as well as his speeches and interviews related to that theme, were widely circulated and publicized.[120] It was reported that Mao's collection of writings on "paper tigers" was sold out as soon as it appeared and the PLA were said to be keenly discussing Mao's writings and citing facts from their own fighting experiences to prove the correctness of Mao's conclusions. According to the *Liberation Army Gazette*, on 4 November the PLA General Political Department arranged for all units to study Mao's works on "paper tigers."[121] By 19 November 1958, it was reported that PLA personnel throughout the country were energetically studying Mao's writings.[122]

In the early '50s, the Soviet Union perceived the Chinese as ideological partners. But in 1958, the Chinese had achieved a degree of economic and political stability and were gradually exhibiting their independence vis-à-vis the Soviet Union.[123] China began to pursue its own interests in the region. During Veljko Micunovic's last meeting with Khrushchev as the Yugoslavian ambassador to the Soviet Union on 8 October 1958, Khrushchev argued that it was not a coincidence that the Russians had taken the north and the Chinese the south of Asia. The two great powers were protecting each other's rear; and that as long as both sides observed Marxist-Leninist principles, relations would continue as they had been.[124] But the Russians were already having second thoughts. According to Aleksandr Kaznacheev, a new period of Soviet policy began to emerge in 1958–1959 when the Soviet Union gradually abandoned the earlier agreement on the division of interests.[125] He cited many examples from his experiences while working in the Russian embassy in Burma to support his claim. The Russians were, however, not very successful in Burma. He also referred to the Soviet Union's generous military assistance in terms of weaponry to Indonesia. As for the Vietnamese Communists, the growing Sino-Soviet rivalry could not have escaped their notice; but they were intent on not being drawn into the growing Sino-Soviet discord. Meanwhile, they were able to benefit from the competition between China and the Soviet Union, who were both ready to help their protégé advance toward socialism.

VII

Sino-Vietnamese relations, particularly in the autumn and winter of 1958, were clearly very good. The Vietnamese Communists were not just urged to learn from Mao's military writings, they were also called upon to learn from China's agrarian revolution. On 3 September, the *VNA* circulated an article written by Le Duan that described the Chinese experience in glowing terms. The article said that the infinitely rich experience of China had taught the Vietnamese "a brand new concept of the road to socialist construction" (a reference to the Great Leap Forward) and that it bore testimony to the fact that once the full force of the peasants had been reorganized and reactivated, once they were free ideologically, their revolutionary, positive spirit and their creative capabilities were immeasurable in socialist construction.[126] On 18 October 1958, *Nhan Dan* published the first installment of a lengthy article by Le Thanh Nghi, minister of industry, on some lessons to be drawn from the high tide of socialist construction in China. It evaluated very highly the Great Leap Forward on the basis of the Rectification Campaign and pointed out that learning from the Chinese, the Vietnamese people had made many new changes in their countryside and their enterprises. The second and final installment was published on 20 October.[127]

In November 1958, the organ of the Vietnamese People's Army began to publish Mao's writings on "Imperialists and all Reactionaries are Paper

Tigers." Serialized publication of a summary of the same collection started in the newspaper *Thoi Moi* on 10 November.[128] It was also announced that the first volume of Mao's *Selected Works* in Vietnamese would be published on 26 December 1958. Mao's writings were praised as "classics of Marxism-Leninism linked with the practice of the Chinese Revolution."[129]

One of the major preoccupations of the PLA in 1958 and 1959 was the drive to strengthen party control over the armed forces.[130] This was also true of the VPA. In November 1958, the General Political Directorate, under Nguyen Chi Thanh, completed the study of the politico-military role of the VPA during the period of struggle against the French. The study confirmed the primacy of party leadership. According to the study, the highest principle of party leadership was collective leadership. The history of the army was first and foremost the history of the party leading the army both in times of war and peace. Even with the modernization and regularization of the army, this principle must always be respected. The study recommended the strengthening of party committees in the military. In the same month, the Central Military Committee held a conference for political commissars in the VPA to disseminate the guidelines regarding the role of politics in the military. The aim of the conference was to clarify the responsibility of the political organization in the VPA and to affirm the leadership of the party vis-à-vis the military.[131]

Chinese influence was evidently growing in North Vietnam. According to the Hungarian diplomat Janos Radvanyi, who visited Hanoi in late 1958 on a routine inspection tour to report on the functioning of the Hungarian Embassy there, he learned of the growing Chinese influence from Jozsef Kertesz who was acting as the Hungarian chargé d'affaires. Jozsef was particularly active on the diplomatic social scene and had learned from private sources that Chinese economic aid was beginning to exceed Russian aid and Chinese popularity was definitely growing. Back in Budapest, Janos Radvanyi reported what he thought was a novel but important observation, but according to him, nobody seemed to take it seriously.[132] The British consul-general also noted this increase in Chinese influence. In his annual report for 1958, he wrote, "Although no opportunity was lost of stressing the essential nature of Soviet help and support, there was a noticeable increase in Chinese influence over the years, almost certainly against the wishes of the Vietnamese people."[133]

Five

January 1959–May 1959

I

Nineteen fifty-nine was a particularly significant year. Both Communist and non-Communist sources regarded 1959 as the year that marked the intensification of the Communist armed struggle against the Diem regime. The year began with the "Huong Lap incident," which suddenly erupted toward the end of December 1958.[1] On 28 December, Pham Van Dong sent a message of protest to Phoui Sananikone regarding Laotian violation of Vietnamese territory and air space since 13 October 1958.[2] On 29 December, the North Vietnamese claimed that at the instigation of the United States, the Laotian armed forces had on several occasions encroached upon North Vietnamese land and air space. Planes of the Laotian air force were alleged to have repeatedly violated Vietnamese air space over Nghe An, Thanh Hoa, and Son La Provinces. Laotian troops were also alleged to have intruded into Quang Tri Province, in particular the Huong Lap area, which the North Vietnamese claimed they had historical and documentary proof was Vietnamese territory. According to the Vietnamese, the Laotian authorities in the Tchepone area had recently established a number of military posts in the vicinity of Huong Lap and had massed troops there. In the last few days, they had also sent threatening messages to the Vietnamese local administration of Huong Lap. They further claimed that the situation was seriously threatening the security of Vietnamese living along the Vietnamese-Laotian border.[3]

A second message of protest was sent on 1 January 1959 that claimed a new violation by the Laotian armed forces. Apparently, at 5:00 A.M. on 31 December 1958, a unit of the Laotian army entered the territory of

Tarua hamlet in the Huong Lap district and opened fire on the local Vietnamese guards. It was also claimed that the activities of the Laotian forces in the area had been intensified.[4] The RLG in its reply of 2 January denied all the accusations and instead countercharged that Vietnamese troops had occupied Laotian territory in Tchepone.[5] On 5 January, Pham Van Dong sent a third note to his Laotian counterpart stating that the situation had not improved.[6] On the same day, the RLG replied and asserted that the areas referred to by the Vietnamese were Laotian territory and therefore the VPA should withdraw immediately from the area concerned. On 6 and again on 7 January, the RLG issued a statement claiming that the DRV's accusations might be connected with the news being spread in Vientiane that the government "would exert pressure to dissolve a certain political party legally founded in Laos," an obvious reference to the NLHX. The North Vietnamese denied the allegation and again claimed that Huong Lap belonged to them. They also denied the reports of the last few days by a number of American, Thai, and South Vietnamese news services and newspapers that three battalions of the VPA had penetrated ten kilometers into Laotian territory.[7] A new note sent on 8 January claimed that the Huong Lap area had been Vietnamese territory since the Le Dynasty.[8] On 9 January, Sisouk Na Champassak, secretary of state for information, RLG, said that the DRV troops had encroached upon Laotian territory in Tchepone because the NLHX was anxious about being outlawed, and the DRV's motive was to compel the ISCC in Laos to resume its activities.[9] This was denied by the Vietnamese on 14 January.[10] The RLG on the same day announced that it had reported the incident to the United Nations and was ready to welcome neutral observers to the disputed area at any time.[11] At this point, the Huong Lap incident ended as abruptly as it started.

That the North Vietnamese and the RLG had unresolved border differences was not new; but the dispute over the Huong Lap area was unexpected. If we recall, during Souvanna Phouma's visit to Hanoi in August 1956, it was agreed that any territorial disagreements between the two countries would be settled through peaceful negotiations. Soon after the visit, a North Vietnamese and a Laotian frontier investigation team arrived in Nong Het, between the Vietnamese province of Nghe An and the Laotian province of Xieng Khouang.[12] Commenting on this survey, an editorial in *Nhan Dan* had remarked that there were reasons for hope that agreement could be reached. It further added that the fixing of the border was a very complex question, aggravated by the fact that the two countries had so long been under foreign domination; but now conditions were favorable for the settlement of the border question.[13] After a week of survey, the teams had issued a joint-declaration stating that they had held their first meeting on 29 September 1956 and had agreed on a working routine. Both sides were said to have found that their viewpoints had much in common. The last meeting had taken place on 4 October 1956, and it was reported that the teams would submit the results of their survey to their respective governments.[14] The truth was that both sides could not agree to the proper line for the frontier, and the only decision reached was that each delegation should report back to its own government. Apparently, agreement could have been reached if the RLG had conceded to a plebiscite in the disputed border area; but as it was under the effective control of the Vietnamese Communists, the result would have been against the RLG.[15]

Nothing more was heard until September of the following year, when it was reported that on 14 September 1957, a delegation from the RLG arrived in Hanoi by special plane. The delegation was in Hanoi to discuss the question of the frontier between the two countries in the Muong Sok and the Nam Can areas.[16] The arrival of the delegation was welcomed by the Vietnamese as "a good expression of the ever-improving relations between the DRV and the Kingdom of Laos."[17] The discussion lasted from 16 September until 2 October 1957. On 22 September, it was reported that agreement was reached on the temporary withdrawal of the armed forces of both sides from the Muong Sok and Nam Can areas. From the joint communiqué issued on 4 October 1957, it was evident that there remained outstanding questions that were not resolved. Both parties deemed it necessary to consult their respective governments in order to carry on the talks in the near future.[18] A *Nhan Dan* editorial on 5 October 1957 welcomed the communiqué as "the fruit of the spirit of frankness, cordiality and mutual understanding" and expressed the conviction that with the goodwill and efforts of both governments, the frontier problem could be settled in accordance with the joint statement by the two premiers in August 1956.[19] Again nothing more was heard about the issue; then in 1958, Souvanna Phouma was replaced by the anti–communist Phoui Sananikone.

According to British sources now available, during the time of the Huong Lap incident there were North Vietnamese troops in the disputed area; the largest involved patrols up to two platoons in the area north of Tchepone near the 17th parallel.[20] North Vietnamese troops had started moving into the Tchepone area about 20 December 1958, but their presence was only discovered some days later. Incursions were also reported in the region near Routes Nationales 12 and 7.[21] Two other incursions by North Vietnamese troops were reported to have occurred on or about 29 December 1958. The first involved an area stretching some 7 miles south of the frontier about 21 miles northeast of Tchepone. There were elements of one battalion occupying three positions in the area. The forward troops were holding the line of Sephbang Hieng and the Nam Se River. A company of Laotian troops south of the river kept them under observation. The second was the occupation by North Vietnamese troops of unknown strength of a section about 2 miles south of Frontier Route Number 12. They were also kept under observation by a company of Laotian troops.[22] According to French reports, on 8 January 1959, three North Vietnamese penetrations in Laos were withdrawn, to be followed by three new ones — of which one was in the area south of Tchepone and the other two were at the latitudes of Vinh and Xieng Khouang. These penetrations went 10 to 15 miles inside Laotian territory.[23] However, according to U.S. sources these incursions by the DRV troops posed no serious military threat.[24] The British embassy in Saigon was of the view that the DRV incursions into Laos were either for the convenience of communication with the North Vietnamese detachments there, or else they could be genuine mistakes in the dense jungle area.[25] In my view, whatever the reasons for the North Vietnamese movement of troops into this part of Laos, Hanoi had no prior intention to start a border dispute with Laos during this time. But after North Vietnamese troops were discovered in the frontier area by units of the Laotian armed forces, Hanoi decided to quickly accuse the Laotians of intrusion before the latter could accuse them.

The immediate result of the Huong Lap incident was that it strengthened the hand of Phoui Sananikone in Laos. Addressing the Laotian National Assembly on 12 January 1959, he spoke of the serious threat caused by the concentration of North Vietnamese troops at certain points along the Laotian border. On 14 January 1959, the Laotian National Assembly voted 28-16 to give his government special powers for a year.[26] Ten days later, Phoui introduced his new cabinet, which did not have any NLHX representative in it. On 11 February, at a press conference, he announced that his government considered the Geneva Agreement pertaining to Laos as fully accomplished; the ISCC had completed its task and henceforth Laos would not tolerate any interference in its internal affairs.[27] The North Vietnamese and Chinese believed that Laos would either join SEATO or the Americans would set up a military mission in the country.[28]

II

In the midst of the Huong Lap incident, the Lao Dong Party held its 15th Plenary Session in Hanoi, less than two months after the 14th Session was held in November 1958. The 15th Plenary Session was divided into two parts: The first was a closed-door meeting, followed by an enlarged one. We do not know the exact dates of the whole session except that it took place in January 1959. We can surmise that it must have taken place after Le Duan returned from his visit to the South in early January. It is highly likely that the closed-door meeting ended before 11 January 1959, because on that day Le Thanh Nghi, who was a member of the politburo, arrived in Beijing to join the DRV economic delegation that had been in China since December 1958.[29] Nghi, who was minister of industry and director of the industrial section of the DRV's Premier Office, was also the leader of the economic delegation. He would have remained in Hanoi for the closed-door meeting before proceeding to Beijing.

We still have no knowledge of the proceedings of the closed-door meeting, except that the resolution to liberate South Vietnam from imperialism and feudalism and complete the people's democratic revolution was adopted. The way to develop the foundation for the revolution in the South was to first use mass uprisings to seize power, and after that to let the current situation determine the course of the revolution. The most important factor was the strength of the masses. The armed forces should play a complementary and supportive role. Because of the American presence, it was anticipated that the struggle would be a protracted one.[30] According to Tran Van Tra, Le Duan's thesis, *Duong Loi Cach Mang Mien Nam,* written almost three years ago, was finally adopted in full.[31]

According to the *CRIMP Document*, although the 15th Plenary Session officially and concisely specified the responsibilities and strategic aims of the revolution in the South, there was insufficient information regarding the revolutionary movement in the South and the experiences of friendly nations to formulate a precise program. Questions such as how the aims and responsibilities of the revolution were to be implemented and what should be the main forms and procedures of the struggle were left unanswered. It was not until two years later that a clear program was eventually formulated.[32] The 15th Plenary Session also discussed the need for a popular front in the South. It saw the struggle to reunite the country as part of the world revolution and believed that a Vietnamese victory would encourage struggles for liberation in Asia, Africa, and Latin America. The need to offer assistance to Laos and Cambodia was highlighted.

We do know now that the enlarged meeting that followed was chaired by Ho and attended by representatives from the Nam Bo Regional Committee, the interprovincial committee of Interzone V, and representatives from all the party committees from the provinces in Central Vietnam,[33] and that it ended on 13 January 1959.[34] In his closing address, Ho said; "The task of saving our country is a responsibility of the whole party.... [We] must consider the southern region of Vietnam as part of our country's revolution and to see our country's revolution as part of the world's revolution.... We must spread out and fly high the flag of peace because that has great benefit for us. But peace does not mean that we do not prepare our military forces.... If we organize our political strength well, when the need comes to resort to arms, it will not be difficult."[35]

It is important to note that although the 15th Plenary Session officially sanctioned the resumption of armed struggle, political struggle was still regarded as the most important. The strategy was to depend primarily on the political strength of the masses in the South — that is, mass uprisings supported by the people's armed forces. How massive a military force to employ would depend on the circumstances and must be tailored to further the political cause. The Central Committee also anticipated that the mass uprisings would eventually develop into a prolonged armed struggle, in which they were confident of victory.

After the 15th Plenary Session, all the southern members of the Central Committee who were in charge of the various regions in the South, the representatives from the Nam Bo Regional Committee, and the interprovincial committee of Interzone V were entrusted with the urgent responsibility to return to the South to prepare and guide the revolution.[36] Significantly, the decision of the 15th Plenary Session was not made public until five months later on 13 May 1959.

III

Soon after the 15th Plenary Session, Vo Nguyen Giap lodged a protest with the ISCC against the so-called Phu Loi incident. It was reported that on 18 January 1958, immediately upon learning of the Phu Loi incident, Giap had met the Indian chairman of the ISCC and the head of the Canadian delegation.[37] The very next day, a "Committee to Struggle against the Phu Loi massacre" was formed by the Central Committee of the Vietnam Fatherland Front. Between 20 to 23 January, thousands of North Vietnamese participated in demonstrations against the incident.[38]

Apparently, on 1 December 1958, over a thousand political prisoners, either Communists or Communist sympathizers, were alleged to have been intentionally poisoned by the South Vietnamese authorities and to have died in the Phu Loi prison in Thu Dau Mot Province, 33 kilometers from Saigon. On 27 January, Pham Binh, the DRV Charge d'Affaires to China, held a press conference in Beijing in which he described the Phu Loi incident as "the most atrocious massacre ever recorded so far in the world in peacetime, comparable only to the mass murders practiced by the Hitlerite fascists and the outrages against prisoners of war in Koje Island committed by the U.S. aggressors of the Korean War. The massacre ... was part of the U.S. plot to perpetuate Vietnam's partition and turn South Vietnam into an American colony and military base. It was also a typical example of the so-called 'denounce and exterminate Communists policy.'"[39] The North Vietnamese protest against the Phu Loi incident lasted till March 1959.

According to the British embassy observers in Saigon, the deaths in Phu Loi prison as a result of food poisoning were caused either by negligence on the part of the prison authorities, by accident, or both; but it was not a massacre and the number of deaths there did not approach the scale alleged by Hanoi.[40] Whatever the truth may be, the incident was exploited to its fullest and was used to fan widespread indignation in the North. The British embassy in Saigon believed that the incident was blown up by the North because the North Vietnamese were discomforted by the calmness prevailing in the South and the satisfactory results of Diem's security drive.[41] According to a Vietnamese Communist source, at the end of 1958 and in early 1959 Diem's policy of terror in the South had reached its height.[42] Wilfred Burchett described the period 1958–1959 as the "blackest, most hopeless years for the people in South Vietnam."[43] The British consulate-general in Hanoi thought that Hanoi wanted to use the incident to rally more support from the Soviet Union and China.[44]

We still do not have the facts to confirm either view. There is reason to believe that Hanoi knew about the Phu Loi incident before it took action on 18 January 1959. As we have noted above, Le Duan was in the South on an extensive inspection tour in December 1958 and returned to Hanoi in early January 1959. Also, many Southern cadres were gathered in the North in early January for the 15th Plenary Session. It would be rather unbelievable if neither Le Duan nor any of the Southern leaders heard of the Phu Loi incident of 1 December 1958 until 18 January 1959. Thus there is reason to believe that the incident was deliberately magnified after the decision was taken at the 15th Plenary Session to intensify the revolution in the South. It is also not unreasonable to believe that Hanoi wanted to use the incident to rally support from Beijing and Moscow. We should recall that both the Chinese and the Russians had so far not supported the idea of the resumption of armed struggle in South Vietnam.

IV

According to the *Lich Su Quan Doi Nhan Dan Viet Nam*, in early January 1959, because of the Phu Loi incident, the VPA began intensifying their training. It is very likely that this decision to intensify military training was made at the 15th Plenary Session. The 324th Division and the 305th Brigade stepped up their military exercises to include mobile vehicles in the mountainous and delta terrains, combined assaults with the infantry, and combined infantry-artillery attacks on key enemy positions. A number of detachments from the 305th Brigade also began to train their troops in parachuting. The 330th Division carried out offensive and defensive exercises in delta terrain that had many villages and rivers. The 335th Battalion experimented with offensive and defensive maneuvers in mountainous terrain under varied conditions in preparation to fight in Laos. In Military Zone IV, they were studying and practicing the procedures of organizing and protecting the cadres in the South. In short, the VPA during this time was gearing up for the order to launch the offensive in the South.[45]

The 338th Division, which comprised the regrouped Southern cadres and a number of infantry regiments, was responsible for the training of cadres and fighters for their mission in the South. Tens of thousands of cadres and fighters who either had lived in the South or were familiar with the terrain in South Vietnam started training in preparation to be sent to the South. A number of divisions, mobile infantry brigades directly under the charge of Military Region IV, Northwest Military Region, were in full battle order. All military units were involved in studying the situation in the South and the duties of the revolution.[46]

It was during this time that DRV troops were reported to have encroached into the demilitarized zone between North and South Vietnam. The South Vietnamese government had protested to the ISCC that on 10 January 1959, North Vietnamese troops had entered A Choc, situated in the demilitarized zone south of the demarcation line; and on 16 January, they had occupied Tchepone (to be distinguished from the Laotian town of the same name), a small village on the North Vietnamese side of the demarcation line. According to the Canadian delegate in the ISCC, the North Vietnamese appeared to have permanently occupied Tchepone.[47] But as we have noted above, at the 15th Plenary Session the Hanoi leadership decided that while preparations should be made for an eventual military struggle, a military offensive was not anticipated for the foreseeable future.

In February 1959, the Central Military Committee met in Hanoi to listen to Le Duan explain the decision of the 15th Plenary Session. In the light of the decision to intensify the revolution in the South, the committee discussed the ways that they could quickly develop the base area and the revolutionary armed forces in the South, the role that the North would play in the revolution, and the preparation of the armed forces in the North in readiness to respond to any contingency.

We do not know whether any of the senior military officers had reservations regarding the intensification of the struggle in the South before the modernization of the VPA was completed. We should recall that in mid–March 1958, the Central Military Committee extended the target year for the completion of the military modernization program from 1959 to 1960. At this February 1959 meeting, Le Duan told the senior officers that they did not want to use war to unite the country. But if the Americans made war against them, they must be ready to fight. A war brought on by enemy provocation would be an opportunity for them to unite their country. The Central Military Committee decided that the modernization of the army had to be accelerated.[48] That the Central Military Committee felt it necessary to reemphasize this point would suggest that they were not satisfied with the pace of modernization, or that given the recent decision of the 15th Plenary Session, there was an urgent need to further speed up the pace.

In March 1959, the political bureau of the party issued a directive on the mission of creating a revolutionary base in the Central Highlands, which included the mountainous areas of Interzone V and the jungle and mountain areas of northeast Nam Bo. According to the political bureau, the Central Highlands were a very strategic region and they had to secure it before the U.S.-Diem regime could construct a military complex there. The directive instructed that the base area should be developed principally through political means, which included proselytizing amongst the people, promoting ethnic solidarity and self-sufficiency, the construction of a political administration base, building up of revolutionary armed forces, and campaigning among enemy soldiers. All tasks would be led by the party.

The political bureau further instructed that the armed forces in the South must be developed since only a strong military could defend the bases. For the present, they should be used to help the political struggle advance to the stage whereby it could carry out limited guerrilla warfare. The long-range goal was to strengthen the revolutionary forces in the South and prepare the conditions for advancing to the overthrow of the U.S.-Diem regime, and to become the main force in defending the future revolutionary administration.[49]

V

Ho Chi Minh was in Beijing from 20 to 24 January 1959 on his way to Moscow for the 21st CPSU Congress (27 January–5 February). He was welcomed at the airport by Zhou Enlai, Deng Xiaoping, and Chen Yi. We should recall that this was soon after the 15th Plenary Session. The Chinese were encountering problems of their own at this time. It had become apparent by now that the Great Leap Forward was running into problems. By the time of the 6th Plenary Session of the 8th CCP Central Committee (28 November–10 December 1958), it was becoming increasingly clear that they had overestimated the speed at which socialist development could proceed, and the targets set in August had to be lowered. It was during this plenary session that Mao offered to step down as chairman of the People's Republic, ostensibly so that he could devote more time to the study of theories and policies. At the 1st Session of the 2nd National People's Congress (18–28 April 1959), Liu Shaoqi replaced Mao as Chairman.[50] In Beijing, Ho told a journalist that North Vietnam had no intention of establishing communes on the Chinese model in the immediate future.[51]

Despite their economic problems, the Chinese remained very generous in their economic assistance to North Vietnam. A DRV economic delegation was in China during December 1958 and, as noted earlier, was joined by Le Thanh Nghi, minister of industry and director of the industrial section of the DRV's Premier Office on 11 January 1959.[52] On 18 February, a longterm trade and economic and technical aid agreement was signed between the two countries. Seven separate documents were signed. Besides the usual exchange agreement, the Chinese provided a new loan of 300 million yuan. Repayment of the 300 million yuan loan would begin only in 1967 and would be in the form of commodities. The Chinese also offered a gift of another 100 million yuan to be used for economic development. If we consider the 800 million yuan gift that the Chinese gave in 1955, this was indeed a very generous gesture. At a banquet given in Beijing by Le Thanh Nghi on 19 February in honor of the signing of the agreements, Chen Yi expressed the Chinese people's great admiration for the Vietnamese. He praised the achievements scored by the Vietnamese people in their hard struggle, they were a result of the revolutionary struggle waged by the Vietnamese people themselves. Chinese aid was very small and merely secondary. He recalled that Ho Chi Minh and other Vietnamese comrades had taken part in China's revolution and that the Lao Dong and Vietnamese had extended help and support to China's revolution at every stage. Le Thanh Nghi said that the agreements marked a new and important development in the economic cooperation and fraternal friendship between the two countries.[53] The *Renmin Ribao* editorial on 20 February declared that the signing of the agreements marked the further growth of mutual help and cooperation between China and North Vietnam in the economic field and the strengthening of the lasting, unbreakable fraternal friendship between them.[54]

The Vietnamese also signed two agreements on economic and technical cooperation with the Soviet Union,[55] but in contrast, the amount of credit given by the Russians was very much less. According to the estimation of the Foreign Office, Russian credit amounted to approximately 9 million pounds as compared to the 57 million pounds loaned by the Chinese. The 9 million pounds was also proportionately much less than the first Russian grant (a gift), which was about one-third of the first Chinese grant.[56]

With regard to the Huong Lap incident, Chinese response was very restrained. Only on 17 January did *NCNA* carry a report from Phnom Penh saying that political observers there believed that recent developments in the Laotian situation gave cause for anxiety.[57] On 21 January, while Ho was in Beijing, the commentary in *Renmin Ribao* urged a peaceful solution of the DRV–Laos border issue. Although the commentary on the whole came out in support of the DRV, the Chinese were noncommittal as to which party was right. Their attitude was that the border issue between North Vietnam and Laos was not too complicated and that it was fully possible for both countries to settle it by peaceful negotiation on the basis of respect for each other's sovereignty and territorial integrity.[58]

As for the Phu Loi incident, whether the reports that came from the South were accurate or otherwise did not appear to be important to the

North Vietnamese and Chinese. The Chinese were quick to join the North Vietnamese in the condemnation of the Diem regime. In support of Giap's demand for prompt investigation, the editorial in the *Renmin Ribao* on 20 January 1959 declared that the Chinese people strongly protest against the inhuman crime of the South Vietnamese authorities. It stressed that the massacre of political prisoners was a violation of Article 14c of the Geneva Agreement and Paragraph 9 of the final declaration.[59] Both the North Vietnamese and Chinese media carried numerous reports denouncing the Phu Loi incident. For example, a dispatch from Shanghai reported that over 400 young Vietnamese studying there or undergoing training in the factories had held a meeting of protest on 25 January; and that students of Jiaotong University and the Xinhua stationery store, many of whose native home was South Vietnam, had said that their countrymen were being butchered by the Ngo Dinh Diem bandits simply because they loved their country and hoped for its unification at an early date.[60]

Judging from the media reports, neither the Huong Lap incident nor the Phu Loi incident appeared to have interested the Russians. At the beginning of 1959, the Russians were themselves preoccupied with their 21st CPSU Congress, which began on 27 January 1959. It was only when the congress was over that they paid some attention to the developments in distant Indochina. At the 21st CPSU Congress, Khrushchev insisted that the conclusion drawn at the 20th CPSU Congress in February 1956 that war was not inevitable had been proven correct; and that economic progress in the Soviet Union and the socialist countries would lead to more countries outside the socialist bloc wanting to join the bloc, thereby consolidating the peace-loving forces of the world. War would be unnecessary as a means of solving international issues. When the Soviet Union became the world's leading industrial power and China became a mighty industrial power, and when all the socialist countries together produced half the world's industrial output, the international situation would change radically. The new correlation of power would be so obvious that even the most obdurate imperialists would realize the hopelessness of any attempt to launch a war against the socialist camp.[61] At the congress, Khrushchev also announced a new seven-year economic plan for the Soviet Union.

Ho Chi Minh in his speech during the congress spoke of the tasks and goals of the Vietnamese, which were to fulfill the three-year State Plan, consolidate the North and lead it toward socialism, and achieve national unification on the basis of independence and democracy. He spoke about the Phu Loi incident but made no reference to the recent decision taken at the 15th Plenary Session.[62] We still do not know whether Ho disclosed the decision of the 15th Plenary Session to the Russians privately while he was in Moscow.

Ho left Moscow on 8 February, three days after the end of the 21st CPSU Congress. He returned to Beijing on 9 February. On the evening of 10 February, it was reported that Mao and Liu had "cordial and friendly conversations" with Ho and Hoang Van Hoan.[63] We have no information about Ho and Hoan's activities on 11 February. It is notable that Ho's visit to Beijing was only briefly reported, whereas that of Ajoy Kumar Ghosh, Secretary-General of the Indian Communist Party who arrived in Beijing from Moscow on the same day as Ho, was better publicized. Ho and Hoan left Beijing on the morning of 12 February for Wuhan where they visited an iron and steel company and a meat-packing combine. They then proceeded to Nanning before returning to Hanoi on 14 February.[64] Chen Geng, member of the CCP Central Committee and deputy-chief of the PLA General Staff, was part of the contingent that saw Ho off to Wuhan on 12 February 1959. We should recall that Chen was one of the Chinese military advisers sent to assist the North Vietnamese in June 1950 and that he and Ho Chi Minh had close ties.[65] In April 1956, he led a Chinese military delegation to North Vietnam. From May 1957 till November 1958, Chen was a member of the State Council's Scientific Planning Commission. However, for the whole of 1958 until his appearance on 12 February 1959, he had not been seen in China. The American speculation was that during that period, he could have been in North Vietnam (presumably on a military-related assignment such as the modernization of the VPA).[66]

Chen Geng also met Vo Nguyen Giap when the latter passed by Beijing on his way to Warsaw on 3 March 1959.[67] Giap was in Beijing for a week a month later, from 5 to 12 April. He was on his way home after visiting Poland, Hungary, and Outer Mongolia. He was met by Peng Zhen, Chen Yi, Tan Zheng, Huang KeCheng, Gong ZiRong, and Xiao XiangRong. We do not know of his activities in Beijing except that he lunched with Peng Zhen and Chen Yi.[68]

The Chinese government trade delegation led by Chen Yu, the governor of Guangdong, was in Hanoi from 5 to 19 March to discuss trade exchange for 1959. The delegation visited the Hon Gay coal mines, Haiphong cement plant, Nam Dinh textile mill, and some other enterprises. The delegation met the DRV minister of foreign trade, and an agreement on supplementary orders for 1959 was signed. The British consulate-general in Hanoi believed that the supplementary agreement was necessary because of the dislocation of transport in China that had come about because of the drive for backyard steelmaking. As a result, Guangdong was cut off from its normal source of supplies and could more easily import what it needed by rail from the DRV.[69]

According to a U.S. State Department source, Fang Yi was also present in Hanoi during the visit of the Guangdong trade delegation. He was identified as the economic representative of the Chinese Foreign Trade Ministry stationed in Vietnam. Fang Yi had been an army commander under Ye Fei as well as the vice-chairman of the Fujian Province People's Government from 1949 to 1952. This Hanoi report marked his first public appearance since 13 October 1953 when he was the vice-chairman of the East China Committee on Financial and Economic Affairs. After the 1954 Geneva Conference, he was one of the economic advisers sent by China to help the North Vietnamese develop their economy.[70] Fang was elected an alternate member of the CCP Central Committee at the 2nd Session of the 8th CCP Congress in May 1958. The stationing of an alternate member of the Central Committee in a foreign country was considered unusual. No Chinese Communist diplomatic representative, except the ambassadors to the Soviet Union and India, had an equivalent rank.[71] The U.S. State Department also noted the presence of Chen Geng in the delegation. We do not know whether it was merely a coincidence, but his presence in Hanoi not long after the 15th Plenary Session and the March 1959 politburo meeting of the Lao Dong Party merits attention.

VI

During this period, besides domestic worries, the Chinese were also concerned about all the developments that were taking place in the region during the early months of 1959, and they saw the United States hand in all the activities. By contrast with the Huong Lap incident, the Chinese and the North Vietnamese strongly opposed Phoui's decision to terminate the ISCC in Laos. On 16 February 1959, a long commentary in *Guangming Ribao* stated that the RLG's unilateral action was a violation of the Geneva Agreement and that it was linked to the U.S. scheme to intensify its military interference in Laos. The Chinese were evidently concerned that Laos would join SEATO and the United States would turn Laos into a military base. The commentary noted that China, a close neighbor of Laos and a participant in the Geneva Conference, could not agree to the RLG's unilateral action to tear up the Geneva Agreements; and it opposed U.S. military interference in Laos.[72] On 18 February, Chen Yi issued a statement declaring the Chinese government's opposition to the unilateral repudiation of the Geneva Agreements. The Chinese government asked the cochairmen of the Geneva Conference to take speedy action "in regard to this serious violation of the Geneva Agreements so as to check the U.S. scheme of military intervention in Laos and safeguard peace in Indochina."[73] On the following day, Chen Yi also addressed letters to both the Soviet and British foreign ministers regarding the situation in Laos.[74] We should recall that since July 1958, the ISCC in Laos had been adjourned sine die. Both the North Vietnamese and Chinese emphasized that the letter sent by the cochairmen of the Geneva Conference to the government of India on 31 January 1959 confirmed that the ISCC in Laos, while adjourning its activities sine die, might be convened again according to normal procedure, and it did not mean its dissolution.[75]

The Soviet government sent two notes to the British government on 26 February and 21 March 1959 suggesting that the two cochairmen should request the ISCC in Laos to resume as soon as possible its supervisory duties there.[76] On 25 March 1959, the Soviet Union issued a statement in response to the letters addressed to them as one of the cochairmen of the Geneva Conference by both the North Vietnamese and Chinese foreign ministers regarding the situation in Laos. The Russians entirely shared the Vietnamese and Chinese concerns.[77] On 7 April, the British government stated that it considered that the ISCC in Laos had completed its tasks and it was up to the Laotian government to request the resumption of its activities.[78]

Meanwhile, on 10 March 1959, the PLA crushed an armed rebellion in Lhasa, Tibet. Three days later, on 13 March 1959, the Chinese accused the Laotians of abetting Jiang Jieshi's troops to invade the border areas in Yunnan province. According to the Chinese, the Laotian authorities had been colluding with these troops by permitting the latter to use the Muong Sing region in Laos for espionage and sabotage activities against China. They further revealed that in the past six months, members of the U.S. Military Advisory Group (MAAG) and economic mission had been active in the region of Muong Sing and Nam Tha and were supporting the troops. U.S. secret agents had also established permanent organizations in the region under the pretext of carrying out medical services. The Chinese believed that the United States, Taiwan, and the pro-U.S. elements in Laos hoped to provoke an armed conflict on the Sino-Laotian border to serve as a pretext for American intervention in Laos and the region.[79]

On 20–22 February and again on 26 March 1959, there were skirmishes between the South Vietnamese and the Chinese in the Paracel Islands.[80] The Chinese claimed that on the evening of 20 February, a South Vietnamese gunboat, HQ 225, had conducted reconnaissance activities in the vicinity of the North Island in the Paracels. The next day, the gunboat intercepted Chinese fishing vessels of Southsand Island to gather information about the island group. On the morning of 22 February, the same gunboat sailed to Shenhang Island and over ten armed personnel again boarded Chinese fishing boats. They landed on the island, tore up the national flags flying there, kidnapped 82 fishermen, and stole five fishing boats and other property. The Chinese further claimed that a South Vietnamese reconnaissance aircraft was circling over the Paracels.

On 28 February, a *Renmin Ribao* commentary referred to the SEATO announcement of a large-scale aerial exercise in Thailand at the beginning of March, as well as the joint Thai–U.S. atomic warfare maneuver in northern Thailand in early February in which representatives from South Vietnam, Laos, South Korea, and Taiwan attended as observers; and the large-scale SEATO naval exercise in the Far East scheduled for April 1959. These were perceived as indications of the U.S. scheme "to drag South Vietnam, Laos, and Cambodia into the SEATO bloc and turn them into bases for military provocation against China, the DRV and other peace-loving Southeast Asian countries."[81] To the Chinese, the aerial exercise was intended as a show of strength to intimidate the people of Southeast Asia and a provocation against the Chinese people. They saw a U.S. global plot in the making: "At the same time, the U.S.A had concluded separate bilateral military agreements with Turkey, Iran and Pakistan which would enable it to dispatch troops to the territories of the signatory countries under the pretext of resisting direct or indirect aggression, and carry out indirect intervention.... The U.S.A was trying hard to undermine, even to tear up the Geneva Agreements. It had intensified its subversive activities against Cambodia, was furthering its infiltration into Laos and was conspiring to pull Laos into the SEATO bloc. At the same time, the U.S.A was also instigating South Vietnam to invade China's territory."[82]

Finally on 26 March, the Chinese again claimed that a South Vietnamese aircraft had intruded into the airspace over Shenhang Island and that 16 naval personnel landed on the island, searched and interrogated the Chinese fishermen there, and threatened to destroy their houses. The Chinese believed that all these acts were committed under the direction of the U.S. imperialists.[83] This was how the international scene looked to China in early 1959. Chinese condemnations and diatribes against Western imperialism were noticeably more vocal than the North Vietnamese.

An interview that Mao gave to Anna Louise Strong on 13 March 1959 gives us a glimpse of Mao's thinking during this time. Strong's account of the interview revealed that Mao did not believe that the United States was prepared to go to war with China. Mao explained that during the 1958 Quemoy crisis, the Americans would escort Jiang's ships, but they always stayed three miles away from them and watched while China shelled the ships. In his words, "they stopped at the brink. So now we regard Dulles as our teacher and we also stop at the brink.... We learned from Dulles to avoid the brink of war." Mao conceded that there would always be wars, but he did not believe that there would be a third world war. He also did not think that the stockpile of bombs could be set off by accident, nor would the human race be destroyed by a nuclear war. He insisted that one should not be afraid of the imperialists because that would only provoke them to action. According to him, "one should oppose them, but with care." Regarding the Soviet Union, Mao thought that it would become revisionist and, in his words, try to "strangle" and "choke" China. However, neither of the superpowers would engage in war with China at that time because it would only provide a big advantage to the other. But it was possible that the United States and the Soviet Union together with India and Japan might attack China, although that would require a large amount of preparation.[84]

A month later, in his speech at the 16th Enlarged Session of the Supreme State Conference on 14 April 1959, Mao explained why, if the imperialist forces were but "paper tigers," China did not simply attack Taiwan. In November 1958, Mao had complained that many people both within and outside the party did not understand the "paper tiger" concept. He compared the Quemoy (Jinmen) crisis of August 1958 and the Tibet problem, and explained that Taiwan had signed a treaty with the United States. Thus, unlike the case of Taiwan, the Chinese military could easily move into Tibet, which did not have such a treaty.[85]

It is very likely that Mao would apply the same logic with regard to Vietnam and discourage any military moves into South Vietnam on the part of the North Vietnamese that would provoke the involvement of the United States. But this does not mean that Mao advocated complete forbearance. As he told Louise Anna Strong at their meeting on 13 March 1959, one should oppose the imperialists, but with care. Also, as we have noted above, the Chinese during this time were seeing security threats all around them. Hanoi was a strategic ally. It is thus probable that compared with the summer of 1958, Mao was more receptive to the rather moderate decision of the 15th Plenary Session, but at the same time continued to counsel caution.

From 25 March to 1 April, the CCP Political Bureau held an enlarged meeting in Shanghai to prepare for the 7th Central Committee Plenary session. The outstanding issue was again that of the people's communes. Meanwhile, the production figures were gradually being adjusted downwards. Despite these efforts, problems in the economy continued to surface. From 29 March till about 6 May 1959, China's attention was shifted to Tibet. Despite all the recent protest and outcry over Laos and South Vietnam, at the 1st session of the 2nd National People's Congress, which took place between 18 and 28 April 1959, there was remarkably little reference to Indochina in Zhou's report on foreign policy. Attention was focused on Tibet and Sino-Japanese relations.[86] Also at this session of the 2nd National People's Congress, Mao relinquished his position as chairman of the People's Republic to Liu Shaoqi. China scholars and Mao specialists are in agreement that this move did not substantially diminish Mao's authority; and his influence particularly in the area of foreign affairs remained great.

It was also in March 1959 that the first signs emerged that the Soviet Union had decided to abandon its self-imposed policy of allowing Beijing to oversee the Communist activities in Southeast Asia. This was when the Soviet embassy in Burma received a strong order from Moscow in March to immediately improve relations with all Burmese aboveground Communists and their National United Front. The control of the Burmese Communists had since 1954 been in Chinese hands, with Soviet acquiescence. Aleksandr Kaznacheev recounted that for a long time the Soviet Union had refused to engage a qualified interpreter for the Soviet embassy in Burma, and the excuse was always a lack of funds. But in the spring of 1959, funds became suddenly available: not only would the embassy get interpreters, but several Burmese language specialists as well. According to Kaznacheev, one of the most significant features of the new Soviet policy in Southeast Asia was the almost open support of anti–Chinese actions by the governments of the area and attempts to establish closer ties with India, which was the biggest natural anti–Chinese force in the region.[87]

VII

Meanwhile, in March 1959, there were further indications that Le Duan was the number-two man in North Vietnam. A letter to the

Polish Communist Party was signed by him as "secretary-general." This was the first time he had been publicly addressed as such. It was again Le Duan who headed the Lao Dong Committee that entertained the visiting Indonesian Communist Party delegation led by Secretary-General D. N. Aidit from 28 March to 4 April 1959. He was placed before Truong Chinh, but was described only as a member of the political bureau.[88] This would indicate that Truong Chinh had lost out to Le Duan in the party hierarchy, although as deputy-premier he remained powerful in the government.[89] Truong Chinh was also made chairman of the newly established National Scientific Research Board in December 1958. In spite of having suffered a setback over the agrarian reform debacle, it was he who delivered the report, on behalf of the government, on the issue of agricultural cooperation at the 10th Session of the National Assembly in May 1959; and he also took the lead in the organization of a new and all-embracing course of political education for party and government officials in July 1959.[90]

However, Le Duan was definitely the man in charge of South Vietnamese affairs. Janos Radvanyi was a member of the Hungarian party and government delegation that visited Hanoi between 19 and 26 April 1959. During one of the discussions, the subject of the situation in South Vietnam was raised. According to Radvanyi, Ho yielded the floor to Le Duan, whom he explained was the politburo member in charge of South Vietnamese affairs and had recently returned from an extended tour of the South. According to Le Duan, the situation in the South was gradually turning to the advantage of the North. Political workers and party cadres had been instructed to merge with the peasants in the countryside and the intellectuals in the cities, and when possible to infiltrate the army and government. In the sphere of political agitation and propaganda, party cadres were told to exploit every opportunity to expose the corruption of the Diem regime and to support popular grievances. Although he admitted that there were difficulties, Le Duan appeared confident that the Diem regime would eventually collapse.

During the conversation, Pḥam Van Dong disclosed that the South Vietnamese guerrilla leaders residing in Hanoi were increasing their pressure on the politburo to endorse unrestrained military action in the South. While he understood their feelings, Dong thought that it was folly to begin such an action before the North became strong enough to back it up and before the situation was ripe in the South. Then, according to Radvanyi, "in a half-finished sentence he hinted that the Southern comrades should not be asked to wait too long."[91]

Radvanyi also observed that the Northern leadership regarded the South Vietnamese living in Hanoi, in his words, "like poor relations—to be tolerated but virtually ignored." He had a brief opportunity to converse with Nguyen Huu Tho who flatly insisted that the South was ripe for revolutionary guerrilla activity, but the guerrillas must stay their hand because Hanoi contended that the time was not right for action. According to the *CRIMP Document*, since the end of 1958 and particularly after the Phu Loi Incident, many felt that the situation was ripe for an armed movement against the Diem regime. But the leadership of the Nam Bo Regional Committee hesitated principally because it was against the party line.[92] Tho had asked Radvanyi whether Ho, Pham Van Dong or Le Duan had divulged to the Hungarians any new plans regarding the liberation of the South.[93]

The Hungarian party and government delegation was in Beijing from 29 April to 7 May 1959 after visiting Hanoi from 19 to 26 April. According to Janos Radvanyi, the Chinese were keen to hear about their experiences in Vietnam. Chinese Foreign Minister Chen Yi and Wang Youtien, director of the Soviet and East European Department in the Chinese Foreign Ministry, were particularly interested in what the Hungarians knew of the South Vietnamese situation. Also, Chen Yi expected Ho to begin the reunification process soon. The subject of Vietnam was raised again at a meeting with Mao Zedong. Mao spoke of Ho as an old friend with whom he had enjoyed harmonious relations and blamed Stalin for Ho's difficulties. It was Mao's hope that the Communists would come to power in France, thus making possible the solution of the Vietnam problem within the framework of a French union under Maurice Thorez and Jacques Duclos. Meanwhile, Mao stated that the Chinese would continue to back the Vietnamese in their efforts to liberate the country.[94]

According to Janos Radvanyi, when the Hungarian party and government delegation were in Moscow on 16–17 May 1959 after visiting China, Khrushchev showed no interest at all in Vietnam. If one considered the Russian response to the Middle East crisis in the summer of 1958 and Khrushchev's address during the recent 21st CPSU Congress, it would only be logical to conclude that the Russians would hardly agree with the North Vietnamese decision to intensify the struggle in the South. Indeed, a month later, on 20 June 1959, the Soviet Union rescinded on the Sino-Soviet agreement concluded in October 1957 in which the Russians had agreed to provide China with a sample of the atom bomb and technical data concerning its manufacture.[95] During the conversation with the Hungarians, Khrushchev spoke about the Berlin question, the current

Conference of Foreign Ministers in Geneva, and his low opinion of the Chinese Great Leap Forward. But when Hungarian Prime Minister Munnich enthusiastically tried to tell him about some of the highlights of their Hanoi visit, Khrushchev all but yawned in his face. According to Radvanyi, he found that attitude rather strange "in as much as the 15th Plenum of the Central Committee of the Lao Dong Party in May [?] had for the first time called for an armed struggle against the Diem clique and the Americans.... Yet Khrushchev, for reasons unknown to me, seemed totally unconcerned."[96]

Six

May 1959–December 1959

I

Whatever the differences within the North Vietnamese leadership, or between the Hanoi leadership and the Southern cadres over whether the South was ready for a revolution, a consensus was reached soon after Ngo Dinh Diem promulgated Law 10/59 on 6 May 1959 in South Vietnam. This law provided for the establishment of special military tribunals to try anyone suspected of being involved in Communist activities.[1] Looking back to this period in 1965, Le Duan said, "Before the law was passed, there were only hundreds who were wholeheartedly prepared to fight the enemy. Since the passing of that law, masses regardless of their political inclinations rose against Diem."[2] In his instructions to the Nam Bo Regional Committee on 7 May, Le Duan emphasized the need to concentrate on the establishment of base areas in Nam Bo, particularly in the eastern part, through political work. At the same time, the armed forces and self-defense forces should also be developed.[3]

On 13 May 1959, a week after the passing of Law 10/59, the Hanoi leadership issued a communiqué regarding the decision made at the 15th Plenary Session in January 1959 to reunify the country. According to the communiqué, North Vietnam had completed the people's democratic revolution and was going through a socialist revolution. This was an important change because it determined the direction and the next stage of the development of the Vietnamese revolution. For the North, building socialism was the most urgent task and it was directly related to the struggle for national reunification, which was the most earnest aspiration of the

Vietnamese people. But while North Vietnam had all along respected the 1954 Geneva Agreements, the Diem regime and the Americans had constantly undermined the Agreements. The communiqué paid tribute to the struggle of the southern compatriots and stated in very broad terms that the entire people would unite and strive to achieve reunification.[4] The *Nhan Dan* editorial on the communiqué was somewhat more precise, but equally circumspect. It stated that "the people were determined to struggle resolutely and gallantly and use every means and methods — if necessary — to attain their objectives."[5]

Soon after the communiqué was issued, a unit under the direct charge of the Central Military Committee was formed to study how the North Vietnamese could open a road that could link them with the cadres in the South. On 19 May, about a week after the communiqué of the 15th Plenary Session was made public, Vo Bam, deputy-director of the office responsible for agricultural collectivization, was appointed to head this unit. The purpose of opening this road was to facilitate the movement of cadres, weapons, and other necessary supplies to South Vietnam. This was the beginning of the Ho Chi Minh Trail.[6]

On the same day, Military Transportation Group 559 was formed. Its mission was to construct the first road connecting the North and the South, and to organize the transfer of weapons and supplies to the South, particularly Interzone V. Group 559 consisted of two battalions. The 301st Battalion was composed of 500 cadres and soldiers specially selected from the 305th Division who had previously fought against the French in Interzone V. The other formed in June was the 603rd Battalion, codename "Gianh River Fishing Team," which comprised 107 cadres and soldiers. The 603rd Battalion was responsible for the sea route to the South. According to another official Vietnamese source, Group 759 was formed in July 1959 to study the problem of organizing a maritime route to transport weapons, ammunition, and equipment to the South and was based at the coastal region of Do Son-Haiphong.[7] It started off as a small group of cadres directly under the General Staff, who were assigned to look into the matter. We know now that these included Vo Nguyen Giap, Hoang Tung, and Tran Quang Huy.[8] It is likely that the 603th Battalion and Group 759 were part of the same outfit. U.S. intelligence sources also identified the formation in May of the 70th Battalion, which was sent to the Laotian panhandle. The mission of the 70th Battalion was to transport weapons, ammunition, mail, and supplies along the Laotian trails into South Vietnam as well as to guide infiltration groups and bring the sick and wounded back to the North.[9]

Initially, the instruction given to Vo Bam was to extend the road no farther than the northern bank of the Ben Hai River. But after a meeting in May with Hanh (a member of the Party Committee of Quang Tri Province) and Quyet (a member of the Party Central Committee of Interzone V at Vinh Linh district, on the northern bank of the Ben Hai River at the 17th parallel), Vo Bam agreed with the two southern comrades that the trail would have to be extended as far as Highway 9 to be effective. By the first week of June 1959, a draft plan of the route, to go through the central region south of the 17th parallel, had been drawn up. The draft plan was for nine relay stations, two in the region north of the Ben Hai River and the remainder in Interzone V.

The point where the trail crossed Highway 9, between Khe Sanh and Lower Laos, is described as the "neuralgic point" because that strategic highway "bristled with enemy positions and was controlled day and night by armored patrols."[10] It was the most difficult and dangerous part of the trail. By 20 August 1959, the 301st Battalion had constructed relay station 9 in Pa Lin, west of Thua Thien, which made it possible for the first time to transport 500 kilograms of material, including weapons and ammunition, to Interzone V. To ensure absolute secrecy, the weapons and equipment were camouflaged as products meant for sale. The cadres and soldiers were also instructed to limit their contact with people and avoid unnecessary engagements with the enemy. By the end of 1959, the 301st Battalion had transferred to Pa Lin 1,667 rifles, 788 bayonets, 188 kilograms of explosives, some binoculars, compasses, and topographic maps. This was excluding the 1,174 rifles of all types, bullets, and ammunition that the units carried with them when they maneuvered into the South through the newly built roads. All these weapons and equipment were meant for Interzone V and the newly formed self-defense forces in the Central Highlands and the plains, as well as the provinces in central Vietnam.[11]

Tran Van Tra recounted a meeting between himself, Nguyen Van Vinh, and Le Duan one evening in the summer of 1959. The meeting had its origin in a BBC news bulletin that Tra had chanced to hear. It was a report of a skirmish between a platoon of Diem's forces and a platoon of the Vietcong in the Plain of Reeds. After two hours of fighting, both sides withdrew. There was no report of any casualties. The news of this inconclusive two-hour-long fight amazed Tra, who thought that either the BBC report was inaccurate or the training of the Communist cadres in the South was inadequate. The next day he visited his old friend, Nguyen Van Vinh, and they both agreed that there was an urgent need to train the Communist cadres in the South. This could be done with the help of the regrouped Southern cadres still based in the North, who had been well honed militarily for the eventual reunification of the country. They then decided to convey their views to Le Duan, who, according to Tran Van Tra, was at that point already the first secretary of the Party Central Committee. The initial proposal by Tra and Vinh was for sending 100 young cadres to the South. After much thought, Le Duan said that it would be difficult, as the politburo had not arrived at a decision regarding this matter. Tran and Vinh pleaded for their cause. Le Duan then asked whether the number could be reduced. This time they proposed 50. Again Le Duan was deep in thought. Because this matter had yet to be discussed by the politburo, by right, approval could not be given. But he was prepared to bear the responsibility if the number was smaller. Le Duan came up with the figure of 25. The team of 25 was selected by June 1959. By 25 December 1959, they were ready to move into the South. By this time, the Party Central Committee had given its blessing.[12]

Tra's account is particularly revealing for two reasons: Firstly, it shows that during this period the Hanoi leadership was still very cautious about escalating the struggle in the South; secondly, it gives us a glimpse of the extent of Le Duan's authority and how decisions were made by the North Vietnamese leadership.

II

At about the time when the North Vietnamese made public their decision to renew the struggle in the South, in Laos, 1,500 Pathet Lao troops refused to be integrated into the Royal Laotian Army.[13] The November 1957 agreement reached between the RLG and the Pathet Lao had specified that the Pathet Lao troops would be demobilized and integrated into the Royal Laotian Army and receive ranks and positions in accordance with the procedures of the government. But there were disagreements between the two armies over the proportion of Pathet Lao officers in the integrated army and over the rank to be conferred on Colonel Singkapo Chounlamany[14] of the Pathet Lao army.

On 11 May 1959, Singkapo Chounlamany refused to accept the rank of colonel given to him and failed to turn up for the award ceremony in Vientiane, on the pretext that there were irregularities in the integration procedure. Souphanouvong also made a similar charge. Over on the Plaine des Jarres, 500 Pathet Lao troops boycotted a similar ceremony on the same day. The government reacted by ordering an alert in the areas where the Pathet Lao troops were stationed. The two Pathet Lao units, stationed at Xieng Khouang and Luang Prabang, were encircled by the Royal Laotian Army and their supply lines were cut. The Pathet Lao troops were given a choice of either accepting the new ranks and being integrated into the national army or surrendering their weapons in order to be discharged as civilians within 24 hours. Failure to do either would be an act of treason. When the deadline had passed, only 50 of the Pathet Lao troops had come forward. It was reported on 17 May that the RLG had sent the police to encircle the residences of Souphanouvong and other NLHX leaders in Vientiane. On the same day, the DRV Foreign Ministry issued a statement accusing Phoui Sananikone's government of serious violation of the Geneva Agreements and the creation of tension in Indochina. The North Vietnamese proposed that the ISCC in Laos should resume its duties and called upon the cochairmen of the Geneva Conference to take appropriate measures to prevent any worsening of the situation in Laos. The statement further added that as a signatory of the Geneva Agreements and a neighboring country that had a common boundary of over 1,000 kilometers with Laos, the DRV was very anxious over the gravity of the developments in Laos. On 18 May, the Chinese Foreign Ministry issued a statement that was almost identical to that of North Vietnam's.

On 17 May at 10:00 A.M., the first Pathet Lao battalion, consisting of 750 Pathet Lao troops stationed south of Luang Prabang, surrendered. A letter from Souphanouvong written some weeks earlier found on the battalion commander instructed him to delay integration till after the Laotian elections; but Souphanouvong subsequently changed his mind and ordered the battalion to comply. During the night of 18–19 May, the second Pathet Lao battalion, which was stationed in a former French Foreign Legion camp on the Plaine des Jarres — the Thong Mai Hin camp — escaped into the mountains. Information provided by the RLG and not contradicted by any foreign military attaché showed that the battalion had fled into the virtually inaccessible mountainous areas in eastern Xieng Khouang, with many of them crossing over into North Vietnam.[15] We do not know whether the escape of the second battalion was authorized by Souphanouvong or by higher echelons either in Sam Neua or Hanoi. What followed was a series of military engagements between the Royal Laotian Army and the Pathet Lao, with the assistance of the North Vietnamese.

In an interview on 21 May in Saigon, Laotian Foreign Minister Khamphan Panya, who was at the time visiting South Vietnam at the invitation of the South Vietnamese government, declared the RLG's intention to outlaw the NLHX. He also said that the RLG would seek help not only from SEATO but from any other international organization or any stronger anti-Communist nation. According to an AFP report on 24 May, the South Vietnamese and Laotian governments had agreed on civil and military security cooperation and the transportation of supplies from South Vietnam to Laos through Saigon and Da Nang. On 25 May 1959, after a special cabinet meeting, the RLG announced that it would use force to annihilate the Pathet Lao. The Thai foreign minister then visited Laos at the invitation of the RLG from 27 to 29 May. On 27 May, the deputy-minister of information stated that the NLHX leaders in Vientiane would be placed under closer surveillance[16] and that Pathet Lao sympathizers would be severely punished. The lines were clearly drawn between the Pathet Lao, North Vietnam, and China on the one side and the RLG, the United States, South Vietnam, and Thailand on the other.

On 28 May 1959, it was reported that there had been a clash involving the RLG forces that had been deployed in the mountainous region between Xieng Khouang and the Vietnamese border. Hanoi Radio stated that the troops and police of the DRV had been ordered to strengthen their defense along the Laotian border and to be alert for any provocations. Fighting was again reported on 29 May in the Muong Ngan area. According to the Pathet Lao 2nd Battalion, they had reached the Muong Ngan region by 30 May. The fighting was particularly serious on those two days. Not long after that, the battalion succeeded in moving to the southeastern part of Xieng Khouang Province. On 10 June, it was reported that the Pathet Lao 2nd Battalion had safely reached its former revolutionary bases. *Nhan Dan* hailed the battalion's safe withdrawal as "a new epic of the Laotian people.... Like fish returning to water, the Pathet Lao Battalion Number 2 is again enjoying the devoted help of the local people." To the North Vietnamese, the battalion was justified to continue their self-defense fight because the government of Phoui Sananikone on the orders of the U.S. imperialists had reneged on the Geneva Agreements.[17] Sporadic fighting persisted throughout May, June, and July 1959.

III

While the Ho Chi Minh Trail was being built and the fighting in Laos was going on, Ho Chi Minh was in the Soviet Union, ostensibly on vacation. There was no report of Ho's departure from Hanoi for Moscow.[18] The first knowledge that Ho was in Moscow was a one-sentence report that he had arrived by TU 104 on 2 July 1959 to spend his summer holiday in the Soviet Union.[19] At Moscow, he was met by Voroshilov (chairman of the Presidium of the Supreme Soviet), Mukhitdinov (secretary of the CPSU Central Committee), Mikhail Geogadze (secretary of the Presidium of the Supreme Soviet), and Vladmir Servemov (deputy-foreign minister).[20] We know that Ho spent the whole of July in the Soviet Union and that he arrived in Baku on 23 July.[21] Other than that, we have no information about his activities. Khrushchev was in Poland for ten days in July, from 14 to 23 July; and U.S. Vice-President Richard Nixon was in Moscow from 23 July till 2 August. While in the Soviet Union, Ho could not have missed all the favorable publicity in the Russian media regarding Khrushchev's impending visit to the United States from 15 to 28 September 1959 at the invitation of President Eisenhower, which was announced in July. Khrushchev was so eager to visit the United States that he postponed an earlier invitation to make an official visit to Scandinavia during that time in order to accept Eisenhower's invitation without change.[22]

In China, from 2 July to 1 August, an enlarged meeting of the Political Bureau of the CCP Central Committee was being convened in Lushan to review the progress of the Great Leap Forward, which as we have noted before had run into trouble. It was this meeting that witnessed a clash between Mao Zedong and Peng Dehuai, basically over the Mao-inspired economic construction of China — the Great Leap Forward — that consequently led to the disgrace of Peng.[23] There was a Soviet dimension in the Mao–Peng dispute.[24] During Peng Dehuai's visit to Eastern Europe from 22 April to 13 June 1959, he was believed to have expressed his opposition to the Great Leap Forward to Khrushchev when they met in Tirana on 25 May 1959. Khrushchev subsequently made an anticommune speech in Poland on 18 July 1959 that was published by the Soviet news media on 21 July, while the Lushan Plenum was in session, thus giving the impression that he was supporting Peng Dehuai. The 8th Plenary Session of the 8th Central Committee followed closely after the Lushan meeting from 2 to 16 August 1959. At this session, Peng Dehuai and his supporters were relieved of all their administrative posts.[25] Stuart Schram stressed that the Lushan Plenum was a turning point toward a greater emphasis on class struggle.[26] According to Laszlo Ladany, the plenum changed the political climate in China. Two months after the meeting, there was a blackout on news out of China. Prior to this, it was possible for non–Chinese to subscribe even to provincial newspapers, but from November 1959, only the *Renmin Ribao* and *Hongqi* were allowed to be disseminated outside China.[27]

Ho Chi Minh left Moscow on 1 August 1959, a day before Nixon concluded his visit to the Soviet Union. He arrived at Urumchi at 10:15 A.M. on the same day.[28] Because the 8th Plenary Session was called by Mao at such short notice (on 23 July when Ho was in Baku), Ho took a leisurely tour of parts of northwestern China while waiting for it to end.[29] He toured Xinjiang (1–4 August), Jiuquan and Lanzhou in Gansu Province (4–7 August), and Xian and its vicinity in Shaanxi Province (7–8 August). Ho finally reached Beijing on 13 August. He was received by Chen Yi, Liu Lantao, alternate member of the Secretariat of the CCP Central Committee, and He Wei.[30] The Chinese sources did not disclose where Ho was between 8 and 13 August. It is possible that Ho was at Lushan during that time, when the 8th Plenary Session of the CCP 8th Central Committee was in still in session.[31]

While in Beijing and waiting for the 8th Plenary Session to end on 16 August, Ho visited the Ming Tomb Reservoir, the Summer Palace, and the Temple of Heaven. On 18–19 August, it was reported that he was visiting places near Beijing and receiving Vietnamese students. On 19 August, he also visited the recently completed military museum.

As far as we can tell, it was not until 21 August that Ho met any of the Chinese leaders in Beijing. On that day, he met both Liu Shaoqi and Zhou Enlai,[32] and he attended a banquet in his honor in the evening given by Liu in which Zhou Enlai, Peng Zhen, Nie Rongzhen, Wang Jiaxiang, and He Wei were present. After 21 August, there was no further report of Ho's activities until his departure on 25 August. He was seen off by Zhou Enlai, Peng Zhen, and Chen Yi. According to a Chinese source, Ho had discussions with Liu Shaoqi, Zhou Enlai, and other Chinese leaders regarding Vietnam.[33] The British consulate-general in Hanoi believed that Pham Van Dong might have joined Ho in Beijing during this time. Dong was absent from Hanoi between 15 and 26 August without explanation.[34] While in China, Ho (and perhaps Dong as well) must have discussed with the Chinese the situation in South Vietnam.

The Chinese were concerned about the developments in South Vietnam and Laos. They believed that the United States was trying to make both South Vietnam and Laos part of SEATO. The increase of U.S. military advisers and personnel, the shipment of U.S. arms and ammunition, the number of U.S. missions to South Vietnam; the proliferation of airfields and the construction of a highway system linking South Vietnam, southern Laos, and Thailand were all perceived as "war preparations." The Chinese also suspected that the Pentagon was plotting to smuggle atomic weapons into South Vietnam and of using South Vietnam as a base to intervene in Laos and Cambodia.[35]

In Han Suyin's account, Ho, during his meeting with Zhou in August 1959, expressed concern about the projected Khrushchev–Eisenhower summit and its implications for Vietnam. Ho also informed Zhou of the plan to form a liberation front in South Vietnam and the use of military means to achieve the reunification of the country. Zhou assured Ho that by the end of the year — that is, 1959 — China would give approximately $500 million worth of weaponry, equipment, and funds to support the liberation struggle.[36] A Chinese source noted that after the promulgation of Law 10/59, when the North Vietnamese proposed an armed defense struggle in the South, China supported the idea.[37] According to Hoang Van Hoan, when the North Vietnamese eventually made public the decision to renew the struggle to unify the country on 13 May 1959,[38] the Chinese considered it "a reasonable idea and agreed to provide military aid."[39]

We do not know to what extent the Chinese promise of military aid to Ho at this time was a response to what they saw as American war preparations in the region or to emphasize to Moscow that Beijing was free to implement its own policies, regardless of Soviet views. But as far as we can tell, the Chinese did not deliver the military aid at the end of 1959.

Ho returned to Hanoi on 26 August and was reported to have been met at the airport by Pham Van Dong and Truong Chinh.[40] All in all, Ho was away from North Vietnam for almost two months at a time when the North Vietnamese were assisting the Pathet Lao in a civil war against the RLG.

A week after Ho's return to Hanoi, on 1 September, which was also the occasion of the 14th anniversary of North Vietnam's National Day, seven senior officers in the VPA were promoted, including Nguyen Chi Thanh, head of the General Political Department, promoted to General. The VPA now had two full generals, the other being Vo Nguyen Giap. Van Tien Dung (general chief of staff) and Chu Van Tan (political commissar of the Viet Bac sector) were promoted to senior-generals; Nguyen Van Vinh (deputy-defense minister), Hoang Van Thai, Tran Van Tra (both assistant general chief of staff), and Song Hao (deputy-head of the General Political Department) were all made major-generals.[41]

IV

Meanwhile, the fighting continued in Laos. The DRV protested against the many aerial intrusions of the RLG's reconnaissance planes into its airspace. Fighting between the RLG troops and the Pathet Lao intensified in mid–July in the provinces of Xieng Khouang and Sam Neua. There was a brief two-week lull in the fighting from 11 August 1959 with both sides claiming they had the upper hand. On 26 August 1959, the U.S. government decided that it would provide the RLG with "emergency aid" in the form of weapons and money. Fighting then resumed in Laos toward the end of the month and into September 1959. It briefly stopped when the United Nations (UN) fact-finding mission arrived in Laos in mid–September.

In China, right up to about 27 July 1959, there was a steady stream of reports and commentaries regarding the developments in Laos, not unlike those of North Vietnam. The Chinese placed the blame for the crisis in Laos squarely on the Americans and the Phoui Sananikone government. After 27 July 1959, there was a notable absence of original Chinese comments. Most of the NCNA items were recapitulations of reports from Hanoi. Although the Chinese continued to report on Laotian developments, they were based on North Vietnamese and Western press reports.[42] No doubt the Chinese continued to be interested in the happenings in Laos; but as we have noted, during this time there were more important developments at home that required their immediate attention. But by the middle of August, the Chinese were able to turn their attention back to Laos and the new developments along the Sino-Indian border. The Sino-Indian border dispute had been brewing since early 1959, and relations between Beijing and New Delhi further deteriorated in the autumn.[43]

According to the U.S. embassy in Laos, a map study of the villages and military posts attacked since mid–July showed that all the military activities took place along the Laotian border adjacent to North Vietnam. There were no incidents reported along the borders that Laos shared with Thailand, Burma, South Vietnam, Cambodia, or even China. It identified six salients in which military activities took place: southeast of PhongSaly Province, starting at Sop Nao just inside the border and extending southwest to Muong Khoua; northwest of Sam Neua Province from Muong Peu through Muong Son to as far as Pong Sa Thone; north of Sam Neua town from Xieng Kho to as far south as Muong Het; further east in Sam Neua Province; southeast Laos; and the DRV border east of Thakhek.[44] Although the embassy could not offer proof of any direct

North Vietnamese involvement at that time, there was much circumstantial evidence.[45] The U.S. State Department, however, found no evidence of Chinese involvement in the fighting.

Throughout, Hanoi adamantly denied the charges that some of its military units were involved in the fighting in Laos. On 4 September 1959, the Permanent Mission of Laos to the United Nations requested that a UN emergency force be dispatched to Laos as soon as possible to halt the aggression along the northeastern frontier of Laos by elements of the DRV. On 5 September, the UN secretary-general asked the president of the Security Council to convene urgently to consider the request. The Security Council met on 7 September to consider the request against the sole opposition of the Soviet Union, whose representative objected to discussing the Laotian request. The Russians felt that the RLG in cooperation with the ISCC in Laos could and must restore order in the country on the basis of the 1954 Geneva Agreements and the Vientiane Agreements of 1956 and 1957, without interference from the outside. The Russians further charged that the Phoui Sananikone government had disregarded those agreements and hampered the work of the ISCC. In an oblique reference to the United States, the Russian representative claimed that the actions of the RLG were linked with foreign interference in the domestic affairs of Laos, designed to turn the country into a foreign base for strategic and military operations in Southeast Asia. This was also the position of both North Vietnam and China. The Soviet Union, however, did not exercise its veto on this occasion. According to British sources, the Soviet attitude in discussions with the British government from May 1959 to early September and in the Security Council on 7 September indicated that the Russians were not deeply interested in Laos and would like to see the situation stabilized.[46] Khrushchev was scheduled to make his first visit to the United States on 15 September 1959.

Russian objection notwithstanding, the Security Council decided to appoint a subcommittee including Argentina, Italy, Japan, and Tunisia to look into the matter. The subcommittee visited Laos from 15 September 1959 to 13 October 1959. It found evidence of rifles and submachine guns of Chinese origin, hand grenades wrapped in Chinese newspapers, uniforms typical of Chinese military attire, and medicines labeled as Chinese government supplies.[47] But the conclusion reached by the subcommittee was that the ensemble of information assembled by the RLG did not clearly establish whether there had been crossings of the frontier by regular troops of the DRV.[48]

However, Langer and Zasloff in 1970 were able to establish that the North Vietnamese were involved in the fighting during the summer of 1959. Their principal source of information was an intelligence officer of the rank of captain in the G-2 section of the Royal Laotian Armed Forces whom they interviewed over an eight-month period.[49] A North Vietnamese economic cadre's notebook also revealed that in May 1959, which coincided with Hanoi's announcement to resume armed struggle and the establishment of the Ho Chi Minh Trail, Hanoi began to pay greater attention to the revolutionary movement in Laos.[50] In 1980, the North Vietnamese finally admitted their involvement. They revealed that in 1959, they and the Pathet Lao agreed to the organization of a delegation of Vietnamese military specialists to work alongside the Pathet Lao forces. In September 1959, Group 959 was thus formed, whose mission was to serve as specialists for the Pathet Lao forces, organize the logistics and the supply of Vietnamese material, and to directly command the Vietnamese volunteer units operating in Sam Neua, Xieng Khouang, and Vientiane. Group 959 continued to function till 1973.[51] In 1994, a Vietnamese source recounted that from the moment the decision was taken to open the Ho Chi Minh Trail for the purpose of infiltration, it was understood that Laos and Cambodia would be involved in the Vietnamese struggle.[52]

V

In China too, there were some major changes in the military. On 17 September 1959, Lin Biao assumed the post vacated by Peng Dehuai as the new defense minister and Luo Ruiqing became the new chief of general staff.[53] Four new vice-defense ministers were also appointed; one was Chen Geng, whom we have noted had very close ties with the North Vietnamese.[54] As we have stated above, evidence to date suggests that the dismissal of Peng Dehuai was because of his disagreement with Mao over purely economic issues. However, one should note that unlike Mao, Peng was also in favor of reducing party control over the military and closer military corroboration with the Soviet Union. The dismissal of Peng and the appointment of Lin Biao provided Mao with another opportunity to ensure that the PLA forge an independent course in military and strategic matters, a goal that, we should recall, he had spelled out at the 2nd Enlarged Conference of the Military Affairs Committee on 28 June 1958. We should also recall that after the Taiwan Strait crisis in autumn 1958, Mao's military writings were widely studied in the PLA.

Soon after Lin Biao became the new minister of defense, he put forward a plan to build China into one of the strongest socialist countries in the world. For the PLA, it meant diligently studying and applying the military teachings of Mao Zedong. This was the thrust of his article published in *Hongqi* on 1 October 1959, which was entitled, "Take Giant Strides, Holding High the Red Flag of the Party's General Line and the Military Thinking of Mao Tse-Tung."[55] Lin Biao called for strict party control over the armed forces. According to him, political work remained the lifeblood of the army and the human factor, not equipment, was the decisive factor in warfare.

This was also the military line expounded by Vo Nguyen Giap in his article, "People's War, People's Army," published about two months later, on 22 December 1959 on the occasion of the 15th anniversary of the VPA.[56] However, this did not mean that the Vietnamese were following the Chinese line blindly. According to Giap in the same article, "in China and Vietnam, as well as in the U.S.S.R., the revolutionary wars and armies have common fundamental characteristics: their popular and revolutionary nature, and the just cause they serve. The Vietnamese revolutionary war and army, however, have their own characteristics. ...In combining the invaluable experiences of the Soviet Union and People's China with its own, our Party has always taken into account the concrete reality of the revolutionary war in Vietnam, which has enabled it to enrich the theories of the revolutionary war and army."[57]

In contrast, in the Soviet Union in December 1959, at a Central Committee meeting, Khrushchev put an end to the arguments regarding Soviet defense policy that had been going on since 1956. Khrushchev decided that in any future war, nuclear weapons would be decisive. Plans were made to reduce the Soviet military by 1,200,000 men. The Strategic Rocket Force was formed in the same month and it became the premier Soviet service branch. From 1960 onward, until Khrushchev was ousted, the ground forces were gradually downgraded.[58]

One month after Ho returned from China, he made another trip to Beijing on 26 September as head of the DRV government delegation to commemorate the 10th anniversary of the PRC. He was accompanied by Vo Nguyen Giap and Ung Van Khiem, senior vice-minister for foreign affairs, a number of government officials, and seven army officers. We do not know whether those seven army officers were the same ones who were promoted recently, but it is very likely that they were. The visit would be an opportunity for the newly promoted military officers of both countries to get to know each other better. In 1961, Marshal Ye Jianying recalled that this visit of the North Vietnamese military delegation led by Giap contributed immensely to enhancing the brotherly relationship of the VPA and the PLA.[59]

They traveled in two Chinese IL-14 planes. The North Vietnamese delegation led by Ho arrived in Beijing on the afternoon of 26 September and was met at the airport by Liu Shaoqi, Soong Jingling, Dong Biwu, and Zhou Enlai. On the morning of 27 September, Ho visited the newly reconstructed Tiananmen grounds and the new Beijing railway station. On the same day, there was a meeting between Lin Biao and the DRV military delegation. Also present at the meeting were other generals, of whom Luo Ruiqing, Tan Zheng, and Xu Guangta were specifically mentioned. The meeting was described as having taken place in "an atmosphere of warm friendship." That same evening, while Ho and Giap dined with Soong Jingling, Lin Biao feted the DRV military delegation. During the mass rally on 28 and 29 September, where 83 countries were represented and 60 congratulatory speeches were delivered, Ho Chi Minh was the second speaker after Khrushchev. In his speech, Ho described the relationship between North Vietnam and China as brotherly and as close as lips and teeth. He spoke of common struggle of both countries for independence and the special significance of the Communist victory in China for the Vietnamese people. But he did not forget to acknowledge the Russian influence and help for the Vietnamese cause as well.

Sino-Soviet relations, however, continued to deteriorate.[60] We should recall that on 20 June 1959, the Soviet Union suddenly rescinded the Sino-Soviet agreement on new technology for national defense concluded in October 1957 in which the Russians had agreed to provide China with a sample of the atom bomb and technical data concerning its manufacture.[61] The Soviet Union also failed to support the Chinese in the continuing Sino-Indian border dispute conflict, which began in July 1959, but instead called upon both sides to settle their misunderstanding in a friendly way.[62] While the Chinese appeared prepared to condone Vietnamese neutrality in the Sino-Indian dispute (which was understandable, as Hanoi needed to maintain the goodwill of India, which chaired the ISCC), they felt that the Russians in siding with the Indians had brought the differences between China and the Soviet Union into the open before the whole world.[63] To crown it all, the Chinese were incensed by Khrushchev's visit to the United States.

Immediately after his visit to the United States from 15 to 28 September, Khrushchev flew to Beijing to join in the celebration of the 10th anniversary of the PRC on 29 September.[64] Khrushchev came with a plan to solve the Taiwan issue and to accomplish two missions on behalf of Eisenhower and Nehru, which he conveyed to Mao on the evening of 30 September 1959, but he was completely rebuffed by Mao. In the end, he told the Chinese that he would withdraw all the Russian experts in China and pressed the Chinese to repay their debts owed to the Russians.[65] Gromyko recalled that during the talks with the Chinese during this visit, deep differences once again emerged between the two parties.[66] In his memoirs, Khrushchev recalled that he did not relish this trip to Beijing,[67] and Jiang Qing described the visit as "tedious and painful."[68]

We do not know whether Ho Chi Minh had any discussions with Khrushchev in Beijing. We only know that Ho met with old friends and acquaintances of the 8th Route Army whom he had known during the period of the struggle against the French. On the night of 1 October, Liu Shaoqi and Zhu De visited Ho Chi Minh at his guest house, and they had a warm and friendly conversation. On 3 October, Ho attended the first National Sports Meet at the People's Sports Stadium along with Zhou Enlai, Soong Jingling, Dong Biwu, Deng Xiaoping, and He Long. In the evening, Ho met Mao and had a cordial conversation before proceeding to a cultural performance.[69]

Ho and Giap returned to Hanoi after the celebration on 4 October 1959, possibly without Ung Van Khiem and the army officers.[70] Ho's departure was reported in great detail by the Chinese. He was sent off by Liu Shaoqi, Soong Jingling, Dong Biwu, and Lin Biao. Ho reviewed a guard of honor of the army, navy and air force, after which a group of Young Pioneers presented the Vietnamese delegation with bouquets. Before boarding the plane, Ho embraced Liu, Soong Jingling, Dong Biwu, and Lin Biao. It was further reported that he mounted the plane amidst a burst of applause, and at the door, Ho smilingly waved back at those seeing him off.[71]

Meanwhile, in Hanoi, the North Vietnamese apparently made a very special effort to celebrate the 10th anniversary of the Chinese Revolution and the founding of the PRC. As observed by the British consul-general in Hanoi, "the praise, the thanks, the decoration in the streets, the special committees and the meetings all went far beyond the natural esteem of one free country for another.... The Vietnamese succeeded in making very clearly their position as a Chinese vassal."[72]

VI

Given Khrushchev's preference for a policy of peaceful coexistence, it can be assumed that the Russians did not actively support the North

Vietnamese decision to intensify the struggle in the South, but there is no evidence that they did anything to stop them. The Chinese, on the other hand, accepted that there could be a nonpeaceful transition to socialism, and unlike the Russians, they did not fraternize with the U.S. imperialists. According to Kenneth T. Young, sometime in late 1959 or early 1960 Beijing decided to put the struggle against imperialism before negotiation. This was evident in the Sino-American ambassadorial talks during this time, in which the Chinese rebuffed all American approaches to improve relations. This Chinese attitude was in contrast to that of August 1956 and also that of the first half of 1958 when the Chinese expressed grave concern after the Warsaw Talks were suspended with the departure of Ambassador Alexis Johnson in December 1957.[73] Also in August 1959, the Chinese promised military aid for the Vietnamese Communist struggle in the South. However, this did not mean that Beijing was prepared to go to war for the reunification of Vietnam. Beijing had its own reservations about Hanoi's decision to renew their struggle but was prepared to support it as long as it was limited in nature.

A conversation between Mao Zedong and the temporary Soviet Charge d'Affaires to China, S. F. Antonov, on 14 October 1959 reveals Mao's assessment of the international situation during this time. Mao told him that China had no intention of starting a war with the United States over Taiwan. According to Mao, the Chinese could wait 10–20 years — even 30–40 years. From the experience of the shelling of Jinmen and Mazu in 1958, Mao felt that the United States too was not prepared to go to war with China. The most dangerous enemies, in Mao's view, were West Germany and Japan. As for the United States, the United Kingdom, and France, Mao thought that on the whole they supported the maintenance of the status quo.[74]

On 17 October 1959, at the farewell banquet for the visiting Burmese cultural and goodwill delegation, Chen Yi once again emphasized China's need for a peaceful environment and the continued relaxation of the world situation for her to engage in national reconstruction. In his speech, Chen Yi said: "China, a vast country and with a big population, needs a long period to solve its own problems completely.... China needs all the more peaceful coexistence with the Southeast Asian countries that have common borders with China.... Peaceful means can be sought to settle disputes between countries and disputes can definitely be settled by peaceful means."[75]

Notwithstanding the reservations of the Soviet Union and China, in South Vietnam, following the announcement of the communiqué of the 15th Plenary Session in May 1959, the struggle for reunification was gathering a momentum of its own. The most outstanding of the uprisings took place in Tra Bong, a mountainous district in the western part of Quang Ngai province. The Tra Bong uprising was regarded as one of the first local uprisings in the transition phase of the revolution in the South in 1959, and it involved the Interzone Party Committee, Provincial Party Committee, the surrounding districts in Quang Ngai and Quang Nam Provinces, and the provincial and interzone armed forces.[76] On 28 August 1959, 16,000 ethnic minority people in Tra Bong, with the support of the 339th platoon, started an uprising under the leadership of the District Party Committee and the Provincial Party Committee. Among other things, they eliminated the Diem administrations in 16 villages, forced the abandonment of seven posts, killed 161 traitors, and set up revolutionary administrations in the hamlets and villages. The uprisings then spread to the neighboring villages in the districts of Son Tra, Ba To, and Minh Long. On 26 September 1959, two companies of the 23rd Division were ambushed by the Communists, 12 soldiers were killed, and all the weapons were confiscated.[77] The U.S. embassy in Saigon, in a special report on the internal security situation in South Vietnam in January 1960, noted that for the first time there were attacks by the Communists on large South Vietnamese Army units.

Pham Van Dong was reported to have told French Consul Georges-Picot in a conversation on 12 September 1959, "You must remember we will be in Saigon tomorrow, we will be in Saigon tomorrow." Again in November 1959, on two occasions, Dong told the Canadian commissioner of the ISCC in Hanoi, Erichson-Brown, that the Vietnamese would drive the Americans into the sea. But Vo Nguyen Giap later saw Erichson-Brown to "reassure" him that the intentions of the DRV were peaceful.[78]

According to the *CRIMP Document* it was only in October 1959 that the armed struggle was launched.[79] A recent Vietnamese source revealed that because of the difficulties of the journey, the Southern representatives to the 15th Plenary Session did not return to the South till September 1959 and it was not till the following month, in October, that they began putting the decisions made in January into practice.[80] The resolution of the 15th Plenary Session was apparently not fully disseminated to the provinces in the Nam Bo and Interzone V until December 1959.[81] According to North Vietnamese historian Tran Huu Dinh, by the end of 1959 the leadership organization of the Nam Bo Regional Committee had returned from Cambodia to South Vietnam to organize the resistance movement in Nam Bo.[82]

Seven

January 1960–July 1960

I

In January 1960, the decision of the 15th Plenary Session of the Lao Dong Central Committee to launch mass uprisings in the South moved into full swing. The week of 17–24 January 1960 was one of uprisings in Ben Tre: 47 villages in the districts of Mo Cay, Giong Trom, Chau Thanh, Ba Tri, and Thanh Phu all revolted at the same time. By 19 January, the Communists succeeded in taking control of the villages. With the weapons captured at Binh Khanh, they were able to arm three squads to support the uprisings in the districts of Minh Tan, Thanh Phu, and Mo Cay. They also managed to create a number of platoons and their first company, the 264th Company. Although these started off as unarmed mass uprisings, in the process the people in Ben Tre acquired guns and were able to build up their armed forces. In this way, they were able to apply the strategy of combining the political and the armed struggle. On 21 January, the Diem regime sent an amphibious battalion into Phuoc Hiep village to recapture Dinh Thuy and Binh Khanh, but they were surrounded by the 264th Company and armed squads of the three villages. A number of the marines were killed and the weapons were captured. In February, the Ben Tre Provincial Committee gathered all the armed soldiers at Bao Island, which comprised the districts of Giong Trom, Ba Tri, and Chau Thanh, and formed their second company, the 269th Company. On 4 February, the Ben Tre Provincial Committee and the Mo Cay District Committee organized 200 women from Phuoc Hiep village and 5,000 women from the adjoining villages into resistance groups.[1] According to the *Lich Su Quan Doi Nhan Dan Viet Nam*, the practice of attacking the enemy by combining the political struggle with the armed struggle was first applied during the Ben Tre uprisings.[2] From the uprisings in Ben Tre onward, concerted uprisings swept across the provinces of Nam Bo.

According to Le Duan, "the simultaneous uprisings that broke out during this period [end of 1959–beginning of 1960] marked an important leap forward. They moved the South Vietnamese revolution to the offensive and the revolutionary high tide developed in all areas with the coordination of both forms of political and armed struggles.... Armed struggle and political struggle together are the fundamental form of violence of the South Vietnamese revolution, and coordinating armed struggle with political struggle is the fundamental law of the method of the South Vietnamese."[3]

Terrorism and guerrilla actions that in the past had been considered by the U.S. Country Team as a long-term threat to the viability of the Diem regime were now South Vietnam's "number-one problem."[4] However, the Northern leadership at this time was not yet prepared to further raise the stakes with the Diem regime. Apparently, in the first nine months of 1960, there were problems within the VPA. Unfortunately, that is as much as we can tell. There is a conspicuous information gap in the *Lich Su Quan Doi Nhan Dan Viet Nam* regarding what the army was doing for the first nine months of 1960. According to the Czech ambassador, as reported by British sources in April, there was "quite a serious malaise" in the army and many units were dispersed to different parts of the country. Giap had been traveling around the country inspecting them and finding out what was upsetting them.[5] This would partially account for Giap's sporadic absence from public view during the large part of 1960. Giap was present at the meeting on the evening of 5 January 1960 to celebrate the 30th anniversary of the party. He was reported to have paid a visit to cadres and combatants of the "Cuu Long" Division with Truong Chinh during Tet. He had urged the soldiers to continually raise their socialist awareness, step up their training, and be prepared to protect peace and smash the enemies' plots. He spoke of the unification of the country and promised that the day would come when the North could spend Tet with the Southern compatriots. On 21 January, Giap attended a press conference where he made known that he had written to the ISCC, requesting it to intervene with the South Vietnamese authorities to rescind Law 10/59. He did not appear at all throughout the visit of the GDR government delegation at the end of January 1960. When the delegation visited the Army Museum on the afternoon of 26 January, they were attended to by Major-General Nguyen Van Vinh, deputy-minister of national defense. *NCNA*, but not *VNA*, reported that Giap attended the meeting of the Political Consultative Committee of the Warsaw Treaty Organisation in Moscow (4–5 February 1960). From Moscow, Truong Chinh, who was head of the Vietnamese delegation to the meeting, went to Beijing where he stayed till 12 February 1960 before returning to Hanoi.[6] We have no account of Truong Chinh's activities in Beijing. Nor is it clear whether or not Giap went to Beijing with Truong Chinh. Both Giap and Nguyen Chi Thanh were present at the Soviet Army Day reception in Hanoi hosted by the Soviet military attache on 23 February. After that there was no news about Giap until 16 April, when it was reported that he had written to the ISCC Chairman protesting the reinforcement of the MAAG in South Vietnam. Giap's disappearance coincided with the promulgation and implementation of the Military Obligation Law in April 1960. The decision on compulsory military service, we should recall, was made at the 12th Plenary Session in March 1957. The Military Obligation Law was part of the plan of the Hanoi leadership to transform the VPA into a professional army. Under this new law, the VPA was no longer a volunteer army. This meant that troops could now be recruited and mobilized to build up the armed forces as quickly as was needed in preparation for the eventual confrontation with the U.S.–Diem forces. It was also now possible to have a large, powerful, and trained reserve force, while reducing the standing army, thus economizing on manpower and material that could then be channeled into economic construction.[7]

In an effort to curb the enthusiasm and the overconfidence of the more militant group of Southern cadres and to control the struggle in the South, on 28 March 1960 a letter was urgently sent by the Regional Party Committee to all the party branches in the South warning against any premature intensification of the military struggle. The letter reiterated that the party's policy remained one of "strongly pushing the political struggle ahead and combining it to the right degree with armed activities." The time was not yet ripe for a direct revolution to overthrow the Diem regime because, while the enemy was weak and demoralized, they still possessed the capacity to retaliate in a massive way. In short, the leadership felt that the balance of forces was still not to their advantage, and any premature resort to violence would only put the Communist forces in a dangerous and vulnerable position.[8] At the same time, it was announced that the party's 3rd Congress would be held in September 1960 and one of the items on the agenda was to discuss the line and task of the party and the people at the present stage of the revolution.[9]

Meanwhile, in Cambodia in mid-March 1960, Sihanouk had written what was described as an "important" editorial that was published in the *Nationalist*, as well as broadcast in full over Phnom Penh radio. He claimed that he had documentary evidence to prove that the Pracheachon Party and the Khmer Communist paper *L' Observateur* were colluding with the Hanoi government in the attempt to carry out a revolution to end "the feudal regime of the princes."[10]

II

However, in 1960 it was neither the Vietnamese Communists' intensification of the struggle in the South nor Sihanouk's concern about Hanoi's support for the Communists in Cambodia that made the headlines. Rather, it was developments in Laos that were a major cause of concern. The crisis in Laos was essentially brought about by the struggle for power between the Pathet Lao and the RLG. Given the close link between the Pathet Lao and the Vietnamese Communists, and the importance of the Ho Chi Minh Trail to the growing struggle in the South, it was to be expected that the North Vietnamese would be deeply involved in the events there. In early 1960, the troops operating on the Ho Chi Minh Trail started to take a shortcut near Khe Sanh by crossing a privately owned coffee plantation. But on one of the trips, some rifles were inadvertently left at relay station 5. This led to a regiment-sized sweep of the area by Diem's troops. When Vo Bam reported this incident to Le Duan, the latter proposed that they try to find an alternative route that would attract less enemy attention. The alternative route that Vo Bam came up with was to go south down the western side of the Truong Son Range, on Laotian territory.[11]

In Laos, on 25 December 1959, the pro–American Committee for the Defense of National Interests (CDNI) and the Royal Laotian Army carried out a coup that forced the Phoui Sananikone government to resign. The *Nhan Dan* article of 3 January accused the U.S. imperialists of instigating and abetting the coup, and declared that Laos was threatened by fascism. On the same day, the *NCNA* also carried a summary of the *Nhan Dan* article. On 5 January, a DRV government spokesman again accused CDNI of colluding with the U.S. imperialists to turn South Vietnam and Laos into U.S. military bases. A provisional government was formed on 7 January 1960, headed ostensibly by elder statesman Kou Abhay. However, the real power behind the provisional government was General Phoumi and the CDNI. The first direct Chinese comment appeared in the *Remmin Ribao* of 8 January. The commentary, which described the members of CDNI as warlords, shared the views of the Vietnamese.[12] On 11 January, the new government declared that it would uphold the policy of peace and neutrality.

Although the North Vietnamese continued to criticize the Laotian government as being run by extremist members of the military, Pham Van Dong on 14 January cabled the new Laotian Prime Minister greeting the formation of the new government. Dong also expressed the hope that under Kou Abhay, the Geneva Agreements would be upheld and relations with North Vietnam would improve.[13] Pham Van Dong's reply of 15 January to Kou Abhay's telegram (of 13 January) alleging that hundreds of Laotians had been abducted by North Vietnam was also exceptionally mild. In an interview with *AFP*, General Phoumi, the Laotian defense minister, stated that North Vietnam had practically ceased its provocations and that the tone of the Hanoi Radio broadcasts had become less aggressive than during the past months, particularly during the days when the High Command of the Laotian armed forces were running the country.[14] As observed by the British consulate-general in Hanoi, in contrast to the hysteria of August-September 1959 over the issue of the integration of the Pathet Lao forces into the Royal Laotian Army and the escape of the 2nd Battalion, this time the North Vietnamese took the coup fairly calmly.[15]

On 30 January 1960, the Laotian Council of Ministers announced that general elections would take place on 24 April 1960. By introducing extremely stringent electoral laws, the RLG did all it could to prevent a repetition of the 1958 supplementary election results. The NLHX, the Vietnamese, and the Chinese all denounced the new Laotian electoral laws. They also called for the release of Prince Souphanouvong and the other NLHX leaders who were still imprisoned. On 5 March, Pham Van Dong wrote to the cochairmen of the Geneva Conference concerning the grave situation in Laos. On 8 March, he sent a letter to the chairman of the ISCC in Laos regarding the elections. In his letter, Dong described the scheduled elections as completely contravening the Geneva and Vientiane Agreements. He accused the RLG and the U.S. imperialists of trying to exclude the NLHX Party and prevent its legal political activities. He also called for the unconditional release of the jailed leaders of the NLHX.[16] On 18 March, it was reported that there were no NLHX candidates listed for the coming elections. The Vietnamese accused the Laotian authorities of having practically banned the NLHX. The next day it was reported that a certain number of NLHX members who submitted their candidacies before 5:00 P.M. on 20 March would be allowed to stand as candidates.[17] After all the complaints that the electoral law was unfair and weighted against them, the NLHX in the end fielded nine candidates. According to British sources, the NLHX had on 8 March asked permission to see their imprisoned leaders to obtain their ruling on whether the NHLX should take part in the election or not. The RLG government refused to accede to the request but agreed to transmit their written communication. Souphanouvong had subsequently given his permission and also expressed his keenness to stand for the elections as well. However, the RLG ruled that none of those imprisoned were allowed to participate in the elections.[18] We do not know whether Hanoi approved of the NLHX taking part in the elections, or even whether it was consulted. But there is also no indication that they objected. The Chinese showed their reservations after the nominations had closed in a *Renmin Ribao* commentary of 23 March that accused Phoumi Nosavan of trying to inveigle the other members of the NLHX Party into laying down their arms by allowing the NLHX to participate in the elections without any handicap.[19]

According to British embassy sources in Vientiane, over the past few months the 2nd Battalion as well as other elements that had been trained in North Vietnam had returned to Laos and spread thinly in advantageous position all over the country. It was reckoned that between 200 and 400 regular units had been infiltrated into southern Laos and that central and northern Laos could have been similarly reinforced. The British officials were of the view, based on the disposition of the guerrilla forces that was taking place, that the Pathet Lao were either preparing to launch an immediate offensive or holding their resources in reserve for early action upon short notice.[20]

The decision of those NLHX members to participate in the elections despite the odds against them, intentional or not, provided a cover for the Pathet Lao forces to perfect their insurrectional machinery. It also fitted in with Hanoi's decision during this time not to embark on an open offensive.

Meanwhile, the North Vietnamese continued to profess their desire to improve relations with the RLG. On 19 April 1960, Pham Van Dong wrote again to Kou Abhay reiterating the DRV's desire to normalize relations. The letter noted with regret that relations were not good because of the interference of foreign imperialism. Dong further expressed concern over the continued detention of the NLHX leaders and the conduct of the electoral campaign.[21]

Not surprisingly, the RLG won a landslide victory on 24 April 1960. On 21 April, General Phoumi Nosavan had told the British ambassador that the results of the elections were already a foregone conclusion.[22] Besides the promulgation of the new electoral laws, which were deliberately weighted against the left-wing parties, and the mopping-up operations conducted by the Royal Laotian Army during the course of the election campaign, the election itself was blatantly rigged, apparently with assistance from CIA agents. To cite just one example, in Sam Neua, the Pathet Lao home base, the NLHX candidate was reported to have received only 13 votes compared to the 6,508 votes of the RLG candidate.[23]

In short, Hanoi's unwillingness to allow the situation in South Vietnam and Laos to develop into a full-scale war was because the leadership recognized that the North was still not ready for a confrontation against a Diem-American or an RLG-American combination. North Vietnam had yet to complete its socialist transformation, after which it could serve as a firm, reliable, and powerful rear base for the revolution in the South.

III

Apart from the internal constraints that inhibited an escalation of the armed struggle in the South and in Laos, the Hanoi leadership also could not ignore the views of Beijing and Moscow. Any direct military confrontation with the Diem regime or the RLG would necessarily involve the Americans. The North Vietnamese realized that they could take on the Americans only with the backing of both the Soviet Union and China.

The Chinese did not object to the Vietnamese struggle in the South in principle. As noted earlier, according to Kenneth T. Young, sometime in late 1959 or early 1960 Beijing decided to put armed struggle against imperialism before negotiation. [24] But they did not approve of escalating the fighting in South Vietnam. We should recall that in August 1959, at a meeting with Ho Chi Minh in Beijing, Zhou had agreed to support the struggle in the South by providing the Vietnamese Communists with military aid at the end of 1959. As far as we know, the Chinese did not keep their promise. It is very likely that Beijing was concerned that giving military aid to the Vietnamese Communists at this time would further fuel the fighting in the South. Two occurrences at the end of 1959 and early 1960 seemed to suggest that Sino-Vietnamese relations during this period were not as warm as they were during autumn 1959. One was that Pham Van Dong's report on foreign policy at the 11th Session of the DRV National Assembly (18–31 December 1959) made only passing reference to China, whereas much emphasis was placed on the achievements of the Soviet Union.[25] And second, according to French Delegate-General Monsieur Chambon, Ho Chi Minh in his speech at a New Year's gathering with the diplomatic corp on 1 January 1960 made no mention at all of China but went out of his way to lavish praise on the Soviet Union. At that gathering, Ho personally asked Chambon, who was the only Western representative, whether he had understood his speech, as though Ho was trying to draw Chambon's attention to his remarks.[26] British officials in Hanoi observed that until March 1960, North Vietnamese reports on China were perfunctory and scarce, whereas much publicity was given to Khrushchev's activities.[27]

The message that the CCP Central Committee sent to its Lao Dong Party counterpart on 5 January 1960 on the occasion of the latter's 30th anniversary gave credit to the Lao Dong Party for leading the Vietnamese people in carrying out the land reforms, in rehabilitating the economy, in waging the socialist revolution, and in the struggle for the peace, reunification, independence, and democracy of Vietnam. The Chinese believed that the Vietnamese leadership would attain even greater achievements in the socialist transformation in the North and in the struggle against the sabotage of the Geneva Agreements and obstruction of the realization of the country's reunification by U.S. imperialism and the Ngo Dinh Diem clique, in the cause of building a peaceful, unified, independent, democratic, and prosperous Vietnam. No specific comment was made regarding the decision of the 15th Plenary Session or about armed struggle.[28] Nor did the Chinese media carry any report or comment about the developments in the South.

At the pre-summit meeting of the Political Consultative Committee of the Warsaw Treaty Organisation held in Moscow on 4–5 February 1960, which Truong Chinh and Vo Nguyen Giap attended,[29] the Chinese representative, Kang Sheng, also failed to mention in his speech the Communist struggle that was intensifying in South Vietnam. There was a brief reference to U.S. support for the reactionary forces in Laos. Sino-Indonesian and Sino-Burmese relations received special mention, but there was no reference to Vietnam. Kang Sheng's speech was extremely anti–Soviet both in tone and implications.[30] He argued that the strategy of the United States, to win victory through peace, was actually aimed at wrecking the unity of the socialist camp. China sympathized with and supported the national democratic movement of the peoples in Asia, Africa, and Latin America and strived to have long-term friendly relations with the nationalist countries in Asia and Africa on the basis of the Five Principles of peaceful coexistence. The Declaration of member states of the Warsaw Treaty issued at the end of the meeting also stressed that all states should do everything in their power to create a situation facilitating the success of the coming East-West talks and urged all other countries to promote the success of the talks by refraining from any steps capable of complicating these negotiations.[31]

In the early months of 1960, the Chinese were reassessing their foreign policy strategy. In the first three months of the year, three work conferences on foreign affairs were held: in Shanghai in January, Canton in February, and Hangzhou in March. At the Hangzhou work conference, Mao delivered a speech indicating that there were some in the Chinese leadership who were concerned about China's increasing isolation.[32] Sino-Soviet relations were strained; China had been very critical of the peace overtures of the Soviet Union to the West; it had border problems with some of its neighbors, and there was still an outstanding dispute with Indonesia over the overseas Chinese population there. Efforts were made to resolve some of these problems, for example, border agreements in principle were signed with Burma in January 1960 and with Nepal in March 1960. It was also reported that a Sino-Indonesian joint committee for implementing the treaty of dual nationality had been set up and had held its first meeting on 27 January 1960. On the last morning of the 2nd Session of the National People's Congress (30 March–10 April 1960), Zhou Enlai delivered an unscheduled foreign policy report behind closed doors. According to British sources, Zhou's report was not on the agenda and was included at the last minute.[33] Only a summary of what Zhou said was made public and no hint of what was not publicized had leaked out. In the published report, there was almost no mention of Laos, Vietnam, Korea, or the Middle East. The stress was on China's peaceful foreign policy and its willingness to develop friendly cooperation on the basis of the Five Principles.[34] Thus China too was not in favor of any conflict in the region during this time. Soon after the congress and in the wake of Khrushchev's trip to Asia — India, Burma, Indonesia, and Afghanistan between 11 February 1960 and 5 March 1960 — Zhou embarked on a tour of Burma (15–19 April), India (19–25 April), Nepal (26–29 April), Cambodia (5–9 May) and North Vietnam (10–14 May). While Khrushchev did not visit Cambodia and North Vietnam on his Asian tour, Zhou Enlai included both countries in his.[35] The two objectives of Zhou's Asian tour were to publicize China's foreign policy of peaceful coexistence and to resolve outstanding issues with its neighboring countries.[36]

Zhou's visit to Cambodia from 5 to 9 May 1960 at the invitation of Sihanouk merits attention. Burma, India, and Nepal all had common borders with China, and the visits to these countries were essentially to resolve as much as possible the boundary questions and to conclude treaties of friendship and mutual nonaggression.[37] There was, however, no serious problem between Beijing and Phnom Penh. Indeed, Sino-Cambodian relations were described as a stabilizing factor in Cambodia's neutrality.[38] According to a Chinese Foreign Ministry source, this was both a return visit on the part of the Chinese (Sihanouk paid his second visit to Beijing in July 1958) and the first Chinese visit to Cambodia since the two countries established diplomatic relations in July 1958.[39] According to one article in *Realites Cambodgiennes*, "at a time when our nation was threatened, it would be comforting to see the arrival of the representative of a great power. This would serve as a reminder that Cambodia was not alone."[40]

Zhou arrived in Phnom Penh on 5 May.[41] On the same day, the *Phnom Penh Home Service* reported that a violent clash that lasted three hours had taken place on the morning of 3 May 1960 between two battalions of the Khmer Royal Armed Forces in cooperation with a provincial guard unit and "an important group of Vietnamese" who had crossed the Cambodian border opposite Chau Doc. The report specified that Type-81 mortars and machine guns of the South Vietnamese Armed Forces were used in the attack.[42] According to British officials in Saigon, it was probably a group of Hoa Hao insurgents (Regiment Nghia Quan), who were also attacked by South Vietnamese troops when they recrossed the border.[43]

In his welcome speech, Sihanouk alluded to the difficulties that were created by "certain powerful neighboring countries" and expressed concern about the threat of armed conflicts in the region.[44] In his press article on Cambodia's foreign relations published in the *Nationalist*, Sihanouk stated that he neither had the time nor the means to be critical of China's problems with Tibet and the Sino-Indian border issue. He explained that Cambodia was faced with a serious threat from South Vietnam and Thailand, whereas China had never threatened Cambodia.[45] In the joint statement issued at the end of the visit, both parties expressed satisfaction with their relationship so far, the Chinese endorsed Cambodia's policy of strict neutrality, and Zhou again encouraged the overseas Chinese in Cambodia to abide strictly by the laws and regulations of the country.[46] The Chinese again offered to provide Sihanouk with whatever armaments and military equipment he needed. According to U.S. intelligence, Zhou Enlai offered to supply fighter planes to Cambodia.[47] On 2 July 1960, Sihanouk disclosed that during his visit, Zhou had given an informal guarantee that China would support Cambodia in the event of any threat to her frontiers.[48] On 10 July, Sihanouk sent three of his sons to Beijing for their education.[49]

IV

Zhou's inclusion of North Vietnam in his tour was said to be in response to an invitation extended to him to visit the country by Pham Van Dong on 4 April 1960. In his letter to Zhou, Dong said that the visit would help strengthen further the friendship and relations of cooperation between the two brotherly countries and would greatly inspire the Vietnamese people in building socialism and in their struggle for national reunification. In his letter of acceptance, Zhou replied that he was very happy to visit Vietnam again at a time when "the brotherly Vietnamese people, under the leadership of the Vietnam Lao Dong Party and the DRV government have won brilliant achievements in socialist construction and transformation and are striving to achieve the three-year plan successfully." Zhou did not mention the struggle in the South.[50]

On 20 April, shortly before Zhou's visit, Le Duan — in a speech on the occasion of Lenin's 90th birthday anniversary — made it very clear that Hanoi was not ready to risk a full-scale war in the South at that time. According to Le Duan, the situation in the South was complex. Although the law governing the South was that of a colonial and feudal regime and should logically follow the road to liberation prescribed by Lenin, the people's democratic revolution of the South was taking place at a time when the world and internal situation had undergone fundamental changes. In the world, the forces of socialism were gaining supremacy while capitalism was weakening. This meant that there were growing possibilities to frustrate imperialism and maintain a lasting peace. Also, North Vietnam, the firm base for the revolution in the South, had already been completely liberated and was advancing toward socialism. Therefore, according to Le Duan, "in the present conjuncture when the possibility exists to maintain a lasting peace in the world and create favorable conditions for the world movement of socialist revolution and national independence to go forward, we can and must guide and restrict within the South the solving of the contradiction between imperialism and the colonies in our country."[51]

On 1 May it was announced that the Chinese delegation led by Zhou Enlai would visit the DRV from 9 to 12 May 1960.[52] Because of poor weather conditions, the Chinese delegation rested for a day in Nghe An Province before arriving in Hanoi on the morning of 10 May 1960. The Chinese delegation included Chen Yi (vice-premier and minister of foreign affairs), Chang Hanfu (vice-minister of foreign affairs), Wang Guangwei (vice-chairman, State Planning Commission), Chang Yan (deputy-director, Office of the State Council in charge of Foreign Affairs), Qiao Guanhua (assistant minister of foreign affairs), Lo Jingzhang (deputy-director, Secretariat of the Premier of the State Council) and Chen Shuliang (director, Second Asian Department, Ministry of Foreign Affairs).

The delegation was met at the airport by Pham Van Dong, Le Duan, Truong Chinh, Phan Ke Toai, Pham Hung, and Ton Duc Thang. Giap was conspicuously absent during Zhou Enlai's visit from 10 to 14 May. When he had reappeared on May Day, it was thought that his pressing work in the army might have come to an end.[53] Between 4 and 6 May, he headed the Vietnamese delegation that entertained the visiting Algerians. A joint communiqué was signed by Bil Qasim Karim, leader of the Algerian delegation, and Giap on 6 May. After that, there was again no news of his activities.

From the airport, the Chinese delegation proceeded to the presidential palace where they were received by Ho Chi Minh. In the afternoon, Zhou visited the Thang Long cigarette factory, the Sao Vang rubber goods factory, and the Hanoi soap factory, as well as attending a joint rally sponsored by the three factories. (All three factories were built with Chinese aid.) After that he laid a wreath at the grave of Vietnamese heroes in Mai Dich. The day ended with a state banquet given by Pham Van Dong. Pham Van Dong's banquet speech is illuminating for its details regarding the assistance given by the Chinese in the economic and cultural development of Vietnam. According to Dong, the Chinese had helped in the repair of railways, irrigation systems, and factories; given large quantities of consumer goods to stabilize prices and ensure the livelihood of the people; built industries for producing farm implements, which were practically nonexistent in Vietnam in the past, as well as consumer goods factories; built farms for cultivating tropical industrial crops and livestock farms; and built many conservancy projects such as the large-scale Bac Hung Hai irrigation system. Currently, the Chinese were helping to lay the preliminary foundation of the metallurgical and chemical industries and to build more electrical power enterprises. They were also helping to draw up plans for the taming and developing of the Red River. Of the 72 factories built with Chinese aid, 31 had been completed and put into operation. Zhou, in his speech, recalled the pledge made by the United States at the 1954 Geneva Conference that they would not resort to armed force to undermine the Geneva Agreements and expressed the firm conviction that the sacred aspirations of the Vietnamese people to reunify the country would be fulfilled. In general, the speeches professed the friendship and solidarity between the two fraternal countries.

The next morning was taken up by talks between the two governments. There is strong evidence that Chinese economic assistance was a major topic of discussion. Besides the very strong economic representation on the North Vietnamese side, the Chinese delegation included Wang Guangwei, vice-chairman of the State Planning Commission, who apparently only joined the delegation for the trip to Hanoi; and Fang Yi, China's economic representative in Vietnam. On the same day, Chen Yi, accompanied by Deputy Premier Pham Hung, visited the scenic spot in Vinh, passed through Haiphong, and toured several islands on board a Vietnamese gunboat.

In the afternoon, the first of three meetings between the Chinese delegation and the Lao Dong Party delegation led by Ho Chi Minh took place. In the evening at the Chinese Embassy, Zhou met the Chinese specialists working in North Vietnam.

On the morning of 12 May, Zhou visited the Hanoi Polytechnic College where he suggested a friendly emulation drive between the Chinese and Vietnamese students for training more proletarian intellectuals who were both "red and expert." At noon, Zhou visited the Nhan Chinh agricultural cooperative where he stressed the value of more and bigger cooperatives and the importance of the local people's militia.

In the afternoon, a second round of talks took place between the Chinese delegation led by Zhou and the Vietnamese Communist Party delegation led by Ho Chi Minh. Also present at the talks were Chen Yi and Chang Hanfu, vice-minister of foreign affairs. They discussed the current international situation and bilateral relations. The report on the high-level talks gave no details except that both sides arrived at completely identical views on all questions discussed.[54]

On 13 May, the last day of the Chinese visit, the Chinese delegation attended a large rally in Ba Dinh Square. At this rally, Ho spoke of China achieving its economic plan in three years instead of five, of the smooth progress of the Soviet Union's seven-year plan, and the successful completion of North Korea's five-year economic plan and exhorted the Vietnamese to learn from the examples of the three countries. After the rally, the third and final round of talks between the two parties took place.

Lunch was held at the Chinese embassy in Hanoi, and Ho Chi Minh was also present. During lunch it was reported that Chen Yi and Ton Quang Phiet had recited "poems of friendship." Later in the day, Zhou received representatives of the Vietnam-China Friendship Association and overseas Chinese in Hanoi. In the evening, the Chinese delegation attended a farewell banquet at the presidential palace hosted by Ho, after which they watched a cultural performance. At the end of the visit, a joint communiqué was signed.[55] From the many press reports and commentaries, the visit was clearly successful. Sino-Vietnamese relations were described as "close as the teeth and the lips."

The three rounds of talks on 11, 12, and 13 May are significant. This series of high-level meetings between the North Vietnamese and Chinese is most likely the same as the one referred to in the official Vietnamese source published in 1980. In that Vietnamese account, during the Sino-Vietnamese meeting in May 1960, the Chinese had told the North Vietnamese that both military struggle and political struggle were equally important. But whether it was a political or a military struggle, there was no question of winning political power immediately. Even if Diem was overthrown, there were still the Americans to contend with. The struggle would therefore have to be protracted. The North could support the South politically and help them in formulating policies, but it must principally nurture in them the spirit of self-reliance. When the chances of success were certain, the North could then aid the South militarily by secretly supplying arms. But in general, it should not lend direct assistance.[56]

The Chinese delegation left Hanoi for Nanning on the morning of 14 May. On arrival, they were received by Wei Guoqing, secretary of the CCP Committee of the Guangxi Zhuangzu Autonomous Region and chairman of the Region. The Chinese delegation was in Wuhan on 16 May and returned to Beijing on the morning of 17 May.[57]

Meanwhile, the U.S. U-2 spy plane was shot down by the Russians on 1 May 1960. The incident was made public only on 5 May when Khrushchev disclosed that the Russians had shot down the plane near Sverdlovsk in central U.S.S.R. At this point in time, there was no indication that the forthcoming Paris summit between Khrushchev and Eisenhower would be canceled as a result of the U-2 incident. Khrushchev arrived in Paris on 14 May as scheduled for his meeting with Eisenhower. On 16 May, it was evident that the Paris summit was not beginning on schedule. On 17 May, the final decision to cancel the Paris summit was taken. At 10:00 P.M. it was made known that the much-heralded summit meeting in Paris between Khrushchev and Eisenhower that was supposed to have begun the day before would not take place.[58] The Chinese had all along opposed Khrushchev's attempts for a rapprochement with the Americans. The U-2 incident that scuttled the summit must have vindicated the Chinese, who had consistently argued that the U.S. imperialists were unreliable and untrustworthy, as well as those within the Soviet leadership who had reservations about the summit. The U-2 episode raised questions about the infallibility of Khrushchev's strategy of peaceful and friendly competition with the West, which he had persistently championed since the 20th CPSU Congress in February 1956, and provided Khrushchev's opponents within the Kremlin the opportunity to remove some of Khrushchev's staunchest supporters in the Central Committee Secretariat. It also strengthened the position of Kozlov and Suslov. Unlike Khrushchev, they were more inclined to improving Soviet relations with China than with the West.[59] Soon after the aborted summit, the Soviet Union began to adopt a more aggressive and uncompromising foreign policy. This was characterized by "less reliance on negotiations with the West in favor of mass propanganda campaigns, political agitation, and other forms of direct action by Communist forces in the free world, backed up by vigorous missile-flexing diplomacy."[60] Some examples include the breaking off of the ten-nation disarmament talks in Geneva on 27 June 1960, championing the Castro regime in the U.S.–Cuban dispute, and renewing Soviet pressure on the Berlin issue. But Khrushchev had not abandoned his goal for peaceful coexistence with the West.

On 17 May, Ho Chi Minh, accompanied by He Wei, arrived in Nanning for a three-day visit; he also spent his 70th birthday there. On 20 May, Wei Guoqing, who we should recall was head of the Chinese Military Advisory Mission to North Vietnam in the early '50s and a very old friend of Ho, delivered to Ho a birthday telegram from Mao, Zhu De, and Zhou Enlai. It was a very complimentary telegram: Ho was described as the founder and leader of the Lao Dong Party, the most beloved leader of the Vietnamese people, the most outstanding fighter in the international Communist movement, and China's favorite friend. It praised Ho for dedicating all his energy and revolutionary experience in fighting to achieve peace, unity, independence, and democracy for the Vietnamese workers. As such he was loved and respected by everyone in the world.[61]

We do not know whether, in the wake of the aborted Paris summit, Ho also made a trip to Beijing for further discussions with the Chinese leaders. According to a Chinese source, in mid–May 1960, the North

Vietnamese and Chinese leaders met first in Hanoi and then in Beijing to discuss the question of revolutionary struggle in the South. During their discussions, Zhou Enlai told Pham Van Dong that the South must be liberated. Both Zhou Enlai and Deng Xiaoping were of the view that there must be a combination of political and military struggle. Because the situations in the cities and the countryside were different, there must be flexibility in the strategy. In the cities, political struggle should dominate but it must be supplemented by military strength. In the countryside, military struggle could take precedence but there was also the need for political support. Pham Van Dong was in agreement.[62] In 1980, at the nadir of Sino-Vietnamese relations, the Vietnamese chose to interpret this as evidence of Chinese opposition to the uprisings in the South. However, in May 1960, the Chinese viewpoint coincided with the thinking of the Hanoi leadership.

These meetings in May could be the point in 1960 referred to by Hoang Van Hoan, in which, according to Hoan, the Chinese, after being fully apprised of the situation in South Vietnam, expressed explicitly that they were not as well informed as the Vietnamese were, which was why they had held on to the view that the time was not ripe for the Vietnamese Communists to expose their strength; but they now saw the correctness of the Vietnamese position for armed struggle in the South and would fully support it.[63]

Not long after the discussions between the North Vietnamese and Chinese leaders in Hanoi and Beijing and the failure of the Paris summit, on the night of 23–24 May 1960, after being detained for ten months, Souphanouvong and the other 15 NHLX prisoners escaped from Phone Kheng police camp outside Vientiane. We have no evidence to implicate either the North Vietnamese or the Chinese in the escape.[64] The British Ambassador in Laos was of the view that Prince Souphanouvong feared assassination and the escape was planned and executed without the knowledge and against the wishes of the Hanoi leadership.[65] The consequence of the escape of the NHLX leaders was that it heightened the already highly tense relations between the Pathet Lao and the RLG. According to a British assessment, the Pathet Lao were now — and before the escape of the NLHX leaders — in a position to launch a very effective military campaign.[66] At the end of June 1960, British sources again confirmed that the Pathet Lao were in a position to score rapid successes against the Royal Laotian Army and administration if they chose to step up the level of their military activity.[67]

V

About a month after the aborted Paris summit, on 14 June, a North Vietnam–Soviet Union economic agreement was signed in Moscow. The Soviet Union would assist the North Vietnamese in the production of perennial tropical crops and their industrial processing; by providing technical assistance in the organization of state farms and in the reconstruction of existing state farms; in organizing a repair workshop to serve the state farms; and by building a tea factory and enterprises for processing coffee and canning fruits. The Soviet Union also gave a long-term loan of 350 million rubles on "very favorable conditions" to cover the supply of Soviet equipment, machines and other material. The loan was to be returned in kind in ten years beginning in 1970 at an interest rate of 2 percent.[68] The *Nhan Dan* editorial of 16 June 1960 said that the aid was all the more valuable because the DRV was still economically backward and lacked equipment and technical workers.[69] According to an assessment by the U.S. State Department, the impact of the Soviet aid program on North Vietnam's economy had been substantial, although it was probably exceeded by the Chinese assistance. However, it was difficult to accurately pinpoint the Soviet contribution because of the paucity of available information and also because several of the projects were being jointly assisted by the U.S.SR and the Eastern Bloc countries. In the view of the State Department, China was more appropriate to the technological capabilities of the North Vietnamese because of the inability of the backward Vietnamese economy to fully absorb the complex type of Soviet industrial assistance offered under the 1955 grant and 1959 credit. Also, Vietnam being the only bloc country in the tropical region, the Chinese experience was more applicable to the North Vietnamese; for example, the Russians lacked experience in tropical agriculture.[70] It was not reported who negotiated the agreement on behalf of the North Vietnamese, but we do know that Le Duan was in Moscow during this time. On 15 June, the day after the economic agreement was signed, the Vietnamese delegation led by Le Duan left Moscow for Bucharest to attend the 3rd Congress of the Communist Party of Romania.[71] Le Duan was absent throughout the visit of the Albanian delegation to North Vietnam from 12 June. It is possible that he was in Moscow, where he would have the opportunity to assess the mood of the Russians in the wake of the aborted Paris summit. As far as we can tell, the failure of the Paris summit did not alter Moscow's preference for a peaceful solution to the Vietnam problem. Although there is no report of Le Duan in Beijing, it is very likely that Le Duan stopped over in Beijing before proceeding to Moscow.

On 20 June 1960, the 3rd Congress of the Communist Party of Romania was convened.[72] It was initially just a routine congress of a minor Communist state. Therefore, very few parties besides Eastern Europe sent their top leaders. Ho himself did not attend but was represented by Le Duan.[73] Khrushchev's intention to attend the congress was announced only when he arrived in Bucharest on 18 June, two days before the congress commenced. The Bucharest conference is significant because the Russians used the occasion for a major attack on the Chinese. At the conference, they distributed an eight-page circular letter detailing the shortcomings of the Chinese. This was the first detailed presentation of the Soviet case against China intended for the eyes of senior party members in the Communist bloc. The Chinese Communists were accused of reneging on what was agreed upon at the 1957 Moscow Conference. Peng Zhen, the leader of the Chinese delegation, rebutted the accusations and countercharged the Russians with the same transgression. The communiqué issued at the end of the Bucharest conference on 24 June 1960 was couched in such a way as to conceal the differences in the bloc. It reaffirmed the correctness of the Marxist-Leninist theses of the declaration and the manifesto of peace adopted by the Communist and workers' parties in Moscow in November 1957. At the same time, it was decided that during the annual celebration of Lenin's revolution in November 1960, a conference of all the parties would be convened in Moscow to settle their outstanding differences. The Vietnamese refused to take sides in the Sino-Soviet dispute. On 28 June, *Nhan Dan* published the full text of the Bucharest communiqué with an editorial entitled "To strengthen solidarity and unity of mind among the brother-parties is constantly our foremost task."

About a month after the Bucharest conference, on 16 July 1960, while the Central Committee of the CCP was in session (5 July–10 August 1960) discussing the economy, the Soviet Union informed the Chinese that it was withdrawing all Soviet advisers from China. According to the Chinese, without prior consultation the Soviet government recalled 1,390 experts working in China and terminated 343 contracts for the service of Soviet experts and 257 projects of scientific and technical cooperation. The Soviet government also ordered their experts to take back with them all blueprints and technical data, thus leaving large numbers of construction projects uncompleted.[74] August 1960 thus saw a large exodus of Soviet experts from China.[75] The Russian decision compounded the already difficult economic situation in China brought about by the Great Leap Forward and recent severe natural calamities. According to the official Chinese account, this was the most difficult period in its history.[76]

We do not know whether Le Duan went to Beijing after leaving Bucharest, but he was back in Hanoi for the first session of the 2nd National Assembly from 7 to 15 July 1960. On the first day of the session, Pham Van Dong delivered his report on the government's work in the first six months of 1960, which — among other things — covered the subjects of national reunification and the DRV's foreign policy. Dong did not expect an easy and quick victory in the struggle for reunification, but he believed that, under the leadership of the Soviet Union and China, the collapse of imperialism was inevitable. He again highlighted the significance of the 1957 Moscow Declaration, which was recently reaffirmed in the Bucharest communiqué. On 9 July, *Nhan Dan* once more published the full text of the Bucharest communiqué together with the complete 29 June 1960 editorials of *Pravda* and *Renmin Ribao* concerning the Bucharest communiqué.[77]

With regard to North Vietnamese — Cambodian relations, Dong stated that the DRV was resolved to support Cambodia's policy of peace and neutrality. As for Laos, the DRV was clearly concerned about the situation there because it directly threatened the security of the DRV and peace in Indochina. Nevertheless, it would appear from Dong's report that Hanoi was adopting a wait-and-see policy in the hope that the situation in Laos would improve. On the subject of reunification, Pham Van Dong emphasized that the reunification of the country was a sacred task of the Vietnamese people. He identified the United States as the enemy. According to Dong, to fulfill the task of reunifying the country the Vietnamese had to struggle against the U.S. imperialists, for "the U.S. imperialists, and their lackeys are precisely the source of the misery and poverty and all other disasters which our compatriots in the South are enduring." He refuted the accusation that the anti–Diem struggle in the South was initiated by the North. Dong explained that the patriotic and anti–Diem movement in South Vietnam had a tradition of revolutionary struggle.[78]

During the 2nd National Assembly, Giap was elected in absentia to the Presidium of the Assembly and Truong Chinh was appointed chairman of the National Assembly Standing Committee. Giap was also appointed chairman of the National Scientific Research Commission, with Truong Chinh as the vice-chairman. There had been no news on Giap since 6 May 1960. He was absent during the visit of the Albanian delegation in June. It was General Nguyen Chi Thanh who attended the banquet for the Albanian visitors on 12 June.[79]

That the Hanoi leadership did not see the need for the North to involve itself directly in the Southern struggle at this point of time was also highlighted in a speech by Major-General Nguyen Van Vinh at the High Command Office, published in the VPA's newspaper *Quan Doi Nhan Dan* on 8 July 1960. Vinh said that there was no need for the North to organize the overthrowing of the U.S.–Diem administration because it was the task of the South Vietnamese. Citing examples of the recent successes in the Southern struggle, he added that the South Vietnamese Communists were more than capable of doing it.[80] This was true up to a point, but the North continued to provide indirect assistance to the struggle in the South. In a Special National Intelligence Estimate of 23 August 1960, the U.S. Country Team reported that in the first five months of 1960, Vietnamese Communist terrorism had continued to intensify, and support from North Vietnam appeared to have increased. In particular, senior cadres and military supplies such as communication equipment were believed to be moving south through Laos and Cambodia and by junk along the eastern coastline.[81]

Sometime around the end of July 1960, the Central Committee of the Lao Dong Party held its 18th Plenary Session to hear Le Duan's report on the Bucharest conference. Again Giap was not mentioned as being present at this plenary session. Nor was he reported to have attended the All-Army Party Congress from 17 to 21 July, although Ho Chi Minh was present at the closing of the congress. The main speech at the congress was delivered by Nguyen Chi Thanh. According to a British source, Giap could be visiting Algeria.[82] The decisions of the 18th Plenary Session were published in a communiqué on 14 August 1960. The communiqué emphasized the need for solidarity and unity of the socialist camp and stated that the Vietnamese Communists would do their best to strengthen the unity of the socialist camp. While conceding that peace was possible and a new world war could be avoided, the Hanoi leadership at the same time stressed the need to be constantly watchful of the perfidious imperialist schemes. As long as imperialism persisted, there was always the likelihood of war. The Vietnamese Communists would also do their utmost to preserve their national unity against U.S. imperialism. The 18th Plenary Session also decided that the 3rd Party Congress would be held from 5 September 1960.[83]

In South Vietnam, in July 1960, the Nam Bo Regional Committee held its 5th Plenary Session in War Zone D to evaluate the uprisings carried out so far. Encouraged by the successes to date, the committee decided that pressure should be intensified and opportunities should be created for even more uprisings. The date 23 September 1960, the 15th anniversary of the resistance in the South, was chosen for the start of a salvo of simultaneous uprisings throughout the country. A similar decision to launch a new wave of armed activities from September 1960 to assist the masses to attain self-rule was also made by the provincial committees of south-central Vietnam and Interzone V. Thus, from the middle of September 1960 till the beginning of 1961, mass uprisings instigated and led by the Communists and supported by armed units swept over the South.[84]

Eight

August 1960–December 1960

I

In Laos, at 3:00 A.M. Vientiane time on 9 August 1960, the "revolutionary forces" led by Captain Kong Lae, commander of the 2nd Paratroop Battalion, successfully carried out a coup in Vientiane.[1] It is believed that Kong Lae had no political affiliation and he carried out the coup on his own initiative.[2] His stated reasons for the coup were to put a stop to the civil war, to eliminate corruption amongst public servants, including military commanders and officials, and to rid the country of foreign armed forces, specifically those of the United States. He believed that it was the Americans who had bought government officials and army commanders and brought about civil war and dissension in the country. The Revolutionary Committee would maintain the neutrality of Laos and establish friendly and neighborly relations with all countries.[3]

Hanoi Radio first broadcast the news of the coup at 11:00 A.M. (GMT) on 9 August, providing a summary of the communiqués issued by the Revolutionary Committee. A *VNA* report of the coup at 2:00 A.M. (GMT) on the same day was based on the monitoring of Vientiane radio.[4] Also on 9 August the Central Committee of the NLHX issued a statement in support of the Revolutionary Committee, which was also published in the *Lao Hak Xat Bulletin* the same day.[5] We cannot be sure whether this statement by the NLHX was issued with the prior approval of Hanoi or Beijing. Until 10 August, no report of the coup in Laos had been monitored from Beijing radio or the *NCNA*. The NLHX statement was not reported by the *VNA* and *NCNA* until 12 August.

At this time, the Pathet Lao was under the charge of Kaysone Phomvihan and his close associate Khamtay Siphandon. Kaysone had very close ties with the Hanoi leadership. Souphanouvong and the other members of the Pathet Lao leadership who had escaped from prison were still making their way back to Sam Neua. According to Souphanouvong's account, after his escape on the night of 23–24 May 1960, he along with Singkapo and Nouhak Phoumsavan headed back toward Sam Neua on foot. On the morning of 9 August, they heard the news of the Kong Lae coup on the transistor radio they had with them. It was then decided that he should go ahead as quickly as possible and try to reestablish contact with Kong Lae. After another seven days of travel with only snatches of sleep, he managed to get close enough to Vientiane to establish contact with Kong Lae, who sent a helicopter to fetch him.[6] That would have been sometime around 16–17 August. It is not clear from Souphanouvong's account whether he went to Vientiane or Sam Neua.

On 10 August *Vientiane Home Service* announced that the military coup had been successfully accomplished.[7] At 11:17 P.M. (GMT) Hanoi Radio carried a two-minute dispatch on the coup, quoting the Revolutionary Committee, and at 2:48 P.M. (GMT) it gave a background talk on the sufferings of the Laotians brought about by the Somsanith government.[8]

On the afternoon of 11 August, at a rally, Kong Lae announced that Souvanna Phouma had been chosen to be premier of the Revolutionary Government. The choice of Souvanna Phouma would certainly please both the Chinese and Vietnamese Communists. We should recall that Souvanna Phouma had all along been the preference of the Chinese and the Vietnamese to lead Laos in the short term. Kong Lae's announcement was followed by the first direct indication of support by the North Vietnamese in a *Hanoi Home Service* commentary of 11 August 1960 at 2:52 P.M., which stated that the coup and the policy of peace and neutrality were compatible with the Laotian people's aspirations. The commentary added that the Vietnamese people were following the developments in Laos and were confident that the Revolutionary Committee would achieve its goals.[9]

It was also not till 11 August at 5:12 P.M. (GMT) that the *NCNA* informed the local press that information about the coup was to be transmitted. The first mention of the coup in the *Beijing Home Service* was in a news bulletin at 9:05 P.M. (GMT). The coup was the only foreign news, and it consisted of reports from Hanoi on the coup, Kong Le's message to the people, and a report on developments on the Laotian situation.[10]

At 6:20 P.M. (GMT), the *NCNA* gave a report of the coup that included summaries of the communiqués and messages issued by the Revolutionary Committee, emphasizing the anti–U.S. parts of Kong Lae's statement. Other *NCNA* reports covered all the developments that had taken place since the coup. On 12 August, the Beijing papers gave prominence to the Laotian coup, stating that a Revolutionary Committee had seized power and had announced a policy of neutrality, opposition to U.S. interference in Laotian affairs, and the ending of the civil war. The papers also published Kong Lae's message to the nation.[11] Also on 12 August, the *VNA* and *NCNA* finally reported the 9 August 1960 statement of support by the NLHX. Subsequent Chinese reports consisted of similar straightforward reporting of the developments in Laos, datelined Hanoi. From the Chinese response to the coup, the British embassy in Beijing was of the view that the Chinese were taken by surprise by the events in Laos and did not immediately support Kong Lae.[12]

On 15 August, it was reported that the incumbent government had submitted its resignation to the king and the latter had appointed Prince Souvanna Phouma to form a new government. The next day Souvanna Phouma presented his new government to the National Assembly. In his policy statement, Souvanna Phouma declared that he planned to implement the agreements he had reached with the Pathet Lao in 1957 that had been derailed by his predecessors. This was good news for the Communists. On 17 August, the paratroopers handed over the administrative functions to Souvanna Phouma and his cabinet. On 18 August, Pham Van Dong sent his greetings to Souvanna Phouma expressing the DRV's readiness to establish friendly relations in all fields with Laos. On the same day, the DRV government issued a statement supporting Souvanna Phouma.[13] There followed negotiations between Phoumi Nosavan and Souvanna Phouma at Savannakhet on the one hand and between the Pathet Lao and Souvanna Phouma on the other. The first clear indication of Chinese support came in the form of a very long commentary in the *Renmin Ribao* of 19 August.[14] The coup was hailed as a blow to U.S. imperialism.

On 23 August, a 12-minute statement by Souphanouvong endorsing the new government's domestic and foreign policies was broadcast. Souphanouvong also stated that the NLHX was ready to negotiate with the RLG on all outstanding issues in the spirit of the 1957 Vientiane Agreement. He further called upon all the Laotian people to support Souvanna Phouma against U.S. imperialism and the Phoumi Nosavan "rebels."[15] By now, Souphanouvong would have arrived back in Sam Neua.

During this period, there were reports that the U.S.–backed Phoumi Nosavan was regrouping his forces in preparation for an offensive to retake Vientiane. There were reports too that the Thais, who had not recognized the new Laotian government, might intervene militarily to forestall a Communist takeover of Laos. If Phoumi Nosavan were to launch a counteroffensive, a war in Laos would be inevitable. Also, American or SEATO involvement could not be discounted. The North Vietnamese would find it difficult not to be embroiled in a war. It was at this time that, after almost four months of absence from public view, Vo Nguyen Giap, the most well known Vietnamese military figure, finally reappeared on 27 August at a "cordial evening party" given by the State Scientific Research Board.[16] It was reported that he was replacing Truong Chinh as chairman of the board.

II

It was in the midst of the uncertainties in Laos and the worsening Sino-Soviet relations, which we noted in the previous chapter, that Ho Chi Minh made a secret trip to Moscow. The Ministry of Foreign Affairs in Hanoi denied knowledge that Ho had even visited Moscow.[17] But Ho's presence in Moscow on 15 August 1960 was inadvertently revealed by the Hungarian Party newspaper, *Nepszabadsag*.[18] In Moscow, he visited the Hungarian exhibition.[19]

In 1981 Hoang Van Hoan disclosed that in August 1960, Ho Chi Minh — accompanied by himself and Xuan Thuy — made a trip to Yalta, where they met Khrushchev. Ho's intention was to help reconcile the two Communist giants. However, the trip was a failure. During their meeting, Ho was constantly interrupted by Khrushchev, who clung to his anti–Chinese position.[20]

There was no indication that the North Vietnamese were preparing to involve themselves directly in Laos at this stage. British officials in Vientiane also reported that the Pathet Lao had shown astonishing forbearance during this time when they could have easily taken advantage of the crisis in Laos to seize power.[21] They were hoping that Souvanna Phouma, who had all along been their choice amongst the non-Communist Laotian leaders, would succeed. The situation appeared to have improved for the Pathet Lao soon after Souvanna Phouma became prime minister. Besides the decision to adhere to the 1957 Vientiane Agreement, on 3 September the Prime Minister's Office announced that all charges made against Souphanouvong and the other NLHX leaders would be dropped because of lack of sound evidence. The Communists, however, were acutely concerned about U.S. or SEATO interference. On 5 September 1960, Ung Van Khiem, vice-minister of foreign affairs, told the French consulate-general that the DRV was against American presence in Laos, but they did not mind French military advisers there.[22]

The Chinese were at this time even less prepared for any upheavals, particularly near their borders. In a speech on 1 August 1960 at the Swiss National Day reception, Zhou expressed the Chinese concern about being encircled by a hostile military bloc, specifically SEATO, and floated the idea of a peace pact of mutual nonaggression amongst countries in Asia and around the Pacific, including the United States, which would turn the whole region into an area free of nuclear weapons. Chen Yi, in his speech at the same reception, once again emphasized China's need "for a peaceful international environment for a long time to come."[23] Zhou, in a conversation with Edgar Snow on 30 August 1960, said that the idea of a peace pact of mutual nonaggression was not a new one. But to mention it again in August 1960 had significance because there were rumors that China had abandoned its policy of peaceful coexistence, which was untrue. But at the same time, the Chinese made a 180-degree turn regarding negotiations with the Americans. The Chinese were no longer prepared to discuss any other matter until the primary issue of Taiwan was settled. This was apparently conveyed to Edgar Snow in the same interview even before the U.S. State Department was aware of it. During that interview, Zhou told Snow that a peace pact of mutual nonaggression could not be concluded without the participation of China and the United States. He expected that it would take a long time for both countries to resolve their differences, but China still wanted to settle disputes through peaceful negotiations.[24]

The 100th meeting of the Sino-American ambassadorial talks that took place on 6 September 1960 was, in the words of Kenneth T. Young, "an historic occasion in the twelve-year history of the talks, for it marked their transition from the diplomacy of negotiation to that of stalemate. That day was the dividing point."[25] However, regarding the situation in Laos, the British embassy's assessment was that the Chinese were not inclined to intervene, even politically to any extent, as long as the United States did not intervene more directly. The British observed that the Chinese were confident that the strength of the Pathet Lao could prevent the RLG from gaining a firm grip on the country and thus frustrate any attempts by the United States to turn Laos into an effective anti–Communist base.[26]

III

In Hanoi, the 3rd Party Congress of the Lao Dong Party opened as scheduled on 5 September 1960. According to the *Lich Su Quan Doi Nhan Dan Viet Nam*, the congress was a milestone in the country's revolutionary struggle. It took place at a very opportune time. After five years of struggle, the North had completed the restoration of its economy and was on the road toward socialism, while the uprisings in the South were expanding and progressing satisfactorily. The dual revolutionary strategy envisaged by the Central Committee was thus becoming clearer by the day. In Laos, after the escape of the 2nd Battalion, a political-cum-military struggle was developing. In the world, the socialist system was in the ascendant. The VPA was also intensifying its preparation for the eventuality that it was called upon to move into South Vietnam and Laos.[27]

As stated by Le Duan in his political report, the objective of the 3rd Party Congress was to define the line for carrying out the socialist revolution in the North, the completion of the national people's democratic revolution throughout the country, and the struggle to achieve national reunification. The congress would also decide upon the basic orientation for the building of the party and the strengthening of the party leadership to meet the new requirements of the revolution. According to Le Duan, Vietnam's revolution at the present stage had two strategic tasks: One was to carry out a socialist revolution in the North, and the other was to complete the national people's democratic revolution through the eradication of the colonial and semifeudal regime in South Vietnam. These two tasks were closely connected. They exerted mutual influence upon each other and also stimulated each other's development. They shared a common goal, which was the reunification of the country.

The immediate task of the revolution in the South was to achieve the unity of the whole people, to strive to achieve a united bloc of workers, peasants and soldiers, and to bring into being a broad national united front with the worker-peasant alliance as the basis, directed against the U.S.–Diem regime. The struggle for national reunification would be gradual and it might take different forms, depending on the changing circumstances. As for the North, the task was to carry out the socialist transformation of agriculture, handicraft, small trade, private capitalist industry, and commerce, and to carry out socialist industrialization by giving priority to the rational development of heavy industry while striving to develop agriculture and light industry.[28]

Pham Van Dong, in his speech on the DRV's foreign policy, stated that the DRV were determined to strengthen further the brotherly friendship, the solidarity and unity of mind, cooperation, and mutual assistance within the socialist bloc. He praised the Soviet Union and China alike for their unflinching struggle against U.S. imperialism. He reiterated the desire of the DRV to establish friendly relations with Cambodia on the basis of the Five Principles of peaceful coexistence. He said that the DRV was also willing to establish friendly relations with Laos if the Laotian government respected the Geneva and Vientiane Agreements.[29]

According to Vo Nguyen Giap in his speech at the congress, economic construction in the North had become the central task of the party, which was why it was necessary for the defense budget to be reduced and military effectives cut appropriately so that manpower and material resources could be concentrated on economic construction. This is the strongest indication that the modernization process of the VPA had slowed down since around January 1960 and priority had been shifted back to the economic construction of the North.[30] This could explain the malaise in the VPA we noted in 1960. There are also some indications that there was confusion within the VPA regarding the pace of military modernization. We should recall that the decision to modernize the army was made at the 12th Plenary Session of the Lao Dong Central Committee in March 1957. The understanding then was that military development must be in tandem with the country's economic development. In mid–March 1958, the Central Military Committee decided to accelerate the process of modernization, but it was still tied to the pace of the country's economic performance. The target year for the completion of the military modernization program was adjusted from 1959 to 1960 in line with the three-year economic plan (1958–1960). Soon after the 15th Plenary Session of the Lao Dong Party Central Committee, in February 1959, it was decided that the process of military modernization had to be further accelerated. At the 3rd Party Congress, it was decided that the modernization of the VPA would need to be intensified. The dual revolutionary strategy spelled out during the congress was to be the military objective and the basis on which the VPA set its direction in the new period.[31]

During the congress, the Vietnamese Communists were caught between their two mentors, who used the occasion to present once again their divergent views regarding the correct global strategy for the socialist camp.[32] Publicly, the North Vietnamese tried their very best to keep a balance between the Soviet and Chinese points of view, as was evident in Pham Van Dong's foreign policy speech and the balanced treatment in the Vietnamese press of both the speeches of the Soviet and Chinese representatives to the Congress.

Xuan Vu, a former North Vietnamese war reporter and propaganda chief, recounted that in 1960, the people in the North began to learn about the differences between China and the Soviet Union through loud street-corner radio speakers. From 8:00 to 8:30 each night, the loudspeakers would broadcast *Radio Peking* on a direct hookup. From 8:30 to 9:00 P.M., it would be *Radio Moscow*. The two stations began to abuse each other. The Chinese would insult Khrushchev, and the Russians in turn would insult Mao. Some nights the programs would be serious — dealing with issues of revisionism and abstract political analyses. On others, the mutual denunciations would get vitriolic and crude. This apparently continued through the year until the North Vietnamese authorities finally cut it off. The huge billboard above the corner of Pho Hue and Trang Tien Streets, the city's biggest intersection, which read, "See full Communism in this generation" and displayed three happy faces, including a Caucasian worker, a peasant, and an intellectual, was also removed. "Maybe the Caucasian faces were too symbolic. Someone might think we were taking sides," Xuan Vu remarked.[33]

The Chinese representatives to the 3rd Lao Dong Party Congress were Li Fuchun (Beijing's top economic official), who was also head of the Chinese delegation, Marshal Ye Jianying, and Liao Chengzhi (deputy-director of the State Council's Office of Foreign Affairs and chairman of the Overseas Chinese Affairs Commission). The delegation from the Soviet Union was headed by Mukhitdinov, secretary of the CPSU Central Committee and full member of the Presidium. It was reported by *TASS* that on 11 September, a meeting took place between the Soviet delegation and the party and government leaders of the DRV. The further expansion of relations between the DRV and the Soviet Union, the international Communist and workers' movement, and international relations were discussed in an "exceptionally warm and cordial atmosphere."[34] On the same day, in the afternoon, Ho Chi Minh attended a farewell lunch at the Chinese embassy in Hanoi hosted by the Chinese delegation.[35] It is notable that these two events were not reported by *VNA*.

According to Bui Tin, within the Lao Dong leadership there were serious arguments regarding the Russian and Chinese positions. Truong Chinh was one of those who from the beginning supported the Russian position regarding peaceful coexistence and anti–Stalinism expounded by Khrushchev at the 20th CPSU Congress. On the other hand, Le Duan was inclined toward the Chinese point of view, which opposed the resolutions of the 20th CPSU Congress; and he was able to carry the politburo and the central committee with him. Those who held contrary views were branded as "revisionists" and "opponents of the Party."[36] The confirmation of Le Duan as the first-secretary of the Lao Dong Party at the 3rd Party Congress put to rest for the moment any more doubts as to who was next in line after Ho Chi Minh in the Hanoi leadership. One other point worth mentioning is the elevation of Tran Quoc Hoan, minister of public affairs, to alternate member of the Lao Dong Party Politburo. Like Hoang Van Hoan, Tran Quoc Hoan, as far as we know, was very close to the Chinese, particularly with his Chinese counterpart Kang Sheng.[37]

Unknown to most at this time, in Cambodia, the Khmer People's Revolutionary Party (KPRP) held its 2nd Party Congress at the end of September 1960, about two weeks after the 3rd Lao Dong Party Congress, in a room at the Phnom Penh railway station. This meeting was convened under orders from Hanoi. At this congress, the name of the party was changed to the Workers' Party of Kampuchea. The existence of the party, however, remained a secret. We now know that at this meeting, there were differences between Pol Pot (Saloth Sar) and his group, who championed a more militant struggle against imperialism and Sihanouk on the one hand, and the senior leaders of the party who continued to advocate political struggle within the framework of Sihanouk's regime on the other. Despite Sihanouk's moves against individual Cambodian Communists during the months July to September 1960, the latter view prevailed. Again, this was in line with the policy advocated by Hanoi. One other significant point to note is the addition of Son Ngoc Minh in the new central committee, which already included Tou Samouth (the secretary of the party), Saloth Sar, Nuon Chea, Keo Meas, Sao Phim, and Ieng Sary. Except for Ieng Sary, all of the others were already members of the Indochina Communist Party. Son Ngoc Minh was appointed in absentia as he was still in Hanoi, having recently attended the 3rd Lao Dong Party Congress incognito.[38]

Not long after both the congresses, in early October, Ho Chi Minh left for a vacation on Hainan Island where he stayed for almost a month. At Hainan, he visited factories, farms, various organizations, military units, shops, kindergartens, and the Institute of Tropical Condiments. He also visited the foot of Wuzhishan (Mt. Five Fingers), Luhuitao Peninsula, and Tianya Haijiao (literally, "edge of the sky, rim of the sea"). It was said that throughout his stay at Hainan Island, he was constantly mingling with the local people and was always in the public eye.[39]

IV

While the Lao Dong 3rd Party Congress was in session, in Laos, tension continued to mount. But the situation now was more advantageous to the Pathet Lao than in 1957. This was particularly so when the negotiations between Souvanna Phouma and Phoumi Nosavan came to naught and armed confrontation was imminent. On 10 September, Phoumi Nosavan broadcast from Savannakhet the formation of a Revolutionary Committee headed by Prince Boun Oum. Without sufficient troops of his own, Souvanna Phouma needed the Pathet Lao forces. Thus on 16 September, Souphanouvong, in his message to Souvanna Phouma, could confidently declare that the NLHX was ready to cooperate with the government headed by Souvanna Phouma and that the Pathet Lao armed units would resolutely oppose the Phoumi Nosavan-Tiao Boun Oum rebel clique. He also called upon all military units and administrative organizations in Laos to obey the orders of Souvanna Phouma's government. Finally, he proposed the establishment of diplomatic relations with the Soviet Union, China, and North Vietnam.[40]

The Phoumi Nosavan offensive to retake Vientiane began with the move on Paksane on 19 September. Two days later on 21 September, the Soviet Union, which had so far made only brief reference to the situation in Laos, issued a government statement condemning the U.S. and their allies in the aggressive bloc for interfering in the domestic affairs of Laos.[41] The next day, the Soviet government issued another statement accusing the Thais of aiding the forces of Phoumi Nosavan.[42] That the Russians had suddenly taken a very active interest in Laos deserves attention. We have noted that after the aborted Paris summit in May 1960, the Soviet Union began to adopt a more aggressive and uncompromising foreign policy.[43] It was believed that Khrushchev confirmed this policy shift at the 3rd Congress of the Communist Party of Romania in Bucharest in June 1960. By adopting a more militant foreign policy, Moscow also hoped to undercut support for the Chinese within the Communist bloc.[44] According to President Eisenhower, there was some indication that the Soviet Union was concerned over Communist pressures in Laos and in Southeast Asia emanating from China and North Vietnam.[45] Perhaps by taking an active role in Laos, the Soviet Union hoped to forestall any Chinese–North Vietnamese initiatives of which they might not approve. Indeed, on 2 May 1961, the Soviet ambassador to Thailand told Marshal Sarit that Soviet activities in Laos were in part meant to keep China from intervening in that country.[46] On 27 September, the Pathet Lao radio hailed the Soviet statement of 22 September and called upon the government of Souvanna Phouma to establish diplomatic relations with the Soviet Union as soon as possible because that would benefit the Laotian people.

The Phoumi Nosavan offensive failed, and his troops were forced by Kong Lae's paratroopers — with the assistance of the Pathet Lao — to retreat down the Mekong Valley to the south bank of the Ca Dinh River. On 26 September, the Pathet Lao armed forces, in coordination with Vietnamese volunteer troops, captured the city of Sam Neua and thus controlled almost the whole province. This gave the Pathet Lao a large base area that bordered North Vietnam and could be expanded north, south, and west. According to an official Vietnamese source, the capture of Sam Neua placed Hanoi in an advantageous position to organize and coordinate the revolution in Laos until complete victory in 1975.[47] According to British officials at Vientiane, with the retreat of the Savannakhet forces, Souvanna Phouma now saw no urgency to seek a compromise with Phoumi Nosavan. But at the same time, the Pathet Lao strength had increased throughout the country. The British assessment was that Souvanna Phouma had lost any control he had over Kong Lae and Kong Lae was completely dependent on the Pathet Lao.[48]

Although the Pathet Lao were in an even stronger position to take control of a large part of Laos, on 3 October the NLHX Central Committee appointed Phoumi Vongvichit, Nouhak Phoumsavan, and Singkapo Chounlamany to negotiate with Souvanna Phouma's government on the basis of the 1957 Vientiane Agreement. The proposal of the NLHX for immediate negotiations with the government of Souvanna Phouma was welcomed by *Nhan Dan* as "fully conforming to the interests of Laos and peace in Indochina."[49] This was consistent with the strategy pursued by Hanoi at this time. On 19 October, during the negotiations with the Laotian government, the NLHX delegation put forward a six-point proposal that included the establishment of diplomatic relations with China and North Vietnam.[50] The negotiations dragged on for almost a month.

Meanwhile, on 6 October it was announced that Laos had opened diplomatic relations with the Soviet Union. We should recall the Russians had been hoping for this diplomatic foothold in Laos since June 1956. The Soviet ambassador to Cambodia, A. N. Abramov, would concurrently serve as ambassador to Laos. The next day, the United States suspended its cash grant to Souvanna Phouma's government. U.S. Assistant

Secretary of State for Far Eastern Affairs Graham Parsons flew into Laos on 12 October to meet Souvanna Phouma. The United States presented Souvanna Phouma with three conditions before they would resume aid to Laos. These were: suspension of the negotiation with the NLHX, reconciliation with the Phoumi Nosavan faction, and the transfer of the Laotian capital from Vientiane to Luang Prabang, all of which Souvanna Phouma found unacceptable.[51] By 15 October, it was clear that the talks between Graham Parsons and Souvanna Phouma had failed. This was the turning point, because Souvanna Phouma could no longer balance the Communists with the Americans, which was crucial for realizing his policy of neutrality. Furthermore, the Americans were supporting the Phoumi Nosavan faction. Slowly but reluctantly, Souvanna Phouma, isolated by the Americans, was pushed closer and closer to the Communists. On 27 October, Souvanna Phouma stated at a press conference that he had in principle accepted Soviet aid.

V

During the Laotian crisis, important developments were taking place within the Communist bloc. We should recall that at the Bucharest conference in June, it was decided that a major conference to settle the dispute between the Soviet Union and China would be held in November 1960 to coincide with the October Revolution celebration. A preparatory commission was set up to formulate a new policy declaration that would reconcile both the Chinese and Russian differences. The commission met in Moscow from 30 September until 22 October. The Chinese were represented, by Deng Xiaoping and Peng Zhen. The North Vietnamese were also represented but we do not know by whom. As in Bucharest, but to an even greater extent, high Soviet functionaries were told to convince the delegates of the correctness of the Soviet position. The preparatory commission was unable to draft a declaration that satisfied all parties. Before the November conference began, the delegates were told that at the preparatory meeting, China had been supported by Albania, North Vietnam, and Indonesia; on the issue of the personality cult, the Chinese, Albanians, and Indonesians had disagreed with the Russians; on the question of whether or not factional activities within the bloc should be reflected in the declaration, the Chinese had been supported by the Japanese, North Korean, Indonesian, North Vietnamese, and Australians.[52]

The Vietnamese apparently also found Mao's ideas of revolutionary warfare appealing. On 30 September 1960, Volume IV of Mao Zedong's works was published in China. Volume IV covers the civil war period of 1945–1949. According to John Gittings, while Mao's writing on the "Paper Tigers" had appeared to be intended mainly for a domestic audience, this particular volume was regarded as equally relevant for all who were fighting for national independence and who might be corrupted by Soviet modern revisionism.[53] According to Lin Biao, the publication of the book was of great importance not only to the Chinese people but also to the international working-class movement. This was because Volume IV was a reflection of the victory of Marxism-Leninism in a big country that had the largest population in the world. Mao's ideas of revolutionary warfare, of how people's revolutionary forces that were inferior numerically and in equipment could defeat the counterrevolutionary forces that were numerically superior, would always remain vitally relevant.[54] In Hanoi, it was reported that Volume IV was completely sold out as soon as it appeared in the bookshops on 29 October 1960.[55]

On the afternoon of 2 November, Ho Chi Minh arrived in Beijing on his way to attend the October Revolution anniversary celebration and the Moscow Conference. His stopover in Beijing was prominently reported in the Chinese press.[56] While in Beijing, he met Mao, Liu Shaoqi, Zhu De, Deng Xiaoping, and Peng Zhen. Liu, Deng, and Peng Zhen would also be attending the Moscow Conference. It was reported that he had a cordial talk with Mao, Liu, Zhou Enlai, Deng Xiaoping, Zhu De, Peng Zhen, Chen Yi, Li Fuchun, Li Jingquan, and Yang Shangkun; and he was guest of honor at a banquet given by Mao. Ho left for Moscow on 4 November with Le Duan, Nguyen Chi Thanh, and Tran Quang Huy, an alternate member of the Lao Dong Central Committee.[57]

The Moscow Conference lasted from 10 November to 1 December. According to Oleg Penkovsky, 90 percent of the conference time was spent on the Soviet-Chinese differences.[58] The issues were very complex and I shall therefore focus on the points that mattered most to the Vietnamese Communists. The Chinese accused the Russians of helping the national bourgeoisie to seize power. The Russians argued that in the present phase, maneuvering was necessary; but it did not mean that they had lost sight of the ultimate objective of destroying imperialism. While military preparedness was necessary, the ideal was disarmament. The Chinese believed that the correct way forward was to support local wars for national liberation. The Russians thought this would only lead to another world war. They attacked the Chinese for paying lip service to the idea of peaceful coexistence while insisting that war was inevitable. To the Russians, it was either peace or war, there was no middle way.[59]

On 21 November, Ho was received by Khrushchev and it was reported that they had a "cordial and friendly conversation." In his memoirs Khrushchev recounted that this meeting took place during the concluding stages of the conference when the Chinese were refusing to sign the declaration because they objected to one point in the document. Ho Chi Minh appealed to Khrushchev to accede to the Chinese because, according to Ho, China was a big country with a big party and they could not allow a schism in the Communist movement. Khrushchev retorted that the Soviet Union was by no means a small country, to which Ho replied, "For us, it is doubly difficult. Don't forget, China is our neighbor."[60] Ho also successfully persuaded Liu Shaoqi to meet privately with Khrushchev so as to produce an agreed conference statement.[61]

Sino-Soviet differences were not resolved. But Ho's intervention may have ensured that the 1960 Moscow Statement issued at the end of the conference was a compromise between the Russian and Chinese positions, which suited the North Vietnamese well enough. The Five Principles of peaceful coexistence were once again emphasized as the correct policy to pursue, while at the same time, national liberation wars were recognized as progressive and had revolutionary significance, and thus should be supported. How these two policies were to be reconciled in practice was not made clear. It was also accepted that colonial countries could achieve their independence through armed struggle as well as by nonmilitary methods, depending on the specific conditions of the individual countries. The Moscow Statement declared that in the countries where the imperialists had established war bases, it was necessary to step up the struggle for their abolition, which was an important factor for fortifying national independence, defending sovereignty, and preventing war. The Statement noted that there could be no true independence unless a determined struggle was waged against imperialism and the remnants of feudalism by all the patriotic forces of the nations united in a single national-democratic front. But again there was no indication of the concrete steps that should be taken within the bloc to help achieve all the above.[62] Nevertheless, the Moscow Declaration of 1960 in principle provided the North Vietnamese with the "license" to continue with their policy.

VI

While the Moscow conference was going on, the forces of Phoumi Nosavan gained control of Luang Prabang on 10 November. The NLHX submitted a new three-point proposal on 14 November, which again included the condition that the government should receive aid from the Soviet Union and conduct trade with China and North Vietnam.[63] On 16 November, it was confirmed that General Ouane Rattikone, one of only two generals in Vientiane, had defected to Savannakhet. On the same day, it was announced that the NLHX and the government of Souvanna Phouma had reached an agreement on the basis of the Vientiane accord. Besides the immediate inclusion of the Pathet Lao in a Government of National Reconciliation, it was also agreed that a delegation would be sent to China and the DRV for the purpose of establishing friendly relations.[64] Events then moved on at a fast pace.

On 18 November Pham Van Dong, referring to reports that the Laotian government had decided on 16 November to take steps to improve Lao–DRV relations, declared that the DRV would do the same.[65] The next day, the Chinese expressed similar sentiments. The Chinese statement made no mention of the establishment of diplomatic relations between Laos and the Soviet Union and the acceptance of Soviet aid.[66] The Souvanna Phouma–Souphanouvong joint communiqué was issued on 23 November. On 24 November, Souvanna Phouma in a message to Pham Van Dong proposed to send a friendship mission to Hanoi. He also sent a telegram to Zhou Enlai with a similar proposal. As a first step in the promotion of good relations with the DRV, the Laotian government permitted border trade with the DRV. This move could not have pleased the North Vietnamese more. Not surprisingly, the decision was warmly welcomed by the Pathet Lao. On 28 November, Souvanna Phouma cabled Pham Van Dong thanking him for allowing the border people to barter across the DRV–Lao frontier.

The next day, *NCNA* carried a broadcast from Vientiane (dated 21 November) stating that the Laotian government delegation led by Souvanna Phouma would be visiting China, North Vietnam, and Burma.[67] We noted above that the decision to send friendship missions to China and North Vietnam was taken at a cabinet meeting on 16 November. On 2 December, it was announced that the plane carrying the delegation to Beijing would stop over in Hanoi on 10 December for refueling and that the Laotian delegation would be visiting North Vietnam from 18 to 21 December after their trip to Beijing.[68]

Sometime during the last week of November, Souvanna Phouma had asked the Soviet ambassador for supplies of petrol and oil.[69] On 23 November, Abramov informed Souvanna Phouma of the Soviet government's decision to provide fuel and other lubricating oils, which would reach Vientiane in the next few days. Souvanna Phouma then made a request for sugar, which Abramov promised to convey to the Soviet government.[70] On 29 November, it was announced that the first shipment of the Soviet gift of 5,000 tons of petrol, which was approximately equivalent to four months of normal consumption in Vientiane, was expected to reach Vientiane via Hanoi at the end of November. The first supply eventually arrived on 3 December 1960. Regular flights delivering fuel from Hanoi to Vientiane began on 4 December.

The Chinese followed the developments in Laos very closely but until the end of 1960, the Laotian situation was not accorded front-page treatment in the Chinese papers.[71] They were unwilling to take any initiative of their own that might involve them deeply in the civil war and were obliged at this time to let the Russians and North Vietnamese take the lead. The Chinese ambassador in Moscow told his British counterpart at the end of November that China was satisfied with the developments so far. There was reasonable hope that Laos would become a genuinely neutral state, which was all that China wanted of her. China had objected to previous attempts to turn Laos into a base against her. But the Chinese were not yet entirely convinced that the danger had been removed.[72]

Meanwhile, Ho and his delegation left Moscow on 2 December and arrived back in Beijing on 3 December. In Beijing, he was treated with the highest ceremony.[73] Ho, Le Duan, Nguyen Chi Thanh, and Tran Quang Huy had a cordial meeting with Mao in the evening. Also at the meeting were Zhou Enlai, Zhu De, Deng Xiaoping, Peng Zhen, Chen Yi, Li Fuchun, He Long, Luo Ruqing, Hu Qiaomo, and Liao Chengzhi. The same evening, Ho also attended a banquet in his honor; Hoang Van Hoan was also in Beijing at this time.[74] In the afternoon, Le Duan and Nguyen Chi Thanh met members of the CCP Central Committee.

The DRV economic and trade delegation led by Ly Ban and Ngo Minh Loan (both deputy-heads of the delegation) was apparently already in Beijing when Ho arrived. It was reported that Nguyen Duy Trinh, head of the economic and trade delegation, who arrived in Beijing on the same day as Ho, was met by Ly Ban and Ngo Minh Loan.[75] On the evening of 4 December, it was reported that Ho, Mao, and some Chinese leaders had attended a concert together. The next day, Ho and the Vietnamese delegation met Vietnamese students and trainees at the DRV Embassy. Le Duan, accompanied by Bo Yibo, visited the National Industrial and Communications exhibition.

Zhou Enlai met the North Vietnamese economic delegation on 5 December. The economic delegation stayed in China till 11 December when it then proceeded to the Soviet Union and the Eastern bloc countries. Meanwhile Ho, Le Duan, Nguyen Chi Thanh, and Tran Quang Huy left Beijing for home on 6 December. A large send-off party included high-ranking officers of the PLA. Before boarding the plane Ho, accompanied by Zhou, reviewed a guard of honor.[76]

VII

Two days after the Vietnamese left Beijing, at 5:00 A.M. (GMT), Savannakhet radio announced that the "Vientiane Revolutionary Committee" had seized power from the Souvanna Phouma government that morning.[77] The coup was led by Colonel Kouprasith Abbay and the objective was to help the Phoumi Nosavan faction assume power. The fight for Vientiane between Kong Lae's paratroopers and the forces of Phoumi Nosavan began.[78] As a consequence of the coup, the friendship visit to Hanoi was led by Khaamsouk Keola, minister of public health, instead of by Souvanna Phouma; and the trip to Beijing had to be shelved.[79] Pham Van Dong cabled Souvanna Phouma stating that the DRV would continue to support him as the only legal government of Laos.[80] The DRV government issued a statement on 10 December condemning the Americans for interfering in Laos.

On 9 December, Souvanna Phouma left for Phnom Penh. According to British officials in Vientiane, Souvanna Phouma had been resisting pressure from the Pathet Lao to ask the Russians for arms. But as soon as he left, Quinim Pholsena flew to Hanoi to negotiate for the supply of Soviet arms. Three days later, the first consignment reached Vientiane.[81]

On 12 December, the Laotian National Assembly withdrew its support for the Souvanna Phouma government and the Laotian King temporarily entrusted the administration of the country to the Revolutionary Committee headed by Prince Boum Oum.[82] The new government was immediately recognized by the United States and Thailand. The North Vietnamese ambassador to China met Zhou in Zhongnanhai to discuss the Laotian situation on 12 December.[83] The following day, Pham Van Dong sent a message to Vientiane stating that the DRV continued to regard Souvanna Phouma as the only legitimate government and condemned the U.S. plot to set up a new puppet government.[84] The Soviet Union also sent a note to the United States protesting their intervention in the domestic affairs of Laos.[85]

According to British sources in Vientiane, the Pathet Lao did not participate in the fighting for Vientiane.[86] American officials in Vientiane also did not find any evidence of direct North Vietnamese intervention in the battle for the city of Vientiane. On the other hand, there were evidences of Thai support, which included participation of troops and provision of supplies for the attack on Vientiane, as early as 9 December.[87] According to the U.S. State Department, however, during the battle for Vientiane, Soviet IL-14 aircraft flew in 105mm howitzers, ammunition, gasoline, combat rations, and other war materials. North Vietnamese military personnel were also landed and parachuted in to augment Kong Lae's forces outside, but not in Vientiane itself. Soviet heavy transport aircraft had been transiting China into Hanoi and Haiphong, backing up the airlift into Laos.[88] On 15 December, Kong Lae and his forces withdrew from Vientiane.

VIII

While the situation in Laos deteriorated, Sino-Cambodian relations continued to improve. The first report that a Cambodian delegation led by Sihanouk would be visiting China was made on 9 December. Sihanouk paid a state visit to China from 14 to 26 December at the invitation of Liu Shaoqi and Zhou Enlai.[89] This was his third visit to China since February 1956. (The second visit was in August 1958.) The main purpose of this trip was to sign a treaty of friendship and nonaggression between the two countries, as proposed by the Chinese side during Zhou Enlai's visit to Phnom Penh in May. In a series of conversations with Malcolm MacDonald in Cambodia, sometime during the week before 19 August 1960, Sihanouk told him of his intention to sign such a treaty along the lines as those signed between the Chinese and the Burmese, Indonesians, and Nepalese on his next visit to Beijing. Sihanouk described the proposed treaty as "innocuous documents that he could not refuse." He asked MacDonald to pass the information to the British and American governments. Sihanouk emphasized that he was still staunchly anti-Communist. The Cambodians had nothing in common with the Russians, did not understand them, and did not like them. He did not wish for any closer relations with Moscow than were necessary and prudent. On the other hand, the Cambodians did feel friendly toward the Chinese. This was partly because there was some Chinese blood in many Cambodian's veins. Moreover, the Chinese were behaving correctly and cooperatively with Cambodia and he hoped to maintain this attitude. In Sihanouk's calculation, if he made some innocuous concessions to the Chinese proposals for friendlier relations, Cambodia's independent future would be more secure. He was, however, very concerned about Thai and South Vietnamese designs on Cambodian territory. He believed that it was the Thais and the South Vietnamese who were the cause of all the difficulties in Cambodia's relations with the West. The only real Communists in Cambodia, in his view, were a number of young though clever intellectuals. Sihanouk told MacDonald that he did not wish to get any military aid from the Soviet Union or China, preferring Western assistance. Moscow and Beijing had for the last two years offered to send him any type of modern armaments he liked, but he had consistently and firmly refused. He needed to train pilots but did not want to send them for training in the Soviet Union or China.[90] By the time of Sihanouk's visit to China, he was still more concerned about the threats to Cambodian security from Thailand and South Vietnam than from the Communists.[91]

In Beijing, Sihanouk had talks with Liu Shaoqi on 15 December, Zhou Enlai on the afternoon of 16 December, and Mao Zedong on 17 December, which were all described as cordial and/or friendly. In all the speeches made by both parties during the visit, the Five Principles of peaceful coexistence were constantly emphasized. The situation in Laos was a major concern for both the Chinese as well as the Cambodians. In his banquet speech on 18 December in honor of Sihanouk, Zhou Enlai said that the Chinese as a close neighbor of Laos and one of the guarantors of the Geneva Agreements resolutely opposed any aggressive acts aimed at subverting and splitting Laos. He further added that the Chinese were closely following the developments there.[92] According to British sources in Beijing, the Chinese press was following the events in Laos closely but did not give the situation particular prominence.[93] In contrast, Sihanouk's visit to China was accorded much publicity and the Chinese made great efforts to extend the warmest hospitality to Sihanouk and his delegation.

In line with its policy of peaceful coexistence, during this period Beijing also signed the arrangement for the implementation of the treaty concerning the question of dual nationality with the Indonesians in Djakarta on 15 December 1960; and the instruments of ratification of the Sino-Burma Boundary Treaty with the Burmese in Rangoon on 4 January 1961.[94] Thus, apart from their border dispute with India, Laos was emerging as the immediate security problem for the Chinese.

IX

Meanwhile, the situation in Laos was such that the Kong Lae forces and the Pathet Lao were receiving military supplies from North Vietnam and the Soviet Union[95] while the Phoumi Nosavan faction was receiving supplies from the United States. Both sides claimed to be the legitimate government.[96]

On 14 December, in a message to the cochairmen of the Geneva Conference, Nehru proposed that the International Commission in Laos be reactivated.[97] On 15 December, as the Kong Lae forces withdrew from Vientiane, the Chinese government issued a statement saying that they would do their utmost to uphold the Geneva Agreements and check U.S. imperialist interference in Laos. The statement further added that the Chinese supported the Vietnamese and Soviet positions regarding Laos. Another meeting took place between Zhou Enlai and the North Vietnamese ambassador to China in Zhongnanhai on 16 December to discuss Laos.[98] On 17 December, the DRV Foreign Ministry issued a statement calling for the reconvening of the Geneva Conference.

On 22 December, the Soviet Union delivered a note to the British government proposing that a new conference involving all the participants of the 1954 Geneva Conference be convened to resolve the situation in Laos and that the ISCC should resume its activity as suggested by the Indian Prime Minister.[99] On 24 December, Pham Van Dong wrote to the cochairmen of the Geneva Conference with the same purpose. The *Renmin Ribao* of 25 December carried the full text of the Soviet note in its foreign news page along with an editorial in support of it. The next day, *Renmin Ribao* carried the full text of Pham Van Dong's letter to the cochairmen of the Geneva Conference. On 27 December, the day after he returned from China, Sihanouk in his opening address at the 10th National Congress of the Sangkum stated that the countries responsible for the Laotian situation and the participants of the 1954 Geneva Conference should hold a conference as soon as possible. He also proposed that the United States, Thailand, Burma, and South Vietnam should attend the conference.[100]

On 1 January 1961, Sihanouk wrote to the two cochairmen of the 1954 Geneva Conference and other heads of government regarding the need for a new enlarged conference on Laos that would include Thailand, South Vietnam, and Burma. On 6 January, Ho Chi Minh responded positively to Sihanouk's proposal. Khrushchev also expressed support for a new conference in his letters of 7 January to Sihanouk, Pham Van Dong, and Souvanna Phouma.[101] The British prime minister replied on 13 January 1961, stating that the proposal would be seriously considered. However, in the interim, it was necessary to stop the fighting in Laos. The British preference was for an immediate reactivation of the ISCC. After that, if a conference was still deemed necessary, it could then be convened. On 14 January, Zhou Enlai replied to the letter from Souvanna Phouma of 30 December 1960 and the telegram from Pham Van Dong of 4 January proposing an international conference on Laos. Zhou condemned U.S. aggression in Laos and expressed support for the idea of a new conference.[102] The next day, on 15 January, in the Chinese reply to Sihanouk's letter of 1 January 1961, Zhou concurred with Sihanouk that an enlarged conference should be urgently convened. Khrushchev wrote to the British prime minister on 20 January stating that while the Soviet Union supported the reactivation of the ISCC, the existing situation in Laos differed from that of 1954 and therefore it was necessary to urgently convene a conference. The next day, the British sent to the Russians a proposed joint message from the cochairmen of the Geneva Conference requesting that India, as Chairman of ISCC, send a representative to Laos as soon as possible on an exploratory mission to propose to the Laotian king the reactivation of the commission. The Russian reply on 18 February 1961 was that there was no necessity to consult the Laotian king as he was at the present time a prisoner of the Phoumi Nosavan–Boun Oum rebels, and in any case the legal government of Souvanna Phouma had already agreed that the ISCC should resume its duties.[103]

Meanwhile, the Vietnamese Communists' revolutionary struggle to reunify Vietnam and the developments in Laos were becoming increasingly interrelated.[104] We should recall that the North Vietnamese operating on the Ho Chi Minh Trail were now using the route going south down the western side of the Truong Son Range in Laotian territory. The Pathet Lao had requested their Vietnamese Communist counterparts to transport some of their supplies to southern Laos and to build up revolutionary organizations wherever the trail extended.[105] At that time, of course, the North Vietnamese vehemently and persistently denied being directly involved in the fighting in Laos. We now know that at the beginning of 1961, the North Vietnamese sent a number of infantry, artillery, and engineer battalions belonging to the 316th and 335th Brigade (Northwest Military Region), the 325th Division, and 271st Regiment (Military Region IV) into Laos. A total of 12,000 North Vietnamese troops were in Laos at this time serving as military advisers, assisting in the creation of armed units, and training the Pathet Lao. The North Vietnamese also helped the Pathet Lao establish a military training school. They also provided arms and ammunition. According to the *Lich Su Quan Doi Nhan Dan Viet Nam*, the united struggle of Laos and Vietnam against the common enemy — the American imperialists was a special relationship based on the traditional closeness of the two countries and the spirit of proletarian internationalism between the two parties and armies. And it was this unity that created the condition for the success of both the revolutions in Vietnam and Laos.[106]

Since the November 1960 agreement between Souvanna Phouma and Pham Van Dong to open the DRV–Laos border for frontier trade, it had become very much easier for the North Vietnamese to carry out their plans in Laos. At the end of January 1961, it was reported by Pathet Lao radio that trade relations between Laos and the DRV were developing favorably. The local government in Phong Saly, Luang Prabang, Sam Neua, Xieng Khouang, Cammon, and other provinces was said to have organized the Laotian people to take their goods to the borders in exchange for daily necessities, table salt, farm implements, and "other items."[107] It is quite possible that "other items" such as small arms and ammunition could have been smuggled across the border as well.

According to U.S. State Department sources, since the withdrawal of the neutralists from Vientiane on 15 December 1960, at least 180 sorties had been monitored in the general area of Vang Vieng, Phong Hong, Sam Neua, and Xieng Khouang. Besides war material, substantial numbers of North Vietnamese personnel were also parachuted into those areas.[108] Pathet Lao–North Vietnamese forces captured Tha Vieng and Tha Thom on 12 and 18 January respectively. Both places were regarded as the southern gateway of Xieng Khouang. Thabun, the strategic point controlling the approaches to Xieng Khouang, and the Plaine des Jarres also fell into their hands.

Souvanna Phouma passed through Hanoi on 21–22 February and 24–26 February 1961 on his way to Xieng Khouang and then to Phong Saly, but no publicity was given to his visits. In February too, Pham Van Dong and Souvanna Phouma agreed to the exchange of economic and cultural missions between the two countries. He was again in Hanoi on 30 April 1961.[109] Sisana Sisane, editor of the Pathet Lao newspaper *Lao Hak Xat,* also visited Hanoi and Beijing in February after attending the Afro-Asian Solidarity conference at Cairo. In March, Quinim Pholsena, the neutralist Laotian minister of national defense, finance and foreign affairs, and He Wei, the Chinese ambassador to the DRV, agreed on the exchange of economic and cultural missions between Laos and China.[110]

On 7 March, the Pathet Lao–North Vietnamese forces took control of Xala Phukhun, an important road junction north of Vientiane. The North Vietnamese–Pathet Lao forces were assisted to a large extent by the continued Soviet airlift into Laos. While the fighting continued, the North Vietnamese kept up the call for a new conference to resolve the Laotian crisis. According to Australian intelligence sources, the Pathet Lao were not taking advantage of the slow pace of Phoumi Nosavan's advance. If the Pathet Lao had wanted to, they could probably have defeated Phoumi quickly with Vietnamese assistance, but they were holding back.[111]

Thus at the end of 1960 and early 1961, it was Laos rather than South Vietnam that was the focus of international concern. In the view of President Eisenhower, if Laos should fall to the Communists, then it would just be a matter of time before South Vietnam, Cambodia, Thailand, and Burma would follow. Laos was the key to the entire area of Southeast Asia. Vietnam, in comparison, was considered less critical.[112]

Nine

December 1960–October 1961

I

While the world's attention was focused on Laos, in South Vietnam, the mass uprisings continued unabated. We should recall that the 5th Plenary Session of the Nam Bo Regional Committee in July 1960 had decided to launch a new series of simultaneous uprisings from 23 September 1960. But on 14 September uprisings had already started in the provinces of Ca Mau, Rach Gia, Soc Trang, Vinh Long, Chau Doc, Long Xuyen, and Can Tho (in west Nam Bo). These were followed on 23 and 24 September by the provinces of Long An, Ben Tre, Kien Phong, and Kien Tuong (in central Nam Bo). Uprisings also occurred in east Nam Bo from Tay Ninh, Ben Cat, Dau Tieng, Cu Chi, Hoc Mon to Lai Thieu, Thu Duc, Tan Binh, Di An, Nha Be, and Binh Chanh, surrounding the cities of Saigon–Gia Dinh, Trung Bo, and Interzone V. All these uprisings were along the lines of the Ben Tre uprisings which had taken place at the beginning of the year. It was still predominantly a political struggle supported by guerrilla squads that served as assault teams. Their role was to assist the mass uprisings by protecting the people, killing the enemy, and destroying the enemy's administrative apparatus, thus compelling the enemy to capitulate.[1]

On 20 December 1960, two weeks after Ho returned from Beijing, the National Liberation Front for South Vietnam (NLFSV) was formed at Tan Lap village, Chau Thanh District (now Tan Bien District, Tay Ninh Province).[2] The Chinese were the first to recognize it. We should recall that the united front strategy was discussed during the 15th Plenary

Session in January 1959 and it was raised during the meeting between Ho Chi Minh and Zhou Enlai in Beijing in August 1959. Subsequently, in autumn 1959, Nguyen Van Hieu went to North Vietnam to discuss the platform of the united front with Ho Chi Minh. By the end of that year, the manifesto and political program was completed and the date for the inaugural meeting was also decided.[3] The intention to establish a united front was officially announced by Le Duan in his political report during the recent 3rd Party Congress in September.

Some form of organization was also clearly needed to coordinate those armed forces mentioned above. A military committee for all the zones, provinces, hamlets, and villages was therefore established as the command center to help the party to provide guidance to all the armed units in the South. It was also responsible for recruitment and logistics. In accordance with the decision of the Party Central Committee, the armed forces in the South were to be called "the Army for the Liberation of South Vietnam."

According to the directive of the Central Military Committee of 1 January 1961, the Army for the Liberation of South Vietnam was a part of the VPA, founded, developed, educated, and led by the party. It was to be both a fighting army as well as a production army, and was expected to continue with the tradition of heroic struggle, the spirit of uprisings, and service to the people. To accomplish its task, the army was to form three categories of soldiers: a main force, a regional force and a guerrilla force. Its mission was to resolutely realize the program and line of the party, which was to liberate the South from imperialist oppression and feudalism and to attain independence and freedom. Although this was an urgent task, it must be carried out realistically depending on the circumstances and the existing practical capability of the army.[4]

Eisenhower was perhaps right to be more concerned about Laos than South Vietnam falling to the Communists during this time, but the Communist threat in South Vietnam was by no means insignificant.[5] Brigadier General Lansdale paid an intensive visit to South Vietnam between 2 and 14 January 1961. In his report to the U.S. Secretary of Defense, he remarked that the Vietnamese Communists were much farther along toward accomplishing their objective of controlling South Vietnam than he had realized from the reports received in Washington. Lansdale's findings indicated that the Communists dominated much of South Vietnam's 1st and 5th Military Regions, as well as other areas. Thousands of Communists had infiltrated the most productive area of South Vietnam and controlled most parts of it except for the narrow corridors protected by Diem's military and paramilitary forces. The Communists also controlled most of the region from the jungle foothills of the High Plateau north of Saigon all the way south down to the Gulf of Siam. The only area still not controlled by the Communists was the Saigon-Cholon area.[6]

The gap between the formation of the National Liberation Front of South Vietnam on 20 December 1960 and the first *VNA* and *NCNA* reports of 29 January 1961 on its formation deserves attention. From about the end of December 1960 to the beginning of January 1961, the Lao Dong Party Central Committee met to review the work of the three-year plan (1958–1960) and to decide on the tasks for 1961. During this session, Le Duan presented a report on the November 1960 Moscow Conference and expounded on the Moscow Statement, which we should recall affirmed the validity of national liberation struggles. He also spoke of the need for creating a "broad front ... to create conditions for the seizure of power by the working class and for socialist transformation."[7]

On 6 January 1961, Khrushchev gave a report of the November 1960 Moscow Communist Conference at the general meeting of party organizations of the Higher Party School, Academy of Social Sciences, and the Institute of Marxism-Leninism attached to the CPSU, which could not have pleased the North Vietnamese more. In his speech, Khrushchev addressed the issue of the wars for national liberation, which, he argued, would continue to exist as long as imperialism and colonialism existed. Wars for national liberation were not only admissible but inevitable. The Vietnamese situation was cited as an example. Khrushchev posed the question of why the U.S. imperialists, while wanting to help the French colonialists in every way, nevertheless decided against a direct intervention in the war in Vietnam. The answer, according to him, was because the U.S. knew that if they helped France with armed forces, Vietnam would get appropriate aid from China, the Soviet Union, and other socialist countries, which could then lead to a world war. The position of the Soviet Union was that it would "fully support such just wars and march in the front ranks of the peoples waging liberation struggles." This was the strongest indication ever of Soviet support for the North Vietnamese cause.[8] But soon after J. F. Kennedy's inauguration on 20 January 1961, Khrushchev began dropping hints of a meeting with the new president. With the exception of this 6 January speech, the other signals Khrushchev sent to the newly elected U.S. president were the most conciliatory since the U-2 incident.[9]

Sino-Soviet relations, however, continued to sour beneath the surface. According to Jan Sejna, in early 1961 Soviet intelligence obtained copies of a secret letter circulated to party cadres in China that marked the opening of an internal propaganda campaign to brief the cadres on the subject of Sino-Soviet disagreements. The letter blamed the Soviet Union for the disunity in the Communist movement, for planning a military attack on China, for being the cause of China's economic problems, and for abandoning Communism while falsely claiming to be the vanguard of Marxism.[10]

We are only beginning to learn of the different perceptions of the Soviet Union held by various personalities within the Chinese leadership and the roles they played in determining the development of Sino-Soviet relations. For example, it is believed that Mao, Deng, Peng Zhen, and Kang Sheng were most suspicious of the Russians, whereas Zhou and Liu Shaoqi favored a more cautious and moderate approach toward the Soviet Union.[11] We know even less of the Soviet side, except that Khrushchev distrusted his Ministry of Foreign Affairs, which had many officials who were loyal to Molotov and were uneasy about Khrushchev's overtures to the West. He also did not trust the KGB. The KGB chairman was thought to oppose Khrushchev's tough policy toward China and his rapprochement with the United States. According to Beschloss, on 11 February 1961, Khrushchev was suddenly called back to Moscow while he was touring the Soviet farming regions. It was believed that his rivals in the Presidium had convened a meeting and demanded a more tough-minded policy toward the United States.[12]

On 20 January 1961, Nguyen Duy Trinh and the North Vietnamese economic and trade delegation returned to Beijing after having only been to Moscow, Budapest, and Bucharest.[13] Hoang Van Hoan was still in Beijing during this time. We should recall that the delegation led by Trinh had been in Beijing from 3 to 11 December 1960 before it left for the Soviet Union and Eastern Europe. On 29 January, while Trinh was still in Beijing, both Hanoi and Beijing finally reported the "recent" formation of the National Liberation Front of South Vietnam.[14]

Two days later, on 31 January, an economic agreement and protocol with China was signed. According to a Chinese source, the start of North Vietnam's first five-year economic plan (1961–1965) coincided with the period of China's "three economically difficult years." Despite that, the Chinese continued to assist North Vietnam's economic development.[15] Under the economic agreement, the Chinese would provide the DRV with a long-term loan of 141,750,000 RMB. The DRV would use this loan within seven years (1961–1967) to pay for the equipment and technical assistance to be provided by China. China would also help the DRV build or expand 28 industrial and transport enterprises in fields such as metallurgy, power generating, light industry, and railways. According to the protocol on the mutual supply of goods for 1961, the Chinese would supply the North Vietnamese with steel products, cotton, automobile tires, bituminous coal, raw material for the chemical industry, mechanical equipment, medicines, and so on. In return, the DRV would supply China with anthracite, apatite, timber, cement, chromate, poultry, livestock, fruits and so on.[16]

In his speech at the farewell banquet for the Vietnamese delegation on 31 January, Zhou again referred to Laos. He said that the peace in Indochina had been destroyed in recent months by the U.S. imperialists, Thailand, and South Vietnam. The expansion of the civil war in Laos was threatening the peace in Southeast Asia and the security of North Vietnam and China. As a result, the Chinese attached great importance to the developments in Laos. Zhou believed that even with the reactivation of the ISCC, it was necessary to convene an international conference.

The editorial in *Renmin Ribao* on 1 February hailed the Sino-Vietnamese aid agreement as evidence of the further strengthening of the unbreakable friendship between the two interdependent fraternal countries. The *Nhan Dan* editorial of the same day gave details of the agreement and expressed North Vietnamese gratitude for the Chinese assistance. The editorial also referred in passing to the economic cooperation agreement signed with the Soviet Union and the other socialist bloc countries.[17] In an article in *Nhan Dan* on 3 February 1961, the DRV minister of light industry said that in the last three years, China had not only given the DRV long-term loans but also helped to build and restore many enterprises in the country.[18]

After Beijing, the North Vietnamese economic delegation led by Nguyen Duy Trinh returned to Eastern Europe via Moscow. This included another visit to Bucharest, followed by Tirana, where Trinh represented the Lao Dong Party at the 4th Albanian Workers' Party Congress; then Warsaw. He also visited the Leipzig Fair in the GDR before proceeding to Sofia and Prague. We do not know whether the delegation stopped in Moscow again, but it is mostly likely that it did. According to British sources, economic aid from the Soviet Union and Eastern Europe for North Vietnam in 1961 was greater than that from China.[19] This is not surprising given the economic crisis in China during this period.

Also on 31 January 1961, the politburo of the Lao Dong Party issued a directive regarding the direction and tasks of the struggle in the South.

In the assessment of the politburo, the North was gradually becoming more capable of defending itself as well as serving as a base area for the revolution to liberate the South. At the same time, the revolution in the South was developing along the path of a general uprising and there was no possibility that the revolution would develop in a peaceful manner. The strategy was to step up both the political and military struggles until they were at par, and to attack the enemy both politically and militarily. Taking into consideration the variation in strengths in different areas and the diverse topographical characteristics in the South, the politburo instructed that in the jungle and mountainous areas, the emphasis should be on military struggle; in the lowland areas, military and political struggles should go hand in hand; and in the urban areas, the stress should be on political struggle. According to the official North Vietnamese account, the 31 January 1961 resolution "provided very important strategic guidance for the revolution in the South."[20]

In a letter of 7 February 1961 to the comrades in the South, Le Duan presented his conception of the revolutionary struggle in the South, which essentially amplified the recent 31 January 1961 resolution. According to him, the revolutionary struggle, at this point of time should not follow the Chinese pattern of protracted armed struggle in which the countryside would first surround the cities, to be followed by the military forces liberating the whole country. Rather, in South Vietnam and Laos as well, the strategy would include separate but coordinated uprisings with the objective of establishing base areas, emphasizing the use of guerrilla warfare, and building up to a general mass uprising in the final stage. The most important aspect was to use political struggle supported by armed struggle to regain the authority for the masses. Political struggle was to play the leading role at this present stage.

According to Le Duan, the immediate task was to build up the armed forces. In his assessment, although at that time the Communists had the absolute advantage over the U.S.–Diem clique in the political struggle, their armed forces were still relatively few in number. For example, they did not have the forces to control the strategically important Central Highlands. Even if they were able to capture the cities, they would still not be able to keep them. Le Duan was ever conscious that it was not just the Diem clique that they were confronting but the Americans as well.

In his letter, Le Duan once again emphasized the need to control the Central Highlands. The region of the Central Highlands was pivotal to the Communist strategy. It was from this region that any attack against the enemy would be launched. It was also important as a base area to build and protect the revolutionary forces. The countryside and the delta areas in the vicinity of the Central Highlands were their main strategic objectives — the cities could be left to the last. Regarding this matter, he had already discussed it with the comrades in Interzone V. Finally, Le Duan revealed that in 1961 the Party Central Committee would assist Interzone V and Nam Bo to establish 12 battalions. In addition it would supply Nam Bo with sufficient cadres for seven battalions.[21] A week later, on 15 February 1961, the revolutionary armed forces in the South were united under the new name, "the Armed Forces for the Liberation of South Vietnam."[22]

On 25 February the politburo in Hanoi approved the military plan prepared by the Central Military Committee and the Ministry of National Defense. The plan identified four main tasks. The first was, to increase the military strength to enhance the defense of the North, establish an air-defense force, lay the foundation for an air force and navy, and to complete the regularization and modernization of the VPA. The second task was to construct the armed forces in South Vietnam. Infantry troops in the districts were to be organized into platoons. Infantry troops in the provinces were to be organized into companies and battalions. It was also proposed that 10 to 15 regiments should be combined with a number of artillery units to counter the enemy's defense, tanks, and aircrafts. The third task was to assist the Pathet Lao to train and develop its armed forces, to consolidate and construct the liberated areas. Vietnamese troops would be sent to Laos whenever the need arose. The fourth task was to organize the military command system in South Vietnam so as to improve communication from the Central Committee to the provincial and district committees down to the village cells. The military regions in South Vietnam were also to be quickly organized. The politburo entrusted the Central Military Committee with the responsibility for the military task in South Vietnam. Speaking at the politburo meeting on 25 February, Ho reiterated that the VPA was a people's army. The war was a people's war. The army must always be close to the people. While weaponry and technical skills must be constantly improved, the army must always live just like the ordinary people.[23]

In March 1961, the General Staff decided on a new battle order: The 325th Division, 341st Brigade, 244th Regiment would operate in Military Region IV; the 316th and 335th Brigades and 148th Regiment would operate in the Northwest Military Region. This was to ensure that troops were ready at hand to move into Battlefield "B," which was South Vietnam, and Battlefield "C," which was Laos, at short notice. The 338th

Division was established as a special training division for the training of all soldiers who were assigned to operate in South Vietnam. In the years 1959–1963, the majority of the cadres and soldiers that fought in the South were Vietnamese forces recruited in the South, regrouped troops in Interzone V, and those who had previous experience fighting in the South, armed with rifles and a number of DKZ trench mortars.[24]

In the same month, the Central Military Commission formed a committee to review the overall strategy of the VPA. The task of the committee was to sum up the experiences of the armed struggle, the military strategy in the resistance war against the French, and the role of the VPA in the dual missions of national construction and warfare. Lieutenant-General Hoang Van Thai, member of the Party Central Committee and deputy-chief of staff, was appointed to head the committee.[25] We should recall that a similar study had already been carried out by the General Political Directorate under Nguyen Chi Thanh and its conclusions disseminated at a conference of political commissars in November 1958. One of the recommendations of the Thanh study had been the strengthening of party committees in the military.[26]

According to British intelligence, the army's military role was given more emphasis after March 1961.[27] According to the *Lich Su Quan Doi Nhan Dan Viet Nam*, the first five years in the development of the Vietnamese People's Army, from 1955–1960, had seen the army grow from many scattered units of infantry equipped with inferior weaponry to a regular and relatively modern army. Those five years were the foundation years. In 1961, the many new military commitments that the VPA had to undertake revealed the limitations of the VPA in the areas of organization, weaponry, military science, and strategy. The objective of the second five-year plan for the military, from 1961–1965, was to produce a truly modern army that could fight effectively in the battlefields of Vietnam and Indochina. Another objective was to speed up the development of military units so that they would be ready when the war expanded.[28]

It is worth noting that in 1961 when the VPA's military role was given more attention, Nguyen Chi Thanh, the only other four-star North Vietnamese general besides Vo Nguyen Giap, was transferred from the army, where he was director of the VPA General Political Directorate, to manage the Ministry of Agricultural Cooperatives.[29] He was replaced by his deputy, General Song Hao.[30] According to P. J. Honey, from early March 1961 the North Vietnamese press ceased to refer to Thanh by his military title but as the "Rural Affairs Chairman of the Party Central Committee."[31] We should recall that four months earlier, in November

1960, Nguyen Chi Thanh (together with Le Duan and Tran Quang Huy) had accompanied Ho Chi Minh to Beijing and the Moscow Conference. We do not know whether Thanh was given any other undisclosed assignments. Six months later, from 28 to 30 September 1961, he was in Beijing after attending the 4th National Congress of the Nodong Dang (North Korean Workers' Party) in Pyongyang. While Thanh was in Pyongyang, he would have met Deng Xiaoping and Kang Sheng, who were also in the North Korean capital to ensure that the North Koreans did not swing to the Soviet side in the Sino-Soviet dispute.[32] In contrast, Giap appeared to have become more influential. An English edition of his essay, *People's War, People's Army*, first published on 22 December 1959, was issued in 1961.[33]

II

On 7 March 1961, the Pathet Lao–North Vietnamese forces captured Xala Phukhun, an important road junction north of Vientiane. What followed was a series of diplomatic maneuverings between Washington and Moscow. In the United States, preparations were made for a gradual increase of American military involvement in Laos. At the same time, Kennedy, through the American ambassador to the Soviet Union, Llewellyn Thompson, informed Khrushchev that the United States was prepared to withdraw completely from Laos and accept a genuinely neutral Laos if the Communists agreed to do the same. This message was also conveyed to the Chinese through the Warsaw channel[34] and to the North Vietnamese via the Soviet channel.

China's perception of Laos and the Laotian situation during this period is revealed in a document entitled "Concerning the Struggle of the Laotian People" distributed with Issue Number 13 (20 March 1961) of the *Bulletin of Activities* circulated by the General Political Department of the PLA. According to the document, the geographical position of Laos was very important. The United States described Laos as the "stopper of the bottle of the Indochina Peninsula." Because of this, the United States was doing all it could to prevent China from having any influence in Laos. Although the United States had yet to develop a modernized military base in Laos, the Chinese were convinced that it was planning to use Laos as a base to attack China. Reference was made to the 1954 Geneva Conference, which foiled the American plan of extending imperialism into the region. The document also recalled with approval the attempts of Souvanna Phouma to establish a neutral government in 1957 and the integration of the Pathet Lao forces with the Royal Laotian Army. It blamed the American imperialists for interfering in the internal affairs of Laos and the subsequent collapse of the neutral government.

Regarding the forces of Kong Lae and the Pathet Lao, the Chinese were of the view that they were stronger than those of Phoumi Nosavan but that their numbers did not compare with the latter. The Kong Lae–Pathet Lao forces still needed a period of time to increase their strength and to conduct military training. Although the political situation seemed favorable, the enemy forces still occupied a fairly strong military position. The Chinese believed that the Laotian question depended for its solution on how the armed struggle developed: Could the Kong Lae–Pathet Lao forces prevent the enemy's strength from increasing? Could they destroy the enemy? Would it be soon or not? All these questions would affect the situation in the political struggle. The Chinese answer was that a solution could not be seen for sometime and the difficulties were still very numerous.

According to the same document, China, the Soviet Union, and North Vietnam wanted a peaceful solution to the Laotian question in accordance with the principles and spirit of the Geneva Conference. But because the current situation was very different from what it was in 1954, the Chinese government believed that there ought to be a conference to discuss the peaceful neutrality of Laos. China approved of reviving the activities of the International Supervision and Control Commission, but only after the international conference that would lay down the duties and power of the ISCC. Also, whether it was the international conference or the ISCC, those involved must deal only with the de jure government of Souvanna Phouma. On the prospect of an international conference, the Chinese believed that the United States was dragging its feet until such time that it had the military advantage before agreeing to a conference.[35]

It was not till April 1961 that the two cochairmen finally reached a consensus regarding the issue of the ISCC and the international conference on Laos. We should recall that on 7 March, the Pathet Lao–North Vietnamese forces captured Xala Phukhun, which led to a series of diplomatic maneuverings between Washington and Moscow. While American military forces were put on alert in Okinawa and Thailand, thus giving the impression that the United States would intervene in Laos, Kennedy in a press conference on 23 March expressed support for an international conference on Laos on the condition that there was an immediate ceasefire.

On the same day, the British handed the Russians an aide memoire with the same proposal. From their conversations with Khrushchev, both the American ambassador to the Soviet Union, Llewellyn Thompson, and the British ambassador, Frank Roberts, believed that Khrushchev did not want the conference indefinitely postponed.[36] On 1 April, Moscow replied to the British aide memoire of 23 March 1961, suggesting that Great Britain and the Soviet Union should issue an appeal for a ceasefire simultaneously with the commencement of the international conference.[37] Four days later, on 5 April, the British ambassador gave the Soviet deputy foreign minister responsible for Southeast Asia — Georgi M. Pushkin-draft texts for an appeal for a ceasefire in Laos, a report to Nehru concerning the ISCC, and an announcement of the conference. Roberts made it very clear that the ceasefire must be verified before the commencement of the conference.[38] After a delay of over two weeks, Soviet Foreign Minister Gromyko finally handed a draft message to the British ambassador calling for a ceasefire in Laos and a draft text of a proposed message to the government of India on recovening the ISCC for Laos on 16 April.[39]

Meanwhile, in Hanoi, the Central Military Committee, with the consent of the Central Committees of the Lao Dong Party and the NLHX, approved the plan for Military Region V and Transportation Group 559 to expand the military campaign into the region of Route Number 9 and southern Laos, in order to support the Pathet Lao in south Laos and Group 559 to the west of Truong Son.[40] Taking part in this operation were the 325th Infantry Division, the 19th battalion border defense troops in Military Region IV, the 927th Battalion from Ha Tinh Province, and the Pathet Lao forces. The campaign was under the command of the 325th Division and Group 559. The operation began on 11 April 1961, despite an appeal on 4 April by the Russians to the Vietnamese "to help create a favorable atmosphere for negotiations."[41]

However, this did not mean that the Vietnamese Communists had decided to launch a full-scale war in both South Vietnam and Laos. On 20 April 1961, Le Duan wrote another letter to the comrades in the South in which he once again emphasized the primary role of the political struggle and the supportive role of armed struggle in the current situation in the South. He reiterated the necessity of building up the armed forces. According to Le Duan, previous experience showed that uprisings would not be successful if the enemy's military was not defeated. He pointed out that the Diem regime had advocated an increase of 450,000 troops. However, he was certain that the Communists would finally defeat the Diem troops. At the same time, he cautioned against taking the enemy's strength lightly or despising the enemy. It is clear from Le Duan's letter that the North Vietnamese leadership did not expect an early or an easy victory. Le Duan stressed that the cadres must understand that the struggle would be long and difficult, and therefore everyone must be psychologically prepared for hardships and sacrifices in the process of liberating their country.[42]

III

While the military activities in Laos were going on, a Laotian delegation that included Souvanna Phouma, Souphanouvong, and Quinim Pholsena visited the Soviet Union (16-21 April), China (22-26 April) and Hanoi (26-28 April). The Russians impressed upon Souvanna Phouma that they sincerely desired a neutral Laos.[43] In Beijing on 23 April, the Laotian leaders had talks with Zhou Enlai "in a cordial and friendly atmosphere." It was revealed in the joint statement issued at the end of the visit that the subject of remnant KMT troops in the Sino-Laotian border areas was discussed and that both parties had agreed that the troops had to be cleared from Laotian territory. The Chinese also agreed to assist the Laotians to build a highway that would link their countries. Both countries also established formal diplomatic relations at the ambassadorial level.[44] Despite Gromyko's 19 April assurance to the British that there would be an immediate ceasefire,[45] on 23 April North Vietnamese–Pathet Lao troops captured Vang Vieng, which lay on the road connecting Vientiane and Luang Prabang. The Laotian delegation met Mao Zedong in Hangzhou on 24 April. From Hangzhou, the Laotians went to Kunming on 25 April before proceeding to Hanoi.

A secret document entitled "Several Important Problems Concerning the Current International Situation" issued with Issue Number 17 of the *Bulletin of Activities* on 25 April 1961 (for the study and reference of cadres at and above the regimental level) throws light on the thinking of the Chinese leadership with regard to their foreign policy during this period. The document raised the question of how China could solve world problems such as the issues of imperialism and decolonization, the question of disarmament, the ban on nuclear tests, East-West relations, and the reorganization of the United Nations. From the Chinese point of view, there were three possible ways. The first was by sharing the spoils. China would not accept this arrangement and was determined to object to it. China did not want "one inch of land from others." The second way was through peaceful coexistence. The present position was to stand firm against the United States and maintain peaceful coexistence with as many other countries as possible. The Chinese were pleased with their achievements in this respect, but the document went on to state that "peaceful coexistence is a transitional form; peaceful neutralism is also a transitional form, and sooner or later imperialism will conclude [sic] its life, and sooner or later Socialism will be realized throughout the world." The third way was to help increase the strength of the socialist camp and to develop and deepen national independence movements.

On the issue of national democratic revolutionary movement, the PLA document of 25 April discussed the situation in Africa, which it described as both the current center of the anticolonialist struggle and the East-West struggle for the control of an intermediary zone; and went on to the problems of the Congo, Cuba, and Laos. No mention was made of the North Vietnamese struggle.[46]

While the Laotian delegation was in Beijing, on 24 April the Geneva cochairmen finally issued a joint appeal for a ceasefire; they proposed that the Indian government convene the ISCC and announced that an international conference for settling the Laotian problem would be convened in Geneva on 12 May 1961. On the morning of 25 April, senior members of the ISCC for Laos who were in Moscow on their way to New Delhi and Indochina had a consultative meeting with officials of the Soviet Ministry of Foreign Affairs, presided over by Deputy Foreign Minister Georgi M. Pushkin. From the meeting, it was clear that the principal objective of the Russians was a political settlement to the Laotian problem. They feared that the conflict might escalate into a world war and were determined to avoid a military confrontation with the United States. To achieve this end, the Russians were prepared to make concessions in favor of the neutral elements in Laos at the expense of the left. They expected the new Geneva Conference to last no longer than six weeks. The ISCC was instructed by the cochairmen after arriving in Laos to contact all the parties and arrange an effective ceasefire, and to ensure that lines dividing the different groups were clearly fixed and controls instituted. The Russians did not invite representatives from Beijing, Hanoi, or the NLHX to this meeting. In fact, the Soviet government did not even hold preliminary discussions about the responsibilities of the ISCC with them.[47]

The Laotian delegation reached Hanoi on 26 April. That morning they met Ho Chi Minh. In the afternoon they had talks with Pham Van Dong "in an atmosphere of cordiality, friendship and mutual understanding." There was no report of their activities on 27 April. According to the joint communiqué issued at the end of the visit, Souvanna Phouma expressed understanding and support for the Vietnamese efforts to reunify their country. Pham Van Dong, in turn, stressed Hanoi's desire for a neutral and independent Laos. Both pledged to uphold the Five Principles of peaceful coexistence. Hanoi also agreed to help build and repair a number of communication lines in Laos, to train Laotian technicians, and to send specialists to Laos.[48]

On 27 and 28 April 1961, the British made two approaches to Gromyko, warning him that any further military moves by the Pathet Lao would endanger the chances of a conference and that an effective ceasefire should be arranged at once. The British further added that it was becoming hourly more difficult to avoid the impression that the delay was deliberate.[49] According to Kenneth T. Young, Kennedy used the ambassadorial channel in Warsaw to warn the Chinese that if a ceasefire did not precede the prospective Geneva Conference, the United States would be compelled to intervene militarily. Beijing replied that it was serious about wishing to negotiate and that it hoped that the Americans would cooperate in working out a satisfactory agreement for the neutralization of Laos.[50] The North Vietnamese–Pathet Lao operation in southern Laos that began on 11 April 1961 was successfully completed by 8:00 A.M. on 3 May 1961, the ceasefire deadline.

The ISCC arrived in Laos on 8 May 1961 and on 11 May reported to the cochairmen that there had been a general and demonstrable cessation of hostilities since the ceasefire order of 3 May 1961. By this time, the combined North Vietnamese–Pathet Lao forces were already in control of the provinces of Sam Neua, Phong Saly, Xieng Khouang, a large part of Luang Prabang, the strategic Plaine des Jarres, and Highways 7, 8, 9, and 12. The control of these highways was particularly important because it would safeguard the Truong Son Road and the activities of Transportation Group 559.[51] Highway 7 was the main supply route leading from North Vietnam, through the villages of Ban Ban and Khang Khay, to the Plaine des Jarres. Highway 9, just south of the 17th parallel, connected Savannakhet (where the Vietnamese set up a storage depot), through Tchepone, with Quang Tri Province. Any intention to build a land bridge through Laos linking Thailand and South Vietnam would require the use of this particular highway. According to Denis Warner: "Thanks to the lightning campaign before the ceasefire, the Pathet Lao in this region now holds all the interior trails and roads leading to South Vietnam and Cambodia. It would require a considerable military campaign to dislodge them, especially since the area is vital to the success of any uprising in South Vietnam."[52]

It is worth noting that in June 1961, a Soviet military mission led by General Antinov, the Soviet Army chief of general staff, was in Hanoi to study means of strengthening the DRV armed potential. One hundred new tanks were to be sent to the Vinh region, an airfield was also to be constructed there, and a subterranean depot was to be built in the Thanh Hoa sector to conceal armaments. The North Vietnamese had constructed a railway at Lao-Kay to allow the passage of Soviet war material into North Vietnam from China. These included tanks and MIGs, which were transported in component parts by night. Soviet specialists would then reassemble them in factories in the jungles of Thanh Hoa and Vinh. British sources also revealed that in July, a thousand Communist cadres from South Vietnam returned to the North. These cadres were to be to sent to the Soviet Union to undergo training in subversive warfare. At the same time, three thousand other cadres were to replace them in the South, passing through Laos.[53] On 27 July 1961, the Party Command and Command of Interzone V were formed; and the first main force regiment of the revolutionary armed forces, designated Q.761, was established in eastern Nam Bo.[54] It would appear that as long as the North Vietnamese did not aggravate the situation in Laos or allow their struggle to escalate into an international conflict, the Soviet Union was prepared to assist in the modernization of the VPA.

IV

On the eve of the Geneva Conference on Laos, Ho Chi Minh again took a vacation in China where he spent his 71st birthday. This was the second year in succession that he spent his birthday in China. He arrived in Guilin on 15 May by plane. Traveling with him on the same plane was He Wei. On that afternoon, he climbed the Diecai Shan (Folded Brocade Hill), sailed down the Li River, and visited the Rong Caves. On reaching the town of Yangshuo, Ho climbed the Wang Jiang Tower. The next day was spent sailing up the Li River back to Guilin. On 17 May, Ho went to Nanjing where he paid his respects at the Sun Yat Sen Memorial. From Nanjing he continued to Wuxi, north of Suzhou, to visit Taihu Lake. Ho's next stop was Hunan. There he visited Shaoshan village where Mao was born, Changsha, the Yuelu Hill, Aiwanting (Loving Dusk Pavilion), the Hunan Number One Teacher's Training School, which Mao attended between 1913 and 1918, and where he taught in 1920–21, sailed down the Xiang River, and visited Long Island or Long Sandbank situated in the middle of the Xiang River. During this trip to China, Ho visited all the places he had been during his younger revolutionary days.[55]

The International Conference on the Settlement of the Laotian Question began on 16 May 1961 and ended only on 23 July 1962. The conference dealt essentially with the international aspects of the Laotian problem. Running parallel to the conference in Geneva was a separate series of meetings and negotiations amongst the factions in Laos, represented by the three Laotian princes. Their task was to work out a compromise for a coalition government in the country. The Chinese delegation was headed by Chen Yi, China's deputy premier and foreign minister. The Soviet delegation was led by Deputy Foreign Minister Giorgi Pushkin. Unlike the Russians, who expected the conference to be over in about six weeks, the Chinese arrived in Geneva expecting a prolonged stay.[56]

The North Vietnamese delegation was led by Foreign Minister Ung Van Khiem; but the pro-Chinese Hoang Van Hoan, a veteran of the 1954 Geneva Conference, was the special adviser to the North Vietnamese government delegation.[57] Souvanna Phouma's Laotian government delegation was led by the neutralist, Quinim Pholsena, and the delegation of the NLHX was headed by Phoumi Vongvichit. Throughout the duration of the Geneva Conference, the Communist bloc presented a facade of complete solidarity.

While the Geneva Conference was going on, Khrushchev and Kennedy met in Vienna on 3–4 June 1961. We now know from the private discussions at Vienna that Khrushchev was keen on improving relations with the United States and wanted to avoid any international conflict. He was not very interested in Laos and told Kennedy that the Soviet Union had no desire to assume responsibilities in remote geographical areas such as Laos. Both Kennedy and Khrushchev agreed to prod their clients to cooperate with the commission policing the ceasefire. Khrushchev also pledged to do his utmost to influence the Laotian forces to establish a truly neutral government. At Vienna, Khrushchev and Kennedy did not discuss Vietnam.[58]

However, two days after the Vienna meeting, on 6 June 1961, the North Vietnamese–Pathet Lao forces captured Ban Padong, a base of the Royal Laotian Government situated a few miles southwest of Xieng Khouang. The North Vietnamese did not inform the Russians nor elicit their assistance in the battle at Ban Padong during May and early June 1961.[59] The non-Communist countries accused the Communists of breaking the ceasefire agreement and as a consequence of this attack, the Geneva Conference had to be adjourned; it resumed only on 12 June 1961. Souvanna Phouma and Souphanouvong, who were on their way to Geneva, arrived in Moscow from Beijing on the day that Ban Padong was captured. It was reported that they were received by Khrushchev in the Kremlin. Khrushchev would presumably have told them that Moscow supported a truly neutral Laos and wanted the Geneva Conference to succeed.

From the account by Marek Thee (the Polish representative on the ISCC) of a three-day visit to Hanoi from 9 to 11 June 1961, we have an idea of Hanoi's perception of the Laotian crisis during this period. Marek Thee had discussions with a number of North Vietnamese Foreign Ministry officials, with Vietnamese specializing in Laotian affairs, and most notably with Pham Hung, the acting prime minister and also a member of the politburo. (Thee did not provide the date for this meeting with Pham Hung, but it was most likely on 11 June when Prime Minister Pham Van Dong was leading a government delegation to China from 11 to 16 June.)

According to Pham Hung, Laos and Vietnam were bound together by fate. The current problem was not one of strategic planning but historical inevitability. The North Vietnamese saw the developments in Laos within the context of the developments in South Vietnam. To them, Indochina formed a unified strategic arena. In their assessment, the situation was fluid and the struggle was expected to be protracted. According to Thee, the Vietnamese on principle avoided linking the Laotian problem with East-West negotiations. They were determined that considerations other than those that were a direct consequence of the IndoChinese struggle should not be allowed to interfere with "local" strategy. Hanoi also suspected that the negotiations on Laos were meant to disguise the growing American intervention in South Vietnam. Thus any agreements reached at the Vienna summit meeting between Khrushchev and Kennedy on 3–4 June 1961 did not alter their own priorities. Nor should such agreements be allowed to hamper military operations such as the battle for Ban Padong, which was to protect their liberated areas.

Thee learned that Hanoi had very close contacts with the Pathet Lao and that strategic planning was a joint enterprise. The North Vietnamese bore the brunt of the struggle in Laos and they were involved in giving military support and economic and technical help, as well as political counsel. In Hanoi there was an interdepartmental body in constant touch with Laos. Hoang Van Hoan was from 1961 in charge of the secret CP38

Committee responsible for directing operations in Laos and Cambodia.[60] Apart from the publicly known economic and cultural representation, there was a confidential military aid committee responsible for channeling supplies and aid to Kong Lae's forces and the Pathet Lao. North Vietnam also provided the nucleus for assault units in the main battles and military staff officers assisted in military planning; for example, the battles at Tha Thom and the most recent at Ban Padong. About 20,000 Vietnamese were employed in Laos, cleaning and repairing roads and also as drivers. Between February and May 1961, because of the intensification of the fighting, the Vietnamese had lost some seven hundred dead and wounded soldiers and auxiliary personnel in Laos. Regarding the Sino-Soviet rift, the North Vietnamese avoided talking about the subject in public. But in private conversations, they admitted that the rift was detrimental to their struggle.[61]

Soon after the battle at Ban Padong, which almost led to a breakdown of the Geneva Conference, a DRV government delegation led by Pham Van Dong visited China from 11 to 16 June 1961, on the first leg of a tour to North Korea, Mongolia, the Soviet Union, Czechoslovakia, Poland, and Bulgaria.[62] The delegation included Deputy-Premier Le Thanh Nghi, Le Van Hien (vice-chairman of the State Planning Commission), Pham Binh (chief of the General Affairs Department of the Foreign Ministry), Hoang Bao Son (chief of the Asian Department of the Foreign Ministry), Nguyen Viet Dung (chief of the Protocol Department of the Foreign Ministry) and Phan Van Su (deputy chief of the Soviet Union and East European Department of the Foreign Ministry). They arrived in Wuhan on 11 June. Deputy Foreign Minister Luo Guibo (who was also the first Chinese ambassador to North Vietnam) had gone from Beijing to Wuhan to meet Pham Van Dong and accompany him to Beijing. The next afternoon, the delegation met Liu Shaoqi and had talks with Zhou Enlai, Li Fuchun, Luo Ruiqing, Luo Guibo, Fang Yi, and He Wei (the current Chinese ambassador to North Vietnam). This was followed by a reception given by Liu Shaoqi. The delegation also attended a banquet given by Zhou, a party given by the China-Vietnam Friendship Association and the Ministry of Culture, and saw a Beijing opera.[63] Pham Van Dong and Zhou Enlai had another meeting in the Diaoyutai Guesthouse on 13 June. We have no information of the delegation's activities on 14 June, but it was reported that Mao had a cordial and friendly talk with Pham Van Dong and the other Vietnamese delegates on the morning of 15 June, the last day of the visit. According to Chinese sources, during this meeting Mao expressed firm support for the armed struggle being waged in the South. Zhou Enlai said that the South must be liberated but the strategy must be flexible and take different forms. He again stressed the need to combine both political and military struggle, and the use of legal as well as nonlegal means of struggle. Pham Van Dong was of the same view.[64] On the afternoon of 15 June, the Vietnamese called at the China-Vietnam Friendship Association and attended a rally in the Great Hall of the People.

Before the farewell banquet, Zhou and Dong signed a joint communiqué stating that the two premiers "held intimate talks and reached complete identity of views on important international questions of common interest to the two countries and on the question of further consolidating and developing the friendship and cooperation between the two countries." Both premiers reiterated firm support for the liberation movement of the oppressed nations. Regarding Vietnam, Zhou Enlai stated that the Chinese government fully supported the DRV's opposition to U.S. interference and aggression and resolutely supported the peaceful unification of Vietnam. The communiqué further added that for the people in the southern part of Vietnam to struggle against U.S. aggression and the suppression and persecution by the Ngo Dinh Diem clique was their sacred right in striving for national liberation, democracy, and freedom.[65] Zhou invited the Vietnamese delegation to visit China again on their way back from Europe. From Beijing, the delegation proceeded to Pyongyang (16–22 June 1961), Ulan Bator (22–26 June 1961), and then to the Soviet Union (26 June–5 July 1961).

Pham Van Dong was thus in Moscow about three weeks after the Vienna meeting between Khrushchev and Kennedy. His delegation arrived in Irkutsk on 26 June and proceeded to Moscow where they met Khrushchev on 27 June. It was officially reported that they discussed the question of cooperation between the Soviet Union and North Vietnam and international questions of interest to both countries.[66] On the same day, Dong called on Leonid Brezhnev and attended a luncheon in his honor. On 28 June, there was a Soviet-Vietnam Friendship rally in the Kremlin. The Vietnamese delegation then visited Leningrad from 29 June to 1 July. Meanwhile, on 30 June, Souphanouvong arrived in Moscow from Geneva on his way back to Laos and was received by Khrushchev. It was reported that they had a "warm and friendly talk." He left Moscow for Beijing on 1 July.

On 3 July, another meeting took place in Moscow between Khrushchev and the Vietnamese delegation. We have no knowledge of what transpired at this meeting, but given what we now know of the conversations between Khrushchev and Kennedy in Vienna, it is very likely that Khrushchev made clear to Dong his views regarding Laos and the need to prevent the revolutionary struggle in Vietnam from escalating into a major war. They signed a joint communiqué on 4 July. In his farewell speech at the airport, Khrushchev said that they were very satisfied with the results of the talks and that basically the communiqué confirmed once more the unanimity of their views, both with regard to Soviet-Vietnamese relations and international problems.[67] But according to British sources, nothing conclusive seemed to have resulted from the visit; Pham Van Dong failed to spark Russian enthusiasm for Hanoi's stepped-up campaign against the "American-Diem authorities."[68] According to A. N. Abramov, the Soviet ambassador to Laos, Khrushchev's primary concern was to do everything possible to cement the alliance between the Pathet Lao and Souvanna Phouma to achieve a coalition government. Souphanouvong, while not in disagreement, was more hard line and less prepared to make concessions that disadvantaged the Pathet Lao. The North Vietnamese, on the other hand, were particularly concerned about South Vietnam and tended to ignore the international context.[69]

A week after Dong left the Soviet Union, on 12 July, another delegation from North Vietnam arrived in Moscow at the invitation of the CPSU Central Committee. This time it was the Lao Dong Party delegation led by Le Duc Tho, member of the political bureau and secretary of the Lao Dong Party Central Committee.[70] We do not have any information regarding this visit other than that its purpose was for the Vietnamese to acquaint themselves with the organizational work of the CPSU.[71]

After Moscow, Pham Van Dong and the Vietnamese delegation proceeded to Prague (5–17 July 1961) and Warsaw (17–23 July 1961). The last stop of the delegation was Sofia, but for reasons still unknown, Pham Van Dong did not go to Bulgaria: The Vietnamese delegation to Sofia was led by Le Thanh Nhgi.[72] A communiqué issued by the DRV Council of Ministers on 31 July 1961 stated that Dong's tour had ended successfully on 23 July 1961.[73]

Pham Van Dong was later reported to have returned to the Soviet Union sometime at the end of July for a vacation and stayed till 12 August. He was reported as being received by Khrushchev on 27 July at Sochi, where they both had a friendly conversation. Khrushchev also gave a dinner in honor of Pham Van Dong.[74] The previous meeting between Khrushchev and Pham Van Dong had been exactly a month before, on 27 June. In the interval, the Russians had become deeply concerned about developments in NATO and Berlin. Speaking at a Kremlin reception for graduates of Soviet military academies on 8 July 1961, Khrushchev announced that the Soviet government had decided to suspend its unilateral reduction of armed forces and would increase defense expenditure in the current year in response to the growing military budgets in the NATO countries. On 25 July, Kennedy in a televised address reaffirmed the rights of the Western allies to be in Berlin and announced that the United States was taking steps to prevent the Communists from driving the Western allies out of Berlin either gradually or by force. What followed was a mass exodus of East German refugees seeking asylum in West Berlin. Two days after Kennedy's televised address, he met Pham Van Dong. Robert M. Slusser in his 1973 study of the Berlin Crisis suggested that after Kennedy's announcement, Khrushchev decided to encourage the struggle in South Vietnam by increasing Soviet aid to North Vietnam.[75] We now know from declassified U.S. material that Khrushchev was "very upset" by Kennedy's speech because he regarded it as an "ultimatum"[76]; but Slusser's hypothesis still cannot be validated.

The day after Dong left Moscow, on 13 August, the East German authorities sealed off the border between East and West Berlin, and began erecting a barbed-wire barrier, the precursor of the Berlin Wall. Thus, from July until September 1962, when both Khrushchev and Kennedy took steps to move back toward negotiations, Moscow and Washington were more concerned about Berlin than Indochina.[77] According to Cyrus L. Sulzberger, who was then Paris correspondent of the *New York Times*, on 5 September 1961 Khrushchev had asked him to convey a message to Kennedy proposing direct contact with the president to resolve the Berlin issue. Khrushchev was of the view that a settlement of the Laotian issue would appeal to Kennedy and thus improve the atmosphere for Berlin.[78]

Meanwhile, Souphanouvong was in Beijing from 2 to 6 July. He met Zhou on the night of 3 July in the Diaoyutai Guesthouse. During the meeting, Zhou expressed the view that the Geneva Conference was unlikely to break down, because the Americans did not want that to happen.[79] After Beijing, Souphanouvong flew to Hanoi. On 7 July, Hoang Van Hoan, special adviser of the North Vietnamese delegation to the Geneva Conference, and Chen Yi arrived back in Beijing from Geneva. The next day Hoan attended a Foreign Ministry reception where Zhou was present, and on the morning of 8 July, there was a meeting between Zhou and Hoang Van Hoan regarding Laos.[80] Hoan left Beijing for home on 11 July; it was subsequently reported that he returned to Geneva on 2 August, presumably by way of Beijing.[81] We now know that on 5 August

1961, he and Kaysone Phomvihane met Zhou in Zhongnanhai. During the meeting, Zhou told them that victory must depend on the strength of the masses: foreign assistance was secondary. Laos had the advantage of being situated near China and North Vietnam, and therefore could depend on both countries for some assistance; but ultimately, as in China's own experience, the Laotians must depend on themselves.[82]

Pham Van Dong was back in Beijing on 12 August 1961 and on the same day had a meeting with Zhou regarding Laos. It was reported that Dong visited the Ming Tombs outside Beijing on 15 August and that he left Beijing for Kunming the next day. Dong spent a day at Xian before reaching Kunming, where he stayed till his return to Hanoi on 21 August. Meanwhile, Le Thanh Nghi, the DRV deputy-premier and a member of the DRV government delegation that had arrived in Beijing before Dong, left for home on 15 August. On 20 August, Ung Van Khiem, foreign minister and formal leader of the North Vietnamese delegation to the Geneva Conference, arrived in Beijing from Moscow and met Zhou Enlai on 21 August before returning to Hanoi on 23 August. From 25 to 27 August, Souvanna Phouma paid an unofficial visit to Hanoi.[83]

The situation in Laos was still rather precarious during this period. Progress at the Geneva Conference was slow and the ongoing negotiations amongst the three Laotian factions in Ban Na Mon were ineffectual. The possibility of renewed fighting could not be discounted. In 1979 and again in 1984, the North Vietnamese disclosed that in August 1961, the Chinese had advised them that the greatest care must be taken to avoid being directly involved in the war in Laos. They also warned of the possibility of U.S. military involvement and its consequences for North Vietnam, Yunnan, and Guangxi. The Vietnamese also claimed that Beijing advocated partitioning Laos horizontally into two zones: a north zone situated along China's southern border that would be controlled by the revolutionary forces; and a south zone controlled by the Phoumi Nosavan faction. To the Vietnamese, the Chinese proposal was aimed at securing the Laotian revolutionary forces' dependence on China and ensuring their own security, while isolating the revolution in South Vietnam. The Laotian revolutionary forces, however, proposed an east zone and a west zone, centered respectively along the Mekong River and the IndoChinese cordillera. The revolutionary forces would control the east zone, which would run north to south and serve as a corridor linking North and South Vietnam through Laos. This was the existing ceasefire line. An east-west division would benefit the revolution in Vietnam.[84]

If this account is true, it would support Malcolm MacDonald's observation that for the first several months of the Geneva Conference, the Chinese were not so keen for an agreement establishing a neutral Laos but gradually became more supportive of it.[85] We do not know exactly when the Chinese changed their minds. It is plausible that their failure to reach an agreement with Hanoi regarding the division of Laos in August 1961 could have led Beijing to reconsider their strategy. As for the North Vietnamese, MacDonald believed that they never wanted an agreement but were compelled by the Russians and the Chinese to accept the neutrality of Laos. (In 1968, Averell Harriman asked the North Vietnamese why they did not honor the 1962 Geneva Agreement regarding Laos. The Vietnamese reply was that they would respect any agreement that they reached voluntarily, but not one that was "forced down our throats by the Russians."[86]) The British officials at Geneva reported that in the last week of August 1961, there were the first signs that the Communist countries might be ready to negotiate seriously with the non-Communist delegation.[87]

At the beginning of September, the Central Committee of the CPSU sent to its Chinese and Vietnamese counterparts a detailed memorandum on the Laotian problem. The memorandum stressed that political errors had been committed, particularly in the alliance between the Pathet Lao and the Neutralists. According to the Russians, Souvanna Phouma and the Neutralists had received inadequate support, thereby causing a weakening in the alliance. The Russians also expressed their dissatisfaction with Hanoi's handling of Soviet aid to Laos: for example, out of 23,000 tons of gasoline delivered by the Soviet Union to Hanoi for Laos, only 990 tons had so far reached the gasoline-starved country. Last but not least, the Russians were impatient with the slow pace of the NLHX's move toward agreement for a coalition government. The Soviet Union wanted a neutral Laos as quickly as possible.[88]

Following the Soviet memorandum, a consultative conference that included representatives from China, the Soviet Union, North Vietnam, and the NLHX was held in Hanoi to iron out the differences. The conference decided that all aid to Laos would continue to be supplied through Hanoi. Hanoi, in turn, would improve on its management of the aid. Quotas were established for both the Neutralists and the NLHX. As for speeding up the agreement to form a coalition government, which the Russians were pushing hard for, the response was lukewarm. The NLHX was fearful, in the words of Marek Thee, "of being unable to cope with the exigencies of a leading role in a sustained alliance with the Neutralists."[89]

In a meeting on 14 September between Soviet Deputy Foreign

Minister Giorgi Pushkin and Averell Harriman, the head of the U.S. delegation at Geneva, Pushkin said that the Soviet Union wanted a truly independent Laos and was ready to come to an agreement that would not only assure the establishment of a really neutral government under Souvanna Phouma, similar to that of Finland, but also ensure the maintenance of the neutral regime. This was regardless of any developments in Berlin. Pushkin added that the Soviet Union would control the North Vietnamese and would support Souvanna Phouma against any political or military aggression from the Pathet Lao. In reply to Harriman's query on how long the neutral regime would be expected to last, Pushkin said that it would be longer than five years and that Laos would be the last country to become Communist. Pushkin also offered to bring Harriman's delegation together with Phoumi Vongvichit in order to talk over Pathet Lao policies. When Harriman emphasized that both the Pathet Lao and Phoumi Nosavan must be compelled to be loyal to the neutral government under Souvanna Phouma, Pushkin was in full agreement.[90]

During a conversation on 7 September 1961 between the British charge d'affaires in Beijing, Michael Stewart, and Chen Yi, the latter said that Laos should be a buffer state like Cambodia, and should be neither a Communist nor an American base. It was therefore inconceivable that either Phoumi Nosavan or Souphanouvong could be prime minister of Laos. The only possibility was Souvanna Phouma.[91]

In conversations in Rangoon on 15 and 16 September 1961, when Harriman briefed Souvanna Phouma about his meeting with Pushkin, Souvanna Phouma said that he would not have depended on the Soviet Union and China if he had not believed that they were sincere in desiring a neutral Laos. Souvanna Phouma was confident that the North Vietnamese could be controlled once a neutral government was formed.[92]

According to Souvanna Phouma's chef de cabinet, Khamchan Pradith, in a conversation with M. Brown (first secretary, head of British chancery, and consul, Laos) in Khang Khay on 23 October 1961, both the Russians and the Chinese wanted a settlement in Laos; but not the North Vietnamese, who had their own reasons for keeping Laos in turmoil. South Vietnam was cited as the reason.[93] Arthur Lall, head of the Indian delegation at the Geneva Conference, in his informal conversations with the Laotian and Chinese delegates at Geneva, formed the impression that the Chinese were sensitive to the Laotian desire for independence. Thus they refrained from sending in Chinese forces because that would only result in a loss of face and influence for China in Laos. He was of the view that both the United States and the Chinese, though looking at the Laotian problem from very different points of view, demonstrated a continuing will to reach agreement.[94]

Meanwhile, according to U.S. intelligence, Pathet Lao and North Vietnamese forces already controlled most of southern Laos, except for towns along the Mekong. And in South Vietnam, a major Hanoi-directed Communist offensive against the Diem regime was under way.[95] According to British intelligence reports, there were grounds for believing that the attacks since early September 1961 in the Pleiku and Kontum areas were carried out by forces from across the North Vietnam–Laotian border. The Vietnamese Communists appeared to be concentrating more forces in the Central Highlands, to which the easiest supply routes run through southern Laos. Movement of the Communist forces to this area from the South were observed in August 1961. The South Vietnamese authorities were of the view that the objective of the Vietnamese Communists was to establish sufficient control in the area of the Central Highlands to enable them to set up a government that could receive aid from the North.[96]

Sometime in October 1961, the Nam Bo Central Committee held an enlarged conference to assess the current struggle against the Diem regime and to spell out the tasks ahead.[97] The conference affirmed the primary importance of the political struggle and the supportive role of armed struggle. It was recognized that the process of advance toward the general uprising required pushing armed struggle to an equal level with political struggle. However, they were acutely concerned that in the process of building up to a general uprising, they must avoid a full-scale war. They were well aware that the enemy still had strong military forces and despite Communist successes, they still did not have the advantage over the Diem regime. The possibility of a full-scale war could come about in two ways: It could be brought about either by the United States, in its efforts to thwart the political struggle, or when the Communist party "strayed from the path leading to the general uprising." This was seen to be a crucial stage in the struggle against the Diem regime because the leadership would need to decide on the correct balance between armed and political struggle. The decision was that political struggle would persist while armed struggle would be increased till it was equal with the political struggle. The pace would depend on the circumstances and the relationship of forces in the different regions. It was proposed that in the plains, political and military struggle could be of the same proportion while in the cities, political struggle was to continue. However, in the mountainous region, military struggle would be primary. The objective was to annihilate the enemy there so that they could expand their base areas. Laos would therefore be an important strategic zone.

Ten

October 1961–July 1962

I

On 11 October, President Kennedy in a news conference in Washington announced that he was sending General Maxwell Taylor to Saigon that week to discuss with Ngo Dinh Diem and American officials on the spot how the United States could better assist South Vietnam against the Communist threat.[1] The announcement added fuel to the prevailing rumor that Diem had written to Kennedy to request American combat troops. Taylor and Walt Rostow, a key foreign and defense adviser to the White House, visited South Vietnam from 18 to 24 October 1961.[2] According to Arthur M. Schlesinger, Jr., the composition of the mission, which was headed by a general and a White House aide and which did not include any high-ranking State Department representative, signified a shift in Washington's perspective of the Vietnam problem from a political to a military one.[3] Thereafter, "the projected American solution (to the Vietnam problem) in 1961–1963 was increasingly framed in military terms."[4]

The mission took place at a time when the Geneva Conference was within sight of an international agreement.[5] During the 40th Restricted Session of the Geneva Conference on 1 November 1961, Chang Hanfu—referring to the visit of General Maxwell Taylor to South Vietnam—claimed that developments in South Vietnam were bound to affect Laos. He accused the United States of ignoring international agreements by sending military personnel into South Vietnam. Chang posed the question: "If the U.S. was allowed to tear up the international agreements on

Vietnam and disregard the international machinery with them, of what use is it for the fourteen countries now gathered in Geneva to reach another international agreement on the Laotian question?" Harriman in turn declared that the Chinese delegate was out of order for raising the subject of South Vietnam at the Laos Conference.[6]

When Kennedy made his announcement, Ho Chi Minh was in Beijing. Ho, accompanied by Le Duan and Xuan Thuy, had arrived in Beijing on 10 October on their way to Moscow to attend the 22nd Congress of the CPSU. We have no information about Vietnamese activities in Beijing on this occasion except that Ho Chi Minh and Le Duan had a "cordial" meeting with Mao, Liu Shaoqi, Zhou Enlai, Zhu De, Chen Yun, Deng Xiaoping, and Peng Zhen on 12 October. This was followed by a banquet.[7] We do not know what was discussed, but it is likely that one topic concerned the implications of the impending visit of General Maxwell Taylor to Saigon. They left for Moscow on the morning of 14 October.

The 22nd Congress of the CPSU took place from 17 to 31 October 1961. At the Congress, Khrushchev denounced Albania as the bastion of Stalinism and for opposing the anti–Stalinist policies that the Soviet Union had initiated since 1956. In a speech on the evening of 19 October, Zhou made clear the Chinese view that any quarrels within the socialist camp should be settled bilaterally and a public denunciation would not contribute to the cohesion of the socialist bloc. China also disagreed with the program spelled out by Khrushchev at the congress, which ran counter to the 1957 Declaration and 1960 Statement on many important questions of principle.[8] Zhou had talks with Khrushchev and other Soviet leaders on 22 October in an attempt to resolve their differences, but they were in vain. The next day, 23 October, before the congress closed, Zhou Enlai returned to Beijing and was warmly welcomed at Beijing airport by Mao personally. After Zhou's departure, the Chinese delegation left Moscow to tour Leningrad and did not return until 31 October, the final day of the congress.

Meanwhile, in his speech on the morning of 21 October, Ho Chi Minh made no reference to the Albanian question. Both he and Le Duan also went on a tour to Estonia (22–23 October), Latvia (24–26 October), and they were reported to be in Lithuania on 27 October.[9] The Soviet Union broke off diplomatic relations with Albania in December 1961. Neither China nor North Vietnam followed suit. The Taylor mission to Saigon thus also coincided with a very tense period in the Communist camp.

Le Duan and Xuan Thuy returned to Beijing on 3 November on their way home from the 22nd CPSU Congress and remained in China until 7 November before returning to Hanoi. Of their activities in Beijing, we know only that they met Zhou and Deng Xiaoping on 6 November.[10] It is very likely that they would have discussed with the Chinese the implications of the Taylor mission to South Vietnam and Hanoi's attitude toward the Sino-Soviet disagreements.

Also on 7 November, the Hanoi papers published appreciations of the "great and far-reaching changes in the Soviet Union over the past 44 years" and praised the new CPSU program spelled out at the congress just ended. The front pages of the newspapers all carried photographs of Khrushchev and Brezhnev. *Nhan Dan* reproduced an article written for *Pravda* by Ho Chi Minh in which he expressed his "firm belief that under the leadership of the glorious CPSU headed by Comrade Khrushchev, the valiant Soviet people will succeed in building Communism."[11]

Meanwhile, Ho Chi Minh had remained in the Soviet Union. He attended a Kremlin reception on the night of 7 November[12] and was received by Khrushchev on 9 November.[13] About a month ago at the meeting at Ban Hin Heup on 8 October, the three Laotian princes had agreed that Souvanna Phouma would be the prime minister of a provisional coalition government, but they failed to reach agreement on the actual composition of the government. Since then there were no further meetings because the three princes could not agree on a venue. At the Kremlin reception on the night of 7 November, Ho reportedly told the Canadian ambassador to the Soviet Union that the prospects at Geneva seemed good, if the three Laotian princes could be brought to complete their recent agreement.[14] (This was also the view of MacDonald and Harriman.[15]) Then on 11 November 1961, just as Ho ended his stay in the Soviet Union, Souphanouvong, in an attempt to force Boum Oum and Phoumi Nosavan back to the negotiating table, suddenly compromised on the conditions for a coalition government and agreed to accept Vientiane, the headquarters of Phoumi Nosavan, as the meeting place. This news was welcomed by Moscow and initially by Hanoi as well.

Ho Chi Minh arrived back in Beijing on 12 November. On 14 November, he had a meeting with Mao, Liu Shaoqi, Zhou Enlai, and Deng Xiaoping. Whereas the Taylor mission had increased the Russian desire for a quick solution to the Laotian problem so as to avoid a confrontation with the United States, it hardened the Chinese attitude as they prepared for a protracted struggle.[16] According to Averell Harriman, Pushkin had agreed that the Russians would assume the responsibility of ensuring that the Communist bloc comply with the Geneva Agreements when they were in place; and that corridor traffic through Laos to South Vietnam would not be permitted.[17] Beijing, on the other hand, was of the view that Souphanouvong should not make any compromises. He Wei, the Chinese ambassador to Hanoi, visited Khang Khay from 14 to 17 November,[18] to argue that the concessions would undermine the gains achieved so far in the negotiations. Besides, having a meeting in Vientiane was a security risk for Souvanna Phouma and Souphanouvong. But the main reason for the Chinese opposition was the continued presence of the Americans in Laos. The Chinese believed that the United States aimed to partition Laos so that it could turn southern Laos into a bridgehead linking South Vietnam and Thailand.[19] The editorial in the *Ta Kung Pao* of 15 November stated that the activities of the United States in South Vietnam were closely related to its plan for military intervention in Laos. South Vietnam served as a springboard for its intervention in Laos. The Chinese were therefore seriously concerned over the extension of U.S. intervention in South Vietnam.[20]

Ho Chi Minh was in China till 16 November before returning to Hanoi. He Wei returned to Hanoi from Khang Khay the day after Ho's return. Soon after He Wei's visit to Khang Khay, the NLHX reversed its previous concession, stating that the time was not ripe for a coalition government and that they would be prepared to meet in Vientiane only when they were satisfied with the security arrangements. Hanoi also changed its position. Sometime between 21 and 24 November, Pham Van Thuyen, chief of North Vietnam's Economic and Cultural Mission to Laos, told Marek Thee that the balance of forces at that time "did not favor a conclusion of the negotiations" and that "only a demonstration of military supremacy could break the deadlock." In this new turn of events, Marek Thee recognized He Wei's line of thinking. But Thee subsequently realized that the situation was more complicated. After a series of discussions in Khang Khay from 21 to 24 November, Thee discovered that there were subtle differences between the perceptions of the Chinese, North Vietnamese, and NLHX. According to Thee, the Chinese were of the view that a new military operation might be unavoidable and was perhaps desirable. The North Vietnamese preferred a status quo, which meant neither a coalition government nor another military operation. As for the NLHX, they thought that they could consolidate and strengthen both their political and military gains achieved so far. Souvanna Phouma, however, was convinced that only military pressure could compel the Boun Oum–Nosavan clique to negotiate. Thee also disclosed that it was after this rift with the Chinese, the Vietnamese, and the Laotians that the Soviet Union decided on a gradual disengagement from Laos.[21]

On 29 November the Chinese Foreign Ministry issued a statement asking all the countries that participated in the 1954 Geneva Conference and all other concerned countries to "pay attention to the grave activities of the U.S. violating the Geneva Agreements and threatening peace." It also called upon the cochairmen of the 1954 Geneva Conference and the ISCC in Vietnam to take measures to check U.S. aggression.[22]

Meanwhile, the Geneva Conference was making progress. On 25 November, there were eight items left on the conference agenda; and by 2 December, only four items remained to be resolved.[23] On 1 December the Chinese seemed to change their mind and assented to the three Laotian princes meeting in Vientiane, the venue which they had previously rejected. When Marek Thee arrived in Khang Khay on the same day, he found the Laotians, Vietnamese, and Chinese all in agreement for a meeting in Vientiane. It was to be a test of U.S.–Vientiane intentions. The meeting of the Laotian princes was eventually scheduled for 27 December 1961.[24]

At a lunch with Marek Thee on 9 December, Nguyen Chinh Giao, chief of the Laos desk in the Central Committee of the Lao Dong Party, revealed that Hanoi's position regarding Laos was closer to that of Beijing than that of the Soviet Union. Beijing insisted that in any coalition government, the NLHX-Neutralists must retain two-thirds of the portfolios. The Soviet Union was prepared for larger concessions. Both Hanoi and Beijing felt that in view of the Vientiane–Thai schemes to preserve Vientiane's military strength, the NLHX must also preserve its own military strength. The Soviet Union advocated immediate unification of the armed forces. Hanoi was apprehensive that Souvanna Phouma might swing to the right; the Soviet Union argued that he should be trusted. Hanoi was also very concerned about the transport difficulties created by the partial withdrawal of Soviet airplanes and the reduction of Soviet aid. The Soviet Union had ceased air deliveries to Tchepone sometime in November-December because it suspected that the North Vietnamese were using the deliveries to support their struggle in South Vietnam, rather than the intended purpose of serving the Laotian units in south Laos.[25]

By 18 December, there were only two items left on the Geneva Conference agenda, namely (a) SEATO protection of Laos and (b) the integration of the Pathet Lao forces in the Laotian Army, which could only be resolved when there was a united Laotian delegation representing a government of national unity in Laos. Both China and North Vietnam called for the complete abolition of SEATO. The Soviet Union was adamant only about the abolition of SEATO protection over Laos. The pivotal issue was the formation of a coalition government. Without a coalition government, neither of the above two items nor the agreements reached at Geneva so far could be finalized. [26]

II

Meanwhile, in Hanoi, the 6th Plenary Session of the Lao Dong Party Central Committee took place between 30 November and 2 December 1961 to hear Ho Chi Minh's report on the recent 22nd CPSU Congress. [27] It was very likely that Laos and the Taylor mission, as well as the Sino-Soviet rift and its implications for the Vietnamese Communist struggle, were also discussed. According to Marek Thee, sometime in early December 1961 the North Vietnamese Politburo met to discuss the Laotian problem. Subsequently, the Polish commissioner residing in Vientiane, Albert Morski, and Marek Thee were invited to Hanoi for a discussion on 16 December.

Not long after the 6th Plenary Session, the *NCNA* and *Beijing Home Service* reported that a Chinese military delegation led by Marshal Ye Jianying would be paying a visit to North Vietnam on the invitation of Vo Nguyen Giap. It was further reported that on 6 December, the delegation attended a banquet given by the Vietnamese charge d'affaires in Beijing. [28] On 8 December, a DRV National Defense Ministry communiqué issued a similar statement, adding that the visit was to coincide with the 17th anniversary of the VPA on 22 December 1961.

Sino-Vietnamese relations in 1961 thus culminated in the visit of the most high-powered military delegation to North Vietnam to date. [29] Four days before the visit, on 11 December 1961, two American helicopter companies landed in Saigon, accompanied by 400 American troops. On 15 December, the Chinese military goodwill mission led by Marshal Ye Jiangying (inspector-general, PLA) arrived in Hanoi. The mission included: Generals Liu Yalou (commander, Chinese Air Force), Xiao Hua (deputy-director, PLA Political Department; director of personnel), Yang Chengwu (deputy-chief of general staff), Huang Yongsheng; Lt. General Xiao Xiangyong (director, General Office of the Ministry of Defense); Vice-Admiral Wu Ruilin; Major General Lei Yingfu, and Senior Colonel Liu Zhongkui. The Vietnamese welcoming party included General Vo

Nguyen Giap, Col. General Van Tien Dung, Maj. Generals Song Hao, Hoang Van Thai, and Tran Van Tra; Brigadier-Generals Tran Quy Hai and Pham Kiet; Deputy Minister of Foreign Affairs Hoang Van Tien; and Tran Duy Hung, Mayor of Hanoi. That evening, in both their banquet speeches, Giap and Ye spoke of the fraternal closeness of China and Vietnam, which was as "close as lips and teeth, sharing the same weal and woe." They also highlighted the close ties between the PLA and the VPA.

The arrival of the Chinese military delegation coincided with the revelation of an exchange of letters between Kennedy and Ngo Dinh Diem on the same day. In his letter, Kennedy agreed with Diem that the current campaign of force and terror waged against the South Vietnamese government was supported and directed by Hanoi. The letter also stated that the United States would immediately increase its assistance to defend South Vietnam. According to Kennedy, he had already given orders to get the programs under way.[30]

The next day, on 16 December, a VPA spokesman was reported by *VNA* to have said that the situation in South Vietnam had become "more serious than ever owing to the U.S.'s first step of armed aggression."[31] On the same day, the military goodwill mission met Ho Chi Minh and Pham Van Dong. They also visited the Vietnamese Revolutionary Museum and in the evening attended a dinner hosted by Ho.

Also on 16 December, Polish Commissioner Albert Morski and Marek Thee were in Hanoi for a discussion with the North Vietnamese. Foreign Minister Ung Van Khiem summed up succinctly Hanoi's perception of the situation. The North Vietnamese believed that the international climate at the time favored a political settlement rather than a renewal of the fighting. However, the balance of forces in Laos was still uncertain, and had not tipped decisively in favor of the NLHX-Neutralists. The intention of the United States was a key factor. Hanoi was of the view that the U.S. opposed a compromise solution and that the United States intended to reassert its dominance in Laos.[32]

We have no knowledge of the activities of the Chinese delegation on 17 December. But on 18 December the delegation, accompanied by Maj. General Tran Van Tra, visited an artillery officer's school. On the same day the military delegation traveled to Nghe An on a visit to the 4th Military Region of the VPA. They stayed in Nghe An from 18 to 20 December. The delegation attended a welcome banquet hosted by the 4th Military Region on 19 December at which Ye Jianying stated that "the U.S. imperialist intervention in and aggression against South Vietnam have become extremely serious" and "the Chinese people would never be indifferent to this adventurist action."[33] They also visited places of historic interest such as Ho Chi Minh's native village, Nam Lien, and attended a performance given by an ensemble of the 5th Interzone. On 20 December they flew back to Hanoi where they attended a program of songs and dances presented by an art ensemble of the General Political Department of the VPA. There was again no report of their activities on 21 December.

The next day, 22 December, was the 17th Anniversary of the VPA. It is notable that the Soviet minister of defense did not send a message on this occasion, as was customary. Ye Jianying, in his personal capacity and on behalf of his four sons, presented Ho with a mottled bamboo fan made during the Ming Dynasty. The military delegation visited a VPA unit on that day and attended the anniversary reception in the evening at which Ho, Pham Van Dong, Truong Chinh, and Le Duan were also present. General Xiao Hua visited the General Political Department on 23 December and again on 24 December. Also on 24 December, General Yang Chengwu, Major-General Lei Yingfu, and Senior-Colonel Liu Zhongkui met Col. General Van Tien Dung. That evening, the delegation was entertained to a "big banquet" by Major-General Bang Giang.[34] On the 25th, the delegation visited Dien Bien Phu, after which they proceeded to Haiphong where they were joined by Vo Nguyen Giap. That evening, they attended a banquet in their honor hosted by the Cholon Military Region of the VPA. On 26 December, they visited the Hon Quang coal basin, a PAVN naval unit, and the Cuc Tho coal mine.

The meeting of the Laotian princes that was scheduled to take place in Vientiane on 27 December failed to materialize because of the intransigence of Boun Oum and Phoumi Nosavan, which meant that a government of national unity could still not be formed and the new Geneva Agreement could not be signed. We should recall that Hanoi and Beijing regarded this meeting as a test of U.S.–Vientiane intentions. The situation in Laos therefore remained uncertain and dangerous. It is notable that we have no information about the activities of the Chinese military delegation on 27 and 28 December.

The next report we have of the delegation's activities is the reception given by He Wei on the evening of 29 December. On 30 December, the Central Committee of the Lao Dong Party received the Chinese military delegation. From the report, it appeared that every member of the Party Central Committee was present except Pham Van Dong and Le Duan. The reception was reported to have proceeded in an atmosphere of extreme cordiality. A farewell reception was held on the same evening.

The Chinese military goodwill mission left Hanoi for Canton on 31 December 1961 after spending two weeks in North Vietnam. In a farewell speech, Giap said that the mission's visit had provided a powerful stimulus to the Vietnamese people's struggle to build socialism and to reunify the country peacefully. Marshal Ye, in his reply, declared that the visit had once again vividly demonstrated that the profound friendship between the Chinese and Vietnamese peoples and armies, based on victorious Marxism-Leninism and proletarian internationalism, was unbreakable, and that they were united by a common ideal and a common cause.

It is reasonable to think that such a high-powered visit must have more important designs than just strengthening goodwill. According to Bui Tin, during the visit the Chinese advocated guerrilla warfare in the mountains and suggested that the southern Communists should fight only at section or company level in order not to provoke American counterattack.[35] Unfortunately, there is not much more that we know. It has been suggested that the visit was a riposte to that of General Maxwell Taylor to South Vietnam in October 1961 and the increased United States buildup in the South. Although Kennedy had not (yet) endorsed Taylor's recommendation of sending ground troops to South Vietnam, by the end of 1961 the strength of the Military Assistance Advisory Group (MAAG) in South Vietnam was three times the number allowed for in the 1954 Geneva Agreements.[36] Given the acute concern of both China and North Vietnam about the military activities of the United States in South Vietnam during this period and the aborted 27 December 1961 meeting of the Laotian princes, it was highly likely that there were discussions on contingency plans in the event of any threat from the United States. One Chinese source disclosed that after the visit of the military delegation, a meeting took place between the Chinese and North Vietnamese leaders in early 1962 regarding Chinese military assistance for the struggle in the South.[37]

One point that we can be certain of is that the visit did not lead to any Sino-Vietnamese military alliance to the exclusion of the Soviet Union. An editorial in the *Quan Doi Nhan Dan* of 3 January 1962 hailed the recent visit as a "brilliant success" and a contribution to the "brotherly solidarity among countries of the socialist camp with the great Soviet Union as center."[38] According to another Chinese source, apart from their difference with the Vietnamese over the handling of the 1956 agrarian debacle, the other significant point of divergence between them before 1965 was the unwillingness of the Vietnamese Communists to join them in denouncing the Soviet Union for deviating from Marxism.[39] North

Vietnam tried its utmost not to get involved in the Sino-Soviet dispute.[40] In January 1962, the Central Committee of the Lao Dong Party sent letters to a number of fraternal parties expressing its concern over the Sino-Soviet differences. The Vietnamese Communists proposed that a meeting be convened among the representatives of Communist and workers' parties to settle their differences and that pending such a meeting, the parties should cease criticizing one another in the mass media.[41]

French Soviet specialists in the Direction d'Europe at the Quai d'Orsay were of the view that since the 22nd CPSU Congress (17–31 October 1961), the North Vietnamese had moved completely into the Chinese fold. The Direction d'Asie of the Quai d'Orsay also noticed a considerable swing toward China in late 1961, but it thought that the North Vietnamese would be very reluctant to provoke the Russians to the point where the latter cut off economic aid.[42] Indeed, on 30 December, an agreement on Soviet loans to North Vietnam involving 3.5 billion rubles for the purchase of Soviet goods was signed in Hanoi between Nguyen Duy Trinh and the Soviet ambassador. It was further reported that the Vietnamese-Soviet Commission for Scientific and Technical Cooperation had recently worked out a joint plan for the first half of 1962, under which the Russians would supply North Vietnam with technical documents on construction, foundries, electrical appliances, forestry, and other areas. In return, the North Vietnamese would assist the Soviet Union in its study of the use of equipment under tropical conditions.[43]

A protocol for commodity exchange and payments for 1962 between China and North Vietnam was signed on 20 January 1962 whereby both countries would do their utmost to provide each other with the commodities needed by their national economies. China would provide the Vietnamese with rolled steel, lead, zinc, coke, soft coal, machinery, machine parts, medicine, cotton, and other raw materials. The Vietnamese would supply China with hard coal, cement, timber, chromate, jute, peanuts, and marine and agricultural products. The signing of the protocol was well publicized in both the Vietnamese and Chinese newspapers.[44] However, as a consequence of the Chinese economic difficulties, China's aid to North Vietnam in 1962 inevitably fell short of its promises and Soviet aid surpassed it.[45]

British officials in Beijing reported that the Chinese internal situation at the end of 1961 was very bad. For the third consecutive year, China had been afflicted with drought and floods. A series of bad agricultural years had not only raised the question of how to feed the population but also crippled a great part of China's light industry, hit nearly three-quarters of its export potential, and seriously affected its foreign exchange earnings. [46] The first six months of 1962 saw little change in the economic situation. Fears for the 1962 harvest were uppermost in all minds. [47] From 11 January to 7 February 1962, the CCP Central Committee held an enlarged working conference in Beijing to discuss the economy. Over 7,000 people attended. According to Liu Shaoqi in his report, 1962 was to be "the most crucial year for readjustment of the national economy," and everyone was exhorted to make the best use of the year. [48] Right through 1962, there were meetings practically every month dealing with the economy.

III

Meanwhile, in South Vietnam, British officials reported that by the end of 1961 it was no longer safe to travel even by day anywhere outside the immediate vicinity of the large towns. By night the dangers were greatly increased. This was especially so in the areas in the Central Highlands where there was a marked increase in Communist strength. Although the Communists were still not strong enough to hold any towns in the area or to make raids to the coast, they had tightened their hold in a number of areas to the north and northeast of Saigon. In these areas, they had established base areas for supplies, training, and even light arms production. The security situation also worsened perceptibly in the Mekong Delta. [49]

On 8 February 1962 the U.S. Military Assistance Command, Vietnam (MACV) was set up in Saigon under General Paul D. Harkins. But it was only ten days later on 18 February that the North Vietnamese government issued a statement that described the setting up of MACV as a most serious act of military aggression in South Vietnam by the United States that created a direct threat to the security of the North and to peace in Southeast Asia and the Pacific. The cochairmen of the 1954 Geneva Conference were requested to urgently study effective measures to end United States aggression in South Vietnam. [50] A few days later, on 24 February, the Chinese Foreign Ministry issued a statement expressing full support. To the Chinese, the armed U.S. imperialist intervention and aggression in South Vietnam constituted a direct threat to the security not only of the DRV but China and the peace of Asia as well. [51] In the later half of February 1962, there was a profusion of articles and commentaries in both the Vietnamese and Chinese mass media condemning U.S. military aggression in South Vietnam. The Russians, however, did not follow suit.

Also in February 1962, the politburo spelled out the tasks of the armed forces in South Vietnam. These were, first, to take the initiative to destroy the enemy. The way to do this was to strike in small groups at the main force of the enemy, at ranger teams, and at military installations and aircraft. Second was to destroy the "strategic hamlet" program devised by the Diem regime.[52] The "strategic hamlet" program initiated during the latter part of 1961 started as scattered efforts. In February 1962, a high-level governmental interagency committee was established in South Vietnam to direct and coordinate the program on a national scale. In mid–March it was formally adopted by Diem, and on 22 March, "Operation Sunrise" was launched in the heavily infiltrated Bing Duong Province, 35 miles north of Saigon. Central to the operation was the forced relocation of peasants into strategic hamlets.

From 16 February to 3 March, the National Liberation Front of South Vietnam held its 1st Congress. The congress agreed that the responsibility of the front was to unite everyone to resolutely struggle against American imperialism and the Diem regime so as to establish a democratic, free, neutral, and independent South Vietnam.[53] However, the first Communist broadcast of the congress and its resolutions was not monitored until 13 April 1962.[54] The time lag deserves attention.

IV

In Laos, the unsettled situation continued to be a source of uncertainty for both Beijing and Hanoi. We should recall that the 27 December 1961 meeting of the three Laotian princes at Vientiane did not take place because of the intransigence of Boun Oum and Phoumi Nosavan. According to the British Foreign Office on 22 January 1962, there was no more work to be done at Geneva except to wait for a united Laotian delegation.[55]

There is indication that the Chinese hoped to have a better control of the situation in Laos themselves, rather than leaving everything in the hands of the North Vietnamese. On 13 January 1962, an air transportation and road-building agreement between China and Laos was signed in Khang Khay between He Wei and Tiao Sisoumang Sisaleumsak, the Laotian Interior and National Economy minister. Under the agreement, a highway would be constructed to link Mengla (Yunnan Province) and Phong Saly Province. The Chinese government would undertake the work of building this highway, as well as bear all the cost involved. This highway when completed would be the first to directly link Laos and China, and it would replace the comparatively longer supply line from China to Laos, which at present had to pass through North Vietnam. The two countries also signed an air transportation agreement. With this agreement, the Chinese could now air-drop supplies into Laos, which had so far been the responsibility of the North Vietnamese.[56]

A month after the aborted 27 December Vientiane meeting and the visit of the Chinese military delegation to North Vietnam, fighting broke out toward the end of January 1962 around the village of Nam Tha, which was held by Phoumi's forces but surrounded by the Pathet Lao. Nam Tha, the capital of Houa Khong Province in northwest Laos, was situated six miles from the Chinese border and eight miles from Thailand. In the last week of January 1962, the troops of Boum Oum–Phoumi Nosavan carried out small-scale offensive operations in the vicinity in an effort to cut the Pathet Lao supply lines between northern and southern Laos.[57] On 1 February 1962, for the first time the airfield at Nam Tha was subjected to mortar fire by the Communist forces. Seven infantry battalions and a number of other units from the North Vietnamese 316th, 335th, and 330th Brigades crossed into Laos to fight alongside the Pathet Lao–Neutralists at Nam Tha. This was the first time since 1954 that the North Vietnamese initiated a military campaign to attack the enemy in its rear area. It was also the first major breach of the ceasefire since the battle at Ban Padong in June 1961.

A meeting between King Savang Vathana and the three Laotian Princes that had been arranged for 2 February 1962 had to be called off at the last minute because Boum Oum refused to attend in view of the fighting in Nam Tha. After some discussions in Moscow between Frank Roberts (the British ambassador to the Soviet Union) and Pushkin (leader of the Soviet delegation at the Geneva Conference), the British and Soviet ambassadors in Laos as well as members of the ISCC flew to Khang Khay on 6 February with the objective of persuading Souphanouvong to agree to a ceasefire.

The main objective of the North Vietnamese–Pathet Lao–Neutralists' military campaign was to force the enemy to return to the negotiating table on conditions favorable to the NLHX. Souphanouvong told the British ambassador that the objective of the military pressure at Nam Tha was political and that there was no intention to capture Nam Tha.[58] According to the British ambassador to Laos, J. M. Addis, during his meetings with Souvanna Phouma and Souphanouvong in February 1962 he had the impression that there was a great deal of strain and difference between them. The atmosphere was unlike his first visits to the Plaine des Jarres in September 1961 and also during the visit of the two princes to Vientiane at the end of December 1961.[59]

Both the Russians and Souvanna Phouma opposed the Nam Tha offensive. Souvanna Phouma's troops were not involved in Nam Tha.[60] Marek Thee revealed that the Soviet Union did not interfere in the Nam Tha campaign. It neither supported nor condemned the military operation. The British ambassador, however, reported that Abramov, the Soviet ambassador to Laos, made great efforts to persuade Souphanouvong to turn off the military pressure at Nam Tha — without success.[61] However, a statement by a junior member of the Soviet embassy in Vientiane revealed that the Chinese and North Vietnamese were encouraging Souphanouvong to continue the military pressure at Nam Tha.[62] The Chinese openly supported this joint North Vietnamese–Pathet Lao offensive. An article in the *Renmin Ribao* of 9 February 1962 explained that to create a favorable political atmosphere for the peaceful settlement of the Laotian question, the Royal Laotian government and the Pathet Lao fighting units had since 3 May 1961 observed the ceasefire order. But, events in the last nine months showed that the United States had made use of the ceasefire to strengthen the Phoumi–Boun Oum forces. It was therefore inevitable and justified that the RLG and the Pathet Lao retaliate. The article further insisted that it was absolutely impermissible that a ceasefire at Nam Tha be a precondition for the resumption of talks amongst the three princes.[63]

The Communists were convinced that Phoumi Nosavan and Boum Oum were doing everything they could to prevent an agreement on Laos; and they were unable to understand why the United States could not impose on Phoumi Nosavan to cooperate. They therefore decided to put military pressure on Phoumi. The Foreign Office also thought that the Russians might no longer be able to hold Souphanouvong and the North Vietnamese if a settlement was not reached soon.[64]

V

Although there was no official commitment to a ceasefire at Nam Tha, the fighting did stop and there was an uneasy lull in Laos[65] that coincided with the visit of the Soviet Communist Party delegation led by B. N. Ponomarev, secretary of the CPSU Central Committee, to Hanoi from 21 February to 2 March 1962. It was announced that the Soviet delegation was making a return visit for one that a North Vietnamese party delegation (led by Le Duc Tho) made to the Soviet Union in July 1961. However, it should be noted that this visit came in the wake of a series of visits to Hanoi by the Russians — for example, the cosmonaut Herman Titov, the Health and Trade Union delegations, and a Soviet vice-minister of foreign trade — not long after that of the Chinese military delegation to North Vietnam. It also took place soon after the formation of MACV and the breakdown of the ceasefire in Laos, as well as during the period of the 1st Congress of the NLFSV.

The Russian delegation was reported to have met with the Lao Dong Party Central Committee on 22 February, although only Ho, Truong Chinh, Pham Van Dong, and Le Duc Tho were mentioned.[66] We do not know what was discussed between the Soviet party delegation and the North Vietnamese, but in his public speeches Ponomarev dwelled much on the program of the CPSU spelled out at the 22nd CPSU Congress. He stressed that the program would enrich not just the Soviet Union; a strong and prosperous Soviet Union would benefit Vietnam and the Communist bloc as well. He also promised Soviet support to North Vietnam. According to British officials based in Hanoi, the North Vietnamese treated the Soviet delegation with great respect, and seemed anxious to demonstrate their support of Soviet leadership and to show that relations were close. Ponomarev was the leading party ideologist with long-standing contacts in the international Communist movement. Since 1953, he had been head of the department of the Central Committee concerned with foreign Communist parties outside the Soviet bloc. It is likely that the Sino-Soviet differences, Albania and the problem of North and South Vietnam, were also discussed. On 23 February, the Soviet delegation met a North Vietnamese delegation led by Le Duc Tho to "exchange experiences on Party work."[67]

On 27 February, when Ponomarev was still in North Vietnam, a Soviet Foreign Ministry official in Hanoi suddenly told British Consul-General J. F. Ford that it was urgent for the cochairmen to convene a conference on South Vietnam.[68] The following day, the North Vietnamese government issued a memorandum that put forward even more insistently the points made on 18 February 1962.[69] On 1 March, the Russian delegation met Ho Chi Minh, Truong Chinh, Pham Van Dong, Pham Hung, Le Duc Tho, and Van Tien Dung.[70] According to British sources, Ho met the delegation no less than four times. Truong Chinh also met the Russians several times in closed meetings. However, Le Duan was not reported to have been present throughout this period.[71] The Russian delegation left for home on 2 March.

After Ponomarev's visit, Sino-Vietnamese relations continued to be good. On 18 March 1962 the inauguration of a new industrial center at Viet Tri–built with Chinese aid and located some 70 kilometers northwest of Hanoi — was described by the North Vietnamese media as a symbol of the close friendship between the two countries.[72] The Vietnamese Communists continued to strike a balance between the Chinese and the Russians. In the same month, the Lao Dong Party and the Communist parties of Indonesia, New Zealand, Sweden, and Great Britain formed a "neutral" group that called for an international Communist meeting to resolve the differences within the movement.[73]

In early March 1962, a four-party conference took place in Hanoi and lasted for a week. It was attended by Ung Van Khiem, He Wei, Kaysone, and Tovmassyan, the Soviet ambassador to North Vietnam. The meeting decided that the situation in Laos was not yet ready for a coalition government. The most important task of the NLHX was to strengthen its alliance with the Neutralists, and at the same time expand its military and political forces. The Chinese particularly emphasized the need for the NLHX to develop its military strength and to consolidate its position in the countryside. It was also decided at the conference to increase unofficial supplies to the NLHX.[74]

Meanwhile, American involvement and commitment in the region inched forward with the announcement on 6 March 1962 of the Rusk-Thanat statement, which guaranteed American defense of Thailand. In the same month, two more battalions and a number of detachments from the North Vietnamese 316th Brigade moved into Nam Tha as reinforcement. Transportation lines in the Northwest Military Region were organized, and transport aircraft from the North Vietnamese 919th Air Force Regiment were utilized to ensure that the necessary supplies reached the battlefield. Infantry Battalions 2 and 4 of the 335th Brigade traveled 12 days and nights continuously, carrying weapons to the battleground.

Abramov, the Soviet ambassador to Laos, returned to Hanoi from Moscow in mid–March. Both Tovmassyan and he were received by Ho Chi Minh and Pham Van Dong on 21 March. Abramov carried a letter from the CPSU to its Chinese, Vietnamese, and Laotian counterparts. The thrust of the letter was that the Russians accepted the conclusions reached at the March conference in Hanoi, and treated them with due understanding since Hanoi and Beijing were nearer to Laos and knew the local conditions better. Thus, the Russians conceded that the latter could better judge what practical steps could be taken in Laos in the near future. According to Marek Thee: "This was a clear statement of disengagement as far as internal Laotian developments [were] concerned. The Asian allies were given a free hand to plan and shape events; this part of the message was received with satisfaction. But resentment grew in Beijing, Hanoi, and Khang Khay against the unwillingness of the Soviet Union to join with its allies in an active IndoChinese policy to defend their most basic national interests."[75]

At the end of March, when Liu Chun, the charge d'affaires of the Chinese mission in Khang Khay, told Abramov that China was in economic difficulties and asked about further Soviet aid to Laos, the Russian was not forthcoming. As Marek Thee observed, the Soviet Union—though it distrusted U.S. motives—was unwilling to adopt a militant line against the United States and therefore chose progressive disengagement. Dean Rusk, Harriman, and the British Foreign Office were convinced that the Russians wanted a settlement in Laos.[76] In a private conversation on 29 March 1962, Dean Rusk remarked that he feared there was little Washington or Moscow could do about Laotian situation. He had the impression that the Russians wanted a settlement, but the Chinese were messing things up.[77]

For reasons still unclear, the Chinese government chose this time to recall its ambassador to North Vietnam. On 15 March it was reported that He Wei would be leaving for home to take up a new post.[78] He left Hanoi for home on 24 March 1962, having served four and a half years as ambassador. Whereas his predecessor, Luo Guibo, was seen off by Truong Chinh when he left his post in December 1957, He Wei was seen off by Nguyen Viet Dung, head of the Protocol Department.[79] In April, He Wei assumed the post of second-secretary of the Party Central Committee of his native province, Honan. It was almost five months later before a new ambassador arrived in Hanoi to replace him. When Luo Guibo left on 2 December 1957, he was replaced in less than a month.

It is possible that the recall of He Wei was related to developments taking place in Beijing at this time. From 27 March to 16 April, the 2nd National People's Congress held its third session in Beijing. This Congress was exceptional in that even foreign Communist correspondents were barred from attending the meetings. Chinese Foreign Minister Chen Yi reportedly told the Hungarian ambassador that a major discussion of Chinese internal policy was in progress and that when the new line had been worked out, foreign Communist colleagues would be told about them.[80] According to British officials who were informed by their "best Chinese contacts," the congress spent two days discussing the need to rehabilitate rightist opportunists, including Peng Dehuai and that this was connected with the Chinese desire for rapprochement with the Soviet Union.[81] On 7 April 1962, the Chinese addressed a letter to the CPSU Central Committee proposing a conference to resolve their differences. The Russians, in their reply on 31 May 1962, agreed in principle to the holding of a new conference. Both sides also agreed to stop their verbal attacks over the mass media. The situation did improve for a period of time.[82] British officials also noted an uneasy period of comparative restraint in Sino-Soviet relations until late summer 1962.[83]

Meanwhile, the Chinese position regarding the situation at Nam Tha was explained to Marek Thee on 26 March at a lunch with Liu Chun, who said that there was a need to strike a tactical blow at the enemy. It would be a period of neither war nor peace. The Chinese were of the view that the Americans would not engage in large operations in Laos as long as the NLHX avoided actions that would aggravate the conflict. The strategy was to hold the initiative in local military operations and, at the same time, to continue the negotiations for a coalition government. One example was Chinese refusal of Souvanna Phouma's request for Chinese jet pilots to defend Laotian airspace. As Liu Chun explained, China did not want to be accused of intervention and also did not want to create a pretext for an escalation of the conflict. This was also the North Vietnamese position, as explained to Marek Thee on 5 April 1962 by Generals Le Chuong and Tong Dy. According to Le Chuong, they did not want to capture Nam Tha by launching a large frontal attack that might provoke a U.S. retaliation.

Also on 5 April, during a farewell call on Chinese Foreign Minister Chen Yi by the British charge d'affaires in Beijing, Michael Stewart, Chen Yi said that the Chinese still hoped for the formation of a united neutral Laotian government under Souvanna Phouma. They accepted that a place would have to be found for Phoumi Nosavan in a united government. China was anxious that the Laotian situation should not become more critical. He also made it clear that China would not expand into Southeast Asia. Expansion southward, even if it were not ruled out on other grounds, would not help to solve China's food and economic problems. Chen Yi, however, discreetly and inoffensively added a warning about South Vietnam. The Chinese would not intervene unless they judged that there was a serious threat to the North Vietnamese regime. The British ambassador noted that the tone of Chen Yi's remarks was in strong contrast with the bellicose Chinese statements published on Laos.[84]

It was around this time that the idea of an international conference to settle the question of South Vietnam was taken up by Sihanouk in an editorial in the Cambodian newspaper *Nationaliste* on 25 March 1962 and in a speech on 5 April at the Ministry of Religious Affairs in Phnom Penh.[85] In a private conversation with a "delicate source," Sihanouk indicated that he had been encouraged by the Chinese to take up the initiative and that the Russians had indicated they would support him.[86]

In a discussion with Marek Thee at the beginning of April, Ambassador Abramov also expressed the view that it might be useful to force the United States to accept negotiations on South Vietnam within the framework of the 1954 Geneva Conference. According to Liu Chun, the charge d'affaires of the Chinese mission in Khang Khay, Beijing more or less shared the same thinking. Chen Yi, in a conversation with Andrei Gromyko, suggested that the Soviet foreign minister could remain as a permanent cochairman. The Chinese hope was to neutralize the whole of Southeast Asia.[87] On 13 April and 14 April respectively, Hanoi and Beijing finally reported the 1st Congress of the NLFSV (16 February–3 March 1962) and its resolutions.[88]

On the non-Communist side, on 15 April 1962 the first U.S. Marine Corps air units arrived in South Vietnam. Based near Soc Trang, 100 miles southwest of Saigon, the 450 Marines and 15 Sikorsky UH-34D combat helicopters were to reinforce the two U.S. Army helicopter companies that were already in South Vietnam. In April, a conference held by the Nam Bo Regional Committee assessed that an all-out military offensive in South Vietnam, which had been anticipated in October 1961, was not yet possible and that the combination of political and military struggle would have to continue for sometime longer.[89]

VI

During March and the first half of April 1962, against the advice of the United States, Phoumi Nosavan reinforced his garrison at Nam Tha to a strength of 5,000 and used Nam Tha as a base for attacks into Pathet Lao–held territories. As a consequence, fighting broke out southeast of Nam Tha on 22 April, each side blaming the other for provoking the fighting. At the end of April 1962, an additional North Vietnamese battalion, Battalion 3 of the 330th Brigade, was sent to join the Pathet Lao–Vietnamese combined forces. On 3 May, the village of Muong Sing, 25 miles northwest of Nam Tha and 5 miles from the Chinese border, was captured by the Pathet Lao–Vietnamese forces. On 6 May 1962, they captured Nam Tha.[90] There was no evidence of Chinese participation.[91]

However, it was believed that Beijing permitted the transit of the Pathet Lao–Viet forces through a salient of Chinese territory in the attack on Muong Sing, while the logistic supplies were furnished by the Soviet–North Vietnam airlifts.[92] The British were of the view that the Nam Tha episode was not provoked by the Communists but engineered by Phoumi Nosavan; and that his retreat to the Mekong, one of the swiftest in military history, was calculated to precipitate a panic in Thailand and force the Americans to back him.[93] However, the Pathet Lao–North Vietnamese forces did not harass or interfere with the withdrawal of Nosavan's troops during the whole of their 120-kilometer retreat to the Mekong at Ban Houei Sai.[94] According to a U.S. intelligence estimate, the fall of Nam Tha—which was also an area of direct security interest to the Chinese—eliminated RLG control of the whole of North Laos and opened the provinces of Western Luang Prabang and Nam Tha (which borders on Burma and Thailand) to Communist domination.[95]

As a consequence of the fall of Nam Tha, the United States on 11 May announced that it was dispatching troops to Thailand and sending elements of the U.S. Seventh Fleet to the Gulf of Siam. On 17 May, 2,800 United States marines arrived in Bangkok to be based at Udorn, 35 miles from Vientiane. A Military Assistance Command for Thailand (MACTHAI) was also established.

During this time, the Chinese were apparently concerned about the collaboration of the Jiang Jieshi brigands with the Phoumi–Boum Oum group. A *Renmin Ribao* commentary of 16 May 1962 entitled "The Chinese People Cannot Remain Indifferent" highlighted the participation of the remnant Guomindang troops in the civil war in Laos. It recalled a 31 January 1961 *UPI* report of the movement of the remnant Guomindang troops from northeast Burma across the border into northern Laos. The commentary claimed that Taiwan had dispatched military personnel and equipment to the Nosavan–Boun Oum group, and drew attention to the presence of a task force from the U.S. Seventh Fleet in the region.[96] On 24 May 1962, the Chinese reported that remnants of Jiang Jieshi's troops on the southwest border of Yunnan had been incorporated into the army of Phoumi Nosavan and had taken part in the Laotian civil war.[97] Unfortunately, we do not have much information regarding the activities of these Nationalist Chinese military units, except that a large number of them were driven into Thailand and Laos by the Burmese Army in January 1961 and again in March 1962 after Ne Win seized power in Burma in a bloodless coup. During a conversation between British Secretary of State for Foreign Affairs. Douglas Home and Chen Yi in Geneva on 12

June 1961, Chen Yi had spoken of the 5,000 Guomindang troops who had been in Laos for 11 years and wanted their withdrawal expedited.[98]

As for the Soviet Union, soon after the fall of Nam Tha, Robert Kennedy sent a private message to Khrushchev telling him that the United States president had relied on Soviet assurances that there would not be any more fighting and now felt that he had been double-crossed. A few days later, Khrushchev replied with the assurance that there would be no more armed action in Laos and that the Soviet Union too was anxious to see the Laotian question resolved peacefully.[99] On 25 May, Khrushchev announced that the Soviet Union still supported the establishment of a neutral Laos despite the presence of American troops in Thailand. Thus, after the fall of Nam Tha, it was clear to all parties concerned that a return to diplomacy was urgently required to diffuse what was perceived to be a potentially volatile situation. On the same day Souvanna Phouma, who was in Paris when Nam Tha fell, announced that he was prepared to return to Laos for new negotiations. Four days later, on 29 May, it was reported that Souvanna Phouma had declared that both Souphanouvong and he were prepared to resume talks with Boum Oum and had set 15 June 1962 as the deadline for the completion of negotiations.[100] Soon after that, on 7 June, negotiations amongst the three Princes reopened. The three Laotian princes finally reached agreement on the coalition government at a meeting in the Plaine des Jarres on 12 June and, on 23 June, the Government of National Union was formed.

Meanwhile, in Cambodia, the British government sent Malcom MacDonald to dissuade Sihanouk from pushing for an international conference on Vietnam. MacDonald was in Cambodia from 11 to 15 May 1962. A conversation that he had with Sihanouk on 12 May gives us some insight into Sihanouk's perception of the regional situation during this period. Regarding Laos, Sihanouk did not think that anyone should foolishly believe that the whole of Laos could be neutral since about a third of the country was under Pathet Lao–Vietnamese Communist control. However, he felt that a neutral government under Souvanna Phouma was not only the best but also the only means to ensure that Laos did not fall completely into Communist hands. But that would require active support from the countries of the free world. Sihanouk did not appear to be very worried about the Communist threat to his country. He was most concerned about the South Vietnamese and the Thais, who were equipped with American weapons, committing territorial aggression against Cambodia. In that situation, Sihanouk said that he would have no choice but to resort to Chinese assistance, which would then mean the end of Cambodia's policy of nonalignment.[101]

VII

Despite the tense atmosphere in the region in May 1962, on 18 May 1962 on the eve of Ho Chi Minh's 72nd birthday, he again visited Nanning. In accordance with Ho's wishes, there was no major celebration of his birthday, except that on the night of 19 May, a small-scale cultural performance organized by the comrades in Guangxi was held on the first floor of the Xiyuan Rest House where he stayed.[102] This was the third year in succession that Ho spent his birthday in China. We know very little about his three consecutive visits to China other than what the Chinese revealed. But it is worth noting that all three visits took place at very significant junctures: In 1960, it coincided with the announcement that the Paris summit had been called off; and in 1961, it coincided with the opening of the Geneva Conference on Laos.

Ho Chi Minh also did not appear in public in Hanoi in June. He did not even attend the Children's Day celebration on 2 June 1962, an event he seldom missed. British officials in Hanoi initially assumed that he was resting in one of the mountain resorts in North Vietnam. However, it was reported in the Indian press on 24 June that he had been seen in a Moscow theatre on 22 June. British officials believed that he went to the Soviet Union to discuss the Vietnamese situation with the Russians.[103] A Chinese source claimed that in response to the North Vietnamese request for military assistance, Khrushchev offered 3,000 guns that the Russians captured from the Germans during the Second World War. Ho Chi Minh said angrily that those guns should be sent to the museum.[104]

After the formation of a Laotian Government of National Union on 23 June, the Geneva Conference on Laos reconvened on 2 July after a five-month interval. The Protocol and the Declaration of the Neutrality of Laos were finally signed on 23 July, very much later than the "six weeks" the Russians had expected when the conference opened in May 1961. In his closing speech, Chen Yi described the peaceful settlement of the Laotian question as having broken through a link in the chain of tensions in Southeast Asia and expressed hope that it would be a new starting point in the relaxation of tensions in the area, a sentiment shared by all the representatives. Chen Yi and Ung Van Khiem, however, did not fail to express their reservations regarding the presence of American troops in Thailand and South Vietnam, which still needed to be resolved.[105] Khrushchev was very pleased with the settlement in Laos but was also concerned about the continued presence of American troops in Thailand. He conveyed to

Kennedy that he understood why the troops were sent but hoped that it was now possible to withdraw them. Kennedy replied that he would withdraw the troops in ten days, to which Khrushchev responded with the message that the withdrawal would mean a great deal to him.[106] In the middle of 1962, Laos finally moved out of center-stage and South Vietnam returned to the forefront after being overshadowed by the former for almost two years.

VIII

Soon after the Geneva Conference, in late July 1962, Bernard Fall had a conversation with Pham Van Dong and Ho Chi Minh in the presidential palace in Hanoi.[107] Ho appeared briefly in the midst of the interview, which surprised Fall since he thought that Ho was vacationing in the Soviet Union at the time. According to Pham Van Dong, the DRV would not take any military action in the South that could give the Americans any pretext for military intervention in North Vietnam. He did not feel that it was necessary at that point in time to intervene militarily. He appeared to be satisfied with the way the war was going there and believed that, given time and patience, American weariness would compel them to withdraw. Meanwhile, the DRV would keep up the publicity about American intervention and Vietnamese resistance. Ho's assessment was that Ngo Dinh Diem was in a very difficult position at that time and had no popular support. Both Dong and Ho agreed that it would be a protracted struggle.

The NLFSV on 1 July 1962 had sent the cochairmen of the Geneva Conference a memorandum backing Sihanouk's proposal for an international conference on South Vietnam, which was endorsed by the North Vietnamese press. On 23 July 1962, the émigré Vietnamese politician Tran Van Huu issued a statement welcoming the newly concluded Geneva Agreements on Laos and urged a similar conference to settle the Vietnamese problem. In his statement, Huu made no reference to Sihanouk. Apparently Huu had been approached by North Vietnamese officials and was being encouraged to play the role of a neutralist Souvanna Phouma in a South Vietnamese coalition government.[108] According to Arthur Lall, many delegates at the Geneva Conference expected that a conference on Vietnam would follow a few weeks after the successful conclusion of the conference on Laos.[109]

Pham Van Dong told Fall that Hanoi was prepared to negotiate.

However, he felt that the situation was not yet ripe for talks because the Diem regime showed no intention to compromise. On 1 August, Chen Yi also said that China supported Sihanouk's proposal for an international conference on South Vietnam, but since very few countries had responded, the time was perhaps not ripe. When the struggle reached a certain stage, a conference would become inevitable.[110] We should recall that it was actually the Chinese who had encouraged Sihanouk to propose such a conference. By 20 August, Sihanouk appeared to have completely lost interest in a conference on Vietnam. Instead, he now began an appeal for an international conference on Cambodia.

From the conversation with Pham Van Dong, Fall gathered the impression that in the immediate future, the DRV would not risk its internal development by military provocation of a kind that would lead to retaliation in the form of undisguised bombing of the northern centers by American planes. The DRV's short-term objective was not reunification of the country. A neutral government that excluded Diem would be acceptable to the North, as long as American military presence was withdrawn as well.[111]

From the above account, it seems that soon after 23 July 1962, Hanoi and Beijing changed their minds regarding an early international conference on South Vietnam. Unfortunately, we do not know the reasons for this. One possibility is that the Communists felt that they were not in a good negotiating position. At the July 1962 Honolulu Conference, U.S. Defense Secretary McNamara was informed by COMUSMACV that there had been "tremendous progress" in South Vietnam in the last six months and that the South Vietnamese Communists could be eliminated in about a year.[112]

It is likely that the new Communist position was taken after discussions in Beijing. Chinese sources have since disclosed that in the summer of 1962, Ho Chi Minh and Nguyen Chi Thanh made a trip to Beijing to request Chinese military assistance. We should recall that in March 1961, Nguyen Chi Thanh, the only other four-star general besides Vo Nguyen Giap, was transferred from the army to head the Ministry of Agricultural Cooperatives. The only other report we have of him in 1961 was on 28 September when he was in Beijing after attending the 4th National Congress of the North Korean Worker's Party in Pyongyang. That it was Thanh who accompanied Ho Chi Minh in summer 1962 might indicate that he had been given a new assignment, most likely to oversee the military struggle in the South.[113] We should also recall that in August 1959 at a meeting with Ho in Beijing, Zhou had promised to provide Hanoi with material support for the struggle in the South by the end of that year; but for reasons still unknown, the Chinese promise had not been fulfilled. In early 1962, the North Vietnamese and Chinese leaders met again to discuss Chinese military assistance for the struggle in the South.[114] In summer 1962, the Chinese finally supplied 90,000 guns of all types to be used for the guerrilla war in the South. According to the Chinese, this was the beginning of Chinese help in promoting the development, strengthening, and expansion of the Communist military arsenal in the South. From this point onward, Chinese assistance increased as the war gradually expanded. When Zhou Enlai recalled Chinese assistance to the Vietnamese struggle in South Vietnam, he cited 1962 as the starting point.[115] (In December 1964, the Americans captured Chinese Communist-manufactured weapons and ammunition in Chuong Thien Province and subsequently in the four Corp areas of South Vietnam as well. These weapons included the 7.62 semiautomatic carbine, 7.62 light machine gun, and 7.62 assault rifle, all manufactured in China in 1962.)[116]

On 27 July 1962, four days after the Geneva Conference ended and almost four months after He Wei was recalled to Beijing, the Chinese finally appointed Zhu Qiwen as the new ambassador to North Vietnam.[117] Zhu arrived in Hanoi on 18 August 1962 and assumed his appointment on 21 August 1962. In August, too, Ho Chi Minh found time to take another vacation in China. This time he spent it at the Stone Forest in Yunnan Province, where he stayed at the Shilin Hotel. He was the guest of Yunnan soprano Du Lihua, whom he got to know in November 1961 when he visited Beijing.[118]

Meanwhile, a letter from Le Duan to the comrades in South Vietnam in July 1962 made clear the Vietnamese Communist strategy at this point. According to Le Duan, although the revolutionary struggle in the South had made much significant progress in the last eight years, there were new difficulties. The American imperialists were determined to prevent South Vietnam from being absorbed into the orbit of socialism and it was their intention to make South Vietnam a springboard to attack the North. South Vietnam was to serve as a wall to prevent the tide of socialism from engulfing Southeast Asia. Therein lay the complexity of the revolution in the South. Unlike Laos, South Vietnam did not share a common border with China. It was thus highly probable that the Americans would be less hesitant about a direct invasion of South Vietnam because unlike Laos, they would not run the risk of colliding with China. The Vietnamese Communists therefore needed to fight cautiously. The twofold task was to protect the peace in order that the North could carry out its socialist construction and at the same time to resolutely resist the Americans and their lackeys so as to liberate the South. North and South Vietnam were interrelated. If they did not struggle against the Americans in the South, the stability and peace of the North could not be assured. And if they did not protect the peace and allow the North to complete its socialist development, the revolution would encounter even more difficulties. Referring to those who emphasized military struggle and underestimated the value of political struggle, Le Duan urged them to evaluate fully their own capability. He warned against underestimating the power of the enemy, who in all aspects — for example, numerical strength, weaponry, transportation, and modern communication — were superior to them. Referring to the struggle in Laos that had "just temporarily ended," he said that the socialist victory there did not come about by coincidence but by following the correct line and strategy, which was to persistently struggle against the imperialists and at the same time to know when to exercise restraint in order to avoid a war between the two opposing camps. Nam Tha was a case in point. The Laotian struggle was therefore an important lesson for the revolution in South Vietnam. Le Duan once again reiterated the importance of combining both the political and military struggle, especially in countering the "strategic hamlet" program. It would be a long struggle, but there was always the possibility that the enemy could be compelled to negotiate or give in at some point when the cost to continue was higher than they were prepared to pay, as had been the case in Laos and Algeria.[119]

Conclusion

The preceding chapters have attempted to trace the development of Vietnamese Communist relations with China between January 1956 and summer 1962, taking into account the interplay of domestic politics, the role of individual leaders and political faction—particularly in Hanoi and Beijing—and the changing international conditions, particularly within the Communist bloc, that impinged on both countries. Admittedly, there are still many gaps that need to be filled and many questions about the relationship during this period that still need to be answered. But pending the release of more archival material, it is my hope that this study has at least contributed a little to furthering our understanding of Sino-Vietnamese relations during the beginning stage of the Second Indochina War. It is also hoped that this thesis has clarified some misconceptions regarding both Sino-Vietnamese relations and the war.

Even before the end of the 1954 Geneva Conference, neither the Hanoi nor the Beijing leadership expected a peaceful reunification of North and South Vietnam; and the United States was identified as the new enemy, replacing the French. Thus, while on the surface the Vietnamese Communists appeared conciliatory and forwarded many proposals for a peaceful reunification, secretly they were preparing for an eventual armed struggle. This strategy of lying low, mustering strength, and keeping in touch with the people while waiting for an opportunity to strike had the support of the Chinese. The Russians, on the other hand, believed that through peaceful coexistence and friendly economic competition, South Vietnam would eventually seek to be unified with the North. Up till 1958, the Hanoi leadership could to an extent reconcile both the Chinese and the Russian approaches with their own since the first stage of the North Vietnamese strategy was to rebuild their economy.

But by mid-1958, Diem's renewed efforts to exterminate the Southern Communists began to adversely affect the revolutionary struggle in the South. By late 1958, Hanoi realized that they could no longer continue to advocate restraint without losing the struggle in the South to Diem.

Hanoi's decision in January 1959 to renew the struggle in the South (which was not made public until four months later in May) coincided with the Huong Lap and Phu Loi incidents as well as the downturn in Sino-Soviet relations. As far as we can tell, Moscow was not in favor of the resumption of armed struggle in South Vietnam but did not object. Khrushchev was trying to balance his desire to improve relations with the United States against his commitment to the Communist fraternity. Beijing reluctantly gave its support. In August 1959 (soon after the Lushan meeting and the 8th Plenary Session of the CCP Central Committee) at a meeting with Ho Chi Minh in Beijing, Zhou Enlai promised to provide Hanoi with material support for the struggle in the South by the end of that year, but for reasons still unknown, the Chinese did not fulfill their promise. Consequently, in the first three months of 1960, Sino-Vietnamese relations were not as warm as before. The announcement in April that Zhou Enlai would visit Hanoi in May 1960 signaled an improvement in the relationship between the two countries. During Zhou's visit on that occasion, an understanding regarding the struggle in the South was apparently reached between the North Vietnamese and Chinese leaders. This series of diplomatic activities should be seen against the buildup to the Paris summit between Khrushchev and Eisenhower, which was aborted at the last moment on 17 May 1960.

From the very beginning it was an Indochina rather than just a Vietnam War. If Cambodia seemed to be rather peripheral in the early years of the war, it was because of Sihanouk's political acumen, and even more so the decisions of both Hanoi and Beijing, although not necessarily for the same reasons. As for Laos, it was definitely of strategic importance to both North Vietnam and China, but for reasons that again were different for Hanoi and for Beijing. Unlike the North Vietnamese, the Chinese were much more ready to accommodate a neutral Laos, if the Americans had allowed it; whereas Hanoi would only countenance a neutral Laos in which the government was prepared to turn a blind eye to its own use of Laotian territory to support its Southern cadres. Much of the Ho Chi Minh Trail was in Laotian territory. If Laos had been neutral and relatively stable like Cambodia, fundamental Sino-Vietnamese differences over Laos might have surfaced. As it happened, because an American presence in Laos was always a possibility, they both campaigned for a neutralization of Laos. An American presence in Laos was the last thing that both the North Vietnamese and the Chinese wanted.

In 1960 and particularly from the Kong Lae coup on 9 August 1960 till the summer of 1962, developments in Laos overshadowed the armed struggle in South Vietnam (which was underway by the end of 1959). Also, it was initially in Laos and not in South Vietnam that the Russians, who had been staunchly opposed to a military solution to the Vietnam problem, found themselves deeply involved after the Kong Lae coup.

Up till the Taylor mission to South Vietnam in October 1961, China was also more concerned about the situation in Laos than in South Vietnam. But after the Taylor mission, Beijing gradually shifted its attention to South Vietnam. Not long after the Taylor mission, a very high-powered Chinese military delegation led by Ye Jianying visited North Vietnam in December 1961, ostensibly to celebrate the 17th anniversary of the VPA. The establishment of MACV on 8 February 1962 added to North Vietnamese and Chinese concerns, while the problem of Laos remained unsettled. Chinese policy regarding South Vietnam only crystallized in July at about the time when the Laotian problem was resolved. In the summer of 1962, Ho Chi Minh and Nguyen Chi Thanh made a secret trip to Beijing, and that was when the Chinese agreed to provide concrete military aid for the struggle in the South.

It is untrue that Hanoi was simply following the instructions of the Chinese or the Russians, or both. In fact, the Vietnamese Communists were remarkably in control of their own decision making, despite being quite dependent on China and the Soviet Union for both economic and military resources. One should not assume that Beijing was always kept well informed or knew every move of the North Vietnamese in advance. Certainly the Vietnamese Communists consulted the Chinese, but the decision of the 15th Plenary Session of the Lao Dong Party to resume armed struggle was made without the prior consent of the Chinese (or the Russians). Also, on many occasions, Hanoi, Beijing, and Moscow were simply reacting to developments in Laos that to a large extent were beyond the control of any of the three governments.

To say this is not in any way to discount the role of China in the Indochina conflict and war. As we have seen in this study, the Vietnamese Communists always made it a point to seek the views of Beijing (and Moscow) and, as far as possible, their concurrence as well. But just as the Vietnamese Communists needed China's support in their war of national liberation, China too needed the Vietnamese. This is an aspect of the relationship that is sometimes overlooked. China's fear of being encircled by the United States and its allies and — as the Sino-Soviet dispute developed, the fear of the Soviet Union — raised the strategic importance of Vietnam in Chinese eyes. Thus by virtue of the geographical proximity of Vietnam and China, the Lao Dong Party, a relatively small party within the Communist camp, became a crucial player, especially to the Chinese, in the growing Sino-Soviet dispute. The relationship was thus mutually beneficial, but they had differences, too. However, Hanoi and Beijing believed that by not discussing controversial and divisive issues openly, it would better serve their respective national interests. As to whether the Sino-Soviet rift provided a "window of opportunity" that the Vietnamese Communists exploited for their own ends, my study shows that at least up till 1962, the Hanoi leadership preferred a united Communist camp and viewed the growing rift between Beijing and Moscow as detrimental to their cause. It should be mentioned that despite the differences between Beijing and Moscow from 1956 to 1962, Beijing did not envisage a split with the Soviet Union.

Many scholars, and this is true up to the early '90s, are greatly influenced by the views of P. J. Honey, for many years the leading Vietnam specialist in the West, regarding North Vietnam's relations with both China and the Soviet Union. For example, the years 1954–1957 were described as the "Chinese phase" in Vietnam's relations with China and Russia, and the years 1957–1961 were described as the "Soviet phase." It was said that in 1957, there was a power struggle between the "pro-Chinese" and "pro-Soviet" factions in the Lao Dong Party; that there was a swing away from Beijing toward closer relations with Moscow; and that, during the Third Lao Dong Party Congress in September 1960, North Vietnam took the side of the Soviet Union against China. My study has shown that that was not how it was. As we have noted, the Chinese have since admitted that although both they and the North Vietnamese did not fully agree on the gravity of the agrarian reform debacle and about Soviet revisionism, Sino-Vietnamese relations in the '50s and '60s were good. My own study therefore supports Carlyle Thayer's view that Vietnamese Communist relations with China and the Soviet Union were not necessarily a "zero-sum game."[1]

Regarding the issue of factionalism within the North Vietnamese leadership and internal party disputes — between Truong Chinh and Pham Van Dong; Truong Chinh and Vo Nguyen Giap; Truong Chinh and Le Duan; Le Duan and Ho Chi Minh; Le Duan and Vo Nguyen Giap; and Vo Nguyen Giap and Nguyen Chi Thanh — it still cannot be fully established. There were disagreements within the leadership on issues such as agricultural and industrialization strategies, military modernization, and the pace of the struggle for reunification. Different personalities might hold views that coincided with those of either Beijing or Moscow, but no one within the leadership (apart from Hoang Van Hoan, who we now know for certain was a Sinophile), can or need be categorized either as pro-Chinese or pro-Russian. Whatever the differences amongst the leaders, their disagreements did not originate from Beijing or Moscow. This is true of Ho Chi Minh, who of all the Vietnamese leaders had the closest ties with the Chinese. Even Truong Chinh, despite the fact that he adopted an alias that meant "Long March," was not pro-Chinese in the same way as Hoang Van Hoan. Indeed, Truong Chinh was one of those who at one stage shared Khrushchev's view of peaceful competition between the two blocs. As for Le Duan, it is wrong to see him simply as the outspoken champion of armed struggle. On the contrary, Le Duan was too much aware of the military power of the United States to advocate callous and unrestrained armed struggle. Indeed, while the 15th Plenary Session officially sanctioned the resumption of armed struggle, it was meant to support and not replace the political struggle. Le Duan, who is often considered to be "pro-Soviet," was in the late '50s and early '60s more attuned to the Chinese viewpoint, which supported the use of armed struggle to achieve national liberation in colonial countries. During the years 1956–1962, the Vietnamese Communist leadership was on the whole cohesive in spite of their differences.

The summer of 1962 is an appropriate point to end this study. In the case of Laos, the conclusion of the one-year long Geneva Conference in July 1962 marked the end of one phase of its postcolonial political experience. The next stage was how to make the 1962 Geneva settlement work. Regarding the issue of the reunification of Vietnam, for a brief period after the successful conclusion of the Geneva Conference on Laos, there were indications that both Hanoi and Beijing (and Moscow as well) were in agreement that through a "low-intensity" type of warfare the Communists could perhaps pressure the United States and South Vietnam to agree to convene another international conference for Vietnam similar to the one for Laos. There were also signs of an improvement in Sino-Soviet relations during this time. In Cambodia, Sihanouk's control of the country remained firm, but within the Khmer Communist underground there was a significant development that would affect Sino-Vietnamese relations in years to come. On 20 July 1962 or thereabouts, Tou Samouth was assassinated. Pol Pot became the acting secretary-general of the party and was subsequently confirmed as secretary-general during the

3rd Congress of the Khmer People's Revolutionary Party on 20–21 February 1963.[2]

The summer of 1962 was therefore a significant point in the Communist struggle. With hindsight, we know that the Laos settlement broke down, the Sino-Soviet rift became public, and an international conference to resolve the Vietnam problem never materialized. But all these must remain the subject of further study.

Chapter Notes

Introduction

1. David G. Marr, *Vietnam* (World Bibliographical Series, Volume 147) (Oxford: Clio Press, 1992), p. 127.

2. Nikita Khrushchev, *Khrushchev Remembers* (London: Andre Deutsch, 1971), pp. 444–445.

3. There are relatively few American scholars who have contributed to our understanding of the Communist side of the Indochina War. The more notable ones are: Douglas Pike, Eugene K. Lawson, Gabriel Kolko, Jon M. Van Dyke, William J. Duiker, W.R. Smyser, and William S. Turley.

4. According to China scholars Michael H. Hunt and Odd Arne Westad, the relationships between China and the Soviet Union, Vietnam, and North Korea "are still consigned to historical limbo" (by the Chinese authorities), regardless of whether the relations were good or bad. See Michael H. Hunt and Odd Arne Westad, "The Chinese Communist Party and International Affairs: A Field Report on New Historical Sources and Old Research Problems" in *China Quarterly*, June 1990, Number 122, p. 269.

Chinese scholar Huang Zheng observed that in recent years not much attention has been given to historical research on Sino-Vietnam relations in China. See Huang Zheng, *Zhongyue Guanxi Shi Yanjiu Ji Gao* (Guangxi Renmin Chubanshe, 1992), p. 315. This is true also on the Vietnamese side.

5. See David Shambaugh, "A Bibliographical Essay on New Sources for the Study of China's Foreign Relations and National Security" in Thomas W. Robinson and David Shambaugh (ed.), *Chinese Foreign Policy: Theory and Practice* (Oxford: Clarendon, 1994); Michel Oksenberg, "Politic Takes Command: An Essay on the Study of Post–1949 China" in Roderick MacFarquhar and John K. Fairbank (ed.), *Cambridge History of China*, Volume XIV (Cambridge: Cambridge University Press, 1989); Michael H. Hunt and Odd Arne Westad, "The Chinese Communist Party and International Affairs: A Field Report on New Historical Sources and Old Research Problems" in *China Quarterly*, Number 122, June 1990; Odd Arne Westad, "Materials on CCP History in Russian Archives" in *CCP Research Newsletter*, Numbers 10 and 11, Spring-Fall 1992; James G.

Hershberg, "Soviet Archives: The Opening Door" and Steven M. Goldstein and He Di, "New Chinese Sources on the History of the Cold War" in *Cold War International History Project Bulletin*, Issue 1, Spring 1992; Mark Bradley and Robert K. Brigham, *Vietnamese Archives and Scholarship on the Cold War Period: Two Reports* (Cold War International History Project, Woodrow Wilson International Center for Scholars, Working Paper Number 7, September 1993); Yang Baoyun, "Presentation concise des resultats de la recherche sur le Laos en Chine" in *Peninsule* 26 (nouvelle serie), 1993.

6. Nayan Chanda, "Research and Destroy: Origins of Vietnam War POW document remain obscure" in *Far Eastern Economic Review*, 6 May 1993, pp. 20–21; Mark Kramer, "Archival Research in Moscow: Progress and Pitfalls" in *Cold War International History Project Bulletin*, Issue 3, Fall 1993, pp. 1, 18–39.

7. For the papers presented at the first conference, see Jayne Werner and David Hunt (ed.), *The American War in Vietnam* (Southeast Asia Program)(New York: Cornell University, 1993); for the papers presented at the second conference, see Jayne S. Werner and Luu Doan Huynh (ed.), *The Vietnam War: Vietnamese and American Perspectives* (New York: M. E. Sharpe, 1993).

8. Ilya V. Gaiduk, *The Soviet Union and the Vietnam War* (Chicago: Ivan R. Dee, 1996).

9. David G. Marr, op. cit., p. 102.

10. Carlyle A. Thayer, *War by Other Means: National Liberation and Revolution in Vietnam 1954–1960* (Sydney: Allen and Unwin, 1989).

11. Ralph B. Smith, *An International History of the Vietnam War, Volume 1: Revolution versus Containment, 1955–61* (London: Macmillan, 1983); *Volume 2: The Struggle for South East Asia, 1961–65* (London: Macmillan, 1985).

12. W.R. Smyser, *The Independent Vietnamese: Vietnamese Communism between Russia and China 1956–1969* (Ohio: Ohio University Center for International Studies, 1980).

13. William J. Duiker, *The Communist Road to Power in Vietnam* (Colorado: Westview, 1981).

14. I am extremely grateful to Professor Chen Jian for sending me a copy of this article before publication.

15. According to Han Suyin, in 1987 when she was in Vietnam, she was told that Hanoi was revising its *1979 White Paper on Sino-Vietnamese Relations*. The new version is not yet available (author's correspondence with Han Suyin, 22 May 1994).

16. In writing this book, Huang had the support of the International Liaison Committee of the Party Central Committee and the Political Affairs and Liaison Department of the PLA. The book is published by the PLA Publishing House.

17. For a discussion of neibu sources, see Flemming Christiansen, "The Neibu Bibliography: A Review Article" and Liu Changyun, "A Preliminary Analysis of the Characteristics of Neibu Materials in the Social Sciences" in *CCP Research Newsletter* Number 4 (Fall-Winter 1989–90), pp. 13–23.

18. Humphrey Trevelyan, *Diplomatic Channels* (London: Macmillan, 1973), p. 85.

19. John Tosh, *The Pursuit of History: Aims, Methods and New Directions in the Study of Modern History* (London: Longman, 1993), p. 66.

Chapter One: January 1956–July 1956

1. For details, see *Documents Relating to British Involvement in the Indo-China Conflict 1945–1965* (Cmnd. 2834), passim. The sequence of events during this period is also encapsulated in *Keesing's Contemporary Archives*, 5–12 July 1958, pp. 16276–16277.

2. *Hanoi Home Service*, 18 January 1956, *SWB/FE/*528, p. 54.

3. *VNA*, 29 and 31 December 1955, *SWB/FE/*523, p. 30.

4. Janos Radvanyi, *Delusion and Reality: Hoaxes and Diplomatic One-Upmanship in Vietnam* (Indiana: Gateway Publishers, 1978), p. 24.

5. *Lich Su Quan Doi Nhan Dan Viet Nam, Tap II— Quyen Mot* (Hanoi: Nha Xuat Ban Quan Doi Nhan Dan, 1988), pp. 11–12; for a brief account of the 6th Plenary Session, which apparently included a closed session, see "Mot Vung Chien Khu Xua" in *Nhan Dan*, 28 August 1993; Cao Van Luong, *Lich Su Cach Mang Mien Nam Vietnam: Giai Doan 1954–1960* (Hanoi: Nha Xuat Ban Khoa Hoc Xa Hoi, 1991), p. 160. According to Cao Van Luong, Ho's view was reiterated at the 8th Plenary Session in August 1955.

6. *Lich Su Quan Doi Nhan Dan Viet Nam*, p. 12 (hereafter cited as *Lich Su...*).

7. Ibid., p. 14.

8. See *Socialist Republic of Vietnam Foreign Ministry White Book on Relations with China* (*Hanoi Home Service*, 6 and 11 October 1979, *SWB/FE/*6238 and 6242). For the replies of the Chinese government and Hoang Van Hoan, see *Beijing Review*, 23 November 1979, 30 November 1979, and 7 December 1979.

9. Hoang Van Hoan, *A Drop in the Ocean: Hoang Van Hoan's Revolutionary Reminiscences* (Beijing: Foreign Languages, 1988), p. 324.

10. Ibid.; Guo Ming (ed.), *Zhongyue Guanxi Yanbian Shishi Nian* (Guangxi Renmin Chubanshe, 1992), p. 65.

11. Hoang, op. cit., p. 324.

12. *Zhongguo Junshi Guwentuan Yuanyue Kangfa Douzheng Shishi* (Beijing: Jiefang Jun Chubanshe, 1990), pp. 141–142.

13. Roderick Marfarquhar, *The Origins of the Cultural Revolution*, Volume I (Oxford: Oxford University Press, 1974), p. 9.

14. *Selected Works of Mao TseTung*, Volume V (Beijing: Foreign Languages, 1977), pp. 235–241; *Beijing Home Service*, 10 January 1956, *SWB/FE/*526, p. 3.

15. John K. Leung and Michael Y. M. Kau (ed.), *The Writings of Mao Zedong, 1949–1976 (Volume II: January 1956–December 1957)* (New York: M. E. Sharpe, 1992), pp. 17–19.

16. Zong Huaiwen (comp.), *Years of Trial, Turmoil and Triumph— China from 1949 to 1988* (Beijing: Foreign Languages, 1989), pp. 56 and 72.

17. Summing-up speech at the sixth expanded plenary session of the 7th CCP Central Committee (September 1955), in *Miscellany of Mao Tse-Tung Thought (1949–1968), Part I* (JPRS 61269-1, 20 February 1974), pp. 14–17.

18. *NCNA*, 30 January 1956, *SWB/FE/*532 (Supplement).

19. *FO 371*/120869, FC 10110/8, 10 February 1956, from Macau to Foreign Office (Secret) and FC 10110/23, 19 February 1956, from Macau to Foreign Office.

20. Ibid.

21. *Documents Relating to British Involvement in the Indochina Conflict 1945–1965* (Cmnd. 2834), pp. 114–115 and 118.

22. See Shao Kuo-kang, "Chou En-lai's Diplomatic Approach to Non-aligned States in Asia: 1953–60" in *China Quarterly*, June 1979, Number 78.

23. *Zhongguo Junshi Guwentuan Yuanyue Kangfa Douzheng Shishi* (Beijing: Jiefang Jun Chubanshe, 1990), p. 143.

24. *Documents relating to British Involvement in the Indochina Conflict 1945–1965* (Cmnd. 2834), pp. 113–114.

25. *Beijing Home Service*, 11 December 1955, *SWB/FE/*518, pp. 11 and 51.

26. *NCNA*, 24 January 1956, *SWB/FE/*530, p. 15 and *NCNA*, 28 January 1956, *SWB/FE/*531, p. 18.

27. *Zhou Enlai Waijiao Huodong Da Shiji* (Beijing: Shijie Zhishi Chubanshe, 1993), p. 136.

28. *VNA*, 1 February 1956, *SWB/FE/*532, p. 44.

29. *Zhou,* op. cit., p. 136.

30. *TASS in English*, 3 February 1956, *SWB/SU/*698, p. 36.

31. *NCNA*, 5 February 1956, *SWB/FE/*533, p. 17; *NCNA*, 9 February 1956, *SWB/FE/*535, p. 13.

32. *Documents Relating to British Involvement in the Indo-China Conflict 1945–1965* (Cmnd. 2834), pp. 115–117; *VNA*, 22 February 1956, *SWB/FE/*538, p. 38.

33. The 20th Congress of the CPSU began on 14 February and closed on 25 February 1956; for the full text of Khrushchev's report on "The International Position of the USSR," see Proceedings of the 20th Congress of the CPSU, *SWB/SU/*16 February 1956, Supplement No. 1, pp. 3–24.

34. *Confidential U.S. State Department Central Files* (hereafter cited as *CUSSDCF*): 751 G. 00/2-1156, 2743, 11 February 1956, State Department to Saigon (Secret).

35. The above summary of Soviet policy in Southeast Asia is taken from Aleksandr Kaznacheev, *Inside a Soviet Embassy: Experiences of a Russian Diplomat in Burma* (Philadelphia: Lippincott, 1962), Chapters 10–11 and 17. Kaznacheev was in Rangoon from 1957 to 1959; One of Kaznacheev's sources is Slava Tarasov, a liaison officer between the Soviet and Chinese embassies in Rangoon.

36. *Documents Relating to British Involvement in the Indochina Conflict 1945–1965*, (Cmnd. 2834), pp. 119–120.

37. *VNA*, 24 February 1956, *SWB/FE/*539, p. 29.

38. *Phnom Penh Home Service*, 10 February 1956, *SWB/FE/*535, p. 40; *Zhongguo Waijiao Guan Huiyi Lu: Xin Zhongguo Waijiao Fengyun*, Volume I (Beijing: Shijie Zhishi Chubanshe, 1944), pp. 59–60.

39. *NCNA*, 18 February 1956, *SWB/FE/*537, p. 10.

40. *CUSSDCF*: 751 H. 00/2-2856, 1108, 28 February 1956, from Phnom Penh to State Department; According to Milton Osborne, he was told by Wilfred Burchett in 1966 that Zhou Enlai offered Sihanouk a guarantee that China would restrain North Vietnam from interfering in Cambodia's domestic affairs. See Milton Osborne, *Sihanouk: Prince of Light, Prince of Darkness* (Sydney: Allen and Unwin, 1994), p. 114; according to Sihanouk in 1973, from 1956, the Chinese had kept their word to respect Cambodia's neutrality. See Norodom Sihanouk

and Wilfred Burchett, *My War with the CIA: Cambodia's Fight for Survival* (Harmondsworth: Penguin, 1973), p. 203.

41. Norodom Sihanouk and Wilfred Burchett, *My War with the CIA: Cambodia's Fight for Survival* (Harmondsworth: Penguin, 1973), pp. 76–80.

42. *CUSSDCF*: 751 H. 00/1-1956,1514, 19 January 1956, from New Delhi to State Department (Secret).

43. *VNA*, 16 February 1956, *SWB/FE/537*, p. 33.

44. *VNA*, 20 February 1956, *SWB/FE/538*, p. 37.

45. David P. Chandler, *Brother Number One: A Political Biography of Pol Pot* (Colorado: Westview, 1992), p. 55.

46. Michael Leifer, *Cambodia: The Search for Security* (New York, 1967), p. 79, cited in Ben Kiernan, *How Pol Pot Came to Power* (London: Verso, 1985), p. 170.

Sangkum Reastr Niyum, or People's Socialist Community, was formed by Sihanouk in 1955; Pracheachon, or People's Group, formed in 1951, was the leading Communist Party in Cambodia.

47. *CUSSDCF*: 751 G. 00/3-1556, 302, 15 March 1956, from Saigon to Foreign Office.

48. *CUSSDCF*: 751 G. 00/4-1656, 334, 16 April 1956, Saigon to State Department: "Country Team evaluation of Vietminh subversive capability in Free Vietnam and the Government's ability to counter this continued threat to its stability" (Secret).

49. See *CUSSDCF*: 751 G. 00/2-2856, 3498, 28 February 1956, from Saigon to State Department (Secret); *CUSSDCF*: 751 G. 00/4-1656, 334, 16 April 1956, from Saigon to State Department: "Country Team evaluation of Vietminh subversive capability in Free Vietnam and the government's ability to counter this continued threat to its stability" (Secret); The weakness of the Vietnamese Communist forces in the South during this period is confirmed by Le Duan in *Duong Loi Cach Mang Mien Nam*. For the full text, see *Race Document Number 1002*.

50. *Documents Relating to British Involvement in the Indochina Conflict 1945–1965* (Cmnd. 2834), p. 120.

51. *NCNA*, 14 March 1956, *SWB/FE/544*, pp. 2 and 11; *Zhou Enlai Waijiao Huodong Da Shiji* (Beijing: Shijie Zhishi Chubanshe, 1993), p. 140.

52. *NCNA*, 20 March 1956, *SWB/FE/546*, p. 17.

53. *Zhongguo Junshi Guwentuan Yuanyue Kangfa Douzheng Shishi* (Beijing: Jiefang Jun Chubanshe, 1990), p. 143.

54. Ibid.

55. *Chen Geng Riji* (Beijing: Jiefang Jun Chubanshe, 1984); Qian Jiang, *Zai Shenbi De Zhanzheng Chung* (Honan Renmin Chubanshe, 1992), pp. 62–75; Wang Xiangen, *Yuanyue Kangmei Shilu* (Jinan Chubanshe, 1992), passim; Hoang Van Hoan, "Distortion of Facts about Militant Friendship Between Vietnam and China Is Impermissible" in *Beijing Review*, 7 December 1979, Number 49, p. 12.

56. Huang Zheng, *Ho Zhiming Yu Zhongguo* (Beijing: Jiefang Jun Chubanshe, 1987), pp. 131–132.

57. *Documents Relating to British Involvement in the Indochina Conflict 1945–1965* (Cmnd. 2834), pp. 93–94.

58. U.S. Department of State, *Working Paper on North Vietnam's Role in the*

South (27 May 1968), Appendices, Item 19 (Translation of a document found on the person of a political officer with Communist forces in Zone 9 of the Western Interzone on 27 November 1956), Item 31 (An intelligence report from an agent of the GVN who had contact with Vietnamese Communist Party members in Saigon area in 1956) and Item 204 (Document purportedly issued probably in late spring 1956 by Lao Dong Party Central Committee for guidance of senior cadres in GVN zone).

59. For an account of the impact of Diem's "denounce the Communists" campaign on the Communists in South Vietnam, see "How Armed Struggle Began in South Vietnam" in *Vietnam Courier* Number 22, March 1974.

60. See U.S. Department of State, *Working Paper on North Vietnam's Role in the South* (27 May 1968), Appendices, Items 19, 31, and 204.

61. Hoang Van Hoan, op. cit., p. 324; Guo Ming (ed.), *Zhongyue Guanxi Yanbian Shishi Nian* (Guangxi Renmin Chubanshe, 1992), p. 65.

62. Hoang Van Hoan, *A Drop in the Ocean* (Beijing: Foreign Languages, 1988), p. 324.

63. *VNA*, 23 March 1956, *SWB/FE/*547, p. 37.

64. *VNA*, 28 March 1956, *SWB/FE/*548, p. 37.

65. *Hanoi Radio*, 25 March 1956, *SWB/FE/*548, p. 37; *FO 371/*123393, DF 1016/20, 2 April 1956, from Vice-Consulate (Haiphong) to Consulate-general (Hanoi).

66. For Mikoyan's visit to Hanoi, see *SWB/FE/*550, pp. 53–60; *SWB/FE/*551, pp. 31–32; *SWB/SU/*714, pp. 34–35; and *SWB/SU/*715, pp. 26–27.

67. David Chanoff and Doan Van Toai, *Portrait of the Enemy: The Other Side of the War in Vietnam* (London: I. B. Tauris, 1986) p. 32.

68. *Documents Relating to British Involvement in the Indochina Conflict 1945–1965* (Cmnd. 2834), pp. 120–123.

69. *FO 371/*123393, DF 1016/24, 3 May 1956, from Vice-Consulate (Haiphong) to Consulate-general (Hanoi).

70. See *SWB/FE/*551, pp. 7–10; *SWB/FE/*552, pp. 19–20.

71. U.S. Department of State, *Working Paper on North Vietnam's Role in the South* (27 May 1968), Appendices, Item 31.

72. *FO 371/*123395, DF 1016/47, 5 October 1956, from Saigon to Foreign Office.

73. Huang Guoan, et al., *Zhongyue Guanxi Jianbian* (Guangxi Renmin Chubanshe, 1986), pp. 190–192; Shi Yingfu, *Mimi Chubing Yare Congling: Yuanyue Kangmei Jishi* (Beijing: Jiefang Jun Wenyi Chubanshe, 1990), p. 13.

74. For details of the relationship between the Vietnamese Communists and the Pathet Lao, see Paul F. Langer and Joseph J. Zasloff, *North Vietnam and the Pathet Lao: Partners in the Struggle for Laos* (Cambridge: Harvard University Press, 1970); Geoffrey Charles Gunn, "Road through the Mountains: The Origins of Nationalism and Communism in Laos, 1930–1954" (Ph.D. Thesis, Monash University, 1985).

75. *VNA*, 24 December 1956, *SWB/FE/*522, p. 59.

76. *NCNA*, 24 December 1955, *SWB/FE/*522, pp. 10–11; also, *NCNA*, 25 December 1955, *SWB/FE/*522, p. 11.

77. *CUSSDCF*: 751 J. 00/1-256, 824, 2 January 1956, from Vientiane to State Department; *FO 371/*123397, DF 1017/13, 4 January 1956, from Vientiane

to Foreign Office; *Vientiane Home Service*, 5 January 1956, *SWB/FE/*525, p. 40; *Paris Radio*, 7 January 1956, *SWB/FE/*525, p. 40.

78. *CUSSDCF*: 751 J. 00/12-3155, 821, 31 December 1955, from Vientiane to State Department (Secret); *FO 371*/123397, DF 1017/13, 4 January 1956, from Vientiane to Foreign Office.

79. *VNA*, 14 January 1956, *SWB/FE/*527, p. 39.

80. *VNA*, 16 January 1956, *SWB/FE/*527, p. 39.

81. *NCNA*, 15 January 1956, *SWB/FE/*527, p. 5.

82. *FO 371*/123440, DF 1043/5, 15 February 1956, from Hanoi to Vientiane.

83. *FO 371*/123399, DF 1017/52, 14 February 1956, from UK High Commission in India to Foreign Office.

84. *CUSSDCF*: 751 J. 00/3-156, 1107, 1 March 1956, from Vientiane to State Department (Secret).

85. *NCNA*, 24 February 1956, *SWB/FE/*539, p. 3.

86. *VNA*, 11 April 1956, *SWB/FE/*552, pp. 46–47.

87. *Documents Relating to British Involvement in the Indochina Conflict 1945–1965* (Cmnd. 2834), p. 123.

88. *TASS in English*, 13 April 1956, *SWB/SU/*718, p. 44.

89. U.S. Department of State, *Working Paper on North Vietnam's Role in the South* (27 May 1968), Appendices, Item 204.

90. *CUSSDCF*: 751 G. 00/4-3056, 30 April 1956, State Department: Memorandum of Conversation (Secret).

91. *Documents Relating to British Involvement in the Indochina Conflict 1945–1965* (Cmnd. 2834), p. 23.

92. *FO 371*/123394, DF 1016/27, 14 May 1956, from Hanoi to Foreign Office.

93. *Documents Relating to British Involvement in the Indochina Conflict 1945–1965* (Cmnd. 2834), p. 123.

94. *FO 371*/129474, DF 1015/228, 19 September 1957, from Foreign Office to Vientiane.

95. *Phnom Penh Radio*, 8 April 1956, *SWB/FE/*552, p. 50.

96. *FO 371*/123420, DF 1023/2, 29 June and 11 July 1956, from Vientiane to Foreign Office.

97. For the full text, see *NCNA*, 4 April 1956, *SWB/FE/*550, pp. 22–30.

98. *Voice of Vietnam*, 27 April 1956, *SWB/FE/*557, p. 58; *Ho Chi Minh: Selected Works*, Volume IV (Hanoi: Foreign Languages, 1962), pp. 153–156.

99. *Selected Works of Mao TseTung*, Volume V (Beijing: Foreign Languages, 1977), pp. 284–307.

100. Ibid., pp. 288–289.

101. *Documents Relating to British Involvement in the Indochina Conflict 1945–1965* (Cmnd. 2834), p. 126.

102. *Moscow in English for Southeast Asia*, 10 May 1956, *SWB/SU/*725, pp. 40–41.

103. *VNA*, 8 June 1956, *SWB/FE/*569, pp. 38–39.

104. Ibid.

105. *NCNA*, 11 May 1956, *SWB/FE/*561, pp. 1–2.

106. See *SWB/FE/*June 1956, Supplements, Numbers 1–3; for Zhou Enlai's address on foreign policy, see *SWB/FE/*July 1956, Supplement, Number 5.

107. U.S. Department of State *Working Paper on North Vietnam's Role in the South* (27 May 1968), Appendices, Item 301: CRIMP Document, p. 2.

The CRIMP Document is believed to be a notebook of a high-level political cadre written sometime around 1963, recording his impressions of Communist policies during the early years of the revolutionary struggle against Diem. It was captured by the Allied forces in early January 1966, during Operation CRIMP north of Saigon.

108. *Vietnam: The Anti–U.S. Resistance War for National Liberation 1954–1975: Military Events* (JPRS 80968, 3 June 1982), pp. 16–17.

109. *Lich Su...*, p. 36; *Ho Chi Minh: Selected Works*, Volume IV (Hanoi: Foreign Languages, 1962), pp. 157–161.

110. *Lich Su...*, p. 77; *Vietnam: The Anti–U.S. Resistance War for National Salvation 1954–1975: Military Events* (JPRS 80968, 3 June 1982), pp. 16–17; "A Party History" (JPRS 75579), *Translations on North Vietnam*, Number 2185 cited in William J. Duiker, *The Communist Road to Power* (Colorado: Westview, 1981), p. 359, n.17; Cao Van Luong, *Lich Su Cach Mang Mien Nam Vietnam: Giai Doan 1954–1960* (Hanoi: Nha Xuat Ban Khoa Hoc Xa Hoi, 1991), p. 88.

111. *VNA*, 12 July 1956, *SWB*/FE/579, p. 38.

112. *CUSSDCF*: 751 G. 00/7-2256, 22 July 1956, from Saigon to State Department.

Chapter Two: August 1956–December 1956

1. *Lich Su...*, pp. 460–461.

2. *Ibid.*, p. 14.

3. *Hanoi Home Service*, 6 September 1956, *SWB/FE/*595, p. 34; *Vietnam: The Anti-U.S. Resistance War for National Salvation 1954–1975: Military Events* (JPRS 80968, 3 June 1982), p. 18; Carlyle Thayer, *War by Other Means: National Liberation and Revolution in Vietnam, 1954–60* (Sydney: Allen and Unwin, 1989), p. 89; Edwin Evariste Moise, "Land Reform in China and North Vietnam: Revolution at the Village Level" (Ph.D. dissertation, University of Michigan, 1977), pp. 381–382.

4. On 2 May 1956, Mao made his famous "hundred flowers" speech to a closed session of the Supreme State Conference. The theme of liberalization in the field of culture was further amplified by Lu Dingyi, Director of the CCP's Propaganda Department on 26 May.

5. *Hanoi Home Service*, 17 August 1956, *SWB/FE/*589, pp. 41–42.

6. *Lich Su...*, pp. 77–78.

7. *Lich Su...*, p. 78; Cao Van Luong, *Lich Su Cach Mang Mien Nam Vietnam: Giai Doan 1954-1960* (Hanoi: Nha Xuat Ban Khoa Hoc Xa Hoi, 1991), p. 89. According to Cao, Le Duan's thesis was completed by August 1956.

The original text is cataloged as Number 1002 in the Race Collection deposited in the Center for Research Libraries. A summary of the thesis can be found in Jeffrey Race, *War Comes to Long An: Revolutionary Conflict in a Vietnamese*

Province (Berkeley: University of California Press, 1973), pp. 75–81; Carlyle A. Thayer, *War by Other Means: National Liberation and Revolution in Vietnam, 1954–60* (Sydney: Allen and Unwin, 1989), pp. 106-109; Gareth Porter, *Vietnam: The Definitive Documentation of Human Decisions,* Volume II (London: Heyden and Son, 1979), pp. 52–53.

8. Vo Tran Nha (chu bien), *Lich Su Dong Thap Muoi* (Hanoi: Nha Xuat Ban Thanh Pho Ho Chi Minh, 1993), p. 190.

9. *VNA*, 2,3,4, and 5 August 1956, *SWB/FE/*585, pp. 38–39.

10. *VNA*, 2 August 1956, *SWB/FE/*585, p. 39.

11. *NCNA*, 5 August 1956, *SWB/FE/*585, pp. 38-39.

12. *VNA*, 6 August 1956, *SWB/FE/*586, p. 44.

13. *CUSSDCF*: 751 J. 00/6-1456, 14 June 1956, "Briefing memorandum on current political situation in Laos" (Top Secret).

14. *NCNA*, 7 August 1956, *SWB/FE/*586, p. 44.

15. *NCNA*, 8 August 1956, *SWB/FE/*586, p. 43.

16. *VNA*, 11 August 1956, *SWB/FE/*587, p. 39.

17. *VNA*, 12 August 1956, *SWB/FE/*587, p. 39.

18. *NCNA*, 8 August 1956, *SWB/FE/*586, p. 6.

19. *Memoirs of Wang Bingnan: Nine Years of Sino-U.S. Talks in Retrospect*, translated in *China Report*, JPRS-CPS-85-079, 7 August 1985, p. 34; Kenneth T. Young, *Negotiating with the Chinese Communists: The United States Experience, 1953–1967* (New York: Mcgraw-Hill, 1968), p. 116.

20. For Souvanna Phouma's visit to China, see *SWB/FE/*589, p. 11; *SWB/FE/*590, pp. 5–12; *SWB/FE/*591, pp. 10–15; *SWB/FE/*592, pp. 2–3. For a first-person account of the visit, see Sisouk Na Champassak, *Storm over Laos: A Contemporary History* (New York: Praeger, 1961), Chapter 5; *Zhou Enlai Waijiao Huodong Da Shiji* (Beijing: Shijie Zhishi Chubanshe, 1993), pp. 155–157.

21. Kenneth T. Young, op. cit., p. 119.

22. *FO 371*/123423, DF 10310/37, 31 August 1956, from Vientiane to Foreign Office. This meeting was the continuation of an earlier meeting which took place on the afternoon of 21 August 1956. See *Zhou Enlai Waijiao Da Shiji* (Beijing: Shijie Zhishi Chubanshe, 1993), p. 156.

23. *NCNA*, 25 August 1956, *SWB/FE/*591, pp. 12–13.

24. *VNA*, 27 August 1956, *SWB/FE/*592, p. 31.

25. For Souvanna Phouma's visit to Hanoi, see *SWB/FE/*592, pp. 29–31; Sisouk Na Champassak, op. cit., Chapter 5.

26. *NCNA*, 31 August 1956, *SWB/FE/*593, p. 7.

27. *FO 371*/123420, DF 10310/22, 8 June 1956, from Vientiane to Foreign Office; Sisouk Na Champassak, op. cit., p. 40.

28. *FO 371*/123438, DF 1042/37, 8 September 1956, from Phnom Penh to Foreign Office (Secret); *FO 371*/120903, DF 1042/52, from Phnom Penh to Foreign Office; *CUSSDCF*: 751 J. 00/9-2556, 1418, 25 September 1956, from Paris to State Department.

29. Wilfred Burchett, *North of the 17th Parallel,* 2nd edition enlarged (Hanoi: Red River, October 1957), p. 301.

30. Hoang Van Hoan, *A Drop in the Ocean* (Beijing: Foreign Languages, 1988), pp. 302–309.

31. Ibid., p. 307.

32. *Vietnam: The Anti-U.S. Resistance War for National Salvation 1954–1975: Military Events* (printing completed 30 May 1980) (JPRS 80968, 3 June 1982), pp. 19–20.

33. For details, see Nhu Phong, "Intellectuals, Writers and Artists" in *China Quarterly*, January-March 1962, Number 9; P. J. Honey, "Ho Chi Minh and the Intellectuals" (originally published in *Soviet Survey* Number 28, April-June 1959) in Wesley R. Fishel (ed.), *Vietnam: Anatomy of a Conflict* (Illinois: F. E. Peacock, 1968); Hoang Giang, "La Revolte des Intellectuals au Vietnam 1956," and Georges Boudarel, "Intellectual Dissidence in the 1950s: The Nhan-Van Giai-Pham Affair," in *The Vietnam Forum* 13 (Yale: Southeast Asia Studies, 1990); Georges Boudarel, *Cent Fleurs Ecloses dan la Nuit du Vietnam: Communisme et Dissidence, 1954–1956* (Jacques Bertoin, 1991); Hirohide Kurihara, "Changes in the Literary Policy of the Vietnamese Workers' Party, 1956–1958," in Takashi Shiraishi and Motoo Furuta (ed.), *Indochina in the 1940s and 1950s* (Ithaca: Cornell University Press, 1992).

34. *CUSSDCF*: 751 G. 00/10-456, 4 October 1956, Department of State: Memorandum of Conversation between Pierre Landy (Counselor, French Embassy) and Paul Kattenburg (Southeast Asia Department, U.S. State Department); *FO 371*/123396, DF 1016/53, 12 November 1956, from Saigon to Foreign Office (Secret); *FO 371*/129706, DV 1016/2, 29 December 1956, from Hanoi to Foreign Office.

35. *VNA*, 29 October 1956, *SWB/FE*/610, p. 39.

36. *FO 371*/123395, DF 1016/52, 31 October 1956, from Hanoi to Foreign Office.

37. *FO 371*/123396, DF 1016/53, 12 November 1956, from Saigon to Foreign Office (Secret).

38. *VNA*, 25 October 1956, *SWB/FE*/610, p. 39.

39. It should be noted that Truong Chinh was vice-chairman of the Agrarian Reform Committee. Pham Van Dong was the chairman.

40. Thanh Tin, *Hoa Xuyen Tuyet (Hoi Ky)* (California: Saigon, 1991), p. 139.

41. Guo Ming, *Zhongyue Guanxi Yanbian Sishi Nian* (Guangxi Renmin Chubanshe, 1992), p. 101; Vo Nhan Tri, *Vietnam Economic Policy Since 1975* (Singapore: ISEAS, 1990), p. 2 and footnote 2.

42. Thanh Tin, *Mat That: Hoi Ky Chinh Tri cua Bui Tin* (California: Saigon, 1993), p. 37.

43. Guo Ming, op. cit., p. 101.

44. Hoang Van Hoan, op. cit., p. 307.

45. According to Faligot and Kauffer, the pro-Chinese Hoang Van Hoan was particularly close to Kang Sheng, who was for many years the head of the Chinese Secret Service. See Roger Faligot and Remi Kauffer, *The Chinese Secret Service* (New York: William Morrow, 1989), p. 179.

46. J.Honey, "Pham Van Dong's Tour," *China Quarterly*, October-December 1961, Number 8.

47. For statistical details of Chinese assistance in North Vietnam's economic development from 1958 to 1960, see Huang Guoan et al, *Zhongyue Guanxi Jianbian* (Guangxi Renmin Chubanshe, 1986), pp. 192–194.

48. For Nguyen Son's death and obituary, see *Hanoi Home Service*, 22 October 1956, *SWB/FE/*608, p. 42.

49. *Saigon Home Service*, 14 November 1956, *SWB/FE/*614, p. 33.

50. *FO 371*/123396, DF 1016/53, 12 November 1956, from Saigon to Foreign Office (Secret).

51. See Liu Shaoqi's political report in *SWB/FE/*September 1956, Supplement Number 1, pp. 18–60.

52. Ibid.

53. See Chen Yi's report on foreign policy, *SWB/FE/*September 1956, Supplement Number 4, pp. 20–22.

54. It is necessary to go into some detail of the discussion regarding the PLA here because it will help our understanding of the similarities and differences between the VPA and the PLA, as well as the Soviet Army, which will be discussed at the appropriate chronological junctures in this thesis.

55. For full text of the speeches of Peng Dehuai and Tan Zheng delivered at the 8th Congress of the CCP, see *SWB/FE/*October 1956, Supplement Number 5, pp. 20–33. Peng's speech was delivered on 18 September 1956 and Tan's on 23 September 1956.

56. Li Zhisui, *The Private Life of Chairman Mao: The Inside Story of the Man Who Made Modern China* (London: Chatto and Windus, 1994), p. 175 and Chapter 18.

57. Strobe Talbot (trans. and ed.), *Khrushchev Remembers: The Last Testament* (London: Andre Deutsch, 1974), p. 280. Also see Enver Hoxha, *The Khrushchevites* (London: Workers', 1976), p. 246.

58. Joseph Rothschild, *Return to Diversity: A Political History of East Central Europe since World War Two* (Oxford: Oxford University Press, 1989), pp. 150–160.

59. For an account of Chinese interest in the Hungarian crisis, see Janos Radvanyi, *Hungary and the Superpowers: The 1956 Revolution and Realpolitik* (Stanford: Hoover Institution Press, 1972), Chapter 2.

60. Fedor Burlatsky, *Khrushchev and the First Russian Spring: The Era of Khrushchev through the Eyes of His Adviser* (London: Weidenfeld and Nicolson, 1991), pp. 89–90; *FO 371*/120873, FC 10110/102, 14 November 1956, from Beijing to Foreign Office.

61. Quan Yanchi, *Mao Zedong Yu Khrushchev: 1957–1959 Zhongsu Guanxi Jishi* (Jiling Remin Chubanshe, 1990), p. 6.

62. Ibid., p. 7.

63. *FO 371*/123427, DF 10338/4, 20 November 1956, from Vientiane to Foreign Office; U.S. Department of State, Division of Research for Far East, report prepared as part of NIE 68-57, 8 July 1957.

64. *FO 371*/123420, DF 1023/6, 15 November 1956, from Vientiane to Foreign Office.

65. *NCNA*, 14 November 1956, *SWB/FE/*615, pp. 37–40.

66. Reports in the British press of fighting in North Vietnam were confirmed by one Vietnamese morse code transmission, one voice broadcast relayed on 16 November 1956, and a broadcast of 17 November from South Vietnam based on AFP and UP reports received through diplomatic channels. See *SWB/FE/*615,

p. 25. The first report from North Vietnam was *VNA*, 16 November 1956, *SWB/FE/*615, p. 28. More information became available on *Hanoi Home Service*, 18 November 1956, *SWB/FE/*616, p. 21 and *Hanoi Home Service*, 27 and 28 November 1956, *SWB/FE/*618, p. 18.

A broadcast from Saigon on 20 November 1956 said that the Vietnamese Communist Radio had just announced that in receiving the delegation attending the Conference of the Catholic Liaison Committee, Ho Chi Minh had said that in addition to the mistakes committed in agrarian reforms, they had infringed on the freedom of belief. He promised to make amends. See *SWB/FE/*616, p. 27.

Also see Edwin Evariste Moise, op. cit., pp. 410–415.

67. David Chanoff and Doan Van Toai, *Portrait of the Enemy: The Other Side of the War in Vietnam* (London: I. B. Tauris, 1986), p. 80; Pham Kim Vinh, *Vietnam: A Comprehensive History* (California: Pham Kim Vinh Research Institute, 1992), p. 338.

68. *The Quynh Luu Uprising* (Saigon: 1958).

69. *FO 371*/129706, DV 1016/2, 29 December 1956, from Hanoi to Foreign Office.

70. Elise Hawtin, "The Hundred Flowers Movement and the Role of the Intellectuals in China: Fei Hsiao-tung: A Case Study" in *Papers on China*, Volume 12 (East Asia Regional Studies Programme, Harvard University, 1958), pp. 147–198; Edward Friedman, "The Revolution in Hungary and the Hundred Flowers Period in China," *Journal of Asian Studies* Volume 25, Number 1, November 1965, pp. 119–122.

71. *CUSSDCF*: 751 G. 00/10-456, 4 October 1956, Department of State: Memorandum of Conversation.

72. North Vietnam, Cambodia, India, Burma, Pakistan, Afghanistan, Nepal, and Ceylon (Sri Lanka).

73. *VNA*, 16 November 1956, *SWB/FE/*615, p. 25; for an account of Zhou's visit to Hanoi from two Chinese sources, see Huang Zheng, *Ho Zhiming Yu Zhongguo* (Beijing: Jiefang Jun Chubanshe, 1987), pp. 225–227 and *Zhou Enlai Waijiao Huodong Da Shiji* (Beijing: Shijie Zhishi Chubanshe, 1993), pp. 169–170.

74. *CUSSDCF*: 751 G. 00/12-1156, 11 December 1956, from Saigon to Department of State.

75. *SWB/FE/*615, p. 25.

76. *VNA*, 18 November 1956, *SWB/FE/*615, p. 22.

77. *CUSSDCF*: 751 G. 00/12-2156, 183, 21 December 1956, from Saigon to Department of State (Secret).

78. *VNA*, 18 November 1956, *SWB/FE/*615, p. 25; *NCNA*, 18 November 1956, *SWB/FE/*615, p. 5; Guo Ming et al., *Xiandai Zhongyue Guanxi Ziliao Xuanbian*, Volume I (Beijing: Shishi Chubanshe, 1986), pp. 162 and 168.

79. *VNA*, 18 November 1956, *SWB/FE/*615, p. 26.

80. Ibid.

81. *Hanoi Home Service*, 19 November 1956, *SWB/FE/*616, pp. 21–22.

82. *VNA*, 19 November 1956, *SWB/FE/*616, p. 22.

83. *VNA*, 20 November 1956, *SWB/FE/*616, p. 22.

84. *NCNA*, 19 November 1956, *SWB/FE/*616, p. 23.

85. *VNA*, 21 November 1956, *SWB/FE/*616, p. 23.

86. *Ibid.* For the definition of "great-nation chauvinism," a phrase coined by the Chinese, see "Broadcast Talk on Chauvinism" in *Beijing Radio*, 11 December 1956, *SWB/FE/*622, p. 11.

87. *NCNA*, 21 November 1956, *SWB/FE/*616, p. 23.

88. *NCNA*, 21 November 1956, SWB/FE/615, p. 22.

89. *NCNA*, 21 November 1956, *SWB/FE/*616, p. 23.

90. Huang Zheng, *Ho Zhiming Yu Zhongguo* (Beijing: Jiefang Jun Chubanshe, 1987), p. 225.

91. *VNA*, 23 November 1956, *SWB/FE/*617, pp. 23-24.

92. *CUSSDCF*: 751.G 00/12-1156, 11 December 1956, from Saigon to Department of State; 751 G. 00/12-2156, 183, 21 December 1956, from Saigon to Department of State: Weekly Report on North Vietnam (Secret).

93. *Socialist Republic of Vietnam Foreign Ministry White Paper on Relations with China, Hanoi Home Service*, 4–6 October 1979, *SWB/FE/*6238/A3/11; *Vietnam: The Anti-U.S. Resistance War for National Salvation 1954–1975: Military Events* (JPRS 80968, 3 June 1982), pp. 20–21.

94. For a Chinese account of Zhou's visit to Cambodia, see *Zhou Enlai Waijiao Huodong Da Shiji* (Beijing: Shijie Zhishi Chubanshe, 1993), pp. 170–171.

95. *NCNA*, 24 November 1956, *SWB/FE/*617, p. 28.

96. *NCNA*, 27 November 1956, *SWB/FE/*618, p. 23.

97. *NCNA*, 27 November 1956, *SWB/FE/*618, p. 1; *Keesing's Contemporary Archives*, 30 March–6 April 1957, pp. 15463–15464.

98. *NCNA*, 27 November 1956, *SWB/FE/*618, p. 25.

99. Ibid., p. 24.

100. *VNA*, 29 November 1956, *SWB/FE/*619, p. 21.

101. *FO 371*/123423, DF 10310/50(A), 29 November 1956, from Hanoi to Saigon.

102. *FO 371*/123423, DF 10310/50(B), 29 November 1956, from Phnom Penh to Foreign Office.

103. *FO 371*/123423, DF 10310/50(B), from Phnom Penh to Foreign Office; *FO 371*/123423, DF 10310/50(A), from Hanoi to Saigon. For a similar Chinese account, see *Zhou Enlai Waijiao Huodong Da Shiji* (Beijing: Shijie Zhishi Chubanshe, 1993), p. 171.

104. Truong Chinh's address to 500 cultural and art workers in Hanoi, *VNA*, 4 December 1956, *SWB/FE/*620, p. 19.

105. "A Party Account of the Situation in the Nam Bo region of South Vietnam from 1954–1960" (undated document captured by U.S. forces in Phuoc Long Province in April 1969), cited in William J. Duiker, *The Communist Road to Power in Vietnam* (Colorado: Westview, 1981), p. 180.

106. *Duong Loi Cach Mang Mien Nam* (Race Document Number 1002).

107. Tran Van Tra, *Nhung Chang Duong Lich Su Cua B2 Thanh Dong, Tap 1: Hoa Binh Hay Chien Tranh* (Hanoi: Nha Xuat Ban Quan Doi Nhan Dan, 1992), p. 153.

108. For a fuller discussion of the 11th Plenary session, see Carlyle A. Thayer, op. cit., pp. 100–111. Thayer's source for this plenary session is an article entitled, "Tang Cuong Doan Ket, Nang Cao Tinh To Chuc Va Boi Duong Chi Khi Dau Trong Toan Dang" in *Hoc Tap*, November-December 1956, Number

11; also see *SWB/FE/*Economic Supplement Number 250 for some details of the economic issues discussed at the session.

109. *Vietnam: The Anti-U.S. Resistance War for National Salvation 1954–1975: Military Events* (printing completed 30 May 1980) (JPRS 80968, 3 June 1982), p. 20; Tran Van Tra, *Nhung Chang Duong Lich Su Cua B2 Thanh Dong, Tap I: Hoa Binh Hay Chien Tranh* (Hanoi: Nha Xuat Ban Quan Doi Nhan Dan, 1992), p. 153; "Tu Nghi quyet lich su den Duong Ho Chi Minh," *Su Kien Va Nhan Chang* Number 4 (17 January 1994), p. 4.

110. Tran Van Tra, *Nhung Chang Duong Lich Su Cua B2 Thanh Dong, Tap I: Hoa Binh Hay Chien Tranh* (Hanoi: Nha Xuat Ban Quan Doi Nhan Dan, 1992), p. 153.

111. Hoang Van Hoan, op. cit., p. 107; also Tran Van Tra, op. cit., p. 152. *Black Paper: Facts and Evidences of the Acts of Aggression and Annexation of Vietnam Against Kampuchea* (Department of Press and Information of the Ministry of Foreign Affairs of Democratic Kampuchea, September 1978) noted that in 1957 (no date given), Le Duan was in transit through Kampuchea.

112. William J. Duiker, *Historical Dictionary of Vietnam* (London: Scarecrow, 1989), p. 87; Tran Van Tra, op. cit., pp. 151, 153.

113. Hoang Van Hoan, *A Drop in the Ocean* (Beijing: Foreign Languages, 1988), p. 307.

114. Thanh Tin, *Hoa Xuyen Tuyet (Hoi Ky)* (California: Saigon, 1991), pp. 139–140.

115. Hoang Van Hoan, opt. cit., p. 326.

Chapter Three: January 1957–December 1957

1. For details of the 6th Session of the DRV National Assembly, see *SWB/*FE/629, p. 21; *SWB/FE/*633, pp. 24–26.

2. Author's correspondence with Dr. Han Suyin: private conversation between Wang Bingnan and Han Suyin.

3. Han Suyin, *Eldest Son: Zhou Enlai and the Making of Modern China, 1898–1976* (London: Jonathan Cape, 1994), p. 260. The Chinese version of this book was published in the PRC before the English edition as *Zhou Enlai Yu Ta De Shiji 1898–1998* (Beijing: Zhongyang Wenxian Chubanshe, 1992).

4. *Annual Report of the Secretary-General on the Work of the Organization*, 16 June 1956–15 June 1957, in *General Assembly Official Records, 12th Session*, Supplement Number 1 (A/3594) (New York, 1957), pp. 51–52.

5. *VNA*, 26 January 1957, *SWB/FE/*634, p. 28.

6. *Annual Report of the Secretary-General ...*, op. cit., p. 52; *Report of the Security Council to the General Assembly*, 16 July 1956–15 July 1957, *Official Records, 12th Session*, Supplement Number 2 (A/3648), p. 74.

7. *General Assembly: Official Records (13th session)— Report of the Security Council*, 16 July 1957–15 July 1958, Supplement Number 2 (A/3901) (New York, 1958), pp. 53–55.

8. *NCNA*, 4 January 1957, *SWB/FE/*628, p. 4.

9. *Intelligence Report Number 7428: Zhou Enlai's Trip and Soviet Policy* (Department of State, Office of Intelligence Research), 30 January 1957.

10. *Beijing Home Service*, 8 January 1957, *SWB/FE/629*, p. 5.

11. For details, see *SWB/FE/*March 1956, Supplement Number 1.

12. Guo Ming (ed.), *Zhongyue Guanxi Yanbian Sishi Nian* (Guangxi Renmin Chubanshe, 1992), p. 66.

13. Ibid., pp. 38–39; *Vietnam: The Anti-U.S. Resistance War for National Salvation 1954–1975: Military Events* (printing completed 30 May 1980) (JPRS 80968, 3 June 1982), pp. 21–22.

14. *Lich Su...*, pp. 38–44.

15. Ibid.

16. Vo Nguyen Giap, "Arm the Revolutionary Masses and Build the People's Army," in *Vietnam Documents and Research Notes*, Document 106, Part II, June 1972.

17. *Ho Chi Minh: Toan Tap, Tap VII (July 1954–December 1957)* (Hanoi: Nha Xuat Ban Su That, 1987), pp. 674–677; *Ho Chi Minh: Selected Works*, Volume IV (Hanoi: Foreign Languages, 1962), pp. 231–234.

18. *Ho Chi Minh: Toan Tap, Tap 7 (July 1954–December 1957)* (Hanoi: Nha Xuat Ban Su That, 1987), pp. 710–712.

19. *FO 371*/129707, DV 1016/25, 31 May 1957, from Hanoi to Foreign Office; *Hanoi Radio*, 17 June 1957, *SWB/FE/677*, pp. 41-42, and *Hanoi Radio*, 27 June 1957, *SWB/FE/679*, p. 29.

20. *FO 371*/129707, DV 1016/48, 3 January 1958, from Hanoi to Foreign Office.

21. *FO 371*/123411, DF 1017/314, 24 November 1956, from Paris to Foreign Office.

22. *Vientiane Radio*, 30 December 1956, *SWB/FE/626*, p. 27.

23. *FO 371*/129468, DF 1015/59, 6 February 1957, from Washington to Foreign Office; *3rd Interim Report of the International Commission for Supervision and Control in Laos (1 July 1955–16 May 1957)* (Cmnd.314), p. 12.

24. *NCNA*, 1 and 2 January 1957, *SWB/FE/627*, pp. 10-11.

25. *FO 371*/129468, DF 1015/59, 6 February 1957, from Washington to Foreign Office.

26. Sisouk Na Champassak, *Storm over Laos: A Contemporary History* (New York: Praeger, 1961), pp. 52–54. Katay was at Lake Success as Head of the Laotian delegation to the 11th United Nations General Assembly.

27. *FO 371*/129481, DF 10310/2, 22 February 1957, from Vientiane to Foreign Office.

28. *VNA*, 16 May 1957, *SWB/FE/666*, p. 35.

29. Telegram from Laos to Department of State dated 10 May 1957, in *Foreign Relations of the United States*, Volume XXI: Cambodia and Laos, 1955–1957 (Washington: U.S. Government Printing, 1990), pp. 914–916.

30. *Zhou Enlai Waijiao Huodong Da Shiji* (Beijing: Shijie Zhishi Chubanshe, 1993), p. 204.

31. *FO 371*/129472, DF 1015/168, 6 June 1957, from Vientiane to Foreign Office (Secret).

32. Fedor Burlatsky, *Khrushchev and the First Russian Spring: The Era of Khrushchev through the Eyes of His Adviser* (London: Weidenfeld and Nicolson,

1991), pp. 94–95; Isaac Deutscher, *Russia, China and the West 1953–1966* (Middlesex: Penguin, 1970), pp. 123–125; Veljko Micunovic, *Moscow Diary* (New York: Doubleday, 1980), Chapter 21; Roger Pethybridge, *A Key to Soviet Politics: The Crisis of the "Anti-Party" Group* (London: George Allen and Unwin, 1962); Martin McCauley, *Nikita Khrushchev* (London: Sphere, 1991); *SWB/SU*/842, pp. 65–83.

33. John Garver, "New Light on Sino-Soviet Relations: The Memoir of China's Ambassador to Moscow, 1955–1962," *China Quarterly*, June 1990, Number 122: Liu Xiao, *Chu Shi Sulian Ba Nian (Eight Years as Ambassador to the Soviet Union)* (Beijing: Zhonggong Dangshi Ziliao Chubanshe, 1986).

34. *VNA*, 5 July 1957, *SWB/FE*/680, p. 35.

35. *VNA*, 30 June 1957, *SWB/FE*/677, p. 46.

36. *VNA*, 3 and 5 July 1957, *SWB/FE*/679, p. 27.

37. *VNA*, 6 July 1957, *SWB/FE*/680, p. 36.

38. *FO 371*/127270, FC 1017/81, 19 July 1957, from Beijing to Foreign Office; telegram from the Consul (Hong Kong) to Department of State dated 29 June 1957, in *Foreign Relations of the United States,* Volume III: China, 1955–1957 (Washington: U.S. Government Printing Office, 1986), pp. 567–569.

For details of the Congress, see *SWB/FE*/June 1957, Supplement.

39. *Socialist Republic of Vietnam Foreign Ministry White Book on Relations with China, Hanoi Home Service*, 4–6 October 1979, *SWB/FE*/6238/A3/11.

40. Zong Huaiwen (comp.), *Years of Trial, Turmoil and Triumph* (Beijing: Foreign Languages, 1989), pp. 80–82.

41. For details of Ho's visit to Pyongyang, see *SWB/FE*/681, pp. 35–40; *SWB/FE*/682, p. 33.

42. *NCNA*, 12 and 13 July 1957, *SWB/FE*/682, p. 5.

43. *TASS in Russian for Abroad*, 13, 14, 15, and 17 July 1957, *SWB/SU*/846, p. 27. For details of Ho's trip to Czechoslavakia, Poland, and East Germany, see *SWB/Part 2A*/847–851, and for his trip to Hungary, Yugoslavia, Albania, and Romania, see *SWB/Part 2B*/851–857.

44. Lester A. Sobel, *Russia's Rulers: The Khrushchev Period* (New York: Facts on File, 1971), p. 125.

45. *TASS*, 27 August 1957, *SWB/SU*/858, p. 24.

46. *General Assembly: Official Records (13th session)— Report of the Security Council*, 16 July 1957–15 July 1958, Supplement Number 2 (A/3901) (New York, 1958), pp. 53-55.

47. *NCNA*, 28 August 1957, *SWB/FE*/695, p. 2; *Zhou Enlai Waijiao Huodong Da Shiji* (Beijing: Shijie Zhishi Chubanshe, 1993), p. 211.

48. *NCNA*, 29 August 1957, *SWB/FE*/695, p. 2.

49. For details of the opening of the Yangtze Bridge, see *SWB/FE*/709, pp. 10–14; *News from Xinhua News Agency*, 16 October 1957, pp. 7 and 9.

50. *NCNA*, 1 August 1957, *SWB/FE*/687, p. 5.

51. *VNA*, 2 July 1957, *SWB/FE*/679, p. 27. Lin was in Hanoi from 2 July 1957.

52. *NCNA*, 1 September 1957, *SWB/FE*/696, p. 5; *NCNA*, 2 September 1957, *SWB/FE*/697, p. 3.

53. *VNA*, 1 July 1957, *SWB/FE/679*, p. 27.

54. *VNA*, 2 September 1957, *SWB/FE/696*, pp. 55-58; *Ho Chi Minh: Selected Works*, Volume IV (Hanoi: Foreign Languages, 1962), pp. 238-247.

55. *VNA*, 14 August 1957, *SWB/FE/691*, p. 54.

56. *NCNA*, 11 August 1957, *SWB/FE/690*, p. 5.

57. *Fourth Interim Report on the Activities of the International Commission for Supervision and Control in Laos* (17 May 1957–31 May 1958) (Cmnd. 541), p. 10.

58. *Vientiane Home Service*, 3 November 1957, *SWB/FE/714*, pp. 57–58.

59. *VNA*, 24 October 1957, *SWB/FE/712*, p. 42.

60. *NCNA*, 24 October 1957, *SWB/FE/711*, p. 4.

61. *Moscow in English for Southeast Asia*, 24 October 1957, *SWB/SU/876*, p. 38.

62. *FO 371*/129477, DF 1015/302, 26 November 1957, from Washington to Foreign Office.

63. *FO 371*/129477, DF 1015/312, 10 December 1957, from Vientiane to Foreign Office.

64. *FO 371*/129478, DF 1015/328, 20 December 1957, from Vientiane to Foreign Office.

65. *FO 371*/135790, DF 1015/5, 17 January 1958, from Vientiane to Foreign Office.

66. *FO 371*/135790, DF 1015/9, 30 January 1958, from Vientiane to Foreign Office.

67. *FO 371*/136118, DV 1016/7, 19 February 1958, from Hanoi to Foreign Office.

68. This interpretation was first put forward by P. J. Honey in "The Position of the DRV Leadership and the Succession to Ho Chi Minh," *China Quarterly*, January-March 1962, Number 9. Also see P. J. Honey, *Communism in North Vietnam: Its Role in the Sino-Soviet Conflict* (Connecticut: Greenwood Press, 1973), pp. 52–59; Jean Lacouture, *Ho Chi Minh* (Middlesex: Penguin, 1968); Robert F. Turner *Vietnamese Communism: Its Origins and Development* (Stanford: Hoover Institution Press, 1975); Daniel S. Papp, *Vietnam: The View from Moscow, Peking, Washington* (North Carolina: McFarland, 1981); Philip B. Davidson, *Vietnam at War: The History 1946–1975* (California: Presidio, 1988); Robert S. Ross, *The Indochina Tangle: China's Vietnam Policy 1975–1979* (New York: Columbia University Press, 1988), p. 20; Michael Lee Lanning and Dan Cragg, *Inside the VC and the NVA: The Real Story of North Vietnam's Armed Forces* (New York: Fawcett Columbine, 1992).

For the only critique of this interpretation so far, see Carlyle Thayer, *The Origins of the National Liberation Front for the Liberation of South Vietnam* (Ph.D. dissertation, Australian National University, 1977), pp. 608-628.

69. *FO 371*/129707, DV 1016/48, 3 January 1958, from Hanoi to Foreign Office.

70. *VNA*, 6 October 1957, *SWB/FE/706*, p. 43; *VNA*, 8 and 9 October 1957, *SWB/FE/707*, pp. 41, 43 and 46.

71. *VNA*, 22 November 1957, *SWB/FE/728*, p. 28.

72. *FO 371*/129707, DV 1016/48, 3 January 1958, from Hanoi to Foreign Office.

73. Guo Ming (ed.), *Zhongyue Guanxi Yanbian Shishi Nian* (Guangxi Renmin Chubanshe, 1992), p. 66.

74. *NCNA*, 15 October 1957, *SWB/FE/*709, p. 11.

75. *VNA*, 12 October 1957, *SWB/FE/*708, p. 35.

76. *VNA*, 18 and 19 October 1957, *SWB/FE/*710, pp. 33–34; *FO 371/*129707, DV 1016/42, 5 November 1957, from Hanoi to Foreign Office.

77. *FO 371/*129707, DV 1016/42, 5 November 1957, from Hanoi to Foreign Office.

78. *VNA*, 23 October 1957, *SWB/FE/*711, p. 39.

79. *FO 371/*129707, DV 1016/42, 5 November 1957, from Hanoi to Foreign Office.

80. *VNA*, 28 October 1957, *SWB/FE/*712, p. 41.

81. *VNA*, 30 October 1957, *SWB/FE/*713, p. 47.

82. Veljko Micunovic, op. cit., pp. 305–311; Otto Preston Chaney Jr., *Zhukov* (Devon: David and Charles, 1972), Chapter XVI. For a recent account of the fall of Zhukov, see William J. Spahr, *Zhukov: The Rise and Fall of a Great Captain* (California: Presidio, 1993), chapters XXIV and XXV.

83. *NCNA*, 27 November 1958, *SWB/FE/*713, p. 15.

84. *VNA*, 31 October 1957, *SWB/FE/*714, p. 51.

85. *Ho Chi Minh: Toan Tap, Tap VII (July 1954–December 1957)* (Hanoi: Nha Xuat Ban Su That, 1987), pp. 674–677; pp. 710-712; *Ho Chi Minh: Selected Works (Volume IV)* (Hanoi: Foreign Languages, 1962), pp. 231–234; *Lich Su...*, p. 47.

86. For details, see Georges Boudarel, "Intellectual Dissidence in the 1950s: The Nhan-Van and Giai-Pham Affair," *Vietnam Forum* 13 (Yale: Southeast Asia Studies, 1990).

87. *Hanoi Home Service*, 5 November 1957, *SWB/FE/*715, p. 45.

88. *CUSSDCF*: 751 G. 000/11-857, 8 November 1957, from Saigon to State Department.

89. Roger Pethybridge, op. cit., pp. 72, 89–90, 128, 152–161; Oleg Penkovsky, *The Penkovsky Papers* (London: Fontana, 1967), pp. 141-145.

90. *CUSSDCF*: 751 G. 00/11-857, 987, 8 November 1957, from Saigon to State Department. In his study, William S. Turley also concluded that Giap favored a lessening of party control over the VPA. See William S. Turley, "Civil-Military Relations in North Vietnam," *Asian Survey* Volume IX, Number 12 (December 1969).

91. *Hanoi Home Service*, 20 December 1957, *SWB/FE/*728, pp. 28–30.

92. For the full text of the 1957 Moscow Declaration, see G. F. Hudson et al.(documented and analyzed), *The Sino-Soviet Dispute* (London: China Quarterly, 1961), pp. 46–56. *SWB/SU/*Supplement, 25 November 1957, contains the full texts of the 12-Party Declaration and the 64-Party Peace Manifesto.

93. *VNA*, 29 April 1958, *SWB/FE/*764, pp. 27–28.

94. *Prague*, 17 November 1957, *SWB/Part 2A/*882, p. 28.

95. John Garver, "New Light on Sino-Soviet Relations: The Memoir of China's Ambassador to Moscow, 1955–1962," *China Quarterly*, June 1990, Number 122; Liu Xiao, *Chu Shi Sulian Ba Nian (Eight Years as Ambassador to the Soviet Union)* (Beijing: Zhonggong Dangshi Ziliao Chubanshe, 1986), p. 305.

96. Quan Yanchi, *Mao Zedong Yu Khrushchev: 1957–1959 Zhongsu Guanxi Jishi* (Jiling Renmin Chubanshe, 1990), pp. 38–41.

97. See Veljko Micunovic, op. cit., p. 319; Jerrold L. Schecter (trans.), *Khrushchev Remembers: The Glasnost Tapes* (Boston: Little, Brown, 1990), p. 152; O. B. Borisov and B. T. Koloskov, *Sino-Chinese Relations 1945–1970* (Bloomington: Indiana University Press, 1975), p. 99.

98. Nie Rongzhen, *Nie Rongzhen Huiyi Lu*, Part III (Beijing: Jiefang Jun Chubanshe, 1984), p. 803.

99. Donald S. Zagoria, *The Sino-Soviet Conflict 1956–61* (New York: Princeton University Press, 1962), pp. 170–171. (Zagoria cites *TASS*, 27 November 1957, as his source.) This visit was also mentioned in the joint editorial of *Renmin Ribao* and *Hongqi*, 6 September 1963. For details of the visit, see *SWB/SU* for the months of November and December 1957.

100. *NCNA*, 18 November 1957, *SWB/FE/*719, p. 6; Donald S. Zagoria, opt. cit., pp. 150–165; Lowell Dittmer, *Sino-Soviet Normalization and Its International Implications, 1945–1990* (Seattle: University of Washington Press, 1992), p. 176.

101. From the Journal of S. F. Antonov (21 October 1959): Summary of a conversation with the Chairman of the CC CPC [Central Committee Communist Party of China] Mao-Tse Tung on 14 October 1959, reproduced in *Cold War International History Project Bulletin*, Issue 3, Fall 1993, pp. 55–58. Antonov was then the temporary charge d'affaires of the Soviet Union in China.

102. For details on Sino-Japanese relations, see Lee Chae-Jin, *Japan Faces China: Political and Economic Relations in the Postwar Era* (Baltimore: Johns Hopkins University Press, 1976), Chapter 2. For a short review of Sino-Japanese relations from 1950 to 1963, see *China News Analysis*, Issue 509, 20 March 1964 For Japanese relations with Vietnam, see Masaya Shiraishi, *Japanese Relations with Vietnam: 1951–1987* (Ithaca: Cornell Southeast Asia Programme, 1990).

103. Strobe Talbot (trans. and ed.), *Khrushchev Remembers: The Last Testament* (London: Andre Deutch, 1974), pp. 254–255.

104. See "The Origin and Development of the Differences between the Leadership of the CPSU and Ourselves," *Beijing Review*, 13 September 1963, Number 37.

105. See, for example, *VNA*, 24 November 1957, and *NCNA*, 24 November 1957, *SWB/FE/*720, pp. 2–7 and 43.

106. Edward Crankshaw, *The New Cold War: Moscow v. Pekin* (London: Penguin, 1963), p. 62.

107. *TASS in English and TASS in Russian for Abroad*, 21 November 1957, *SWB/SU/*883, p. 38.

108. *TASS in English*, 21 November 1957, *SWB/SU/*883, p. 38.

109. *VNA*, 28 November 1957, *SWB/FE/*722, p. 35.

110. *VNA*, 1 December 1957, *SWB/FE/*722, p. 35.

111. *VNA*, 4 December 1957, *SWB/FE/*723, p. 37.

112. *VNA*, 8 December 1957, *SWB/FE/*724, p. 51.

113. *VNA*, 2 December 1957, *SWB/FE/*724, p. 37; *NCNA*, 10 December 1957, *SWB/FE/*725, p. 15; *VNA*, 14 December 1957, *SWB/FE/*726, p. 39.

114. Jan Seljna, *We Will Bury You* (London: Sidgwick and Jackson, 1982), pp. 56–58. The Czech military delegation visited China from 6 to 27 December

1957. Seljna was the former chief of staff to the minister of defense in Czechoslovakia and assistant secretary to the top-secret Czech Defense Council before he defected to the West in February 1968. He was then the highest ranking Communist ever to defect.

115. *FO 371*/129707, DV 1016/48, 3 January 1957, from Hanoi to Foreign Office.

116. *FO 371*/136118, DV 1016/7, 19 February 1958, from Hanoi to Foreign Office.

117. *Lich Su...*, p. 49.

118. "How Armed Struggle Began in South Vietnam," *Vietnam Courier* Number 22, March 1974, pp. 19–24.

119. *VNA*, 1 January 1958, *SWB/FE/*730, p. 41.

120. *Hanoi Home Service*, 17 January 1958, *SWB/FE/*735, pp. 33–34.

121. *Lich Su...*, pp. 85–86.

Chapter Four: January 1958–December 1958

1. *VNA*, 28 January 1958, *SWB/FE/*737, p. 33.

2. *Hanoi Home Service*, 25 February 1958, *SWB/FE/*746, p. 28; *Beijing Review* Volume 1, Number 1, 11 March 1958, p. 20.

3. *NCNA*, 20 January 1958, *SWB/FE/*736, p. 4.

4. *VNA*, 28 January 1958, *SWB/FE/*737, p. 33.

5. *VNA*, 3 March 1958, *SWB/FE/*748, p. 35.

6. *NCNA*, 31 January 1958, *SWB/FE/*757, p. 7.

7. *VNA*, 3 March 1958, *SWB/FE/*748, p. 36; also see Andrew Vickerman, *The Fate of the Peasantry: Premature "Transition to Socialism" in the Democratic Republic of Vietnam* (Yale University Southeast Asian Studies, Monograph Series Number 28, 1986), pp. 130 and 132. Vickerman's study showed that Chinese experience continued to influence land reforms in North Vietnam. But that did not mean that the North Vietnamese adopted Chinese ideas wholesale see Huang Guoan et al., *Zhongyue Guanxi Jianbian* (Guangxi Renmin Chubanshe, 1986), p. 193.

8. *NCNA*, 20 March 1958, *SWB/FE/*752, p. 32.

9. *VNA*, 24 April 1958, *SWB/FE/*763, p. 38.

10. Guo Ming (ed.), *Zhongyue Guanxi Yanbian Sishi Nian* (Guangxi People's Publisher, 1992), pp. 135 and 143.

11. For a detailed analysis of this subject, see Hirohide Kurihara, "Changes in the Literary Policy of the Vietnamese Worker's Party, 1956–1958," in Takashi Shiraishi and Motoo Furuta (ed.), *Indochina in the 1940s and 1950s* (Ithaca: Cornell University Press, 1992); P. J. Honey, "Ho Chi Minh and the Intellectuals," in Wesley R. Fishel (ed.), *Vietnam: Anatomy of a Conflict* (Illinois: F. E. Peacock, 1968).

12. *FO 371*/136119, DV 1016/21, 3 May 1958, from Hanoi to Foreign Office; *FO 371*/136119, DV 1016/24, 4 June 1958, from British Vice-Consulate (Haiphong) to British Consulate-General (Hanoi).

13. *FO 371*/136119, DV 1016/27, 27 May 1958, from Hanoi to Foreign Office; *VNA*, 29 April 1958, *SWB/FE/*764, pp. 27–28.

14. *FO 371/136119*, DV 1016/36, 10 September 1958, from Hanoi to Foreign Office.

15. Zong Huaiwen (comp.), *Years of Trial, Turmoil and Triumph—China from 1949 to 1988* (Beijing: Foreign Languages, 1989), p. 86.

16. Roderick MacFarquhar, *The Origins of the Cultural Revolution, Volume II: The Great Leap Forward 1958–1960* (Oxford: Oxford University Press, 1983), pp. 29–33; *Jianguo Yilai Mao Zedong Wengao*, Volume VII (Beijing: Zhongyang Wenxian Chubanshe, 1992), pp. 45–65.

17. Roderick MacFarquhar, op. cit., pp. 33–34; *Zhongguo Gongchandang Lishi Da Cidian: Shehui Zhuyi Shiqi* (Beijing: Zhonggong Zhongyang Dang Xiao Chubanshe, 1991), p. 167.

18. *NCNA*, 12 March 1958, *SWB/FE/750*, p. 30.

19. *NCNA*, 31 March 1958, *SWB/FE/757*, p. 7.

20. *VNA*, 13 March 1958, *SWB/FE/751*, p. 41.

21. For details of Ho's visit to India and Burma, see *SWB/FE/740*, pp. 29–30; *SWB/FE/741*, pp. 27–33; *SWB/FE/742*, pp. 17–18; *SWB/FE/743*, pp. 41–43; *SWB/FE/744*, pp. 33–36.

22. Speech by Le Duan on 18 March 1958 at the Enlarged Session of the Vietnam Fatherland Front Central Committee; *VNA*, 19 March 1958, *SWB/FE/751*, p. 32.

23. *Keesing's Contemporary Archives*, 19–26 April 1958, p. 16136.

24. For a discussion of India's relations with North and South Vietnam, see D. R. SarDesai, *Indian Foreign Policy in Cambodia, Laos and Vietnam 1947–1964* (Berkeley: University of California Press, 1968), Chapter 4. For the North Vietnam–India joint communiqué, see *SWB/FE/742*, pp. 17–18. For the North Vietnam–Burma joint statement, see *SWB/FE/744*, pp. 33–34.

25. *FO 371/136118*, DV 1016/8, 26 February 1958, from Beijing to Foreign Office.

26. *NCNA*, 8 March 1958, *SWB/FE/749*, p. 6.

27. *VNA*, 9 March 1958, *SWB/FE/749*, pp. 41–42.

28. *NCNA*, 9 March 1958, *SWB/FE/749*, pp. 5–6.

29. Wang Xiangen, *Yuanyue Kangmei Shilu* (Jinan Chubanshe, 1992), pp. 36–37.

30. *NCNA*, 21 December 1957, *SWB/FE/728*, p. 7.

31. *NCNA*, 1 January 1958, *SWB/FE/730*, p. 16.

32. *Lich Su...*, pp. 50–51.

33. *Hanoi Home Service*, 20 March 1958, *SWB/FE/755*, pp. 32–35; *VNA*, 26 March 1958, *SWB/FE/754*, pp. 32–35.

34. *NCNA*, 15 January 1958, *SWB/FE/734*, p. 7.

35. For Nguyen Son's death and obituary, see *Hanoi Home Service*, 22 October 1956, *SWB/FE/608*, p. 42.

36. *VNA*, 7 May 1958, *SWB/FE/766*, p. 33.

37. For full text of Peng Dehuai's speech, see *NCNA*, 22 February 1958, SWB/FE/745, pp. 3-7.

38. *Beijing Home Service*, 18 May 1958, *SWB/FE/769*, p. 14.

39. Zong Huaiwen (comp.), *Years of Trial, Turmoil and Triumph—China from 1949 to 1988* (Beijing: Foreign Languages, 1989), p. 87.

40. *NCNA*, 20 May 1958, *SWB/FE/770*, p. 8.

41. Speech at the Group Leaders' Forum of the Enlarged Meeting of the Military Affairs Committee (excerpts), 28 June 1958, in Stuart Schram (ed.), *Chairman Mao Talks to the People: Talks and Letters (1956–1971)* (New York: Pantheon, 1974), pp. 125–130; Li Deng et al., *Jianguo Yilai Junshi Bai Zhuang Da Shi* (Beijing: Zhishi Chubanshe, 1992), pp. 131–136; *Dang De Junshi Luebian Yu Renmin Jundui Jianshe* (Beijing: Guofang Daxue Chubanshe, 1990),pp. 163–164.

42. *Beijing Home Service*, 3 August 1958, *SWB/FE/791*, p. 1.

43. The meetings took place on 31 July, 1, 2, and 3 August 1958. See *Zhou Enlai Waijiao Huodong Da Shiji* (Beijing: Shijie Zhishi Chubanshe, 1993), p. 239.

44. From the journal of S. F. Antonov (21 October 1959): Summary of Conversation with the Chairman of the CC CPC [Central Committee Communist Party of China] Mao-Tse Tung on 14 October 1959, reproduced in *Cold War International History Project*, Issue 3, Fall 1993, pp. 55–58.

45. Quan Yanchi, *Mao Zedong Yu Khrushchev: 1957–1959 Zhongsu Guanxi Jishi* (Jiling Renmin Chubanshe, 1990), pp. 123–133.

46. Li Zhisui, *The Private Life of Chairman Mao: The Inside Story of the Man who Made Modern China* (London: Chatto and Windus, 1994), pp. 261–262.

47. For full text, see *NCNA*, 3 August 1958, *SWB/FE/792*, pp. 2–4.

48. *VNA*, 5 August 1958, SWB/FE/792, p. 37.

49. *NCNA*, 3 May 1958, *SWB/FE/765*, p. 4.

50. For a firsthand account, see Sisouk Na Champassak, *Storm over Laos: A Contemporary History* (New York: Praeger, 1961), Chapter 7.

51. *NCNA*, 1 June 1958, *SWB/FE/773*, p. 4.

52. *Fourth Interim Report on the Activities of the International Commission for Supervision and Control in Laos (17 May 1957–31 May 1958)* (Cmnd. 541), p. 13.

53. *VNA*, 28 May 1958, *SWB/FE/772*, p. 30.

54. *NCNA*, 1 June 1958, *SWB/FE/773*, p. 3.

55. *NCNA*, 2 June 1958, *SWB/FE/774*, p. 13.

56. *Vientiane Home Service*, 2 June 1958, p. 41.

57. *VNA*, 8 June 1958, *SWB/FE/775*, p. 29.

58. *NCNA*, 13 July 1958, SWB/FE/785, pp. 1–2.

59. *Documents Relating to British Involvement in the Indochina Conflict 1945–1965* (Cmnd.2834), pp. 25, 132.

60. *FO 371*/135792, DF 1015/70, 3 July 1958, from the Australian Legation (Saigon) to Department of External Affairs (Canberra)(Secret).

61. *VNA*, 9 August 1958, *SWB/FE/793*, p. 38.

62. *Vientiane Home Service*, 22 July 1958, *SWB/FE/788*, p. 30.

63. *Vientiane Home Service*, 15 August 1958, *SWB/FE/795*, p. 62.

64. *VNA*, 21 August 1958, *SWB/FE/795*, p. 55.

65. *Vientiane in Thai*, 26 December 1958, *SWB/FE/832*, p. 49.

66. See Sisouk Na Champassak, op. cit., p. 67; *Vientiane in Thai*, 26 December 1958, *SWB/FE/832*, p. 49.

67. *FO 371*/136068, DU 1015/10, 20 February 1958, from Australian Legation (Phnom Penh) to Department of External Affairs (Canberra) (Secret).

68. *FO 371*/129659, DU 1022/2, 29 April 1957, from Phnom Penh to Foreign Office.

69. *FO 371*/136070, DU 1016/1, 10 February 1958, from Phnom Penh to Foreign Office (Secret); *Saigon Radio*, 29 January 1958, *SWB/FE/*738, p. 31.

See Ben Kiernan, *How Pol Pot Came to Power* (London: Verso, 1985), pp. 178–181, for details of the activities of the Cambodian Communists during this time.

70. *FO 371*/136068, DU 1015/10, 20 February 1958, from Australian Legation (Phnom Penh) to Department of Defense (Canberra)(Secret).

71. *Phnom Penh*, April 1958 (exact date not given), *SWB/FE*/759, pp. 46–47.

72. *NCNA*, 31 May 1958, *SWB/FE/*773, p. 43.

73. *Phnom Penh*, 30 June 1958, *SWB/FE/*782, p. 40.

74. *Phnom Penh*, 25 June 1958, *SWB/FE/*781, p. 52.

75. *Hanoi in English*, 28 June 1958, *SWB/FE/*781, p. 52.

76. *Zhongguo Waijiao Guan Huiyi Lu: Xin Zhongguo Waijiao Fengyun*, Volume I (Beijing: Shijie Zhishi Chubanshe, 1994), p. 61.

77. *Zhongguo Waijiao Guan Huiyi Lu: Xin Zhongguo Waijiao Fengyun*, Volume I (Beijing: Shijie Zhishi Chubanshe, 1994), p. 61.

78. *FO 371*/136069, DU 1015/29, 29 July 1958, from Australian Legation (Phnom Penh) to Department of External Affairs (Secret); *FO 371*/136069, DU 1015/31, 19 August 1958, from Phnom Penh to Foreign Office.

79. *Zhongguo Waijiao Guan Huiyi Lu: Xin Zhongguo Waijiao Fengyun*, Volume I (Beijing: Shijie Zhishi Chubanshe, 1994), p. 61.

80. *VNA*, 27 July 1958, *SWB/FE/*789, p. 39.

81. *CUSSDCF*: 751 H. 00/9-358, 29 August 1958, Memorandum of Conversation Involving Son Phuoc Tho, director of Meatophum, and Gordon G. Heiner and Robert S. Barnet, second secretaries, U.S. Embassy (Phnom Penh).

82. *Zhou Enlai Waijiao Huodong Da Shiji* (Beijing: Shijie Zhishi Chubanshe, 1993), pp. 240–241.

83. *CUSSDCF*: 751 H. 00(W)/9-1158, 331, 11 September 1958, from Phnom Penh to Department of State; 751 H/9-358, 302, 3 September 1958, from Phnom Penh to Department of State; *NCNA*, 28 August 1958, *SWB/FE/*799, p. 47.

84. *Zhou Enlai Waijiao Huodong Da Shiji* (Beijing: Shijie Zhishi Chubanshe, 1993), p. 240–241.

85. *CUSSDCF*: 751 H. 00(W)/9-2458, 386, 24 September 1958, from Phnom Penh to Department of State; for Sihanouk's account of the events leading to as well as his visit to China, see Norodom Sihanouk and Wilfred Burchett, *My War with the CIA: Cambodia's Fight for Survival* (Harmondsworth: Penguin, 1973), pp. 102–103.

86. Sihanouk's speech in Paris on 19 November 1960 to an audience of Cambodians living in France, *SWB/FE/*523/B/3; *FO 371*/152692, DU 1015/108, 25 August 1960, from Commonwealth Relation Office (CRO) to Foreign Office: Malcolm MacDonald's Talk with Sihanouk (Secret).

87. For details of Sihanouk's visit to China, see *SWB/FE/*795, pp. 19–22; *SWB/FE/*797, pp. 9–18.

88. *VNA*, 26 August 1958, *SWB/FE/*798, p. 37.

89. *VNA*, 7 August 1958, *SWB/FE/*793, p. 40.

90. *NCNA*, 20 November 1958, *SWB/FE/*822, p. 42.

91. For details of the domestic policies of the Diem regime from January 1957

to December 1958, see Carlyle A. Thayer, *War by Other Means: National Liberation and Revolution in Vietnam 1954–60* (Sydney: Allen and Unwin, 1989), Chapter 6.

92. Hoang Van Hoan, "Distortion of Facts about the Militant Friendship between Vietnam and China is Impermissible," *Beijing Review* Number 49, 7 December 1979, p. 15.

93. Guo Ming (ed.), *Zhongyue Guanxi Yanbian Sishi Nian* (Guangxi Renmin Chubanshe, 1992), p. 66.

94. Ibid., p. 66.

95. "Tu Nghi quyet lich su den Duong Ho Chi Minh," *Su Kien Va Nhan Chung*, Number 4, 17 January 1994, pp. 4 and 32.

96. "How Armed Struggle Began in South Vietnam," *Vietnam Courier* Number 22, March 1974, pp. 19–24; *Vietnam: The Anti-U.S. Resistance War for National Liberation 1954–1975: Military Events* (printing completed 30 May 1980) (JPRS 80968, 3 June 1982), p. 24.

97. *Lich Su...*, pp. 86–87; *Vietnam: The Anti-U.S. Resistance War for National Liberation 1954–1975: Military Events* (printing completed 20 May 1980) (JPRS 80968, 3 June 1982), pp. 25–26.

98. *An Outline History of the Vietnam Workers' Party (1930–1975)* (Hanoi: Foreign Languages, 2nd edition, 1978), p. 81; *VNA*, 8 December 1958, *SWB/FE/*827, pp. 53–54.

99. George Carver, "The Faceless Vietcong," *Foreign Affairs* Volume 44:3 (April 1966); U.S. Department of State *Working Paper on North Vietnam's Role in the South* (27 May 1968), Appendices, Item 36: Interrogation of a Vietcong Infiltrator Captured on 4 April 1964; Janos Radvanyi, *Delusion and Reality: Gambits, Hoaxes and Diplomatic One-Upmanship in Vietnam* (Indiana: Gateway, 1978), p. 23; Carlyle Thayer's interview with Phan The Ngoc from My Tho Province, who was Le Duan's escort officer during part of his trip in late 1958. See Carlyle Thayer, *War by Other Means: National Liberation and Revolution in Vietnam 1954–1960* (Sydney: Allen and Unwin, 1989), p. 222, footnote 85.

100. *Race Document Number 1025: Tinh Hinh Va Nhiem Vu 59* (no date).

101. For a recent account based on newly available Chinese sources, see Zhang Shu Guang, *Deterrence and Strategic Culture: Chinese-American Confrontations, 1949–1958* (Ithaca: Cornell University Press, 1992), Chapter 8.

102. John Garver, "New Light on Sino-Soviet Relations: The Memoir of China's Ambassador (Liu Xiao) to Moscow, 1955–1962," *China Quarterly* Number 122, June 1990, p. 305.

103. From the journal of S. F. Antonov (21 October 1959): Summary of a Conversation with the Chairman of the CC CPC [Central Committee Communist Party of China] Mao-Tse Tung on 14 October 1959 (Top Secret), reproduced in *Cold War International History Project Bulletin*, Issue 3, Fall 1993, pp. 55–58.

104. Li Zhisui, *The Private Life of Chairman Mao: The Inside Story of the Man who Made Modern China* (London: Chatto and Windus, 1994), pp. 270–271.

105. *VNA*, 29 August 1958, *SWB/FE/*799, p. 45.

106. *NCNA*, 1 September 1958, *SWB/FE/*799, p. 45.

107. *NCNA*, 2 September 1958, *SWB/FE/*800, p. 16.

108. *VNA*, 10 September 1958, *SWB/FE/*802, p. 47.

109. Guo Ming (ed.), *Zhongyue Guanxi Yanbian Sishi Nian* (Guangxi Renmin Chubanshe, 1992), p. 147.

110. *VNA*, 22 September 1958, *SWB/FE*/806, p. 37.

111. O. B. Borisov and B. T. Koloskov, *Soviet-Chinese Relations, 1945–1970* (Bloomington: Indiana University Press, 1975), p. 154.

112. John Garver, op. cit., p. 305.

113. *Zhongguo Waijiao Guan Huiyi Lu: Xin Zhongguo Waijiao Fengyun*, Volume I (Beijing: Shijie Zhishi Chubanshe, 1990), pp. 135–138.

Gromyko remembered the meeting differently. According to Gromyko, Mao told him that he expected an American attack on China over the straits crisis. When that happened, the Chinese would retreat inland and the U.S.SR should then "catch them with all its means." Andrei Gromyko, *Memories* (London: Hutchinson, 1989), pp. 250–251.

114. For full text, see *SWB/SU*/962, pp. 1, 7, and 8. For details of Soviet response to the Taiwan Strait crisis, see Donald S. Zagoria, *The Sino-Soviet Conflict 1956–61* (New York: Princeton University Press, 1962), Chapter 7.

115. *NCNA*, 14 September 1958, *SWB/FE*/803, p. 2.

116. Ibid.

117. John Garver, op. cit., p. 305.

118. Stuart R. Schram, "Mao Tse-Tung's Thought from 1949 to 1976," in John Fairbank and Roderick MacFarquhar (eds.), *Cambridge History of China*, Volume XV (Cambridge: Cambridge University Press), p. 63.

119. *Mao Zedong Sixiang Wansui (1969)*: Mao's Speech at the 15th Plenary Session of the Supreme State Conference, 5 September 1958, pp. 226–237.

120. *Peking Review*, Number 36, 4 November 1958, pp. 6–10; Number 37, 11 November 1958, pp. 6–11; *SWB/FE*/817, pp. 2-5.

121. *NCNA*, 4 November 1958, *SWB/FE*/818, p. 20.

122. *NCNA*, 19 November 1958, *SWB/FE*/822, p. 21.

123. See O. B. Borisov and B. T. Koloskov, *Soviet-Chinese Relations 1945–1970* (Bloomington: Indiana University Press, 1975), Chapter 5; *Mao Zedong Sixiang Wansui (1969)*: Speech at an Enlarged Central Work Conference, 30 January 1962, p. 416.

124. Veljko Micunovic, *Moscow Diary* (London: Chatto and Windus, 1980), p. 422.

125. See Aleksandr Kaznacheev, *Inside a Soviet Embassy: Experience of a Russian Diplomat in Burma* (Philadelphia: Lippincott, 1962).

126. *VNA*, 3 September 1958, *SWB/FE*/801, p. 55.

127. *VNA*, 18 October 1958, *SWB/FE*/813, p. 42; *VNA*, 20 October 1958, *SWB/FE*/814, p. 31; *NCNA*, 18 October 1958, *SWB/FE*/813, p. 42.

128. NCNA, 13 November 1958, SWB/FE/821, p. 33.

129. *VNA*, 14 November 1958, *SWB/FE*/821, p. 33.

130. U.S. Department of State, Bureau of Intelligence and Research: *Intelligence Report 8140* (dated 29 October 1959).

131. *Lich Su...*, pp. 60–61.

132. Janos Radvanyi, *Delusion and Reality: Gambits, Hoaxes and Diplomatic One-Upmanship in Vietnam* (Indiana: Gateway, 1978), pp. 14–16.

133. *FO 371*/144387, DV 1011/1, 7 January 1959, from Saigon to Foreign Office.

Chapter Five: January 1959–May 1959

1. The area in dispute was a mountainous, forested, and sparsely populated region situated just north of the 17th parallel, which divided North and South Vietnam, and about 15 miles from the highway between Savannakhet and the South Vietnamese port of Tourane.

2. *VNA*, 2 January 1959, *SWB/FE*/834, pp. 34–35. For a brief account of the Huong Lap incident, see Arthur J. Dommen, *Conflict in Laos: The Politics of Neutralization* (New York: Praeger 1971), pp. 115–116.

3. *VNA*, 29 December 1958, *SWB/FE*/833, p. 55.

4. *VNA*, 2 January 1959, *SWB/FE*/834, p. 35.

5. *Laotian Home Service*, 5 January 1959, *SWB/FE*/835, p. 32.

6. *VNA*, 6 January 1959, *SWB/FE*/835, p. 33.

7. *VNA*, 8 January 1959, *SWB/FE*/836, p. 31.

8. *VNA*, 8 January 1959, *SWB/FE*/836, p. 32.

9. *VNA*, 12 January 1959, *SWB/FE*/837, p. 28.

10. *VNA*, 14 January 1959, *SWB/FE*/837, pp. 28–29.

11. *Laotian Home Service*, 14 January 1959, *SWB/FE*/837, p. 29.

12. *VNA*, 28 September 1956, *SWB/FE*/601, p. 44.

13. *VNA*, 30 September 1956, *SWB/FE*/601, p. 44.

14. *NCNA*, 7 October 1956, *SWB/FE*/603, p. 56.

15. *FO 371*/123440, DF 1043/19, 15 October 1956, from Vientiane to Foreign Office.

16. *VNA*, 14 September 1957, *SWB/FE*/700, p. 49.

17. *VNA*, 17 September 1957, *SWB/FE*/701, p. 52.

18. *VNA*, 4 October 1957, *SWB/FE*/706, p. 44.

19. *VNA*, 5 October 1957, *SWB/FE*/706, p. 45.

20. *FO 371*/143969, DF 10396/1, 2 January 1959, from Vientiane to Foreign Office (Secret).

21. *FO 371*/143957, DF 1015/15, 10 January 1959, from Vientiane to Foreign Office.

22. *FO 371*/143969, DF 10396/2, 5 January 1959, from Vientiane to Foreign Office (Secret).

23. *FO 371*/143957, DF 1015/11A, 8 January 1959, from Washington to Foreign Office (Secret).

24. *FO 371*/143970, DF 10396/23, 23 January 1959, from Washington to Foreign Office (Secret).

25. *FO 371*/144404, DV 1041/5, 27 January 1959, from Saigon to Foreign Office.

26. *VNA*, 16 January 1959, *SWB/FE*/838, p. 36.

27. *Vientiane in French*, 11 February 1959, *SWB/FE*/845, pp. 25–26.

28. *NCNA*, 14 February 1959, *SWB/FE*/846, p. 56; *VNA*, 15 February 1959, *SWB/FE*/846, p. 56.

29. *NCNA*, 11 January 1959, *SWB/FE*/836, p. 10.

30. "Tu Nghi quyet lich su den Duong Ho Chi Minh," *Su Kien va Nhan Chung* Number 4, 17 January 1994, p. 32.

31. Tran Van Tra, *Nhung Chang Duong Lich Su Cua B2 Thanh Dong, Tap I: Hoa Binh Hay Chien Tranh* (Hanoi: Nha Xuat Ban Quan Doi Nhan Dan, 1992), p. 153.

32. U.S. Department of State *Working Paper on North Vietnam's Role in the South* (27 May 1968), Appendices, Item 301: CRIMP Document.
33. *Lich Su...*, p. 89.
34. Cao Van Luong, *Lich Su Cach Mang Mien Nam Vietnam: Giai Doan 1954–1960* (Hanoi: Nha Xuat Ban Khoa Hoc Xa Hoi, 1991), p. 120.
35. *Lich Su...*, pp. 89–91; Cao Van Luong, *Lich Su Cach Mang Mien Nam Vietnam: Giai Doan 1954–1960* (Hanoi: Nha Xuat Ban Khoa Hoc Xa Hoi, 1991), pp. 120-123.
36. *Lich Su...*, p. 98.
37. *VNA*, 18 January 1959, *SWB/FE*/838, pp. 35–36.
38. *VNA*, 20 January 1958, *SWB/FE*/839, pp. 40–41; *Vietnam: The Anti-US Resistance War for National Salvation 1954–1975: Military Events* (printing completed 30 May 1980) (JPRS 80968, 3 June 1982), p. 28.
39. *NCNA*, 27 January 1959, *SWB/FE*/840, p. 14.
40. *FO 371*/144404, DV 1041/6, 28 January 1959, from Saigon to Foreign Office.
41. *FO 371*/144404, DV 1041/10, 30 January 1959, from Saigon to Foreign Office.
42. "How Armed Struggle Began in South Vietnam," *Vietnam Courier* Number 22, March 1974, pp. 19–24.
43. Wilfred Burchett, *My Visit to the Zones of South Vietnam* (Hanoi: Foreign Languages, 1966), p. 17. For a more detailed account of the situation in South Vietnam during this period, see Carlyle Thayer, *War by Other Means: National Liberation and Revolution in Vietnam 1954–60.* (Sydney: Allen and Unwin, 1989), Chapter 7.
44. *FO 371*/144404, DV 1041/10, 26 January 1959, from Consulate-General (Hanoi) to Foreign Office.
45. *Lich Su...*, pp. 74–76.
46. *Ibid.*, p. 93.
47. FO 371/144404, DV 1041/5, 27 January 1959, from Saigon to Foreign Office.
48. *Ibid.*, pp. 91–92.
49. *Vietnam: The Anti-US Resistance War for National Salvation 1954–1975: Military Events* (printing completed 30 May 1980) (JPRS 80968, 3 June 1982). pp. 28–29.
50. Zhong Huaiwen (comp.), *Years of Trial, Turmoil and Triumph — China from 1949 to 1988* (Beijing: Foreign Languages, 1989), pp. 90–95; Roderick MacFarquhar, *The Origins of the Cultural Revolution*, Volume II (Oxford: Oxford University Press, 1983), passim.
51. *FO 371*/144390, DV 1016/7, 6 February 1959, from Consulate-General (Hanoi) to Foreign Office.
52. *NCNA*, 11 January 1959, *SWB/FE*/836, p. 10.
53. *NCNA*, 19 February 1959, *SWB/FE*/848, pp. 10–11.
54. *NCNA*, 20 February 1959, *SWB/FE*/848, p. 11.
55. *NCNA*, 14 March 1959, *SWB/FE*/854, p. 34.
56. *FO 371*/144390, DV 1016/8, 4 March 1959, from Hanoi to Foreign Office; *FO 371*/1444430, DV 11338/3, 16 March 1959, from Hanoi to Foreign Office.

57. *NCNA*, 17 January 1959, *SWB/FE/*838, p. 37.
58. *NCNA*, 21 January 1959, *SWB/FE/*838, p. 13.
59. *NCNA*, 20 January 1959, *SWB/FE/*838, p. 13.
60. *NCNA*, 25 January 1959, *SWB/FE/*839, p. 14.
61. For text of Khrushchev's report at the 21st CPSU Congress, see G. F. Hudson et al.(documented and analyzed), *The Sino-Soviet Dispute* (China Quarterly, 1961), pp. 56–57. For a discussion of the report and its implications for Sino-Soviet relations, see Donald S. Zagoria, *The Sino-Soviet Conflict 1956–61* (New York: Princeton University Press, 1962), Chapter 9.
62. *SWB/SU/*January 1959, Supplement Number 3, pp. 53–54.
63. *NCNA*, 10 February 1959, *SWB/FE/*844, p. 8.
64. *NCNA*, 12 February 1959, *SWB/FE/*844, p. 8; *NCNA*, 13 and 14 February 1959, *SWB/FE/*845, p. 34.
65. *Chen Geng Riji* (Beijing: Jiefang Jun Chubanshe, 1984); Qian Jiang, *Zai Shenbi De Zhanzheng Chung* (Honan Renmin Chubanshe, 1992), pp. 62–75; Wang Xiangen, *Yuanyue Kangmei Shilu* (Jinan Chubanshe, 1992), passim; Hoang Van Hoan, "Distortion of Facts about Militant Friendship between Vietnam and China is Impermissible," *Beijing Review*, Number 49, 7 December 1979, pp. 12.
66. *CUSSDCF*: 651 G. 93/3-2059, 703, 20 March 1959, from Hong Kong to Department of State.
67. Ibid.
68. *NCNA*, 5 April 1959, *SWB/FE/*860, p. 20.
69. *FO 371*/144426, DV 11310/2A, 23 March 1959, from Hanoi to Foreign Office; *NCNA*, 20 March 1959, *SWB/FE/*855, p. 10.
70. Hoang Van Hoan, "Distortion of Facts about Militant Friendship between Vietnam and China is Impermissible," *Beijing Review*, Number 49, 7 December 1979, p. 12; Ling Yuan, "Hanoi-Beijing: Friends, Foes, Friends-to-Be," *Beijing Review* Number 34, 26 August 1985, p. 30; Huang Guoan et al., *Zhongyyue Guanxi Jianbian* (Guangxi Renmin Chubanshe, 1986), p. 190.
71. *CUSSDCF*: 651 G. 93/3-2059, 703, 20 March 1959, from Hong Kong to Department of State.
72. *NCNA*, 15 February 1959, *SWB/FE/*845, pp. 21–22.
73. *NCNA*, 18 February 1959, *SWB/FE/*847, pp. 27–28.
74. *NCNA*, 19 February 1959, *SWB/FE/*848, p. 8.
75. *Documents Relating to British Involvement in the IndoChina Conflict* 1945–1965 (Cmnd.2834), p. 134.
76. *Ibid.*, pp. 135–136.
77. *TASS in English*, 25 March 1959, *SWB/SU/*1019, p. 42.
78. *Documents Relating to British Involvement in the Indochina Conflict 1945–1965* (Cmnd. 2834), pp. 135–136.
79. *NCNA*, 13 and 14 March 1959, *SWB/FE/*853, pp. 14–16.
80. *NCNA*, 27 February 1959, *SWB/FE/*849, pp. 11–12; *NCNA*, 5 April 1959, *SWB/FE/*860, p. 17.
81. *NCNA*, 28 February 1959, *SWB/FE/*849, pp. 10–11.
82. *NCNA*, 8 March 1959, *SWB/FE/*851, pp. 7–8.
83. *NCNA*, 27 and 28 February 1959, *SWB/FE/*850, pp. 11–13; *NCNA*, 5 April 1959, *SWB/FE/*860, pp. 17–18.

84. Tracy B. Strong and Helene Keyssar, "Anna Louise Strong: Three Interviews with Chairman Mao Zedong," *China Quarterly* Number 103, September 1985; Han Suyin's Interviews with Anna Louise Strong in 1964 and 1969 in Han Suyin, *Wind in the Tower: Mao Tsetung and the Chinese Revolution 1949–1975* (London: Jonathan Cape, 1976), pp. 169–170.

85. *Mao Zedong Sixiang Wansui (Long Live Mao Zedong Thought)(1969)*: Speech to Co-operative Heads, 30 November 1958, p. 255, and Speech at 16th Enlarged Session of the Supreme State Conference, 14 April 1959, p. 289.

86. For the full text of Zhou's report, see *SWB/FE/5/C2*, pp. 20–28.

87. Aleksandr Kaznacheev, *Inside a Soviet Embassy: Experiences of a Russian Diplomat in Burma* (Philadelphia: Lippincott, 1962), pp. 85-86, 146-147, 214–216.

88. *FO 371*/144390, DV 1016/10, 7 April 1959, from Hanoi to Foreign Office; *VNA*, 28 March 1959 and 1 April 1959; *NCNA*, 29 and 30 March 1959, *SWB/FE*/589, pp. 20, 37; *VNA*, 4 April 1959, *SWB/FE*/860, pp. 39–40.

89. Truong Chinh and Pham Hung were both appointed deputy-premiers at the National Assembly Session of 16–29 April 1958.

90. *FO 371*/144388, DV 1012/2, 5 December 1959, from Saigon to Foreign Office.

91. Janos Radvanyi, *Delusion and Reality: Gambits, Hoaxes and Diplomatic One-Upmanship in Vietnam* (Indiana: Gateway, 1978), pp. 22–24.

92. U.S. Department of State *Working Paper on North Vietnam's Role in the South* (27 May 1968), Appendices, Item 301: CRIMP Document.

93. Janos Radvanyi, op. cit., pp. 22–24.

94. *Ibid.*, p. 26.

95. "The Origin and Development of the Differences between the Leadership of the CPSU and Ourselves," *Peking Review*, Number 37, September 1963, p. 12.

96. Janos Radvanyi, op. cit., pp. 26–27. Radvanyi followed the American dating of the 15th Plenary Session of the Lao Dong Party. We now know that the plenary session took place in January 1959.

Chapter Six: May 1959–December 1959

1. See *Fascist Terror in South Vietnam: Law 10-59* (Hanoi: Foreign Languages, 1961); "How Armed Struggle Began in the South," *Vietnam Courier* Number 22, March 1974, pp. 19–24.

2. Le Duan, "We Will Surely Be Victorious, the Enemy Will Surely Be Defeated" (no date given), cited in *Lich Su...*, p. 88.

3. Tran Huu Dinh, "Qua Trinh Hinh Thanh Luc Luong Vu Trang va Can Cu Dia O Nam Bo Trong Nhung Nam 1954–1960," *Tap Chi Nghien Cuu Lich Su*, 6:277(11–12, 1994), pp. 5–6.

4. *VNA*, 13 May 1959, *SWB/FE/27/A3/1-3*.

5. *VNA*, 14 May 1959, *SWB/FE/28/A3/3*.

6. The account is from *Lich Su...*, pp. 93–96; *The Ho Chi Minh Trail* (Hanoi: Foreign Languages, 1982); interview with General Vo Bam in *The Economist*, February 1983, p. 70; Brigadier-General Vo Bam, "Opening the Trail,"

Vietnam Courier Number 5, 1984, pp. 9–15; David Chanoff and Doan Van Tai, *Portrait of the Enemy: The Other Side of the War in Vietnam* (London: I.B. Tauris, 1986), pp. 147–148; "Chuyen xoi duong dau tien," *Su Kien Va Nhan Chung* Number 4, 17 January 1994, pp. 6–7.

7. *Vietnam: The Anti-US Resistance War for National Salvation 1954–1975: Military Events* (printing completed 30 May 1980) (JPRS 80968, 3 June 1982), p. 32.

8. "Tu Nghi Quyet lich su den Duong Ho Chi Minh," *Su Kien Va Nhan Chung* Number 4, 17 January 1994, p. 32.

9. U.S. Department of State *Working Paper on the North Vietnamese Role in the War in South Vietnam* (27 May 1968), Appendices, Item 73: Interrogation of a Senior Sergeant, 5th Military Region, Captured in 1964 in Tra Bong District, Quang Ngai Province.

10. *The Ho Chi Minh Trail* (Hanoi: Foreign Languages, 1982), p. 13.

11. *Lich Su*..., pp. 93–96.

12. Tran Van Tra, *Nhung Chang Duong Lich Su Cua B2 Thanh Dong, Tap I: Hoa Binh Hay Chien Tranh* (Hanoi: Nha Xuat Ban Quan Doi Nhan Dan, 1992), pp. 160–162.

13. The events of this episode can be obtained from Sisouk Na Champassak, *Storm Over Laos: A Contemporary History* (New York: Praeger, 1961), Chapter 8; Arthur J. Dommen, *Conflict in Laos: The Politics of Neutralization* (New York: Praeger, 1971), pp. 117–118; Huge Toye, *Laos: Buffer State or Battleground* (London: Oxford University Press, 1968), pp. 124–126. The account here is according to the BBC: *Summary of World Broadcast (Far East).*

14. Biographical data of Singkapo is extremely scanty. He belonged to one of the prominent regional families of Laos — Khammouane/Thakhek. He was a member of the Central Committee of the Free Lao Front (Neo Lao Issara) in the '50s and a member of the Central Committee of the Lao Patriotic Front (NLHX) from 1956.

15. *CUSSDCF*: 751 J. 00/8-1359, 13 August 1959, from Vientiane to Secretary of State.

16. These included Souphanouvong, Singkapo, Phoumi Vongvichit, Nouhak Phoumasavan, Sithone Komadam, Phoun Sipraseuth, and the editor of *Lao Hak Xat*, Khamphay Boupha.

17. *VNA*, 10 June 1959, *SWB/FE*/50/A3/6.

18. *FO 371*/144391, DV 1016/28, 3 August 1959, from Hanoi to Foreign Office.

19. *SWB/FE*/69/4 July 1959/(i).

20. *TASS in Russian for Abroad*, 2 July 1959, *SWB/SU*/69/A3/4.

21. *Moscow Radio*, 28 July 1959, *SWB/FE*/W16/A/4.

22. Strobe Talbot (trans. and ed.) *Khrushchev Remembers: The Last Testament* (London: Andre Deutsch, 1974), Chapter 16; Martin McCauley, *Nikita Khrushchev* (London: Sphere, 1991), p. 86.

23. For details, see Zong Huaiwen (comp.) *Years of Trial, Turmoil and Triumph — China from 1949 to 1988* (Beijing: Foreign Languages, 1989), pp. 97–99; Peng Dehuai, *Memoirs of a Chinese Marshal: The Autobiographical Notes of Peng Dehuai* (Beijing: Foreign Languages, 1984), pp. 485–520; Li Zhisui, *The Private*

Life of Chairman Mao: The Inside Story of the Man Who Made China (London: Chatto and Windus, 1994), Chapter 39.

24. See David A. Charles, "The Dismissal of Marshall P'eng Teh-huai," *China Quarterly* Number 8, October-December 1961; J. D. Simmonds, "P'eng Te-huai: A Chronological Reassessment," *China Quarterly* Number 37, January-March 1969.

25. Zong Huaiwen (comp.), *Years of Trial, Turmoil and Triumph—China from 1949 to 1988* (Beijing: Foreign Languages, 1989), pp. 97–99; Peng Dehuai, *Memoirs of a Chinese Marshal: The Autobiographical Notes of Peng Dehuai* (Beijing: Foreign Languages, 1984), pp. 485–520.

26. Stuart R. Schram, "Mao Tse-Tung's Thought from 1949–1976," in John Fairbank and Roderick MacFarquhar (eds.), *Cambridge History of China*, Volume XV (Cambridge: Cambridge University Press, 1991), p. 71; Li Zhisui, *The Private Life of Chairman Mao: The Inside Story of the Man Who Made Modern China* (London: Chatto and Windus, 1994), pp. 320–321.

27. Laszlo Ladany, *The Communist Party of China and Marxism, 1921–1985: A Self-Portrait* (Stanford: Hoover Institution Press, 1988), p. 253. Laszlo Ladany was the founder-publisher of the *China News Analysis*.

28. *NCNA*, 1 August 1959, *SWB/FE/94/*(i); *FO 371*/144391, DV 1016/33, 7 September 1959, from Hanoi to Foreign Office.

29. *Peking Review* Issue 32, 11 August 1959, p. 21. The most detailed account of Ho's tour of northwest China is in Huang Zheng, *Ho Zhiming Yu Zhongguo* (Beijing: Jiefang Jun Chubanshe, 1987), pp. 151–154.

30. *NCNA*, 13 August 1959, *SWB/FE/103/*(i).

31. Han Suyin, *Zhou Enlai Yu Ta De Shiji 1898–1998*, (Beijing: Zhongyang Wenxian Chubanshe, 1992), pp. 362–363. The English version is *Eldest Son: Zhou Enlai and the Making of Modern China*, 1898–1976, (London: Jonathan Cape, 1994), p. 277. Author's correspondence with Han Suyin. Source of information is from Han Suyin's conversation with Zhou Enlai and a photograph of Ho Chi Minh with Deng Yingchao and Cai Chang, wife of Li Fuchun, taken at Lushan in August 1959.

32. *Zhou Enlai Waijiao Huodong Da Shiji* (Beijing: Shijie Zhishi Chubanshe, 1993), p. 258.

33. Guo Ming (ed.), *Zhongyue Guanxi Yanbian Sishi Nian* (Guangxi People's Publisher, 1992), p. 66.

34. *FO 371*/144391, DV 1016/33, 7 September 1959, from Hanoi to Foreign Office.

35. "The Geneva Agreements Must be Upheld," *Peking Review* Number 30, 28 July 1959, pp. 6–8; "On the Worsening Situation in Laos," *Peking Review* Number 33, 18 August 1959, p. 9

36. Han Suyin, *Zhou Enlai Yu Ta De Shiji 1898–1998*, (Beijing: Zhongyang Wenxian Chubanshe, 1992), p. 363; *Eldest Son: Zhou Enlai and the Making of Modern China, 1898–1976* (London: Jonathan Cape, 1994), p. 277.

37. Wang Xiangen, *Yuanyue Kangmei Shilu* (Jinan Chubanshe, 1992), p. 18.

38. *VNA*, 13 May 1959, *SWB/FE/27/A3/1-3*.

39. Hoang Van Hoan, *A Drop in the Ocean: Hoang Van Hoan's Revolutionary Reminiscences* (Beijing: Foreign Languages, 1988), p. 324.

40. *VNA*, 26 August 1959, *SWB/FE/115/*(i).

41. *VNA*, 1 September 1959, *SWB/FE/121/C/1.*

42. *FO 371*/141246, FC 1015/12, 6 August 1959, from Beijing to Foreign Office.

43. *Keesing's Contemporary Archives*, 21–28 November 1959, pp. 17115-17123.

44. *CUSSDCF*: 751 J. 00/8-1359, 310, 13 August 1959, from Vientiane to State Department.

45. *CUSSDCF*: 751 J. 00/8-1059, 271, 10 August 1959, from Vientiane to State Department (Secret).

46. *FO 371*/141261, FC 10338/21, 16 October 1959, from UK delegate to NATO (Paris) to Foreign Office.

47. *Report of the Security Council Subcommittee Established under the Resolution of 7 September 1959* (Document S/4236), *United Nations Security Council Official Records, 14th Year*, Supplement for October-December 1959 (New York, 1960), cited in Lee Chae Jin, *Chinese Communist Policy in Laos: 1945–1965* (University of California, Los Angeles, Ph.D. Thesis, 1966), p. 141.

48. *Annual Report of the Secretary-General on the Work of the Organization, 16 June 1959–15 June 1960, Official Records, 15th Session*, Supplement Number 1 (A/4390) (New York, 1960), pp. 22–23; *Report of the Security Council to the General Assembly, 16 July 1959–15 July 1960, Official Records, 15th Session*, Supplement Number 2 (A/4494), (New York, 1960), pp. 1–4.

49. Paul F. Langer and Joseph J. Zasloff, *North Vietnam and the Pathet Lao: Partners in the Struggle for Laos* (Cambridge: Harvard University Press, 1970), pp. 67–70, 236.

50. Joseph J. Zasloff, *The Pathet Lao: Leadership and Organization* (Toronto: Lexington, 1973), p. 15.

51. *Vietnam: The Anti-US Resistance War for National Salvation 1954–1975: Military Events* (printing completed 30 May 1980)(JPRS 80968, 3 June 1982), pp. 33–34.

52. "Bieu Tuong Cua Tinh Doan Ket Chien Dau Ba Nuoc Dong Duong," *Su Kien Va Nhan Chung* Number 4, 17 January 1994, p. 6.

53. *Dang De Junshi Luebian Yu Renmin Jundui Jianshe* (Beijing: Guofang Daxue Chubanshe, 1990), pp. 164–165; Li Deng et al., *Jianguo Yilai Junshi Baizhuang Da Shi* (Beijing: Zhishi Chubanshe, 1992), pp. 155–159.

54. *NCNA*, 17 September 1959, *SWB/FE/134/B/1.*

55. Lin Biao's article in *Hongqi* Number 19, 1 October 1959, is translated in *Peking Review* Number 40, 6 October 1959, under the title, "March Ahead Under the Red Flag of the General Line and Mao Tse-Tung's Military Thinking"; *SWB/FE/144/C/14-23.*

56. A brief report of the article is given in *VNA*, 22 December 1959, *SWB/FE/216/B/3.* For the full text, see Vo Nguyen Giap, *People's War, People's Army* (New Dehli: Natraj, 1974), pp. 43–74.

57. Vo Nguyen Giap, *People's War, People's Army* (New Dehli: Natraj, 1974), pp. 45 and 73.

58. For details see Thomas M. Nicols, *The Sacred Cause: Civil-Military Conflict over Soviet National Security, 1917–1992* (Ithaca: Cornell University Press, 1993), Chapter 3.

59. Guo Ming et al., *Xiandai Zhongyue Guanxi Ziliao Xuanbian*, Volume II (Beijing: Shishi Chubanshe, 1986), p. 525.

60. See John Garver, "New Light on Sino-Soviet Relations: The Memoir of China's Ambassador (Liu Xiao) to Moscow, 1955–62," *China Quarterly* Number 122, June 1990.

61. "The Origin and Development of the Differences Between the Leadership of the CPSU and Ourselves," *Peking Review* Number 37, September 1963, p. 12.

62. *TASS in English*, 9 September 1959, *SWB/SU/*127/A3/1.

63. "The Origin and Development of the Differences Between the Leadership of the CPSU and Ourselves," *Peking Review* Number 37, 13 September 1959, p. 12.

64. Strobe Talbot (trans. and ed.), *Khrushchev Remembers: The Last Testament* (London: Andre Deutsch, 1974), p. 263.

65. For details of Khrushchev's visit to Beijing in 1959, see Tracy B. Strong and Helene Keyssar, "Anna Louise Strong: Three Interviews with Chairman Mao Zedong," *China Quarterly* Number 103, September 1985; the memoirs of Khrushchev; and Quan Yanchi, *Mao Zedong Yu Khrushchev: 1957–1959 Zhongsu Guanxi Jishi* (Jiling Renmin Chubanshe, 1990), pp. 211–215.

66. Andrei Gromyko, *Memories* (London: Hutchinson, 1989), p. 252.

67. Strobe Talbot (trans. and ed.), *Krushchev Remembers: The Last Testament* (London: Andre Deutsch, 1974), p. 263.

68. Roxane Witke, *Comrade Chiang Ching* (Boston: Little, Brown, 1977), p. 272.

69. Huang Zheng, *Ho Zhiming Yu Zhongguo* (Beijing: Jiefang Jun Chubanshe, 1987), pp. 154–156. For Ho's speech, also see *Ho Chi Minh: Selected Works*, Volume IV (Hanoi: Foreign Languages, 1962), pp. 366–369.

70. *FO 371*/144393, DV 10310/2, 8 October 1959, from Hanoi to Foreign Office; *VNA*, 4 October 1959, *SWB/FE*/148/C/9. However, according to *NCNA*, 4 October 1959, *SWB/FE/*148/C/9, both the government and the military delegations left Beijing on 4 October 1959.

71. *NCNA*, 4 October 1959, *SWB/FE/*148/C/9.

72. *FO 371*/144393, DV 10310/2, 8 October 1959, from Hanoi to Foreign Office.

73. See Kenneth T. Young, *Negotiating with the Chinese Communists: The United States Experience, 1953–1967* (New York: McGraw-Hill, 1968), Chapters 5 and 9.

74. From the journal of S. F. Antonov (21 October 1959): Summary of a Conversation with the Chairman of the CC CPC [Central Committee Communist Party of China] Mao-Tse Tung on 14 October (Top Secret), reproduced in *Cold War International History Project Bulletin*, Issue Number 3, Fall 1993, pp. 56–58.

75. *NCNA*, 17 October 1959, *SWB/FE/*159/A3/1-2.

76. *Vietnam: The Anti-US Resistance War for National Salvation 1954–1975: Military Events* (printing completed 30 May 1980) (JPRS 80968, 3 June 1982), p. 34; "Cuoc Dong Khoi Tra-Bong (28-8-1959)," *Nghien Cuu Lich Su* Number 138, May-June 1971, pp. 19–27.

77. *The Pentagon Papers as published by the New York Times* (London: Routledge and Kegan Paul, 1971), Chapter 2; *Vietnam: The Anti-US Resistance War*

for National Salvation 1954–1975: Military Events (printing completed 30 May 1980)(JPRS 80968, 3 June 1982), pp. 34–35.

78. "Special Report on Current Internal Security Situation in Vietnam" (7 March 1960), in US Department of Defense, *United States–Vietnam Relations 1945–1967* (Washington, 1971), pp. 1254–1275.

79. Department of State *Working Paper on North Vietnam's Role in the South* (27 May 1968), Appendices, Item 301: CRIMP Document.

80. Vo Tran Nha (chu bien), *Lich Su Dong Thap Muoi* (Hanoi: Nha Xuat Ban Thanh Pho Ho Chi Minh, 1993), p. 196.

81. *Vietnam: The Anti-US Resistance War for National Salvation 1954–1975: Military Events* (printing completed 30 May 1980) (JPRS 80968, 3 June 1982), p. 34.

82. Tran Huu Dinh, "Qua Trinh Hinh Thanh Luc Luong Vu Trang va Can Cu Dia O Nam Bo Trong Nhung Nam 1954–1960," *Tap Chi Nghien Cuu Lich Su* 6:277 (11–12, 1994), p. 4.

Chapter Seven: January 1960–July 1960

1. *Lich Su...*, pp. 107-115. For a first-person account, see Mai V. Elliot (trans.), *No Other Road to Take: Memoirs of Mrs. Nguyen Thi Dinh* (Data Paper Number 102, Southeast Asia Program, Department of Asian Studies, Cornell University, June 1976), pp. 59-77.

2. *Lich Su...*, p. 114.

3. Le Duan, "Under the Glorious Party Banner, for Independence, Freedom, and Socialism, Let Us Advance and Achieve New Victories" (14 February 1970), *Vietnam Documents and Research Notes*, Document Number 77, April 1970.

4. "Special Report on Current Internal Security Situation in Vietnam" (7 March 1960), US Department of Defense, *United States-Vietnam Relations 1945-1967*, (Washington, 1971), pp. 1254-1275.

5. *FO 371*/152746, DV 1016/16, 9 April 1960, from Hanoi to Foreign Office.

6. *NCNA*, 12 February 1960, *SWB/FE/*259/A3/4.

7. *Vietnam: The Anti-US Resistance War for National Salvation 1954–1975: Military Events* (Hanoi, 30 May 1980)(JPRS 80968, 3 June 1982), pp. 40–41.

8. Gareth Porter, *Vietnam: The Definitive Documentation of Human Decisions*, Volume II (London: Heyden and Son, 1979), pp. 59–70. Porter's source is *Race Document 1044*, which is in Vietnamese. An English translation of the same document is in U.S. Department of State *Working Paper on the North Vietnamese Role in the War in South Vietnam* (27 May 1968), Appendices, Item 34.

9. *VNA*, 27 March 1960, *SWB/FE/*296/B/1.

10. *Phnom Penh in French*, 14 March 1960, *SWB/FE/*286/B/4-6.

11. Brigadier-General Vo Bam, "Opening the Trail," *Vietnam Courier* Number 5, 1984, pp. 9–15.

12. *NCNA*, 8 January 1960, *SWB/FE/*228/A3/2-3.

13. *VNA*, 14 January 1960, *SWB/FE/*234/(i).

14. *Vientiane in French*, 19 January 1960, *SWB/FE/*238/A3/3.

15. *FO 371/152323*, DF 1015/86, 11 February 1960, from Hanoi to Foreign Office.

16. *VNA*, 11 March 1960, *SWB/FE/282/A3/3*.

17. *Vientiane Home Service*, 19 March 1960, *SWB/FE/290/B/7*.

18. *FO 371/152325*, DF 1015/111, 18 March 1960, from Vientiane to Foreign Office.

19. *NCNA*, 23 March 1960, *SWB/FE/292/A3/3*.

20. *FO 371/152328*, DF 1015/144, 13 April 1960, from Vientiane to Foreign Office.

21. *VNA*, 19 April 1960, *SWB/FE/313/A3/3*.

22. *FO 371/159811*, DF 1011/1, 23 June 1961, from Vientiane to Foreign Office.

23. Arthur J. Dommen, *Conflict in Laos: The Politics of Neutralization* (London: Pall Mall, 1964), pp. 129–133.

24. See Kenneth T. Young, *Negotiating with the Chinese Communists: The United States Experience, 1953-1967* (New York: McGraw-Hill, 1968), Chapters 5 and 9.

25. *FO 371/152745*, DV 1016/5A, 11 January 1960, from Hanoi to Foreign Office; *VNA*, 23 December 1959, *SWB/FE/217/C/5-7*.

26. *FO 371/152745*, DV 1016/5A, 11 January 1960, from Hanoi to Foreign Office.

27. *FO 371/152745*, DV 1016/13, 8 April 1960, from Hanoi to Foreign Office.

28. *NCNA*, 5 January 1960, *SWB/FE/226/C/1*.

29. *VNA*, 4 February 1960, *SWB/FE/252/A2/1*; *NCNA*, 4 February 1960, *SWB/FE/252/A2/1*.

30. For a discussion of Kang Sheng's role in contributing to the personal feud between Mao and Khrushchev, see John Byron and Robert Pack, *The Claws of the Dragon: Kang Sheng—The Evil Genius behind Mao, and His Legacy of Terror in People's China* (New York: Simon and Schuster, 1992), pp. 252–253.

31. For full text of Kang Sheng's speech and the declaration, see G. F. Hudson et al.(documented and analyzed), *The Sino-Soviet Dispute* (London: China Quarterly Publications, 1961), pp. 63–77.

32. Roderick MacFarquhar, *The Origins of the Cultural Revolution*, Volume II (Oxford: Oxford University Press, 1983), pp. 264, 269–270. MacFarquhar cites Kenneth Lieberthal, *A Research Guide to Central Party and Government Meetings in China, 1949–1975* (New York: International Arts and Sciences, 1976).

33. *FO 371/150407*, FC 1016/18A, 12 April 1960, from Beijing to Foreign Office; *FO 371/150408*, FC 1016/21, 22 April 1960, from Beijing to Foreign Office.

34. For full text of the published version of Zhou Enlai's report, see *SWB/FE/308/C/1-5*.

35. According to a Phnom Penh Home Service commentary of 4 May 1960, Khrushchev had accepted an invitation to visit Cambodia but had not honored his commitment. The commentary did not say when the invitation was extended. See *SWB/FE/327/A3/4*.

36. *Zhongguo Waijiao Guan Huiyi Lu: Xin Zhongguo Waijiao Fengyun*, Volume I (Beijing: Shijie Zhishi Chubanshe, 1994), p. 61.

37. For details of Zhou's tour to Burma, India and Nepal, and the treaties signed, see BBC: *Summary of World Broadcast (Far East)* for April 1960 beginning from *SWB/FE/*310/A3/1 to *SWB/FE/*325/A3/1-3.

38. The description originated from excerpts of reports from *Phnom Penh* and *Realities Cambodgiennes*. See *NCNA*, 3 May 1960, *SWB/FE/*325/A3/3.

39. *Zhongguo Waijiao Guan Huiyi Lu: Xin Zhongguo Waijiao Fengyun*, Volume I (Beijing: Shijie Zhishi Chubanshe, 1994), p. 61.

40. *NCNA*, 3 May 1960, *SWB/FE/*325/A3/3.

41. For an account of Zhou's visit to Cambodia, see *Zhongguo Waijiao Guan Huiyi Lu: Xin Zhongguo Waijiao Fengyun*, Volume I (Beijing: Shijie Zhishi Chubanshe, 1994), pp. 61–65; *Zhou Enlai Waijiao Huodong Da Shiji* (Beijing: Shijie Zhishi Chubanshe, 1993), pp. 277–279.

42. *Phnom Penh Home Service*, 5 May 1960, *SWB/FE/*328/A3/7.

43. *FO 371*/152706, DV 10396/7, 21 May 1960, from Saigon to Foreign Office (Secret).

44. For the full text of Sihanouk's welcome speech, see *NCNA*, 5 May 1960, *SWB/FE/*327/A3/1-3.

45. *NCNA*, 8 May 1960, *SWB/FE/*329/A3/4-5.

46. *NCNA*, 8 May 1960, *SWB/FE/*329/A3/2-3.

47. Memorandum from Director of Intelligence and Research to Secretary of State dated 21 June 1960, in *Foreign Relations of the United States*, Volume XVI: Cambodia and Laos, 1958-1960 (Washington: US Government Printing Office, 1992), p. 364.

48. *Keesing's Contemporary Archives*, 1–8 April 1961, p. 18013.

49. *FO 371*/152697, DV 10310/8, 28 July 1960, from Phnom Penh to Foreign Office.

50. *VNA*, 1 May 1960, *SWB/FE*/323/A3/2.

51. Le Duan, "Leninism and Vietnam's Revolution" in *On the Socialist Revolution in Vietnam*, Volume I (Hanoi: Foreign Languages, 1965), pp. 9–56.

52. *VNA*, 1 May 1960, *SWB/FE/*323/A3/2.

53. *FO 371*/152746, DV 1016/19, 2 May 1960, from Hanoi to Foreign Office.

54. *NCNA*, 13 May 1960, *SWB/FE/*333/A3/1.

55. *NCNA*, 14 May 1960, *SWB/FE/*334/A3/2-6.

56. *Vietnam: The Anti–US Resistance War for National Salvation 1954–1975: Military Events* (Hanoi, 30 May 1980)(JPRS 80968, 3 June 1982), pp. 44–45.

57. For Zhou Enlai's visit to Hanoi, see *SWB/FE/*331/A3/1-4; *SWB/FE/*332/A3/1; *SWB/FE/*333/A3/1-2; *Zhou Enlai Waijiao Huodong Da Shiji* (Beijing: Shijie Zhishi Chubanshe, 1993), pp. 279–280.

58. For details of the U-2 incident leading to the aborting of the Paris summit, see Khrushchev's memoirs; Fedor Burlatsky, *Khrushchev and the Russian Spring: The Era of Khrushchev through the Eyes of His Adviser* (London: Weidenfeld and Nicolson, 1991), pp. 155–157; Harold Macmillan, *Pointing the Way 1959–1961* (London: Macmillan, 1972), Chapter 7.

59. Carl A. Linden, *Khrushchev and the Soviet Leadership, 1957–1964* (Baltimore: Johns Hopkins University Press, 1966), pp. 93–104.

60. U.S. Department of State, Bureau of Intelligence and Research: *Intelligence Report Number 8306* (dated 21 July 1960).

61. For details of Ho's visit, see *NCNA*, 25 August 1979, *SWB/FE*/6208/-A3/3; Huang Zheng, Ho Zhiming Yu Zhongguo (Beijing: Jiefang Jun Chubanshe, 1987), pp. 160–161.

62. Guo Ming (ed.), *Zhongyue Guanxi Yanbian Sishi Nian* (Guangxi Renmin Chubanshe, 1992), p. 67.

63. Hoang Van Hoan, "Distortion of Facts about the Militant Friendship between Vietnam and China Is Impermissible," *Beijing Review* Number 49, 7 December 1979, p. 15.

64. For Souphanouvong's account of the escape, see Wilfred Burchett, *The Furtive War: The United States in Vietnam and Laos* (New York: International, 1963), Chapter X.

65. *FO 371*/159811, DF 1011/1, 23 June 1961, from Vientiane to Foreign Office.

66. *FO 371*/152335, DF 1015/265, 25 May 1960, Record of Conversation between Lord Lansdowne and Prince Khammao, Laotian ambassador to the United Kingdom.

67. *FO 371*/152339, DF 1015/321, 30 June 1960, from Foreign Office to Vientiane (Secret).

68. *Hanoi Radio in French*, 15 June 1960, *SWB/FE*/362/A2/1-2.

69. *VNA*, 16 June 1960, *SWB/FE*/362/A2/2.

70. *FO 371*/152772, DV 1338/1, 2 September 1960, US Embassy: US State Department Information Brief on Soviet Aid to North Vietnam, Number 319.

71. *VNA*, 16 June 1960, *SWB/FE*/362/A2/2.

72. For details of the Bucharest Congress, see Edward Crankshaw, *The New Cold War: Moscow v. Pekin* (Harmondsworth: Penguin, 1965), Chapter 10 (Crankshaw's sources include material published by the French, Italian, and Belgian Communist parties) Allen S. Whiting, "The Sino-Soviet Split," in John Fairbank and Roderick MacFarquhar (eds.), *Cambridge History of China*, Volume XIV (Cambridge: Cambridge University Press, 1989). Whiting cites the document "The Sino-Soviet Dispute and Its Significance," Central Intelligence Agency, 1 April 1961, TS #142274-b (originally Top Secret).

73. Le Duan was reported as the secretary of the Vietnam Workers' Party Central Committee. He was accompanied by Nguyen Van Kinh, member of the Lao Dong Central Committee. Le Duan made a speech on the afternoon of 22 June 1960, the third day of the conference. See *Agerpres in English*, 19 June 1960, *SWB/EE*/C/11. For Le Duan's speech, see *SWB/EE*/367/C/11; *Bucharest Home Service*, 23 June 1960, *SWB/EE*/370/C/23.

74. Zong Huaiwen (comp.), *Years of Trial, Turmoil and Triumph-China from 1949 to 1988* (Beijing: Foreign Languages—1989), p. 102.

75. *FO 371*/150424, FC 10338/31, 15 August 1960, from Beijing to Foreign Office; *FO 371*/150424, FC 10338/39C, 9 September 1960, from Moscow to Foreign Office; *FO 371*/150424, FC 10338/57, 12 September 1960, from Beijing to Foreign Office.

76. Zong Huaiwen (comp.), op. cit., p. 102.

77. *VNA*, 9 July 1960, *SWB/FE*/382/A2/2.

78. *VNA*, 7 July 1960, *SWB/FE*/381/B/1-8.

79. *FO 371*/152747, DV 1016/29, 26 August 1960, from Hanoi to Foreign Office. Giap was not mentioned as present at the opening of the second National Assembly on 7 July. See *VNA*, 7 July 1960, *SWB/FE*/381/B/1.
80. *VNA*, 8 July 1960, *SWB/FE*/382/A3/3.
81. US Department of Defense, *United States–Vietnam Relations: US Perceptions of the Insurgency 1954–1960* (Washington, 1971), pp. 48–52.
82. *FO 371*/152747, DV 1016/29, 26 August 1960, from Hanoi to Foreign Office.
83. *VNA*, 14 August 1960, *SWB/FE*/412/B/1-2.
84. *Lich Su...*, p. 115. September 23, 1940, was when the Bac Son uprising broke out. The first guerrilla unit under the Lao Dong party leadership was also formed on that day.

Chapter 8: August 1960–December 1960

1. *Vientiane Home Service in French* (0515h GMT), 9 August 1960, *SWB/FE*/406/B/1.
2. Interview with Kong Lae in Wilfred Burchett, *The Furtive War: The United States in Vietnam and Laos* (New York: International, 1963), pp. 188–191; *United States Senate, Committee of Foreign Relations Top-Secret Hearings*: Briefing by Dean Rusk, Secretary of State, 28 February 1961.
3. *Vientiane Home Service*, 9 August 1960, *SWB/FE*/407/B/2.
4. *SWB/FE*/407/(i).
5. *NCNA*, 12 August 1960, *SWB/FE*/410/B/10-11.
6. Wilfred Burchett, *The Furtive War: The United States in Vietnam and Laos* (New York: International, 1963), pp. 186–188.
7. *Vientiane Home Service in French* (0346h GMT), 10 August 1960, *SWB/FE*/408/B/3.
8. *SWB/FE*/408/(i).
9. *Hanoi Home Service*, 11 August 1960, *SWB/FE*/409/B/5.
10. *SWB/FE*/409/(i).
11. *SWB/FE*/409/B/5.
12. *FO 371*/152343, DF 1015/390(E), 15 August 1960, from Beijing to Foreign Office.
13. *VNA*, 18 August 1960, *SWB/FE*/414/B/6.
14. *NCNA*, 19 August 1960, *SWB/FE*/415/A3/1-3.
15. *Voice of the Pathet Lao*, 23 August 1960, *SWB/FE*/419/B/6.
16. *FO 371*/152747, DV 1016/29, 26 August 1960, from Hanoi to Foreign Office. On 1 August, the chairman of the ISCC visited Hanoi but did not manage to interview Giap. There was speculation that he could have gone to Algeria, but we do not have any evidence to substantiate this.
17. *FO 371*/152747, DV 1016/36, 24 September 1960, from Hanoi to Foreign Office.
18. P. J. Honey, "The Position of the DRV in the Sino-Soviet Dispute" in *China News Analysis*, 16 March 1962.

19. *FO 371*/150425, FC 10338/70, 10 October 1960, from Beijing to Foreign Office; *FO 371*/152752, DV 10338/2, 2 November 1960, from Hanoi to Foreign Office.

20. Hoang Van Hoan, "Ho Chi Minh's Last Will Was Tampered With," *Beijing Review* Number 37, 14 September 1981; Hoang Van Hoan, *A Drop in the Ocean: Hoang Van Hoan's Revolutionary Reminiscences* (Beijing: Foreign Languages, 1988), p. 314.

21. *FO 371*/152353, DF 1015/563, 3 September 1960, from Vientiane to Foreign Office.

22. *FO 371*/1522353, DF 1015/570, 5 September 1960, from Hanoi to Foreign Office.

23. *NCNA*, 1 August 1960, *SWB/FE*/400/A1/1.

24. Edgar Snow, *The Other Side of the River* (London: Victor Gollancz, 1963), p. 77 and 85–92.

25. Kenneth T. Young, *Negotiating with the Chinese Communists: The United States Experience, 1953–1967* (New York: McGraw-Hill, 1968), p. 233. For the Chinese version of the meeting, see Wang Bingnan, *Nine Years of Sino–US Talks in Retrospect* (JPRS-CPS-85-079, 7 August 1985), pp. 44–45.

26. *FO 371*/152359, DF 1015/683, 26 September 1960, from Beijing to Foreign Office.

27. *Lich Su...*, p. 115.

28. For the full text of Le Duan's political report, see *SWB/FE*/431/C/2-6.

29. *VNA*, 9 September 1960, *SWB/FE*/435/C/3-4; for full text of Pham Van Dong' speech, see *SWB/FE*/439/C/1-3.

30. *VNA*, 9 September 1960, *SWB/FE*/435/C/5.

31. *Lich Su...*, p. 128.

32. *FO 371*/152747, DV 1016/36, 24 September 1960, from Hanoi to Foreign Office; also see speeches by Li Fuchun and Mukhitdinov, the Chinese and Soviet representatives to the Congress in *SWB/FE*/435/C/10-11.

33. David Chanoff and Doan Van Toai, *Portrait of the Enemy: The Other Side of the War in Vietnam* (London: I.B. Tauris, 1986), p. 81.

34. *TASS in English*, 11 September 1960, *SWB/FE*/435/C/11.

35. Huang Zheng, *Ho Zhiming Yu Zhongguo* (Beijing: Jiefang Jun Chubanshe, 1987), pp. 196–197.

36. Thanh Tin, *Hoa Xuyen Tuyet (Hoi Ky)* (California: Saigon, 1991), p. 130. Also, according to Hoang Van Hoan, Le Duan during the early '50s and '60s was inclined to the Chinese view regarding the strategy for unifying Vietnam, and only much later was he persuaded to drift with the anti–China tide. See Hoang Van Hoan, *A Drop in the Ocean* (Beijing: Foreign Languages, 1988), p. 325.

37. For details, see Roger Faligot and Remi Kauffer, *The Chinese Secret Service* (New York: Morrow, 1989).

38. Ben Kiernan, *How Pol Pot Came to Power* (London: Verso, 1985), pp. 189–193, 367 (Kiernan's account is based mainly on the annotated party history by the Eastern Zone Military Political Service, September 1973, and the history of the Communist Party of Kampuchea by Ieng Sary, distributed to cadres in Hanoi, September 1974); David P. Chandler, *The Tragedy of Cambodian History: Politics, War, and Revolution since 1945* (New Haven: Yale University Press, 1991),

pp. 112–115, 205 n.33 (on Son Ngoc Minh's activities, Chandler cites US Central Intelligence Agency, "Communism and Cambodia," no date but probably 1971, p. 29); David P. Chandler, *Brother Number One: A Political Biography of Pol Pot* (Colorado: Westview, 1992), pp. 61–62; speech by Pol Pot on 27 September 1977 in Phnom Penh marking the CPK's seventeenth anniversary, *Phnom Penh Home Service*, 28 September 1977, *SWB/FE*/5629/C2/1-9 and *SWB/FE*/5631/C2/1-6; *Black Paper: Facts and Evidences of the Acts of Aggression and Annexation of Vietnam Against Kampuchea* (Democratic Kampuchea, September 1978), pp. 24–25; Pol Pot's press conference in Beijing, *NCNA*, 3 October 1977, *SWB/FE*/5631/A3-6; To Quyen, "The Kampuchean People's Revolutionary Party, The Vanguard of the Working Class and People of Kampuchea," *Tap Chi Cong San* Number 11, November 1983, pp. 51–67.

39. Huang Zheng, *Ho Zhiming Yu Zhongguo* (Beijing: Jiefang Jun Chubanshe, 1987), pp. 158–159.

40. *Pathet Lao Radio*, 16 September 1960, *SWB/FE*/440/B/5-6.

41. *TASS in English*, 21 September 1960, *SWB/SU*/444/A3/1-2.

42. *Bangkok Home Service*, 6 October 1960, *SWB/FE*/458/A2/3.

43. U.S. Department of State, Bureau of Intelligence and Research: *Intelligence Report Number 8306 (*dated 21 July 1960).

44. United States Department of State, Bureau of Intelligence and Research: *Intelligence Report Number 8307 (*dated 3 August 1960).

45. US Department of Defense, *United States-Vietnam Relations 1956-1960*: Memorandum of Conference on 19 January 1961 between President Eisenhower and President-elect Kennedy on the subject of Laos in United States Department of Defense, pp. 1360-1364.

46. *FO 371*/159846, DF 1015/734, 4 May 1961, from Bangkok to Foreign Office.

47. *Vietnam: The Anti-US Resistance War for National Salvation 1954–1975: Military Events* (Hanoi, 30 May 1980)(JPRS 80968, 3 June 1982), p. 44.

48. *FO 371*/152359, DF 1015/685, 5 October 1960, from Vientiane to Foreign Office.

49. *VNA*, 2 October 1960, *SWB/FE*/455/B/14.

50. *NCNA*, 30 October 1960, *SWB/FE*/477/B/5.

51. *Vientiane Home Service*, 15 October 1960, SWB/FE/465/B/6.

52. Edward Crankshaw, *The New Cold War: Moscow v. Pekin* (Harmondsworth: Penguin, 1965), Chapters 11–12 (Crankshaw's sources include published material by the French, Italian, and Belgian Communist parties); Allen S. Whiting, "The Sino-Soviet Split," in John Fairbank and Roderick MacFarquhar (eds.), *Cambridge History of China*, Volume XIV (Cambridge: Cambridge University Press, 1989). Whiting cites "The Sino-Soviet Dispute and Its Significance," Central Intelligence Agency, 1 April 1961, TS #142274-b (originally Top Secret).

53. John Gittings, *The Role of the Chinese Army* (London: Oxford University Press, 1967), p. 235.

54. Ibid.; also see *NCNA*, 30 September 1960, *SWB/FE*/452/B/8-11.

55. *NCNA*, 1 November 1960, *SWB/FE*/479/(i).

56. *FO 371*/152747, DV 1016/45, 12 December 1960, from Hanoi to Foreign Office.

57. *NCNA*, 2 November 1960, SWB/FE/480/A2/1; Guo Ming, et al., *Xiandai Zhongyue Guanxi Ziliao Xuanbian*, Volume I (Beijing: Shishi Chubanshe, 1986), p. 437.

58. Oleg Penkovsky, *The Penkovsky Papers* (London: Fontana, 1967), p. 242; Allen S. Whiting, "The Sino-Soviet Split," in John Fairbank and Roderick MacFarquhar (eds.), *Cambridge History of China*, Volume XIV (Cambridge: Cambridge University Press, 1989), pp. 518-519.

59. For the Belgian, French, and Italian communist accounts of the debates that took place during the conference, see David Floyd, *Mao against Khrushchev: A Short History of the Sino-Soviet Conflict* (London: Pall Mall, 1964), pp. 286–295.

60. Strobe Talbot (trans. and ed.), *Khrushchev Remembers: The Last Testament* (London: Andre Deutsch, 1971), pp. 444–445.

61. Allen S. Whiting, op. cit., p. 518.

62. For full text of the 1960 Moscow Declaration, see G. F. Hudson et al., *The Sino-Soviet Dispute* (China Quarterly, 1961), pp. 177–205.

63. *Pathet Lao Radio*, 17 November 1960, *SWB/FE*/493/B/4.

64. *Vientiane Home Service*, 17 November 1960, *SWB/FE*/493/B/4; *FO 371*/152382, DF 1022/2, 2 December 1960, from Vientiane to Foreign Office.

65. *VNA*, 18 November 1960, *SWB/FE*/494/A3/1.

66. *NCNA*, 19 November 1960, *SWB/FE*/495/A3/1. Also see *Renmin Ribao* editorial of 21 November 1960 in *SWB/FE*/495/A3/2.

67. *NCNA*, 29 November 1960, *SWB/FE*/503/A3/1.

68. *VNA*, 2 December 1960, *SWB/FE*/506/A3/5-6.

69. *FO 371*/152382, DF 1022/2, 2 December 1960, from Vientiane to Foreign Office.

70. *Vientiane*, 24 November 1960, *SWB/FE*/499/B/4.

71. *FO 371*/152379, DF 1015/1053, 26 December 1960, from Beijing to Foreign Office.

72. *FO 371*/150425, FC 10338/83, 30 November 1960, from Moscow to Foreign Office.

73. *FO 371*/150405, FC 1013/27, 20 December 1960, from Beijing to Foreign Office.

74. *NCNA*, 3 December 1960, *SWB/FE*/507/A3/1; Guo Ming et al., *Xiandai Zhongyue Guanxi Ziliao Xuanbian*, Volume II (Beijing: Shishi Chubanshe, 1986), p. 438.

75. *NCNA*, 3 December 1960, *SWB/FE*/507/A3/2.

76. *NCNA*, 6 December 1960, *SWB/FE*/508/A3/1. For the visit of Ho and his delegation to Beijing, also see *Zhou Enlai Waijiao Huodong Da Shiji* (Beijing: Shijie Zhishi Chubanshe, 1993), p. 295.

77. *Savannakhet Radio*, 8 December 1960, *SWB/FE*/510/B/2.

78. For details of the battle for Vientiane, see Hugh Toye, *Laos: Buffer State or Battleground* (London: Oxford University Press, 1971), pp. 157–164.

79. *NCNA*, 11 December 1960, *SWB/FE*/514.

80. *VNA*, 8 December 1960, *SWB/FE*/511/B/7.

81. *FO 371*/159811, DF 1011/1, 23 June 1961, from Vientiane to Foreign Office.

82. *Savannakhet*, 12 December 1960, *SWB/FE*/514/B/3 and *Savannakhet*, 13 December 1960, *SWB/FE*/515/B/2.

83. *Zhou Enlai Waijiao Huodong Da Shiji* (Beijing: Shijie Zhishi Chubanshe, 1993), p. 295.

84. *Hanoi Radio*, 13 December 1960, *SWB/FE*/515/B/4.

85. *TASS in English*, 13 December 1960, *SWB/SU*/515/A3/1.

86. FO 371/159811, DF 1011/1, 23 June 1961, from Vientiane to Foreign Office.

87. *FO 371*/152375, DF 1015/990, 19 December 1960, from Vientiane to Foreign Office (Secret).

88. *FO 371*/159813, DF 1015/21, 3 January 1961, from Washington to Foreign Office.

89. For details of Sihanouk's visit to China, see BBC: *Summary of World Broadcast (Far East)* for December 1960; *Zhou Enlai Waijiao Huodong Da Shiji* (Beijing: Shijie Zhishi Chubanshe, 1993), pp. 295–297.

90. *FO 371*/152692, DU 1015/107, 20 August 1960, from Saigon to Foreign Office; *FO 371*/152692, DU 1015/108, 25 August 1960, from Commonwealth Relation Office (CRO) to Foreign Office (Secret).

91. Sihanouk's speech in Paris on 19 November 1960 to an audience of Cambodians living in France, *SWB/FE*/523/B/3-4.

92. *NCNA*, 18 December 1960, *SWB/FE*/519/A3/3-4.

93. *FO 371*/152379, DF 1015/1049, 24 December 1960, from Beijing to Foreign Office.

94. *Peking Review* Number 52, 27 December 1960, pp. 9-12; Volume IV, Number 1, 6 January 1961, pp. 13–18.

95. *FO 371*/152379, DF 1015/1057, 27 December 1960, from Hanoi to Foreign Office.

96. *Documents Relating to British Involvement in the IndoChina Conflict 1945–1965* (Cmnd. 2834), p. 26.

97. *Ibid.*, pp. 154-155.

98. *Zhou Enlai Waijiao Huodong Da Shiji* (Beijing: Shijie Zhishi Chubanshe, 1993), p. 296.

99. *Documents Relating to Brtish Involvement in the IndoChina Conflict 1945–1965* (Cmnd. 2834), pp. 156–158. President Eisenhower was, however, certain that the Soviet Union did not want the ISCC to go into Laos. See "Memorandum of Conference on 19 January 1961 Between President Eisenhower and President-Elect Kennedy on the subject of Laos" in US Department of Defense, *United States–Vietnam Relations 1956–1960*, pp. 1360–1364.

100. *NCNA*, 27 December 1960, *SWB/FE*/526/B/3.

101. *TASS in English*, 12 January 1961, *SWB/SU*/538/A3/3.

102. *NCNA*, 17 January 1961, *SWB/FE*/543/B/3.

103. The sequence of events can be followed in the BBC: *Summary of World Broadcast* for this period.

104. United States Department of State *Working Paper on North Vietnam's Role in the South* (27 May 1968), Appendices, Item 301: CRIMP Document.

105. Brigadier-General Vo Bam, "Opening the Trail," *Vietnam Courier* Number 5, 1984, pp. 9–15.

106. *Lich Su...*, pp. 152–153; *FO 371*/159812, DF 1015/2, 1 January 1961, from Washington to Foreign Office; *FO 371*/159824, DF 1015/243, 10 February 1961, from Vientiane to Foreign Office (Secret).

107. *VNA*, 27 January 1961, *SWB/FE/*551/B/4.

108. *FO 371*/159813, DF 1015/21, 3 January 1961, from Washington to Foreign Office.

109. *FO 371*/159826, DF 1015/300, 26 February 1961, from Hanoi to Foreign Office; *FO 371*/159845, DF 1015/6641, 30 April 1961, from Hanoi to Foreign Office.

110. *NCNA*, 9 March 1961, *SWB/FE/*586/(i).

111. *FO 371*/159824, DF 1015/241, 10 February 1961, from Office of the High Commissioner for Australia (London) to Foreign Office.

112. "Memorandum of Conference on 19 January 1961 Between President Eisenhower and President-Elect Kennedy on the Subject of Laos in United States Department of Defense," US Department of Defense, *United States–Vietnam Relations 1956–1960*, pp. 1360-1364; *The Pentagon Papers*, Volume II (Senator Gravel Edition (Boston: Beacon, 1971), pp. 635–637.

Chapter 9: December 1960–October 1961

1. *Lich Su*..., pp. 116–117.

2. Cao Van Luong, *Lich Su Cach Mang Mien Nam Vietnam: Giai Doan 1954-1960* (Hanoi: Nha Xuat Ban Khoa Hoc Xa Hoi, 1991), p.156; *Lich Su*..., p.120; Truong Nhu Tang, *Journal of a Vietcong* (London: Jonathan Cape, 1986), pp. 79–80.

According to Tang, on the morning of 21 December 1960, a special broadcast from Hanoi announcing the formation of the NLF and the good wishes of the Lao Dong Party and North Vietnamese government reached every part of South Vietnam. But the first communist broadcast monitored was that of *VNA* and *NCNA*, 29 January 1961, *SWB/FE*/553/A3/2, which cited a Reuters report, and various papers published in Phnom Penh, as the sources for the "recent" formation of the NLF.

3. Truong Nhu Tang, *Journal of a Vietcong* (London: Jonathan Cape, 1986), pp. 70–74. Also see Carlyle A. Thayer, *War by Other Means: National Liberation and Revolution in Vietnam 1954–60* (Sydney: Allen and Unwin, 1989), pp. 187–188, and 227 n.28.

4. *Lich Su*..., pp. 120–121.

5. "Memorandum of Conference on 19 January 1961 Between President Eisenhower and President-Elect Kennedy on the Subject of Laos," US Department of Defence, *United States–Vietnam Relations 1956–1960*, pp. 1360–1364; *The Pentagon Papers*, Volume II, Senator Gravel Edition (Boston: Beacon, 1971), pp. 635–637.

6. United States Department of Defense; *United States–Vietnam Relations 1945–1967* (Book II/IV/A5/Table IV) (Washington, 1971), pp. 66–77. The NFL Provisional Committee decided to strengthen its presence in the Saigon-Cholon area with the formation of the Saigon/Cholon/Goading Committee on 31 January 1961. See Truong Nhu Tang, *Journal of a Vietcong* (London: Jonathan Cape, 1986), pp. 81–84.

7. *SWB/FE*/539/(i); Lao Dong Party Central Committee Resolution on Moscow Conference, VNA, 12 January 1961, SWB/FE/539/A2/2-6.

Only an extract of Le Duan's report is available. See Le Duan, *On Some Present International Problems* (Hanoi: Foreign Languages, 1964), pp. 9–55.

8. *Moscow Home Service*, 19 January 1961, *SWB/SU/*544/C/1-29.

9. Arthur M. Schlesinger, Jr., *A Thousand Days: John F. Kennedy in the White House* (London: Mayflower, 1967), pp. 254–255; Michael R. Beschloss, *Kennedy v. Khrushchev: The Crisis Years, 1960–63* (London: Faber and Faber, 1991), pp. 63–65, 69.

10. Jan Seljna, *We Will Bury You* (London: Sidgwick and Jackson, 1982), pp. 58–59.

11. John Byron and Robert Pack, *The Claws of the Dragon: Kang Sheng—The Evil Genius Behind Mao and His Legacy of Terror in People's China* (New York: Simon and Schuster, 1992), p. 247.

12. Michael R. Beschloss, *Kennedy v. Khrushchev: The Crisis Years 1960-63*, (London: Faber and Faber, 1991), pp. 77-78, 157-158. Beschloss however did not cite the source for this episode.

13. *NCNA*, 20 January 1961, *SWB/FE/*546/A3/3.

14. *VNA* and *NCNA*, 29 January 1961, *SWB/FE/*553/A3/2.

15. Huang Guoan et al., *Zhongyue Guanxi Jianbian* (Guangxi Renmin Chubanshe, 1986), pp. 194–195.

16. Ibid., pp. 194–195.

17. *NCNA*, 31 January 1961, *SWB/FE/*555/A3/1-5.

18. *VNA*, 3 February 1961, *SWB/FE/*558/A3/2.

19. *FO 371*/166697, DV 1011/2, 15 February 1962, from Saigon to Foreign Office: 1961 Annual Report on North Vietnam.

20. *Vietnam: The Anti-US Resistance War for National Liberation 1954–1975: Military Events* (JPRS 80968), pp. 45–46.

21. Le Duan, *Thu Vao Nam* (Hanoi: Nha Xuat Ban Su That, 1985), pp. 31–38.

22. *Lich Su…*, pp. 116–122. On 15 February 1971, the Vietnamese communists celebrated the tenth anniversary of the unification of the South Vietnamese People's Liberation Armed Forces. See *Liberation Press Agency*, 15 February 1971, *SWB/FE/*3612/A3/5-9.

23. *Lich Su…*, pp. 130–135.

24. *Lich Su…*, pp. 136–138.

25. Hoang Van Thai is believed to be a close friend of Vo Nguyen Giap. See *Vietnam Documents and Research Notes* (Document Number 114, Part 1, July 1973): VWP–DRV Leadership, 1960–1973, pp. 60–61.

26. *Lich Su…*, pp. 60–61.

27. *FO 371*/160123, DV 1016/22, 2 August 1961, FO minutes.

28. *Lich Su…*, p.161.

29. *FO 371*/166697, DV 1011/2, 15 February 1962, from Saigon to Foreign Office (1961 Annual Report for North Vietnam).

30. *Hanoi Radio*, 15 March 1961, *SWB/FE/*593/B/1.

31. P.J. Honey, *Communism in North Vietnam: Its Role in the Sino-Soviet Conflict* (Connecticut: Greenwood, 1973), p.97.

32. John Byron and Robert Pack, *The Claws of the Dragon: Kang Sheng—The Evil Genius Behind Mao, and His Legacy of Terror in People's China* (New York: Simon and Schuster, 1992), p.255–256.

33. Vo Nguyen Giap, *People's War, People's Army*, (Hanoi: Foreign Languages Publishing House, 1961).

34. Kenneth T. Young, *Negotiating with the Chinese Communists: The United States Experience, 1953–1967* (New York: McGraw–Hill, 1968), p. 248.

35. J. Chester Cheng (ed.), *The Politics of the Chinese Red Army* (Stanford: Hoover Institution on War, Revolution, and Peace, 1966), pp. 365–369.

36. Telegram 2366 from Moscow to Department of State dated 1 April 1961 in *Foreign Relations of the United States (FRUS)*, Volume XXIV, 1961–1963: Laos Crisis (Washington: US Government Printing Office, 1994), p.111.

37. See David K. Hall, "The Laos Crisis, 1960–61," in Alexander L. George et al., *The Limits of Coercive Diplomacy: Laos, Cuba, Vietnam* (Boston: Little, Brown, 1971), Chapter 2.

38. *Foreign Relations of the* United States, Volume XXIV, 1961–1963: Laos Crisis (Washington, US Government Printing Office, 1994), p.124.

39. *Ibid.*, p. 135.

40. Brigadier-General Vo Bam, "Opening the Trail," *Vietnam Courier* Number 5, 1984, pp. 9–15.

41. See Roger Hilsman, *To Move a Nation: The Politics of Foreign Policy in the Administration of John F. Kennedy* (New York: Doubleday, 1967), p.133.

42. Le Duan, *Thu Vao Nam* (Hanoi: Nha Xuat Ban Su That, 1985), pp. 39–49.

43. For Souvanna Phouma's visit to Moscow, see *SWB/SU*/616/A3/1; *SWB/SU*/618/A3/1; *SWB/SU*/620/A3/2; *SWB/SU*/621/A3/3.

44. For Souvanna Phouma's visit to Beijing, see *SWB/FE*/621/B/3; *SWB/FE*/622/B/1-4; *SWB/FE*/623/B/3-4; *Zhou Enlai Waijiao Huodong Da Shiji* (Beijing: Shijie Zhishi Chubanshe, 1993), p.310; *China's Foreign Relations: A Chronology of Events 1949–1988* (Beijing: Foreign Languages, 1989), p.191. For details of the road construction, see *Dangdai Zhongguo Jundui De Junshi Gongzuo*, Volume 1 (Beijing: Zhongguo Shehui Kexue Chubanshe, 1989), pp. 560–561.

45. *FO 371*/159931, DF 2231/69, 8 May 1961, Foreign Office minutes.

46. J.Chester Cheng (ed.), *The Politics of the Chinese Red Army* (Stanford: Hoover Institution on War, Revolution and Peace, 1966), pp. 480–487.

47. Marek Thee, *Notes of a Witness: Laos and the Second Indochinese War* (New York: Random House, 1973), pp. 16–18. Thee, whose original name was Gdanski, was a member of the ISCC in Laos.

48. For Souvanna Phouma's visit to Hanoi, see *SWB/FE*/625/B/7; *SWB/FE*/626/B/5-8.

49. *FO 371*/159843, DF 1015/626A, 27 April 1961, from Ankara to Foreign Office (Secret); DF 1015/638/G, 28 April 1961, from Foreign Office to Moscow (Secret).

50. Kenneth T. Young, "American Dealings with Peking," *Foreign Affairs* October 1966, pp. 81–82.

51. *Lich Su...*, p.154.

52. Denis Warner, *Reporting South-East Asia*, (London: Angus and Robertson, 1966), p.171.

53. *FO 371*/160123, DV 1016/22, 2 August 1961, FO minutes.

54. Vietnam: *The Anti–US Resistance War for National Salvation 1954–1975: Military Events* (JPRS 80968), p.47.

55. Huang Zheng, *Ho Zhiming Yu Zhongguo* (Beijing: Jiefang Jun Chubanshe, 1987), pp. 161–163.

56. Marek Thee, *Notes of a Witness: Laos and the Second IndoChinese War* (New York: Random House, 1973), pp. 18–19. The Chinese believed that the United States was using the negotiation and the ceasefire to gain time, increase the military strength of Phoumi Nosavan, and wait for an opportunity to resume its assault against the Pathet Lao and neutralist forces. See document entitled "The Plan and Strategy of the United States, Britain and France with respect to the Laotian Question" distributed with *Bulletin of Activities*, Issue 22, 1 June 1961.

57. Hoang Van Hoan, *A Drop in the Ocean* (Beijing: Foreign Languages, 1988), p.384.

58. Memorandum of Conversation: Vienna Meeting between the President and Chairman Khrushchev, Vienna, 3 and 4 June 1961, in *Foreign Relations of the United States, Volume XXIV, 1961–1963: Laos Crisis* (Washington: US Government Printing Office, 1994), pp. 225–236.

Michael R. Beschloss, *Kennedy v. Khrushchev: The Crisis Years 1960–63* (London: Faber and Faber, 1991), pp. 205, 211–213. Beschloss's account of the private Kennedy-Khrushchev conversations in Vienna is based on the official memoranda of conversations drafted by Kennedy's interpreter, Alexander Akalosky, released by the Archivist of the United States on 5 September 1990.

Roger Hilsman, *To Move a Nation: The Politics of Foreign Policy in the Administration of John F. Kennedy* (New York: Doubleday, 1967), p.136.

59. Marek Thee, *Notes of a Witness: Laos and the Second IndoChinese War* (New York: Random House, 1973), p.131.

60. Hoang Van Hoan, *A Drop in the Ocean* (Beijing: Foreign Languages Press, 1988), p.382.

61. Marek Thee, op.cit., Chapter 9.

62. For the economic reason of Pham Van Dong's tour, see P. J. Honey, "Pham Van Dong's Tour," *China Quarterly* Number 8, October-December 1961, pp. 42-44. Also see *Vietnam Press*, 12 September 1961, *SWB/FE/742/B/1*, which cites an article in *Nhan Dan* (23 August 1961) regarding a DRV National Assembly meeting on 19 August 1961 that discussed the shortcomings in the National Budget and the State Plan for the current year, and the need to overcome economic "difficulties" (not specified in the article).

63. *NCNA*, 12 June 1961, *SWB/FE/664/A3/1*.

64. *Xinhua News Agency*, 21 November 1979; Huang Guoan et al., *Zhongyue Guanxi Jianbian* (Guangxi Renmin Chubanshe, 1986), p.205, 209; Guo Ming (ed.), *Zhongyue Guanxi Yanbian Sishi Nian* (Guangxi Renmin Chubanshe, 1992), p.67.

65. *NCNA*, 16 June 1961, *SWB/FE/668/A3/1-3*; For an account of the visit, also see *Peking Review* Volume IV, Number 24, 16 June 1961, pp. 6–8; *Zhou Enlai Waijiao Huodong Da Shiji* (Beijing: Shijie Zhishi Chubanshe, 1993), pp. 313–314.

66. *TASS in English*, 3 July 1961, *SWB/SU/682/A3/1*.

67. *Moscow Home Service*, 5 July 1961, *SWB/SU/683/A3/4-5*.

68. *FO 371/160127*, Number 47, 1021/24/7, 24 July 1961, from Moscow to Foreign Office.

69. Marek Thee, *Notes of a Witness: Laos and the Second IndoChinese Conflict* (New York: Random House, 1973) p. 124.

70. *TASS in Russian for Abroad*, 12 July 1961, *SWB/SU/690/*A3/2.

71. *VNA*, 14 July 1961, *SWB/FE/693/*(i).

72. *Sofia Home Service*, 23 July 1961, *SWB/EE/700/*A3/1; *Sofia Home Service*, 28 July 1961, *SWB/EE/706/*A3/2.

73. *VNA*, 1 August 1961, *SWB/FE/707/*A2/1-2.

74. *TASS in English*, 27 July 1961, *SWB/SU/706/*A3/1.

75. Robert M. Slusser, *The Berlin Crisis of 1961: Soviet-America Relations and the Struggle for Power in the Kremlin, June–November 1961* (Baltimore: Johns Hopkins University Press, 1973), pp. 92–93. Also see P. J. Honey, "Pham Van Dong's Tour," *China Quarterly* Number 8, October-December 1961, Number 8, pp. 42–44.

76. William Burr, "New Sources on the Berlin Crisis, 1958–1962," *Cold War International History Project* Issue 2, Fall 1992, p.23. Burr did not provide specific references.

77. The sequence of events of the Berlin Crisis can be followed in *Keesing's Contemporary Archives*; Arthur M. Schlesinger, Jr., *A Thousand Days: John F. Kennedy in the White House* (London: Mayflower, 1967), pp. 329–336; Robert M. Slusser, *The Berlin Crisis of 1961: Soviet-American Relations and the Struggle for Power in the Kremlin, June–November 1961* (Baltimore: Johns Hopkins University Press, 1973), Chapters 4–8.

78. C. L. Sulzberger, "The Two K's and Germany," *New York Times*, 6 November 1966, p.10, cited in Robert M. Slusser, op. cit., pp. 209–210; *FO 371/*159947, DF 2231/381, 11 August 1961, Foreign Office minutes: Extract of Moscow telegram 1447 reporting private communication between Khrushchev and Macmillan (Khrushchev told Macmillan that he wanted the Geneva Conference on Laos to succeed); William Burr, "New Sources on the Berlin Crisis, 1958–1962," *Cold War International History Project* Issue 2, Fall 1992, pp. 21–24, 32.

79. *Zhou Enlai Waijiao Huodong Da Shiji* (Beijing: Shijie Zhishi Chubanshe, 1993), p.315.

80. Ibid., p.315.

81. *VNA*, 2 August 1961, *SWB/FE/*708/C/2.

82. *Zhou Enlai Waijiao Huodong Da Shiji* (Beijing: Shijie Zhishi Chubanshe, 1993), p.317.

83. *FO 371/*159867, DF 1015/1105, 25 August 1961, from Hanoi to Foreign Office (Secret).

84. *Socialist Republic of Vietnam Foreign Ministry White Paper on Relations with China*, Hanoi Home Service, 4–6 October 1976, *SWB/FE/*6238/A3/13; *The Chinese Rulers' Crimes Against Kampuchea*, (Ministry of Foreign Affairs, People's Republic of Kampuchea, April 1984), pp. 30–31.

85. *FO 371/*166504, DF 2331/166, 30 July 1962, from MacDonald to Foreign Office: Report on the Geneva Conference on Laos (Secret).

86. Interview with Roger Hilsman, former assistant secretary of state for Far Eastern affairs, in Michael Charlton and Anthony Moncrieff, *Many Reasons Why: The American Involvement in Vietnam* (London: Scolar, 1978), pp. 63-64.

87. *FO 371/*159947, DF 2231/397(A), 30 August 1961, from Geneva to Foreign Office (Secret).

88. Marek Thee, *Notes of a Witness: Laos and the Second IndoChinese War* (New York: Random House, 1973), pp. 193–194.

89. Ibid.

90. *FO 371*/159870, DF 1015/1178, 15 September 1961, from Washington to Foreign Office (Secret).

91. *FO 371*/159948, DF 2231/412, 9 September 1961, from Beijing to Foreign Office.

92. *FO 371*/159872, DF 1015/1204, 21 September 1961, Conversations held in Rangoon between Mr. Harriman and Prince Souvanna Phouma (15–16 September 1961) (Secret).

93. *FO 371*/159877, DF 1015/1317, 27 October 1961, Account of M. Brown's Visit to Khang Khay on 23 October 1961.

94. Arthur Lall, *How Communist China Negotiates*, (New York: Columbia University Press, 1968), pp. 142 and 176.

95. NIE 14.3/53-61, "Prospects for North and South Vietnam," 16 August 1961, in *United States–Vietnam Relations 1945-1967, Book 11*, pp. 245-246, reproduced in Gareth Porter, *Vietnam: The Definitive Documentation of Human Decisions*, Volume 2 (London: Heyden and Son, 1979).

96. *FO 371*/159890, DF 103196/11, 30 October 1961, from the Commissioner-General for South East Asia (Singapore) to Foreign Office (Secret).

97. Gareth Porter, *Vietnam: The Definitive Documentation of Human Decisions*, Volume 2, (London: Heyden and Son, 1979), pp. 119–123. Porter's source is "Nghi Quyet Hoi Nhgi R (mo rong). Thang 10/61," Captured Party Document, Combined Documents Exploitation Centre log number 1706/-KTTL/69.

Chapter Ten: October 1961–July 1962

1. *Public Papers of the President of the United States: John F. Kennedy, 1961* (Washington: US Government Printing Office, 1962), pp. 414–415.

2. In two cables to the president on 24 October and 1 November, Taylor recommended to Kennedy, among other things, the dispatch of US troops to South Vietnam. See *The Pentagon Papers*, Volume II Senator Gravel Edition (Boston: Beacon 1971, pp. 73–127.

3. Arthur M. Schlesinger, Jr., *A Thousand Days: John F. Kennedy in the White House* (London: Mayflower, 1967), p. 435.

4. Arthur M. Schlesinger, Jr., *The Bitter Heritage: Vietnam and American Democracy, 1941–1968* (New York: Fawcett, 1968) p. 40. Also see Michael W. Cannon, "Raising the Stakes: The Taylor-Rostow Mission," *Journal of Strategic Studies* Volume 12, Number 2, June 1989, pp. 125–165.

5. *FO 371*/159950, DF 2231/455, 26 October 1961, from Geneva to Foreign Office: Personal Letter from MacDonald to Sihanouk (Secret); *FO 371*/159951, DF 2231/467, 4 November 1961, from Geneva to Foreign Office: Harriman and MacDonald's meeting with Nehru during his hour's stop at Geneva airport on the morning of 2 November 1961 (Secret).

6. George Modelski, *International Conference on the Settlement of the Laotian*

Question, 1961–62 (Department of International Relations, Australian National University, Working Paper Number 2, 1962), pp. 128–129.

7. Guo Ming et al., *Xiandai Zhongyue Guanxi Ziliao Xuanbian*, Volume II (Beijing: Shishi Chubanshe, 1986), pp. 439–440; *Zhou Enlai Waijiao Huodong Da Shiji* (Beijing: Shijie Zhishi Chubanshe, 1993), p. 324.

8. For details, see "The Origin and Development of the Differences between the Leadership of the CPSU and Ourselves" *Peking Review* Number 37, 13 September 1963, pp. 6–20; Lester A. Sobel, *Russia's Rulers: The Khrushchev Period* (New York: Facts on File, 1971), pp. 212–256.

For Zhou's activities in Moscow, see *Zhou Enlai Waijiao Huodong Da Shiji* (Beijing: Shijie Zhishi Chubanshe, 1993), pp. 325–326.

9. *VNA*, 25 October 1961, *SWB/FE*/780/C2/2; *VNA*, 27 October 1961, *SWB/FE*/781/C/3.

10. *Zhou Enlai Waijiao Huodong Da Shiji* (Beijing: Shijie Zhishi Chubanshe, 1993), p. 326.

11. *VNA*, 7 November 1961, *SWB/FE/*791/C2/6.

12. *FO 371*/159879, DF 1015/1341, 8 November 1961, from Moscow to Foreign Office.

13. *TASS in Russian for Abroad*, 11 November 1961, *SWB/SU/*793/A3/3.

14. *FO 371*/159879, DF 1015/1341, 8 November 1961, from Moscow to Foreign Office.

15. *FO 371*/159951, DF 2231, 4 November 1961, from Geneva to Foreign Office: Harriman and MacDonald's meeting with Nehru during his hour's stop at Geneva airport on the morning of 2 November 1961 (Secret).

16. Marek Thee, *Notes of a Witness: Laos and the Second IndoChinese War* (New York: Random House, 1973), pp. 191–192, 196–201.

17. U.S. Department of State, *Foreign Relations of the United States (FRUS)*, Volume XXIV (Laos Crisis, 1961–1963), Document 219:Telegram from the Delegation to the Conference on Laos to the Department of State, 2 November 1961 (Washington, U.S. Gov. Printing Office, 1994). Also, see W.W. Rostow, *The Diffusion of Power, 1957–1972* (New York: Macmillan, 1972), pp. 287–288.

18. *NCNA*, 14 November 1961, *SWB/FE*/796/C/1-2. In Khang Khay, He Wei met Souvanna Phouma, Pheng Phongsavan, and Kong Lae.

19. Marek Thee, op. cit., pp. 197–198.

20. *NCNA*, 15 November 1961, *SWB/FE/*796/A3/2.

21. Marek Thee, op. cit., pp. 191–192; 196–201.

22. *Peking Review*, Number 48, 1 December 1961, pp. 9-10.

23. *FO 371*/159953, DF 2231/501, 25 November 1961, from Geneva to Foreign Office; DF 2231/519, 2 December 1961, from Geneva to Foreign Office; *FO 371*/159954, DF 2231/527, 4 December 1961, from Geneva to Foreign Office.

24. Marek Thee, op. cit., p. 202.

25. Marek Thee, op. cit., pp. 205–209.

26. *FO 371*/159955, DF 2231/547, 18 December 1961, Foreign Office minutes; *FO 371*/166496, DF 2231/12, 22 December 1961, from Foreign Office to Certain of Her Majesty's Representatives (Secret).

27. *VNA*, 4 December 1961, *SWB/FE*/812/A2/1.

28. *SWB/FE*/816/(i).

29. *Peking Review* 22 December 1961, Volume IV, Number 51, pp. 16–17. For a British account of this visit, see *FO 371*/166713, DV 103110/2, 3 January 1962, from Hanoi to Foreign Office: Visit of Chinese Military Delegation to North Vietnam.

30. *Public Papers of the Presidents of the United States: John F. Kennedy, 1961* (Washington: US Government Printing Office, 1962), pp. 505–506.

31. *VNA*, 16 December 1961, *SWB/FE*/827/A3/4.

32. Marek Thee, op. cit., pp. 205–209.

33. *NCNA*, 20 December 1961, *SWB/FE*/827/A3/3-4.

34. I have not been able to identify Major-General Bang Giang. There is however, one brief reference to a Bang Giang, an ethnic minority leader who rose to become commander of the Viet Bac Military Zone and chairman of the Viet Bac Autonomous Zone Administrative Committee in the 1970s, in William S. Turley, "Origins and Development of Communist Military Leadership in Vietnam," *Armed Forces and Society* Volume 3, Number 2, February 1977, p. 227.

35. Judith Stowe and Do Van (trans. and adapt.), *Following Ho Chi Minh: Memoirs of a North Vietnamese Colonel [Bui Tin]*, (London: Hurst, 1995), p. 45.

36. George McT. Kahin, *Intervention: How America Became Involved in Vietnam* (New York: Anchor, 1987), pp. 138–139.

37. *Zhonghua Renmin Gongheguo dui Wai Guanxi Gaishu* (Shanghai Waiyu Jiaoyu Chubanshe, 1989), p. 89.

38. *VNA*, 3 January 1962, *SWB/FE*/836/A3/2.

39. Guo Ming (ed.), *Zhongyue Guanxi Yanbian Shishi Nian* (Guangxi Renmin Chubanshe, 1992), p. 101.

40. *FO 371*/166716, DV 103138/3, 16 February 1962, from Hanoi to Foreign Office.

41. Vietnam Workers' Party Statement on International Solidarity, *VNA*, 10 February 1963, *SWB/FE*/1173/C1/1-3.

42. *FO 371*/160125, DV 1022/4, 21 December 1961, from Paris to Foreign Office (Secret).

43. *VNA*, 30 and 31 December 1961, *SWB/FE*/834/A2/1.

44. *NCNA*, 20 January 1962 and *VNA*, 21 January 1962, *SWB/FE*/851/A3/2-3.

45. *FO 371*/166712, DV 1022/8, 23 April 1962, from Hanoi to Foreign Office.

46. *FO 371*/158386, FC 1011/1, 3 January 1962, from Beijing to Foreign Office.

47. *FO 371*/170683, FC 1011/3, 17 January 1963, from Beijing to Foreign Office: Annual Economic Report for 1962.

48. Party History Research Centre, CCP Central Committee (comp.), *History of the Chinese Communist Party: A Chronology of Events (1919–1990)* (Beijing: Foreign Languages, 1991), p. 296.

49. *FO 371*/166697, DV 1011/1, 2 January 1962, from Saigon to Foreign Office: Annual Report for 1961.

50. *VNA*, 18 February 1962, *SWB/FE*/875/A3/3-4.

51. *NCNA*, 24 February 1962, *SWB/FE*/880/A3/1-2.

52. *Lich Su…*, p. 196; *Vietnam: The Anti–US Resistance War for National Salvation 1954–1975: Military Events* (JPRS 80968), pp. 48–49.

53. Tran Van Tra, *Nhung Chang Duong Lich Su Cua B2 Thanh Dong (Tap I): Hoa Binh Hay Chien Tranh* (Nha Xuat Ban Quan Doi Nhan Dan, 1992), pp. 241-242; *Vietnam: The Anti-US Resistance War for National Salvation 1954–1975: Military Events* (JPRS 80968), pp. 50-51.
54. *VNA*, 13 April 1962, *SWB/FE*/923/B/3-4.
55. *FO 371*/166497, DF 2231/21, 22 January 1962, Foreign Office minute.
56. *NCNA*, 13 January 1961, *SWB/FE*/845/C/1-3.
57. *Keesing's Contemporary Archives*, 11–18 August 1962, p. 18915.
58. *FO 371*/166430, DF 1015/109/G, 12 February 1962, from Vientiane to Foreign Office (Secret).
59. *FO 371*/166430, DF 1015/117, 16 February 1962, from Vientiane to Foreign Office; *FO 371*/166432, DF 1015/141, 21 February 1962, from Vientiane to Foreign Office.
60. Ibid.
61. *FO 371*/166430, DF 1015/118, 17 February 1962, from Vientiane to Foreign Office; *FO 371*/166432, 28 February 1962, from Vientiane to Foreign Office.
62. *FO 371*/166432, DF 1015/151, 28 February 1962, from Vientiane to Foreign Office.
63. *NCNA*, 9 February 1962, *SWB/FE*/867/C/1-2.
64. *FO 371*/166497, DF 2231/31, 15 February 1962, from Foreign Office to Washington (Secret).
65. *FO 371*/166432, DF 1015/143, 26 February 1962, Foreign Office minutes.
66. *VNA*, 22 February 1962, *SWB/FE*/881/A2/1.
67. *VNA*, 24 February 1962, *SWB/FE*/881/A2/1.
68. *FO 371*/170153, DV 2231/1, 20 September 1963, Foreign Office Minutes.
69. *VNA*, 28 February 1962, *SWB/FE*/884/A3/2-5.
70. *VNA*, 1 March 1962, *SWB/FE*/887/A2/1.
71. *FO 371*/166716, DV 103138/4, 9 March 1962, from Hanoi to Foreign Office.
72. *SWB/FE*/901/(i).
73. Alexander Dallin et al. (eds.), *Diversity in International Communism: A Documentary Record, 1961–1963* (New York: Columbia University Press, 1963), pp. 650–651.
74. Marek Thee, *Notes of a Witness: Laos and the Second IndoChinese War* (New York: Random House, 1973), pp. 240–241.
75. Ibid., pp. 241-243.
76. *FO 371*/166435, DF 1015/201, 30 March 1962, from Washington to Foreign Office; 2 April 1962, from Foreign Office to Washington.
77. Michael R. Beschloss, *Kennedy v. Khrushchev: The Crisis Years, 1960–63* (Boston: Faber and Faber, 1991), p. 395, 761.
78. *VNA*, 15 March 1962, *SWB/FE*/897/A3/4.
79. *NCNA*, 24 March 1962, *SWB/FE*/904/A3/5.
80. FO 371/164895, FC 1016/28, 6 April 1962, from Moscow to Foreign Office.
81. *FO 371*/164895, FC 10/6/33, 25 April 1962, from Shanghai to Foreign Office.

82. Wu Xiuquan's Speech at the Sixth Congress of the Socialist Unity Party of Germany on 18 January 1963 in *Peking Review*, Number 4, 1963; Alexander Dallin et al. (eds.), *Diversity in International Communism: A Documentary Record, 1961–1963* (New York: Columbia University Press, 1963); Vietnam Workers' Party Statement on International Solidarity, *VNA*, 10 February 1963, *SWB/FE/*1173/C1/1-3.

Also see Enver Hoxha, *Reflections on China: Extracts from a Political Diary*, Volume I (1962–1973) (Tirana: 8 Nentori Publishing House, 1979), pp. 7–29.

83. *FO 371*/170653, FC 1011/1, 1 January 1963, from Beijing to Foreign Office: Annual Report of 1962; *FO 371*/171924, NS 1011/1, 8 January 1963, from Moscow to Foreign Office: Annual Report for 1962.

84. *FO 371*/1666435, DF 1015/216, 6 April 1962, from Beijing to Foreign Office.

85. *Phnom Penh Radio*, 6 April 1962, *SWB/FE*/919/A3/1.

86. *FO 371*/170153, DV 2231/1, 20 September 1963, Foreign Office Minutes.

87. Marek Thee, *Notes of a Witness, Laos and the Second IndoChinese War* (New York: Random House, 1973), pp. 245–250.

88. *VNA*, 13 April 1962 and *NCNA*, 14 April 1962, *SWB*/FE/923/B/3-4.

89. Document Number 855 in Douglas Pike, Catalog of Vietcong Documents, Series 20, cited in William J. Duiker, *The Communist Road to Power in Vietnam* (Colorado: Westview, 1981), p. 207, p. 362 n.8.

90. See *SWB/FE/*939/C/1 and *SWB/FE/*940/C/1-2.

91. *FO 371*/166439, DF 1015/282, 10 May 1962, from Commonwealth Relations Office to Foreign Office.

92. Special National Intelligence Estimate (SNIE 58-3-62) dated 9 May 1962 in *Foreign Relations of the United States, Volume XXIV, 1961–1963: Laos Crisis* (Washington: US Government Printing Office, 1994), pp. 726–729.

93. *FO 371*/169802, DF 1011/1, 15 January 1963, from Vientiane to Foreign Office.

94. *FO 371*/166441, DF 1015/335, 16 May 1962, from Vientiane to Foreign Office.

95. Special National Intelligence Estimate (SNIE 58-3-62) dated 9 May 1962 in *Foreign Relations of the United States, Volume XXIV, 1961–1963: Laos Crisis* (Washington: US Government Printing Office, 1994), pp. 726-729.

96. *NCNA*, 16 May 1961, *SWB/FE/*946/C1/1-2.

97. *NCNA*, 24 May 1962, *SWB/FE/*954/C/2.

98. *FO 371*/159941, DF 2231/276, 14 June 1961, Record of conversation between Secretary of State and Marshal Chen Yi on 12 June 1961 at the Villa Mont Fleury, Geneva.

99. Michael R. Beschloss, *Kennedy v. Khrushchev: The Crisis Years, 1960–63* (Boston: Faber and Faber, 1991), p. 397.

100. *Radio of the Laotian Kingdom*, 29 May 1962, *SWB/FE*/958/C/1.

101. *FO 371*/166667, DU 1022/5, 6 June 1962, Notes on Conversation with Prince Sihanouk about Cambodia's Attitude to Present-Day South East Asian Problems.

102. *NCNA*, 25 August 1979, *SWB/FE*/6208/A3/3; Huang Zheng, *Ho Zhiming Yu Zhongguo*, (Beijing: Jiefang Jun Chubanshe, 1987), p. 163.

103. *FO 371*/166709, DV 1016/18, 2 July 1962, from Hanoi to Foreign Office; *FO 371*/166710, DV 1016/30, 2 August 1962, from Hanoi to Foreign Office; the Indonesian consul-general in Hanoi also believed that Ho had visited the Soviet Union in June, see *FO 371*/166710, DV 1016/27, 10 July 1962: Report by the Indonesian Consul-General in Hanoi on political situation in North Vietnam, from Hanoi to Foreign Office; *FO 371*/170088, DV 1011/1, 2 January 1962, from Saigon to Foreign Office: Annual Report of North Vietnam (1962) also confirmed that Ho was in Moscow on 22 June 1962, although dates of arrival and departure were never published.

104. Wang Xiangen, *Yuanyue Kangmei Shilu* (Jinan Chubanshe, 1992), p. 18.

105. George Modelski, *International Conference on the Settlement of the Laotian Question 1961–62* (Department of International Relations, Australian National University, Working Paper Number 2, 1962), pp. 135–136, 140–143.

106. Michael R. Beschloss, *Kennedy v. Khrushchev: The Crisis Years, 1960–1963* (Boston: Faber and Faber, 1991), p. 398.

107. For the transcript of the interview, see Bernard B. Fall (ed.), *Ho Chi Minh: On Revolution (Selected Writings, 1920–66)* (London: Pall Mall, 1967), pp. 352–358.

108. *Journal de Genève*, 24 July 1962, cited by Gareth Porter in Jayne Werner and David Hunt (ed.), *The American War in Vietnam* (Southeast Asia Program)(New York: Cornell University Press, 1993), p. 11, n. 13.

109. Arthur Lall, *How Communist China Negotiates* (New York, Columbia University Press, 1968), p. 180.

110. *NCNA*, 1 August 1962, *SWB/FE*/1012/C1/1.

111. *FO 371*/166710, DV 1016/21, 14 July 1962, from Hanoi to Foreign Office; *FO 371*/1666711, DV 1016/45, 30 July 1962, from Canadian Delegation, ICSC (Saigon) to Foreign Office; FO 371/ 166711, DV 1016/45, 6 August 1962, from Canadian Delegation, ICSC (Phnom Penh) to Foreign Office.

112. *The Pentagon Papers: The Defense Department History of US Decision Making on Vietnam*, Senator Gravel Edition, Volume II (Boston: Beacon, 1971), p. 164.

113. *FO 371*/1666697, DV 1011/2, 15 February 1962, from Saigon to Foreign Office.

114. *Zhonghua Renmin Gongheguo dui Wai Guanxi Gaishu* (Shanghai Waiyu Jiaoyu Chubanshe, 1989), p. 89.

115. Huang Guoan et al., *Zhongyue Guanxi Jianbian* (Guangxi Renmin Chubanshe, 1986), p. 209; Guo Ming (ed.), *Zhongyue Guanxi Yianbian Shishi Nian* (Guangxi Renmin Chubanshe, 1992), p. 69; Wang Xiangen, *Yuanyue Kangmei Shilu* (Jinan Chubanshe, 1992), p. 18; *Dangdai Zhongguo Waijiao* (Beijing: Zhongguo Shehui Kexue Chubanshe, 1990), p. 159; "On Hanoi's White Book," *Beijing Review* Number 47, 23 November 1979; Hoang Van Hoan, "Distortion of Facts about Militant Friendship between Vietnam and China Is Impermissible," *Beijing Review* Number 49, 7 December 1979.

116. *United States Government "White Paper": Aggression from the North: The Record of North Vietnam's Campaign to Conquer South Vietnam* (US Department of State Publication 7839; Far Eastern Series 130) (Washington, D.C., February

1965), reproduced in Marvin E. Gettleman (ed.), *Vietnam: History, Documents and Opinions on a Major World Crisis* (Middlesex: Penguin, 1966), pp. 300–334. There was no report of Chinese weapons captured in the 1961 "White Paper," *A Threat to Peace: North Vietnam's Efforts to Conquer South Vietnam* (US Department of State 7308; Far Eastern Series 110) (Washington, D.C., December 1961).

117. Before being appointed as ambassador to North Vietnam, Zhu Qiwen was ambassador to Bulgaria. Zhu's expertise and previous experience were mainly in the legal field. See *Who's Who in Communist China* (Hong Kong: Union Research Institute, 1965), p. 156.

118. Huang Zheng, *Ho Zhiming Yu Zhongguo*, (Beijing: Jiefang Jun Chubanshe, 1987), pp. 164–165.

119. Le Duan, *Thu Vao Nam* (Hanoi: Nha Xuat Ban Su That, 1985), pp. 50–67.

Conclusion

1. See Carlyle Thayer, *The Origins of the National Front for the Liberation of South Vietnam* (Ph.D. dissertation, Australian National University, 1977), pp. 608–628.

2. The circumstances surrounding Tou Samouth's death remain controversial. See Ben Kiernan, *How Pol Pot Came to Power* (London: Verso, 1985), pp. 197–198, 241; David P. Chandler, *Brother Number One: A Political Biography of Pol Pot* (Colorado: Westview, 1992), pp. 63–64, 206; Serge Thion, *Watching Cambodia: Ten Paths to Enter the Cambodian Tangle* (Bangkok: White Lotus, 1993), Appendix 3: *"About Tou Samouth,"* pp. 222–224.

Bibliography

I. Communist Documentation
- a) Vietnam
  - i) Vietnamese-Language Sources
  - ii) Memoirs and First-Person Accounts (in Vietnamese)
  - iii) English-Language Sources
  - iv) Journals and Periodicals
- b) China
  - i) Chinese-Language Sources
  - ii) Memoirs and First-Person Accounts (in Chinese)
  - iii) English-Language Sources
  - iv) Journals and Periodicals

II. Monitored Broadcasts and Reports

III. Non-Communist Documentation
- i) British Sources
- ii) United States Sources
- iii) United Nations Sources
- iv) Other Sources
- v) Memoirs and First-Person Accounts (in English)
- vi) Journals and Periodicals

IV. Secondary Sources
- i) Books
- iv) Articles

I. Communist Documentation

a) Vietnam

i) Vietnamese-Language Sources

Ban Ngien Cuu Lich Su Dang Thanh Pho Ho Chi Minh, 50 Nam Dau Tranh Kien Cuong Cua Dang Bo Va Nhan Dan Thanh Pho (Nha Xuat Ban Thanh Pho Ho Chi Minh, 1981)

Cao Van Luong, *Lich Su Cach Mang Mien Nam Viet Nam: Gioi Doan 1954–1960* (Hanoi: Nha Xuat Ban Khoa Hoc Xa Hoi, 1991)

Ho Chi Minh: Toan Tap, Tap VII (7/1954–12/1957)(Hanoi: Nha Xuat Ban Su That, 1987)

Le Duan, *Thu Vao Nam* (Hanoi: Nha Xuat Ban Su That, 1985)

Lich Su Dang Cong San Viet Nam, Tap II, De Cuong Bai Giang (Hanoi: Nha Xuat Ban Dai Hoc Trung Hoc Chuyen Nghiep, 1981)

Lich Su Dang Cong San Viet Nam, Tap III, Chuong Trinh Cao Cap (Hanoi: Nha Xuat Ban Sach Gio Khoa Mac-Lenin, 1985)

Lich Su Quan Doi Nhan Dan Viet Nam, Tap II (Hanoi: Nha Xuat Ban Quan Doi Nhan Dan, 1988)

Vo Tran Nha (chu bien), *Lich Su Dong Thap Muoi* (Nha Xuat Ban Thanh Pho Ho Chi Minh, 1993)

ii) Memoirs and First-Person Accounts (in Vietnamese)

Duong Ho Chi Minh: Hoi Ky Truong Son (Nha Xuat Ban Tac Pham Moi/Hoi Nha Van Viet Nam, 1982)

Hoang Van Hoan, *Giot Nuoc Trong Bien Ca* (Nha Xuat Ban Tin Viet Nam, 1986)

Thanh Tin, *Hoa Xuyen Tuyet (Hoi Ky)* (California: Saigon Press, 1991)

____. *Mat That: Hoi Ky Chinh Tri cua Bui Tin* (California: Saigon Press, 1993)

Tran Van Tra, *Nhung Chang Duong Lich Su Cua B2 Thanh Dong, Tap I: Hoa Binh Hay Chien Tranh* (Hanoi: Nha Xuat Ban Quan Doi Nhan Dan, 1992)

iii) English-Language Sources

The Anti–US Resistance War for National Salvation, 1954–1975 (translated by FBIS/US Joint Publications Service, Washington, D.C., June 1982)

Black Paper: Facts and Evidences of the Acts of Aggression and Annexation of Vietnam against Kampuchea (Phnom Penh, September 1978, reprinted in New York)

The Chinese Rulers' Crimes against Kampuchea (Ministry of Foreign Affairs, People's Republic of Kampuchea, April 1984)

Fall, Bernard B. (ed.), *Ho Chi Minh: On Revolution (Selected Writings, 1920–66)* (London: Pall Mall Press, 1967)

Fascist Terror in South Vietnam: Law 10/59 (Hanoi: Foreign Languages Publishing House, 1961)

50 Years of Activities of the Communist Party of Vietnam (Hanoi: Foreign Languages Publishing House, 1980)
Ho Chi Minh: Selected Works, Volume IV: Period from the Re-establishment of Peace in July 1954 to the 3rd National Congress of the Vietnam Workers' Party in September 1960 (Hanoi: Foreign Languages Publishing House, 1962)
Ho Chi Minh: *Selected Writings, 1920–1969* (Hanoi: Foreign Languages Publishing House, 1977)
The Ho Chi Minh Trail (Hanoi: Foreign Languages Publishing House, 1982)
Le Duan, *On Some Present International Problems* (Hanoi: Foreign Languages Publishing House, 1964)
____. *On the Socialist Revolution in Vietnam, Volume I–III* (Hanoi: Foreign Languages Publishing House, 1967)
Le Duan, *The Vietnamese Revolution: Fundamental Problems and Essential Tasks* (New York: International Publishers, 1971)
____. Selected Writings (Hanoi: Foreign Languages Publishing House, 1977)
An Outline History of the Vietnam Workers' Party, 1930–1975 (Hanoi: Foreign Languages Publishing House, 1978)
Socialist Republic of Vietnam Foreign Ministry White Book on Relations with China (Hanoi home service, 4–6 October 1979, SWB/FE/6238 and 6242)
The South Vietnam National Liberation Front (Hanoi: Foreign Languages Publishing House, 1962)
Third National Congress of the Vietnam Workers' Party: Documents, Volume I–III (Hanoi: Foreign Languages Publishing House, 1960)
Truong Chinh: *Selected Writings* (Hanoi: Foreign Languages Publishing House, 1977)
Woddis, John (ed.), *Ho Chi Minh: Selected Articles and Speeches, 1920–1967* (London: Lawrence and Wishart Limited, 1969)

iv) Journals and Periodicals

Nhan Dan
Su Kien Va Nhan Chung
Tap Chi Nghien Cuu Lich Su
Vietnam Courier

b) China

i) Chinese-Language Sources

Dang De Junshi Shilue Zhuanbian Yu Renmin Jundui Jianshe (Beijing: Guofang Daxue Chubanshe, 1990)

Guo Ming, *Zhongyue Guanxi Yanbian Sishinian* (Guangxi Renmin Chubanshe, 1992)
Guo Ming et al., *Xiandai Zhongyue Guanxi Ziliao Xuanbian* (2 volumes) (Beijing: Shishi Chubanshe, 1986)
Han Suyin, Zhou Enlai Yu Ta De Shiji 1898–1998 (Beijing: Zhongyang Wenxian Chubanshe, 1992)
"Huan Nan Zhi Zhong Jian Zhen Qing: Mao Zedong Yu Ho Zhiming," in *Congren Ribao*, 28 November 1993
Huang Guoan et al., *Zhongyue Guanxi Jianbian* (Guangxi Renmin Chubanshe, 1986)
Huang Zheng, *Ho Zhiming Yu Zhongguo* (Beijing: Jiefang Jun Chubanshe, 1987)
____. *Zhongyue Guanxi Shi Yanjiu Ji Gao* (Guangxi Renmin Chubanshe, 1992)
Jianguo Yilai Mao Zedong Wengao, Volume VI (1956–1957), Volume VII (1958) (Beijing: Zhongyang Wenxian Chubanshe, 1992) and Volume VIII (1959) (Beijing: Zhongyang Wenxian Chubanshe, 1993)
Jie (Xie) Lifu, *Yuenan Zhanzheng Shilu* (2 volumes) (Beijing: Shijie Zhishi Chubanshe, 1993)
Li Deng et al., Jianguo Yilai Junshi Bai Zhuang Da Shi (Beijing: Zhishi Chubanshe, 1992)
Mao Zedong Sixiang Wansui (no publisher, August 1969).
Meiguo Dui Yuenan Nanfang De Ganshe He Qinlue Zheng Ce (Beijing: Shijie Zhishi Chubanshe, 1963)
Quan Yanchi, *Mao Zedong Yu Khrushchev: 1957–1959 Zhongsu Guanxi Jishi* (Jiling Renmin Chubanshe, 1990)
Shi Yingfu, *Mimi Chubing Yare Congling: Yuanyue Kangmei Jishi* (Beijing: Jiefang Jun Wenyi Chubanshe, 1990)
Shi Yinghong, *Meiguo Zai Yuenan De Ganshe He Zhanzheng*, 1954-1968 (Beijing: Shijie Zhishi Chubanshe, 1993)
Wang Qi, *Zhonghua Renmin Gongheguo Dui Wai Guanxi Gaishu* (Shanghai Waiyu Jiaoyu Chunbanshe, 1989)
Wang Xiangen, *Yuanyue Kangmei Shilu* (Jinan Chubanshe, 1992)
Xie Yixian, *Zhechong Yi Gongchu—Xin Zhongguo Dui Wai Guanxi Sishinian* (Henan Renmin Chubanshe, 1990)
Xie Yixian, *Zhongguo Waijiao Shi—1949–1979* (Henan Renmin Chubanshe, 1994)
Zhongguo Junshi Guwentuan Yuanyue Kangfa Douzheng Shishi (Beijing: Jiefang Jun Chubanshe, 1990)
Zhonghua Renmin Gongheguo Dui Wai Guanxi Wenjian Ji (Beijing: Shijie Zhishi Chubanshe, ?)
Zhongmei Guanxi Erbainian (Beijing: Xinhua Chubanshe, 1984)
Zhou Enlai Waijiao Huodong Da Shiji (Beijing: Shijie Zhishi Chubanshe, 1993)

ii) Memoirs and First-Person Accounts (in Chinese)

Chen Geng, *Chen Geng Riji (Volume II)* (Beijing: Jiefang Jun Chubanshe, 1984)
Nie Rongzhen, *Nie Rongzhen Huiyi Lu (Part III)*(Beijing: Jiefang Jun Chubanshe, 1984)
Shi Zhe, *Zai Lishi Juren Shenbian: Shi Zhe Huiyi Lu* (Beijing: Zhongyang Wenxian Chubanshe, 1991)
Zhongguo Waijiao Guan Huiyi Lu: Xin Zhongguo Waijiao Fengyun (3 volumes) (Beijing: Shijie Zhishi Chubanshe, 1990, 1991, and 1994)

iii) English-Language Sources

Chen, Jerome (ed.), *Mao Papers: Anthology and Bibliography* (London: Oxford University Press, 1970)
Cheng, J. Chester (ed.), *The Politics of the Chinese Red Army (Kung-tso T'ung-hsun)*(Stanford: Hoover Institution on War, Revolution and Peace, 1966)
China's Foreign Relations: A Chronology of Events, 1949–1988 (Beijing: Foreign Languages Press, 1989)
China's Indisputable Sovereignty over the Xisha and Nansha Islands — Documents of the Ministry of Foreign Affairs of the People's Republic of China (Beijing: Foreign Languages Press, 30 January 1980)
"Chinese Government and Hoang Van Hoan's replies to Vietnam Foreign Ministry White Book," *Beijing Review*, 23 November, 30 November, and 7 December 1979; 12 October, 19 October, and 2 November 1981
Communist China 1955–1959: Policy Documents with Analysis (Massachusetts: Harvard University Press, 1962)
Concerning the Situation in Laos (Beijing: Foreign Languages Press, 1959)
Deng Xiaoping, "Suggestions on the Drafting of the Resolution on Certain Questions in the History of Our Party since the Founding of the People's Republic of China," *Beijing Review*, 25 July and 1 August 1983
Documents of Chinese Communist Party Central Committee, September 1956–April 1969, Volume I (Hong Kong: Union Research Institute, 1971)
"Facts about Sino-Vietnamese Relations," in *China and the World* (Beijing Review, Foreign Affairs Series I, 1982)
Leung, John K., and Michael Y. M. Kau (ed.), *The Writings of Mao Zedong, 1949–1976: Volume II: January 1956–December 1957* (New York: M. E. Sharpe, 1992)
Liu Suinian and Wu Qungan (ed.), *China's Socialist Economy: An Outline History, 1949–1984* (Beijing Review, 1986)
MacFarquhar, Roderick, Timothy Cheek, and Eugene Wu (eds.), *The Secret Speeches of Chairman Mao: From the Hundred Flowers to the Great Leap Forward* (Massachusetts: Harvard University Press, 1989)

Miscellany of Mao Tse-Tung Thought (1949–1968)(Parts I and II), (JPRS 61269-1; 61269-2, 20 February 1974)
"On Questions of Party History — Resolutions on Certain Questions in the History of our Party since the Founding of the People's Republic of China" (adopted by the 6th Plenary Session of the 11th Committee of the Communist Party of China on 27 June 1981), *Beijing Review* Number 27, 6 July 1981
On Vietnam's Expulsion of Chinese Residents (Beijing: Foreign Languages Press, 1978)
Schram, Stuart (ed.), *Chairman Mao Talks to the People: Talks and Letters (1956–1971)* (New York: Pantheon, 1974)
Zhong Huaiwen (comp.), *Years of Trial, Turmoil and Triumph — China from 1949 to 1988* (Beijing: Foreign Languages Press, 1989)

iv) Journals and Periodicals

News from Xinhua News Agency
Peking Review (subsequently *Beijing Review*)

II. Monitored Broadcasts and Reports

China News Analysis
Far Eastern Economic Review
Jones, Peter, and Sian Kevill, Sian, *Keesing's International Studies: China and the Soviet Union, 1949–84* (Longman Group, 1985)
Keesing's Contemporary Archives (Bristol: Keesing's Publications)
Keesing's Research Report: The Sino-Soviet Dispute (Keesing's Publications Limited, 1970)
Keesing's Research Report 5: South Vietnam — A Political History, 1954–1970 (New York: Charles Scribner, 1970)
Summary of World Broadcasts (Far East, USSR and Eastern Europe series) (Caversham: BBC Monitoring Service)
United States Consulate General, Hong Kong, *Chinese Communist Propaganda Review*
____. *Current Background*
____. *Survey of China Mainland Press*
____. *Extract from China Mainland*
United States Foreign Broadcast Information Service: Daily Report (China)
____. *Magazines* (subsequently from Issue Number 216, 5 July 1960, *Summary from China Mainland Magazines*)

III. Non-Communist Documentation

i) British Sources

British Foreign Office General Political Correspondence (FO 371), 1956–1964 (UK: Public Record Office)

Documents Relating to British Involvement in the IndoChina Conflict, 1945–1965 (Cmnd. 2834)

Reports of the International Commission for Supervision and Control in Laos (Cmnd. 314)

Vietnam, Laos and Cambodia: Chronology of Events, 1945–68 (London: Central Office of Information, 1968)

ii) United States Sources

Confidential United States State Department Central Files, 1956–1959

The Pentagon Papers: The Defense Department History of US Decision Making on Vietnam (The Senator Gravel Edition)(Boston: Beacon Press, 1971)

United States Congress and Senate Committee on Foreign Relations— Top-Secret Hearings, 1959–1966

United States Department of the Army, *U.S. Army Area Handbook for Vietnam* (Washington: US Government Printing Office, 1962)

United States Department of Defense, *United States–Vietnam Relations, 1945–1967* (Washington: US Government Printing Office, 1971)

United States Department of State, *Aggression from the North: The Record of North Vietnam's Campaign to Conquer South Vietnam* (Washington: US Government Printing Office, February 1965)

United States Department of State, *Foreign Relations of the United States (FRUS)*, Volume I (Vietnam, 1955–1957), Volume I (Vietnam 1958–1960), Volume I (Vietnam, 1961), Volume II (Vietnam, 1962); Volume XXI (Cambodia and Laos, 1955–1957), Volume XVI (Cambodia and Laos, 1958–1960), Volume XXIV (Laos Crisis, 1961–1963) (Washington: US Government Printing Office)

United States Department of State, *A Threat to the Peace: North Vietnam's Effort to Conquer South Vietnam* (Washington: US Government Printing Office, December 1961)

United States Department of State, *Working Paper on North Vietnam's Role in the South* (including Appendices)(Washington: US Government Printing Office, 27 May 1968)

United States Office of Strategic Services (OSS)/State Department Intelligence and Research Reports

United States Senate Committee on Foreign Relations, *Background Information Relating to Southeast Asia and Vietnam* (Washington: US Government Printing Office, 1969)
Vietnam Documents and Research Notes (Joint United States Public Affairs Office, Saigon)
Who's Who in North Vietnam (no publisher given but believed to be CIA, November 1972)

iii) United Nations Sources

Cordier, Andrew W., and Wilder Foote, *The Public Papers of the Secretaries-General of the United Nations* (New York: Columbia University Press, 1974)
Djonovich, Dusan J. (ed.), *United Nations Resolutions/Resolutions and Decisions of the Security Council* (New York: Oceana Publications, 1973 and 1989)
United Nations: Annual Report of the Secretary-General on the Work of the Organization
United Nations: Report of the Security Council to the General Assembly

iv) Other Sources

Dallin, Alexander, Jonathan Harris, and Grey Hodnett (ed.), *Diversity in International Communism: A Documentary Record, 1961–1963* (New York: Columbia University Press, 1963)
Kwan Ha Yin (ed.), *China and the United States, 1955–63* (New York: Facts on File, 1973)
Porter, Gareth (ed.), *Vietnam: The Definitive Documentation of Human Decisions* (London: Heyden and Son, 1979)
The Quynh Luu Uprisings (Saigon, 1958)
Sagar, D. J., *Major Political Events in Indo-China* (Oxford: Facts on File, 1991)
Soebel, Lester A., *Russia's Rulers: The Khrushchev Period* (New York: Facts on File, 1971)
_____. *South Vietnam: US-Communist Confrontation in Southeast Asia, Volume I, 1961–65* (New York: Facts on File, Inc., 1973)
Southeast Asia Treaty Organization (SEATO): Record of Progress

v) Memoirs and First-Person Accounts (in English)

Burlatsky, Fedor, *Khrushchev and the First Russian Spring: The Era of Khrushchev through the Eyes of His Adviser* (London: Weidenfeld and Nicolson, 1991)

Chanoff, David, and Doan Van Toai, *Portrait of the Enemy: The Other Side of the War in Vietnam* (London: I. B. Tauris, 1987)

Gromyko, Andrei, *Memories* (London: Hutchinson, 1989)

Hilsman, Roger, *To Move a Nation: The Politics of Foreign Policy in the Administration of John F. Kennedy* (New York: Doubleday, Inc., 1967)

Hoang Van Hoan, *A Drop in the Ocean* (Beijing: Foreign Languages Press, 1988)

Hoxha, Enver, *The Khrushchevites* (London: Workers' Publishing House, 1980)

Karnow, Stanley, "An Interview with General Giap," in Capps, Walter (ed.), *The Vietnam Reader* (London: Routledge, 1991)

Kaznacheev, Aleksandr, *Inside A Soviet Embassy: Experiences of a Russian Diplomat in Burma* (Philadelphia: Lippincott, 1962)

Lall, Arthur, *How Communist China Negotiates* (New York: Columbia University Press, 1968)

Langer, Paul F., and Joseph J. Zasloff, *The North Vietnamese Military Adviser in Laos: A First Hand Account* (California: Rand Corporation, 1968)

Li Zhisui, *The Private Life of Chairman Mao: The Inside Story of the Man Who Made Modern China* (London: Chatto and Windus, 1994)

Mai V. Elliot (transl.), *No Other Road to Take (Khong Con Duong Nao Khac): Memoir of Mrs. Nguyen Thi Dinh* (Ithaca: Cornell University, Department of Southeast Asian Studies, Southeast Asia Program, Data Paper Number 102, June 1976)

Maneli, Mieczyslaw, *War of the Vanquished* (New York: Harper and Row, 1971)

Macmillan, Harold, *Riding the Storm, 1956–1959* (London: Macmillan, 1971)

____. *Pointing the Way, 1959-1961* (London: Macmillan, 1972)

Micunovic, Veljko, *Moscow Diary: A Revealing Memoir about the Communist World when Khrushchev Ruled* (New York: Doubleday, 1980)

Peng Dehuai, *Memoirs of a Chinese Marshall— The Autobiographical Notes of Peng Dehuai, 1898–1974* (Beijing: Foreign Languages Press, 1984)

Penkovsky, Oleg, *The Penkovsky Papers: The Russian Who Spied for the West* (London: Fontana Books, 1967)

Phathanothai, Sirin, *The Dragon's Pearl* (New York: Simon and Schuster, 1994)

Radvanyi, Janos, *Hungary and the Superpowers: The 1956 Revolution and Realpolitik* (Stanford: Hoover Institution Press, 1972)

____. *Delusion and Reality* (Indiana: Gateway Limited, 1978)

Schecter, Jerrod L. and Vyacheslav V. Luchkov, *Khrushchev Remembers: The Glasnost Tapes* (Boston: Little, Brown, 1990)

Arthur M. Schlesinger, Jr., *A Thousand Days: John F. Kennedy in the White House* (London: Mayflower, 1967)

Seljna, Jan, *We Will Bury You* (London: Sidgwick and Jackson, 1982)

Sihanouk, Norodom, and Wilfred Burchett, *My War with the CIA: Cambodia's Fight for Survival* (Harmondsworth: Penguin Books, 1973)
Sisouk Na Champassak, *Storm over Laos: A Contemporary History* (New York: Praeger, 1961)
Souvannaphouma Prince Mangkra, *L'Agonie du Laos* (Plon, 1976)
Stowe, Judy, and Do Van (translated and adapted), *Following Ho Chi Minh: The Memoirs of a North Vietnamese Colonel [Bui Tin]* (London: Hurst, 1995)
Strong, Tracy B., and Helene Keyssar, "Anna Louise Strong: Three Interviews with Chairman Mao Zedong," *China Quarterly* Number 103, September 1985
Talbot, Strobe, *Khrushchev Remembers* (London: Sphere Books, 1971)
____. *Khrushchev Remembers: The Last Testament* (London: Andre Deutch Limited, 1974)
Thee, Marek, *Notes of a Witness: Laos and the Second IndoChina War* (New York: Random House, 1973)
Truong Nhu Tang, *Journal of a Vietcong* (London: Jonathan Cape, 1986)
Wang Bingnan, *Nine Years of Sino-US Talks in Retrospect* (JPRS-CPS-85-079, 7 August 1985)
"We Lied to You" (interview with Generals Vo Nguyen Giap and Vo Bam), in *The Economist*, 26 February 1983
Wu Xiuquan, *Eight Years in the Ministry of Foreign Affairs (January 1950–October 1958): Memoirs of a Diplomat* (Beijing: New World Press, 1985)
Young, Kenneth T., *Negotiating with the Chinese Communists: The United States Experience, 1953–1967* (New York: McGraw-Hill, 1968)

iv) Journals and Periodicals

Cold War International History Project Bulletin
Current Scene
Issues and Studies
The World Today

IV. Secondary Sources

i) Books:

Adams, Nina, and Alfred W. McCoy, *Laos: War and Revolution* (New York: Harper and Row, 1970)
Adelman, Jonathan R., *The Revolutionary Armies: The Historical Development of the Soviet and Chinese People's Liberation Armies* (Westport: Greenwood Press, 1980)

Barnet, Richard J., *Intervention and Revolution: The United States in the Third World* (London: Granada, 1970)

Barnett, A. Doak, *China's Far West: Four Decades of Change* (Boulder: Westview Press, 1993)

Beresford, Melanie, *Vietnam: Politics, Economics and Society* (London: Pinter, 1988)

Beschloss, Michael R., *Kennedy and Khrushchev: The Crisis Years, 1960-1963* (London: Faber and Faber, 1991)

Blaufarb, Douglas S., *The Counterinsurgency Era: US Doctrine and Performance, 1950 to the Present* (New York: Free Press, 1977)

Bloodworth, Dennis, *The Reporter's Notebook* (Singapore: Times Books International, 1988)

Borisov, O. B., and B.T. Koloskov, *Soviet-Chinese Relations, 1945–1970* (Bloomington: Indiana University Press, 1975)

Boudarel, George, *Cent Fleurs Ecloses dan la Nuit du Vietnam: Communisme et Dissidence, 1954–1956* (Jacques Bertoin, 1991)

Brown, Archie (ed.), *The Soviet Union: A Biographical Dictionary* (London: Weidenfeld and Nicolson, 1990)

Burchett, Wilfred, *North of the 17th Parallel* (Hanoi: Red River Publishing House, 1957)

____. *Mekong Upstream* (Hanoi: Red River Publishing House, 1957)

____. *The Furtive War: The US in Vietnam and Laos* (New York: International Publishers, 1963)

____. *My Visit to the Liberated Zones of South Vietnam* (Hanoi: Foreign Languages Publishing House, 1966)

____. *The China Cambodian Vietnam Triangle* (London: Zed Press, 1981)

Byron, John, and Robert Pack, *The Claws of the Dragon: Kang Sheng—The Evil Genius Behind Mao, and His Legacy of Terror in People's China* (New York: Simon and Schuster, 1992)

Cable, James, *The Geneva Conference of 1954 on IndoChina* (New York: St. Martin's Press, 1986)

Caldwell, Malcolm, and Lek Hor Tan, *Cambodia in the Southeast Asian War* (New York: Monthly Review Press, 1973)

Cameron, Allan W. (ed.), *Vietnam Crisis: A Documentary History, Volume I: 1940–1956* (Ithaca: Cornell University Press, 1971)

Castle, Timothy Neil, *At War in the Shadow of Vietnam: US Military Aid to the Royal Lao Government, 1955–1975* (PhD dissertation, University of Hawaii, 1991)

Caulkins, Laura Marie, *Sino-Vietminh Relations, 1948–1952* (unpublished PhD dissertation, University of London, 1990)

Chanda, Nayan, *Brother Enemy: The War after the War* (London: Harcourt Brace Jovanovich, 1986)

Chandler, David P., *The Tragedy of Cambodian History: Politics, War, and Revolution since 1945* (New Haven: Yale University Press, 1991)

____. *A History of Cambodia* (Boulder: Westview Press, 1992)

____. *Brother Number One: A Political Biography of Pol Pot* (Boulder: Westview Press, 1992)

Chang, Gordon H., *Friends and Enemies: The United States, China and the Soviet Union, 1948–1972* (Stanford: Stanford University Press, 1990)

Chang Pao-min, *Beijing, Hanoi and the Overseas Chinese* (Berkeley: University of California, Center of Chinese Studies, China Research Monograph Number 24, 1982)

Chang, Parris H., *Power and Policy in China* (Iowa: Kendall/Hunt, 1990)

Charlton, Michael, and Anthony Moncrieff, *Many Reasons Why: The American Involvement in Vietnam* (London: Scolar Press, 1978)

Conquest, Robert, *Power and Policy in the USSR: The Study of Soviet Dynasties* (London: Macmillan, 1962)

Crankshaw, Edward, *The New Cold War: Moscow v. Pekin* (Middlesex: Penguin Books, 1965)

Davidson, Philip B. (Lt. General, Retired), *Vietnam at War: The History, 1946–1975* (California: Presidio Press, 1988)

Deutscher, Issac, *Russia, China and the West, 1953–1966* (Middlesex: Penguin Books, 1970)

Dickie, John, *Inside the Foreign Office* (London: Chapmans, 1992)

Dittmer, Lowell, *Sino-Soviet Normalization and Its International Implications, 1945–1990* (Seattle: University of Washington Press, 1992)

Domes, Jurgen, *The Internal Politics of China, 1949–1972* (London: Hurst, 1973)

Dommen, Arthur J., *Conflict in Laos: The Politics of Neutralization* (New York: Praeger, 1971)

____. *Laos: Keystone of IndoChina* (Boulder: Westview Press, 1985)

Donnell, John C., and Melvin Gurtov, *North Vietnam: Left of Moscow, Right of Peking* (California: Rand Corporation, 1968)

Dudley, Williams, and David Bender (ed.), *The Vietnam War: Opposing Viewpoints* (San Diego: Greenhaven Press, 1990)

Duiker, William J., *The Communist Road to Power in Vietnam* (Colorado: Westview Press, 1981)

____. *China and Vietnam: The Roots of Conflict* (Institute of East Asian Studies, University of California at Berkeley, IndoChina Research Monograph I, 1986)

Duker, Pollack Jonathan, *Perception and Action in Chinese Foreign Policy: The Quemoy Decision* (2 volumes)(PhD dissertation, University of Michigan, 1976)

Eayrs, James, *In Defence of Canada, (Volume V) IndoChina: Roots of Complicity*, (Toronto: University of Toronto Press, 1983)

Elliot, David William Penn, *Revolutionary Reintegration: A Comparison of the Foundation of Post-Liberation Political Systems in North Vietnam and China* (PhD dissertation, Cornell University, 1976)

Errington, Elizabeth Jane, and B. J. C. McKercher, *The Vietnam War as History* (New York: Praeger, 1990)

Fairbank, John, and Roderick MacFarquhar (ed.), *Cambridge History of China (Volume 14), Part 1: The Emergence of Revolutionary China 1949–1965* (Cambridge: Cambridge University Press, 1989)

____. *Cambridge History of China (Volume 15), Part 2: Revolutions within the Chinese Revolution 1966–1982* (Cambridge University Press, 1991)

Faligot, Roger, and Remi Kauffer *The Chinese Secret Service* (New York: William Morrow, 1989)

Fall, Bernard, *Vietnam Witness, 1953–66* (London: Pall Mall, 1966)

____. *The Two Vietnams: A Political and Military Analysis* (London: Pall Mall, 1967)

____. *Last Reflections On a War* (New York: Doubleday, 1967)

____. *Anatomy of a Crisis: The Laotian Crisis of 1960–1961* (New York: Doubleday and Company, 1969)

Ferrell, Robert H., *The Eisenhower Diaries* (New York: W. W. Norton, 1968)

Field, Michael, *The Prevailing Wind: Witness in IndoChina* (London: Methuen, 1965)

Fishel, Wesley R. (ed.), *Vietnam: Anatomy of a Conflict* (Illinois: F. E. Peacock, 1968)

George, Alexander L., et al., *The Limits of Coercive Diplomacy: Laos, Cuba, Vietnam* (Boston: Little, Brown, 1971)

Gettleman, Marvin E. (ed.), *Vietnam: History, Documents and Opinion on a Major World Crisis* (Middlesex: Penguin Books, 1966)

Gettleman, Marvin and Susan, and Lawrence and Carol Kaplan, (eds.), *Conflict in IndoChina: A Reader to the Widening War in Laos and Cambodia* (New York: Random House, 1970)

Gittings, John, *The Role of the Chinese Army* (London: Oxford University Press, 1967)

____. *The World and China: 1922–1972* (London: Eyre Methuen, 1974)

Goldstein, Martin E., *American Policy Towards Laos* (New Jersey: Associated University Press, 1973)

Griffith, William E., *The Sino-Soviet Rift* (Massachusetts: MIT Press, 1964)

Gunn, Geoffrey Charles, *Road through the Mountains: The Origins of Nationalism and Communism in Laos, 1930–1954* (PhD dissertation, Monash University, 1985)

Gurtov, Melvin, *Hanoi on War and Peace* (California: Rand Corporation, 1967)

Gurtov, Melvin, and Byong-Moo Hwang, *China Under Threat: The Politics of Strategy and Diplomacy* (Baltimore: John Hopkins University Press, 1980)

Halliday, Jon (ed.), *The Artful Albanian: The Memoirs of Enva Hoxha* (London: Chatto and Windus, 1986)
Han Suyin, *Wind in the Tower: Mao Tsetung and the Chinese Revolution 1949–1975* (London: Jonathan Cape, 1976)
____. *Eldest Son: Zhou Enlai and the Making of Modern China, 1898–1976* (London: Jonathan Cape, 1994)
Hannah, Norman B., *The Key to Failure: Laos and the Vietnam War* (London: Madison Books, 1987)
Hearden, Patrick J. (ed.), *Vietnam: Four American Perspectives* (Indiana: Purdue University Press, 1990)
Hinton, Harold C., *Communist China in World Politics* (London: Macmillan, 1966)
____. *China's Turbulent Quest: An Analysis of China's Foreign Relations since 1949* (Indiana: Indiana University Press, 1973)
Hoffman, Erik P., and Frederick J. Fleron, Jr., *The Conduct of Soviet Foreign Policy* (New York: Aldine, 1980)
Hollingworth, Clare, *Mao* (London: Grafton Books, 1987)
Honey, P. J. (ed.), *North Vietnam Today: Profile of a Communist Satellite* (New York: Praeger, 1962)
____. *Communism in North Vietnam: Its Role in the Sino-Soviet Dispute* (Connecticut: Greenwood Press, 1973)
Hood, Steven J., *Dragons Entangled: IndoChina and the China-Vietnam War* (New York: M. E. Sharpe, 1992)
Hsieh, Alice Langley, *Communist China's Strategy in the Nuclear Age* (New Jersey: Prentice-Hall, 1962)
Hudson, G. F., Richard Lowenthal, and Roderick MacFarquhar, *The Sino-Soviet Dispute* (London: China Quarterly, 1961)
Jacobs, Dan N. (ed.), *The New Communisms* (New York: Harper and Row, 1969)
Jacques, Marcuse, *The Peking Papers: Leaves from the Notebook of a China Correspondent* (London: Arthur Barker, 1968)
Joffe, Ellis, *Party and Army: Professionalism and Political Control in the Chinese Officer Corps, 1949–1964* (Massachusetts: Harvard University Press, 1965)
Kahin, George McT., *Intervention: How America Became Involved in Vietnam* (New York: Alfred A. Knopf, 1986)
Kalb, Marvin, and Elie Abel, *Roots of Involvement: The US in Asia, 1784–1971* (London: Pall Mall, 1971)
Karnow, Stanley, *Vietnam: A History* (London: Penguin Books, 1988)
Keith, Ronald C., *The Diplomacy of Zhou Enlai* (New York: St. Martin's Press, 1989)
Kiernan, Ben (ed.), *How Pol Pot Came to Power* (London: Verso, 1985)
____. *Burchett Reporting the Other Side of the World, 1939–1983* (London: Quartet Books, 1986)

Kirk, Donald, *Wider War: The Struggle for Cambodia, Thailand and Laos* (New York: Praeger, 1971)

Klein, Donald, and Anne Clark *A Biographical Dictionary of Chinese Communism* (Cambridge: Harvard University Press, 1971)

Kolko, Gabriel, *Vietnam: Anatomy of War, 1940–1975* (London: Unwin Hyman, 1987)

Lacoutre, Jean, *Vietnam: Between Two Truces* (London: Secker and Warburg, 1966)

____. *Ho Chi Minh* (Middlesex: Penguin Books, 1968)

Ladany Laszlo, *The Communist Party of China and Marxism, 1921–1985: A Self-Portrait* (California: Hoover Institution Press, 1988)

Laid, Zaki, *The Third World and the Soviet Union* (London: Zed Books, 1988)

Langer, Paul F., *The Soviet Union, China and the Pathet Lao: Analysis and Chronology* (California: Rand Corporation, no date indicated)

Langer, Paul F., and J. Joseph Zasloff, *North Vietnam and the Pathet Lao* (Massachusetts: Harvard University Press, 1970)

Lanning, Michael Lee, and Dan Cragg, *Inside the VC and the NVA: The Real Story of North Vietnam's Armed Forces* (New York: Ballantine Books, 1992)

Lee Chae Jin, *Chinese Communist Policy in Laos, 1954–1965* (PhD dissertation, University of California in Los Angeles, 1966)

____. *Japan Faces China: Political and Economic Relations in the Postwar Era* (Baltimore: Johns Hopkins University Press, 1976)

Leifer, Michael, *Cambodia: The Search for Security* (London: Pall Mall, 1967)

Leighton, Marian Kirsh, *The Kremlin and the Vietnam Conflict* (PhD dissertation, Columbia University, 1979)

Leonhard, Wolfgang, *The Kremlin since Stalin* (London: Oxford University-Press, 1962)

Linden, Carl A., *Khrushchev University and the Soviet Leadership, 1957–1964* (Baltimore: Johns Hopkins Press, 1966)

Low, Alfred D., *The Sino-Soviet Dispute: An Analysis of the Polemics* (London: Associated University Press, 1976)

MaCabe, Robert Karr, *Storm over Asia: China and Southeast Asia — Thrust and Response* (New York: New American Library, 1967)

MacAlister, Brown and Joseph J. Zasloff, *Apprentice Revolutionaries: The Communist Movement in Laos, 1930–1985* (Stanford: Hoover Institution Press, 1986)

McCauley, Martin (ed.), *Khrushchev and Khrushchevism* (London: Macmillan Press, 1987)

____. *Nikita Khrushchev* (London: Sphere Books, 1991)

McCoy, Alfred W., *The Politics of Heroin: CIA Complicity in the Global Drug Trade* (New York: Lawrence Hill, 1991)

MacDonald, Peter, *The Victor in Vietnam: Giap* (London: Fourth Estate, 1993)

MacFarquhar, Roderick, *The Origins of the Cultural Revolution, Volume I: Contradictions among the People, 1956–57; Volume II: The Great Leap Forward, 1958–1960* (London: Oxford University Press, 1974 and 1983 respectively)

McGregor, Charles, *The Sino-Vietnamese Relationship and the Soviet Union* (Adelphi Paper 232, International Institute for Strategic Studies, 1988)

McMahon, Robert J. (ed.) *Major Problems in the History of the Vietnam War* (Lexington: Heath and, 1990)

Masaya Shiraishi, *Japanese Relations with Vietnam: 1951–1987* (Ithaca: Cornell Southeast Asia Program, 1990)

Mende, Tibor, *China and her Shadow* (London: Thames and Hudson, 1961)

Mitchum, Chad J., *Right Honorable Alvin Hamilton's "Peace through Trade": The 1961 Sino-Canadian Grain Agreement"* (MA thesis, University of Saskatchewan, 1994)

Modelski, George, *International Conference on the Settlement of the Laotian Question, 1961–62* (Department of International Relations, Research School of Pacific Studies, ANU, 1962)

Moise, Edwin Evaviste, *Land Reform in China and North Vietnam: Revolution at the Village level* (PhD dissertation, University of Michigan, 1977)

Moore, John Norton, *The Vietnam Debate: A Fresh Look at the Arguments* (Lanham: University Press of America, 1990)

Newman, John M., *JFK and Vietnam: Deception, Intrigue and the Struggle for Power* (New York: Warner, 1992)

Nichols, Thomas M., *The Sacred Curse: Civil-Military Conflict over Soviet National Security, 1917–1992* (Ithaca: Cornell University Press, 1993)

O'Ballance, Edgar, *The Wars in Vietnam, 1954–1973* (London: Ian Allan, 1975)

Osborne, Milton, *Sihanouk: Prince of Light, Prince of Darkness* (Sydney: Allen and Unwin, 1994)

Papp, Daniel S., *Vietnam: The View from Moscow, Peking and Washington* (North Carolina: McFarland, 1981)

Pham Kim Vinh, *Vietnam: A Comprehensive History* (California: Pham Kim Vinh Research Institute, 1992)

Pike, Douglas, *Viet Cong: The Organization and Techniques of the National Liberation Front of South Vietnam* (Massachusetts: MIT Press, 1968)

____. *History of Vietnamese Communism, 1925–76* (Stanford: Hoover Institution Press, 1978)

____. *PAVN: People's Army of Vietnam* (California: Presidio Press, 1986)

____. *Vietnam and the Soviet Union: Anatomy of an Alliance* (Colorado: Westview Press, 1987)

Porter, Gareth, *Vietnam: The Politics of Bureaucratic Socialism* (Ithaca: Cornell University Press, 1993)

Post, Ken, *Revolution, Socialism and Nationalism in Vietnam* (4 volumes) (UK: Dartmouth, 1989 and 1990)

Race, Jeffrey, *War Comes to Long An: Revolutionary Conflict in a Vietnamese Province* (Berkeley: University of California Press, 1972)

Randle, Robert F., *Geneva 1954: The Settlement of the IndoChina War* (New Jersey: Princeton University Press, 1969)

Raskin, Marcus G., and Bernard B. Fall, (ed.), *The Vietnam Reader: Articles and Documents on American Foreign Policy and the Vietnam Crisis* (New York: Random House, 1965)

Robbins, Christopher, *Air America* (London, Macmillan, 1979)

____. *The Ravens* (New York: Crown, 1987)

Robinson, Jeffrey, *The End of the American Century: Hidden Agendas of the Cold War* (London: Hutchinson, 1992)

Robinson, Thomas W., and David Shambaugh (ed.), *Chinese Foreign Policy: Theory and Practice* (Oxford: Clarendon Press, 1994)

Rostow, W. W. *The Diffusion of Power, 1957–1972* (New York: Macmillan, 1972)

Rothschild, Joseph, *A Political History of East Central Europe since World War Two* (London: Oxford University Press, 1989)

Rupen, Robert A. and Robert Farrell, *Vietnam and the Sino-Soviet Dispute* (New York: Praeger, 1967)

Salisbury, Harrison E., *Behind the Lines—Hanoi* (London: Secker and Warburg, 1967)

____. *Disturber of the Peace: Memoirs of a Foreign Correspondent* (London: Unwin Hyman, 1989)

____. *The New Emperors: Mao and Deng—A Dual Biography* (London: Harper Collins, 1993)

Segal, Gerald, *The Great Power Triangle* (London: Macmillan, 1982)

____. *Defending China* (London: Oxford University Press, 1989)

Shaplen, Robert, *The Lost Revolution: Vietnam, 1945–1965* (London: Andre Deutsch, 1966)

Shaw, Yu-ming (ed.), *Changes and Continuities in Chinese Communism, Volume I: Ideology, Politics and Foreign Policy* (Boulder: Westview Press, 1988)

Sheehan, Neil, *Two Cities: Hanoi and Saigon* (London: Jonathan Cape, 1992)

Short, Anthony, *The Origins of the Vietnam War* (London: Longman, 1989)

Simmonds, J. D., *China's World: The Foreign Policy of a Developing State* (New York: Columbia University Press, 1970)

Slusser, Robert M., *The Berlin Crisis of 1961: Sino-American Relations and the Struggle for Power in the Kremlin, June–November 1961* (Baltimore: Johns Hopkins University Press, 1973)

Smith, Ralph B., *An International History of the Vietnam War, Volume I: Revolution versus Containment, 1955–61* (London: Macmillan, 1983)

____. *Volume II: The Struggle for Southeast Asia, 1961–65* (London: Macmillan, 1985)

Smith, Roger M., *Cambodia's Foreign Policy* (PhD dissertation, Cornell University, 1964)

Smyser, W. R., *The Independent Vietnamese: Vietnamese Commmunism between Russia and China, 1956–1969* (Ohio: Ohio University Center for International Studies, 1980)

Snow, Edgar, *The Other Side of the River: Red China Today* (London: Victor Gollancz, 1963)

Spahr, William J., *Zhukov: Rise and Fall of a Great Captain* (California: Presidio Press, 1993)

Spector, Ronald H., *Advice and Support: The Early Years of the US Army in Vietnam, 1941–1960* (New York: Free Press, 1985)

Stevens, Richard L., *The Trail: A History of the Ho Chi Minh Trail and the Role of Nature in the War in Vietnam* (New York: Garland, Inc., 1993)

Stuart-Fox, Martin, *Laos: Politics, Economics and Society* (London: Pinter, 1986)

Swearingen, Rodger (ed.), *Leaders of the Communist World* (New York: Free Press, 1971)

Tang Tsou (ed.), *China in Crisis: China's Policies in Asia and America's Alternatives (Volume II)* (Chicago: University of Chicago Press, 1968)

Taylor, Jay, *China and Southeast Asia: Peking's Relations with Revolutionary Movements* (New York: Praeger, 1976)

Thai Quang Trung, *Collective Leadership and Factionalism: An Essay on Ho Chi Minh's Legacy* (Singapore: Institute of Southeast Asian Studies, 1985)

Thayer, Carlyle Alan, *The Origins of the National Liberation Front for the Liberation of South Vietnam* (PhD dissertation, ANU, 1977)

____. *War by Other Means: National Liberation and Revolution in Vietnam, 1954–60* (Sydney: Allen and Unwin, 1989)

Ton That Thien, *The Foreign Politics of the Communist Party of Vietnam: A Study of Communist Tactics* (New York: Crane Russack, 1989)

Townsend, James R., *Politics in China* (Boston: Little, Brown, 1980)

Toye, Hugh, *Laos: Buffer States or Battleground* (London: Oxford University Press, 1971)

Trevelyan, Humphrey, *Diplomatic Channels* (London: Macmillan, 1973)

Turley, William S., *Army, Party and Society in the Democratic Republic of Vietnam: Civil-Military Relations in a Mass-Mobilization System* (PhD dissertation, University of Washington, 1972)

Turley, William S. (ed.), *Vietnamese Communism in Comparative Perspective* (Colorado: Westview Press, 1980)

____. *The Second IndoChina War: A Short Political and Military History, 1954–1975* (Colorado: Westview Press, 1986)

Turner, Robert F., *Vietnamese Communism: Its Origins and Development* (Stanford: Hoover Institution Press, 1975)

Van Dyke, Jon M., *North Vietnam's Strategy for Survival* (Palo Alto: Pacific Books Publishers, 1972)

Vickerman, Andrew, *The Fate of the Peasantry: Premature "Transition to Socialism" in the Democratic Republic of Vietnam* (Yale University Southeast Asia Studies, Monograph Series Number 28, 1986)

Vickery, Michael, *Kampuchea: Politics, Economics and Society* (Australia: Allen and Unwin, 1986)

Wang Gungwu, *China and the World since 1949: The Impact of Independence, Modernity and Revolution* (London: Macmillan, 1977)
Wang, James C. F., *Contemporary Chinese Politics: An Introduction* (New Jersey: Prentice-Hall, 1980)
Warner, Denis, *Reporting Southeast Asia* (Sydney: Angus and Robertson, 1966)
Werner, S. Jayne, and Luu Doan Huynh (ed.), *The Vietnam War: Vietnamese and American Perspectives* (New York: M. E. Sharpe, 1993)
White, Christine Katherine Pelzer, *Agrarian Reform and National Liberation in the Vietnamese Revolution, 1920–1957* (PhD dissertation, Cornell University, 1981)
Whitson, William W., *The Chinese High Command: A History of Communist Military Politics, 1927–71* (New York: Praeger, 1973)
Wilson, Dick, *Chou: The Story of Chou En Lai, 1898–1976* (London: Hutchinson, 1984)
Wise, David, and Thomas B. Ross, *The Invisible Government* (New York: Random House, 1964)
Witke, Roxane, *Comrade Chiang Ching* (Boston: Little, Brown, 1977)
Wu Yuan-li (ed.), *China: A Handbook* (New York: Praeger, 1973)
Yahuda, Michael B., *China's Role in World Affairs* (London: Croom Helm, 1978)
Zagoria, Donald S., *The Sino-Soviet Conflict, 1956–61* (New York: Atheneum, 1964)
Zasloff, Joseph J., *The Pathet Lao: Leadership and Organisation* (Toronto: Lexington, 1973)
Zasloff, Joseph J., and Alan E. Goodman, *IndoChina in Conflict: A Political Assessment* (Lexington: Lexington, 1972)
Zasloff, Joseph J., and Brown MacAlister, *Communism In IndoChina: New Perspectives* (London: Heath, 1975)
Zhang Shu Guang, *Deterrence and Strategic Culture: Chinese-American Confrontations, 1949–1958* (Ithaca: Cornell University Press, 1992)

ii) Articles

Boudarel, Georges, "Intellectual dissidence in the 1950s: The Nhan-Van and Giai-Pham Affair," *Vietnam Forum* Number 13 (Yale University Southeast Asia Studies, 1990)
Cameron, Allan W., "The Soviet Union and Vietnam: The Origins of Involvement," in W. Raymond Duncan, (ed.), *Soviet Policy in Developing Countries* (Toronto: Ginn-Blaisdell, 1970)
Carver, George A., Jr., "The Faceless VietCong," *Foreign Affairs* 44:3, April 1966
Chen Jian, "China and the First Indo-China War, 1950–54," *China Quarterly* Number 133, March 1993
Chen, King C., "North Vietnam in the Sino-Soviet Dispute, 1962–64," *Asian Survey* 4:9, September 1964

———. "Hanoi's Three Decisions and the Escalation of the Vietnam War," *Political Science Quarterly* 90:2, Summer 1975

Christiansen, Flemming, "The Neibu Bibliography: A Review Article," *CCP Research Newsletter* Number 4, Fall-Winter, 1989–90

Crozier, Brian, "Peking and the Laotian Crisis: An Interim Appraisal," *China Quarterly* Number 7, July-September 1961

———. "Peking and the Laotian Crisis: A Further Appraisal," *China Quarterly* Number 11, July-September 1962

Dittmer, Lowell, "China's Search for Its Place in the World," Brantly Womack (ed.), *Contemporary Chinese Politics in Historical Perspective* (Cambridge: Cambridge University Press, 1991)

Dunn, Joe P., "In Search of Lessons: The Development of a Vietnam Historiography," in Lloyd J. Matthews and Dale E. Brown, (eds.), *Assessing the Vietnam War: A Collection from the Journal of the US Army War College* (Washington, D.C.: Pergamon-Brassey's International Defense Publishers, 1987)

Eckstein, Alexander, "On the Economic Crisis in Communist China," *Foreign Affairs* 42:4, July 1964

Fall, Bernard B., "Crisis in North Vietnam," *Far Eastern Survey*, January 1957

———. "The International Relations of Laos," *Pacific Affairs* 30:1, March 1957

Ford, Harold P., "Modern Weapons and the Sino-Soviet Estrangement," *China Quarterly* Number 18, April-June 1964

Friedman, Edward, "The Revolution in Hungary and the Hundred Flowers Period in China," *Journal of Asian Studies*, 25:1, November 1965

Garver, John W., "New Light on Sino-Soviet Relations: The Memoirs of China's Ambassador to Moscow, 1955–62," *China Quarterly* Number 122, June 1990

———. "The Chinese Threat in the Vietnam War," *Parameters*, Spring 1992

Godley, Michael R., "Issues in Contemporary Chinese History," *Asian Studies Association of Australian Review* 13:1, July 1989

Goldstein, Steven M., and He Di, "New Chinese Sources on the History of the Cold War," *Cold War International History Project*, Issue 1, Spring 1992

Griffith, William E., "The November 1960 Moscow Meeting: A Preliminary Reconstruction," *China Quarterly* Number 11, July-September 1962

Halpern, A. M., "Communist China and Peaceful Co-existence," *China Quarterly* Number 3, July-September 1960

———. "The Chinese Communist Line on Neutralism," *China Quarterly* Number 5, January-March 1961

Hawtin, Elise, "The Hundred Flowers Movement and the Role of the Intellectuals in China: Fei Hsiao-tung: A Case Study," in *Papers on China* (Volume 12), (East Asia Regional Studies Program, Harvard University, 1958)

Heder, Stephen, "Kampuchea's Armed Struggle: The Origins of an Independent Revolution," in *Bulletin of Concerned Asian Scholars* 11:1, 1979

Hinton, Harold C., "The Eighth Congress of the Chinese Communist Party," *Far Eastern Survey* 26:1, January 1957

Hirohide Kurihara, "Changes in the Literary Policy of the Vietnamese Workers' Party, 1956–1958," in Takeshi Shiraishi and Motoo Furuta (ed.), *IndoChina In the 1940s and 1950s* (Ithaca: Cornell University Southeast Asia Program, 1992)

Hoang Giang, "La Revolte des Intellectuels au Viet-nam en 1956," *Vietnam Forum* Number 13 (Yale University Southeast Asia Studies, 1990)

Honey, P. J., "Pham Van Dong's Tour," *China Quarterly* Number 8, October-December 1961

Hsieh, Alice Langley, "China's Secret Military Papers: Military Doctrine and Strategy," *China Quarterly* Number 18, April-June 1964

Hunt, Michael H., and Odd Arne Westad, "The Chinese Communist Party and International Affairs: A Field Report on New Historical Sources and Old Research Problems," *China Quarterly* Number 122, June 1990

Joffe, Ellis, "The Conflict between the Old and New in the Chinese Army," *China Quarterly* Number 18, April-June 1964

Klein, Donald W., "Peking's Evolving Ministry of Foreign Affairs," *China Quarterly* Number 4, October-December 1960

Lee Chae Jin, "Communist China and the Geneva Conference on Laos: A Reappraisal," *Asian Survey* 9:7, July 1969

Leifer, Michael, "Cambodia and her Neighbours," *Pacific Affairs* 34:4, Winter 1961–62

Lewis, John Wilson, "China's Secret Military Papers: Continuities and Revelations," *China Quarterly*, Number 18, April-June 1964

Liu Changyun, "A Preliminary Analysis of the Characteristics of Neibu Materials in the Social Sciences," *CCP Research Newsletter* Number 4, Fall-Winter 1989–90

MacFarquhar, Roderick, "Communist China's Intra-Party Dispute," *Pacific Affairs* 31:4, December 1958

McLane, Charles B., "The Russians and Vietnam: Strategies of Indirection," *International Journal* Number 24, Winter 1968

"New China News Agency Review of Selected Documents of the CCP Central Committee," *CCP Research Newsletter* Numbers 10 and 11, Spring-Fall 1992

Oksenberg, Michel, "Sources and Methodological Problems in the Study of Contemporary China," in A. Doak Barnett (ed.), *Chinese Communist Politics in Action* (Seattle: University of Washington Press, 1969)

Phan Thien Chau, "Leadership in the Vietnam Workers Party: The Process of Transition," *Asian Survey*, 12:9, September 1972

Pike, Douglas, "Origins of Leadership Change in the Socialist Republic of Vietnam," in Raymond C. Taras (ed.), *Leadership Change in the Communist States* (London: Unwin Hyman, 1989)

Porter, Gareth D., "The Myth of the Bloodbath: North Vietnam's Land Reform Reconsidered," *Bulletin of Concerned Asian Scholars* 5:2, September 1973

Pringsheim, Klaus H., "China and the Soviet Satellites: New Dimensions in China's Foreign Policy," *China Quarterly* Number 4, October-December 1960

Race, Jeffrey, "The Origins of the Second IndoChina War," *Asian*, 10:5, May 1970

Radvanyi, Janos, "Vietnam War Diplomacy: Reflections of a Former Iron Curtain Official," in Lloyd J. Matthews and Dale E. Brown, (eds.), *Assessing the Vietnam War: A Collection from the Journal of the US Army War College* (Washington, D.C.: Pergamon-Brassey's International Defense Publishers, 1987)

Shabad, Theodore, "Economic Developments in North Vietnam," *Pacific Affairs* 31:1, March 1958

Shao Kuo-kang, "Chou En-lai's Diplomatic Approach to Non-aligned States in Asia: 1953–60," *China Quarterly* Number 78, June 1979

____. "Zhou Enlai's Diplomacy and the Neutralisation of IndoChina, 1954–55," *China Quarterly* Number 107, September 1986

Shaw, Brian, "China and North Vietnam: Two Revolutionay Paths, Part I and II," *Current Scene* 9:11 & 12, 1971

Slusser, Robert M., "America, China, and the Hydra-headed Opposition: The Dynamics of Soviet Foreign Policy," in Peter H. Juviler, and Henry W. Morton (eds.), *Soviet Policy-Making: Studies of Communism in Transition* (London: Pall Mall, 1967)

Smith, R. B., "Cambodia in the Context of Sino-Vietnamese Relations," *Asian Affairs*, 16:Part III, October 1985

Sun, Warren, "The National Defence University's Teaching Reference Materials," *CCP Research Newsletter* Numbers 10 and 11, Spring-Fall 1992

Teiwes, Frederick C., "Interviews on Party History," *CCP Newsletter* Numbers 10 and 11, Spring-Fall 1992

Thayer, Carlyle A., *Revisionism in Communist Vietnamese Historiography: The Issue of Central Party Control over the Southern Party Organisation, 1954–1961* (Canberra: ANU, Research School of Pacific Studies, Department of Pacific and Southeast Asian History Seminar Series, 8 August 1989)

Trager, Frank N., "Never Negotiate Freedom: The Case of Laos and Vietnam," *Asian Survey* 1:11, January 1962

____. "Laos and the Defence of Southeast Asia," *Orbis* 7:3, Fall 1963

Turley, William, "The Vietnamese Army," in Jonathan R. Adelman, *Communist Armies in Politics* (Colorado: Westview Press, 1982)

Weigelin-Schwiedrzik, Susanne, "Party Historiography," in Jonathan Unger, *Using the Past to Serve the Present: Historiography and Politics in Contemporary China* (Armonk: M. E. Sharpe, 1993)

Westad, Odd Arne, "Materials on CCP History in Russian Archives," *CCP Research Newsletter* Numbers 10 and 11, Spring-Fall 1992

Whiting, Allen S., "Quemoy 1958: Mao's Miscalculation," *China Quarterly* Number 62, June 1975

Woodside, Alexander, "Peking and Hanoi: Anatomy of a Revolutionary Partnership," *International Journal* Number 24, Winter 1968

Zhai Qiang, "China and the Geneva Conference of 1954," *China Quarterly* Number 129, March 1992

Zheng Jingzhong, "An Introduction to Developments in Studies of Modern Chinese History in the Last Five Years (1986–90)," in *Chinese Studies in History* 25:2, Winter 1991–92

Zhu Zhenming, "Contemporary Southeast Asian Studies in China: 1980–1990," *Asia Research Trends* Number 2, 1992

Index

Abramov, A. N. 165, 169, 198, 220
Addis, J. M. 217

Battle for Ban Padong 194–196
Battle for Nam Tha: China and 222; Laos and 217–218, 220, 223–225, 230
Bong Souvannavong 60
Boudarel, Georges 64
Boun Oum (Prince) 164, 171, 207, 212–216–218, 224–225
Bucharest Conference (1960) 150–151, 164, 166
Bui Tin 213; on agrarian reform 37; on differences within North Vietnamese leadership 162–163; memoir of 7; on Secretary-General, VCP 48
Burchett, Wilfred 35, 99
Burlatsky, Fedor 41

Cambodia: and China 16–17, 84–95, 141–143; and the KPRP 2d Congress 163; and North Vietnam 17, 35, 85; and the Pracheachon Party 17, 83; and South Vietnam 83, 142; and Thailand 83; and the 3d Sangkum Congress 17, 83
Cao Van Luong 7
Central Highlands 71, 87, 101, 117, 185, 203
Chandler, David P. 17
Chang Hanfu 145, 205
Chen Geng 18–19, 105–106
Chen Jian 5–6
Chen Yi 84, 122, 159, 226, 228; and Andrei Gromyko 223; and British chargé d'affaires 202, 222; and Chinese delegation to Geneva Conference on Laos 194; and Sir Alec Douglas-Home 224–225; and Ho Chi Minh 145–146, 170; and Hungarian ambassador 221; on ISCC in Laos 107; and Janos Radvanyi 112; speaks at banquet for Burmese visitors 130
Chen Yun 22
China: anti-rightist campaign in 57; on the Battle for Nam Tha 222; and Cambodia 16–17, 84–85, 141–143; and 8th Congress 38–39; foreign policy 14, 38–39, 141, 190–191; and Geneva Agreements of 1954 13–15, 28; and Great Leap Forward 76, 79, 102, 121, 150; internal situation (1961–1962) 214–215; and Kong Lae coup 156,

170, 187–188, 202; and Laos 24, 33–34, 106–107, 124, 159, 216–217; and Lushan Plenum 121; and the PLA 78–79, 92, 126–127; and Soviet Union 56, 66–68, 109–110, 128, 150, 181–182; and Tibet 107; trade delegation in Hanoi 105–106; and United States 14, 34, 50, 88, 130, 159
Chu Van Bien 37
Chu Van Tan 73, 123
Conference of Communist and Workers' Parties (1960) 1, 166, 167–168
CPSU Congress: 20th 15–16; 21st 104; 22d 206
CRIMP Document 97, 131

Douglas-Home, Sir Alec 224–225
Duiker, William J. 5, 48
Duong Loi Cach Mang Mien Nam (The Road to the South) 32, 47, 97

8th CCP National Congress 38–39
Eisenhower, Dwight D. 146–147, 177, 180

Fall, Bernard 227–228
Fang Yi 106, 145, 196

Geneva Agreements (1954) 11–12; and Britain 25, 27; and China 13–15, 28; and France 19; and Soviet Union 16, 20–21, 25–27
Geneva Conference 1960 *see* International Conference on the Settlement of the Laotian Question
Great Leap Forward 76, 79, 102, 121, 150
Gromyko, Andrei 25, 89, 190

Han Suyin 23
Harriman, Averell 201–202 , 207, 221
He Wei 73, 122 208, 212, 229; appointed ambassador 69; attends 4-party conference 216; Ho Chi Minh and 147; leaves post 220–221; signs agreement with Quinim Pholsena 176
Ho Chi Minh 37–38, 43–44, 62–63, 70–71, 74, 139, 152, 168, 191; address of 1 January 1960 140; addresses 15th Plenary 98; addresses military 52–53; and Bernard Fall 227; and Chen Geng 19; in China 69, 86, 102, 105, 121–123, 128–129, 139, 147–148, 163, 167, 170–171, 193, 206, 208, 226, 228, 233; in India and Burma 76–77; and Janos Radvanyi 111; and Khrushchev 1–2; and Lao Dong Party 3d Congress 162–163; in Moscow 66, 68, 104–105, 120–122, 158, 168, 206–207; on NLFSV 180; and PLA visit to North Vietnam 211–212; and Ponomarev 219–220; and reunification 26–27, 29; Supports Geneva Conference on Laos 174; visits socialist bloc 56–60; and Zhou Enlai 144–146
Ho Chi Minh Trail 116, 120, 126, 136, 175, 189, 232
Ho Viet Thang 37
Hoang Minh Giam 55
Hoang Quoc Viet 37
Hoang Tung 116
Hoang Van Hoan 6, 13, 20, 42, 46, 48, 57, 63, 105, 123, 148, 158, 163, 170, 182, 199, 235; and CP38 committee 195; elected member of Politburo 27; serves as special adviser to North Vietnamese delegation at Geneva Conference on Laos 194
Hoang Van Thai 123, 186, 211
Honey, P. J. 186, 234
Huang Zheng 7
Hungarian Crisis (1956) 40–41

Huong Lap Incident: 93–96; British reports of 95–96; Chinese response to 103; French reports of 96; Russian response to 104

Ieng Sary 163
International Conference on the Settlement of the Laotian Question 174, 183, 193–194, 196, 200–201, 205–206, 209–210, 226–227
Interzone V 71, 87, 98, 101, 116–117, 131, 153, 185, 193

Jinmen (Quemoy) 88–90

Kang Sheng 140, 163, 187
Katay Don Sasorith 24, 54–55, 60–61
Kaysone Phomvihane 61–62, 156; at 4-party conference in Hanoi 220; and Zhou Enlai 200
Kaznzcheev, Aleksandr 91
Kennedy, John F. 181, 192, 194, 197, 199, 205–206, 211, 213
Khamphan Panya 119
Khamtay Siphandon 156
Khmer People's Revolutionary Party (KPRP) 2d Congress 163
Khrushchev, Nikita 56, 89–90, 121, 123, 125, 158, 168, 187, 225; address of 6 January 1961 181–182; in Beijing 79–80, 128–129; in Bucharest 164; and DRV delegation 197–198; and John F. Kennedy 194; and Janos Radvanyi 112–113; at Moscow Conference 66–68; at 20th CPSU Congress 15; at 21st CPSU Congress 104; at 22d CPSU Congress 206; on Soviet defense policy 127
Kong Lae 155–158, 165, 172; *see also* China: and Kong Lae coup; Laos: and Kong Lae coup
Kou Abhay 136–137
Kouprasith Abbay 171

Ladany, Laszlo 121
Lall, Arthur 202
Lansdale (Brigadier General) 180
Lao Dong Party 2; Politburo meeting (15 Sept 72) 2; 6th Plenary session (1954) 12, 31, 51; 9th Plenary session (enlarged) (1956) 26; 10th Plenary session (1956) 35, 36; 11th Plenary session (1956) 47; 12th Plenary session (1957) 51, 78; 13th Plenary session (1957) 70–71, 75; 14th Plenary session (1958) 87–88, 97; 15th Plenary session (1959) 97–98, 115–16, 131, 133, 161, 179–180, 233, 235; 18th Plenary session (1961) 152; 6th Plenary session (1961) 210; 3rd Party Congress (September 1960) 135, 152, 160–164, 180
Laos 5, 33; and the Battle for Ban Padong 194–196; and the Battle for Nam Tha 217–218, 220, 223–225, 230; and the Committee for the Defense of National Interests 136–137; elections in 80–82; and the Geneva Agreements of 1954 22–24, 96; and the Geneva Conference 1960 (International Conference on the Settlement of the Laotian Question) 174, 183, 193–194, 196, 200–201, 205–206, 209–210, 226–227; and highway construction by China 216–217; and Ho Chi Minh Trail 116–117, 189; and the Huong Lap Incident 93–96; internal developments in 53–56, 60–62, 118–120, 124–125, 136–139; and ISCC 81–82, 96, 106–107, 119, 125, 174–175, 183, 191–192, 217; and the Kong Lae coup 155–158, 164–166, 168–172, 174–177, 187–193, 200, 233; and the November 1957 (Vientiane) Agreement 61, 80, 165; and the Royal Laotian Government

22–24, 33–35, 60, 62, 94–95, 107, 118–120, 123–125, 136–139, 218; and South Vietnam 82; and the Soviet Union 165; and the United Nations 124–125; and the United States Military Advisory Group 107
Law 10/59 115, 205
Le Chuong 222
Le Duan 48, 63, 68–72, 77, 134, 144, 151, 167, 180, 212, 219; address on Lenin's 90th birthday anniversary 143; in Beijing 170–171; confirmed as First Secretary 163; as de facto Secretary General 48; and Duong Loi Cach Meng Mien Nam 32, 47, 97; and 14-point Plan 19, 21; on Geneva Agreements of 1954 12–13; on Ho Chi Minh Trail 136; inspection tour of the South 99; and Janos Radvanyi 110–111; at Lao Dong Party 3d Congress 160; on Law 10/59 115; letter of 7 February 1961 184–185; letter of 20 April 1961 189–190; letter of July 1962 230; on May Day 1958 75; in Moscow 149; at Moscow Conference 1957 65–66; report at 14th Plenary session 87–88; in Russia 206–207; and Tran Van Tra and Nguyen Van Vinh 117–118
Le Duc Tho: attends 20th CPSU Congress 15; in Beijing 18–19; and Giap 65; heads Lao Dong Party Organisation Department 48; in Moscow 198; and Soviet delegation in Hanoi 219
Le Thanh Nghi: article by 91; in China 102–103; elected member of Politburo 37; in Sofia 198
Le Van Luong 37
Li Fuchun 162, 196
Lin Biao 126–127, 129, 167
Liu Chun 221, 222, 223
Liu Shaoqi 15, 38, 40–41, 57, 122, 173, 196, 215
Liu Xiao 56, 88–90
London Talks (April 1956) 25–26
Luo Guibo 57, 69, 196, 221
Lushan Plenum 121
Ly Ban 170

MacDonald, Malcolm 200–201, 207; conversations with Sihanouk 172, 225
Mao Zedong 75–76, 90; with Anna Louise Strong 109; on Chinese economy 13–14, 27; and Jan Sejna 69; with Janos Radvanyi 112; in Moscow 66–68; with Nikita Krushchev in Beijing 79–80, 128–129; with S.F. Antonov 130; with Sihanouk 85, 173; steps down as Chairman of CCP 102; on Vietnamese reunification 57
Marek Thee 125, 201, 208–209, 210–211, 220–221, 222–223
Marr, David 1, 3
Matsu *see* Mazu
Mazu (Matsu) 88–90
Micunovic, Veljko 90
Mikoyan, Anastas 19–21
Morris, Stephen 2
Morski, Albert 211
Moscow Conference of 1960 *see* Conference of Communist and Workers' Parties (1960)

Nam Bo Regional Committee 19, 21, 115, 131, 135, 152 , 203, 223; 2d Conference 47; 3d Conference 86–87
National Liberation Front (NLFSV) 3, 227; 1st Congress 216, 223; formation of 179–180
Neo Lao Hak Xat (NLHX) 23–24, 61, 80–81, 94, 119, 120, 137–139, 148, 155, 159, 165–166, 168, 169, 208, 211, 217, 220; *see also* Pathet Lao
Ngo Dinh Diem 11–12, 82, 181, 211; and Law 10/59 115, 205

Ngo Dinh Nhu 82
Ngo Minh Loan 170
Nguyen Chi Thanh 65, 92, 123, 151–152, 167, 170–171, 186–187, 228, 233
Nguyen Chinh Giao 209
Nguyen Duy Trinh 37, 87, 170, 182–183
Nguyen Huu Tho 112
Nguyen Khang 55, 88, 171
Nguyen Son 38, 78
Nguyen Van Hieu 180
Nguyen Van Linh 47, 86
Nguyen Van Vinh 117–118, 123, 134
Nhan Van-Giai Pham Affair 35–36, 74–75
North Vietnam: and the agrarian reform debacle 35–37; and the Nhan Van-Giai Pham Affair 35–36, 74–75; and the Quynh Luu Uprising 42; and the United Nations 49–50
Nouhak Phoumsavan 156, 165
Noun Chea 163

October Revolution 66
Ouane Rattikone 169

Paracel Islands 89, 108
Parsons, Graham 166
Pathet Lao 22–24, 33–35, 54–55, 60–62, 118–120, 123–124, 126, 136, 148, 156, 158, 172, 189, 192, 217–218, 223, 225; triumvirate of 62; *see also* Neo Lao Hak Xat
Peng Dehuai 39, 67, 78, 121, 126–127, 221
Penkosky, Oleg 167
Pham Hung 66, 69, 144–145, 195, 219
Pham Van Dong 11–12, 15, 23–24, 28, 45, 43, 46, 63, 75, 77, 82, 93–94, 111, 122–123, 131, 137–139, 144, 157, 161, 169, 171, 174–176, 191–192, 196–198, 200, 212, 219–220, 227–228
Pham Van Thuyen 208
Phong Saly 22–23, 33, 53, 61–62, 78, 176, 192, 216
Phoui Sananikone 82, 93, 96, 119, 136
Phoumi Nosavan 136–138, 157, 164–166, 168, 212, 216–218, 224
Phoumi Vongvichit 165, 194
Phu Loi Incident 98–100; British report of 99; Chinese and Russian responses to 104
Pol Pot *see* Saloth Sar
Polish Crisis (1956) 40–41
Ponomarev, B.N. 79, 218–220
Pracheachon Party 17, 83
Pushkin, Giogi 189, 194, 202, 207, 217

Quemoy *see* Jinmen
Quinim Pholsena 171, 176, 190, 194
Quynh Luu Uprising 42

Radvanyi, Janos 92, 111–113
Reading, Lord 25
The Road to the South *see* Duong Loi Cach Mang Mien Nam
Roberts, Frank 189
Royal Laotian Government *see under* Laos
Rostow, Walt 205
Rusk, Dean 221

Saloth Sar 17, 163, 235
Sam Neua 22–23, 33, 53, 61–62, 78, 119, 124, 126, 139, 157, 165, 176, 192
Schlesinger, Arthur M., Jr. 205
Schram, Stuart 121
SEATO 17, 106, 108, 120, 122, 158–159, 210
Sejna, Jan 69, 90, 181
Sieu Heng 17
Sihanouk 53, 83–84, 135–136, 141–143, 163, 222, 232; in China 16–17, 84–86, 172–175; on Geneva Conference on Laos 174; and

Malcom MacDonald 225; proposes international conference on South Vietnam 227; proposes international conference on Cambodia 228; and Vietnamese communists 17
Singkapo Chounlamany 62, 118, 156, 165, 266
Sino-Soviet relations *see* Soviet Union: and China
Sino-U.S. ambassadorial talks 34, 50, 88, 130, 159
Sino-Vietnamese War (1979) 2
Sisana Sisane 176
Sisouk Na Champassak 94
Slusser, Robert M. 199
Smith, R.B. 3–4
Smyser, W.R. 5
Snow, Edgar 159
Son Ngoc Minh 163
Song Hao 123; promoted to Major-General 186, 211
Souphanouvong 23, 53–55, 60, 62, 118–119, 138, 148, 156–157, 159, 169, 190, 197, 199, 217–218
South Vietnam: communist activities in 1957 71–72; communist activities in 1958 86–87; communist activities in 1959 130–131; communist activities in 1960 133–135; communist activities in 1961 215; elections of 1956 11, 18; and Law 10/59 115, 205; and MACV 215, 233; and NLFSV 179–180, 216, 223, 227
Souvanna Phouma 24, 33–35, 41, 54–55, 60, 81, 82, 156–157, 164–166, 169–171, 202, 218; in China 34; in Hanoi 34–35, 176, 191–192, 200
Soviet Union: and China 79–80, 110, 128–129, 150–164, 181–182; and Geneva Agreements of 1954 16, 20–21, 25–27; and Laos 14, 125, 164–165, 169, 172, 187, 190, 194, 201, 202; and military mission in Hanoi 193; at Moscow Conference of 1957 66; Moscow Conference of 1960 166–168; and North Vietnam 20–21, 56, 63, 65–66, 92, 112–113, 129–130, 149, 162–163, 193, 214, 218–220; October Revolution anniversary in 66; at 20th CPSU Congress 15–16; at 21st CPSU Congress 104; at 22d CPSU Congress 206
Spratly Islands 89
Stewart, Michael 202, 222
Strong, Anna Louise 109
Stung Treng Incident 84
Sulzberger, Cyrus L. 199

Tan Zheng 39, 128
Taylor, Maxwell 205–207, 213
Thayer, Carlyle A. 3–4, 234
3d Congress of the Communist Party of Romania *see* Bucharest Conference
3d Sangkum Congress 17, 83
Thompson, Llewllyn 189
Tibet, rebellion in 107
Tong Dy 222
Tosh, John 10
Tou Samouth 17, 235
Tovmassyan 220
Tran Quang Huy 116, 167, 171
Tran Quoc Hoan 163
Tran Van Huu 227
Tran Van Tra 47–48, 97, 211; memoir of 7; meets with Nguyen Van Vinh and Le Duan 117–118; promoted to Major-General 123
Trevelyan, Sir Humphrey 9
Truong Chinh 19, 43, 45, 53, 62–63, 68, 70, 87, 111, 123, 134–135, 140, 158, 212, 219, 221, 235; appointed chairman if National Assembly Standing Committee 151; appointed deputy premier 75; attends 20th CPSU Congress 15; resign as secretary general 36–37

20th CPSU Congress 15–16
21st CPSU Congress 104
22d CPSU Congress 206

U-2 spy plane incident 146–147
Ung Van Khiem 127, 129, 211, 226; attends 4-party conference in Hanoi 220; leads North Vietnamese delegation at Geneva Conference on Laos 194

Van Tien Dung 123, 211, 219
Vienna meeting (1961) 194, 197
Vietnamese communists: and China 18–19, 73–74, 86, 91–92, 102–103, 139–140, 143–149, 166–167, 170, 171, 182–183, 196–197, 213–214, 220; and Laos 24, 33, 34–35, 53, 54–55, 61, 82, 93–96, 120, 126, 137–139, 158, 169, 175–177, 188–189, 192, 194–196, 217, 223–224, 232; and Sihanouk 17; and the Soviet Union 20–21, 56, 63, 65–66, 92, 112–113, 129–130, 149, 162–163, 193, 218–220; strategy for reunification 47–48, 70–72, 86–88, 183–185, 203, 216, 230
Vietnamese People's Army (VPA) 52–53, 78, 100–101, 134–135, 175, 185–186; relations with PLA 77, 92; visit to China 128
Vo Bam 116–117, 136
Vo Chi Cong 87
Vo Nguyen Giap 36–37, 43, 52–53, 62–63, 65–66, 70, 98, 105, 116, 123, 127, 129, 134–135, 140, 151–152, 157, 161, 186–187, 211, 228

Wang Bingnan 34, 49–50
Warner, Denis 192
Wei Guoqing 18, 146

Xieng Khouang 119–120, 124, 126, 176, 192
Xuan Thuy 158, 206–207

Ye Jianying 67, 127, 233; attends 3d Congress of the Lao Dong Party 162; leads Chinese military delegation to North Vietnam 210–213
Young, Kenneth T. 130, 139, 192; on 100th meeting of Sino-American ambassadorial talks 159
Yudin, Pavel F. 15

Zhai Qiang 6
Zhang Shu Guang 6
Zhou Enlai 14, 55, 84–86, 128, 139, 141, 143–145, 159, 170–173, 180, 183, 196–197, 199–200, 206–207; Asian tour of 50–51, 141; meets with Ho Chi Minh in China 122–123; meets with Ho Chi Minh and Nguyen Chi Thanh in Beijing 228–229; visits North Vietnam 42–46, 143–145; visits Cambodia 45–46, 141–142; visits Budapest, Moscow and Warsaw 50–51
Zhu Qiwen 229
Zhukov Affair 64–65